Nationalizing Nature

Today, one-quarter of all the land in Latin America is set apart for nature protection. In *Nationalizing Nature*, Frederico Freitas uncovers the crucial role played by conservation in the region's territorial development by exploring how Brazil and Argentina used national parks to nationalize borderlands. In the 1930s, Brazil and Argentina created some of their first national parks around the massive Iguazu Falls, shared by the two countries. The parks were designed as tools to attract migrants from their densely populated Atlantic seaboards to a sparsely inhabited borderland. In the 1970s, a change in paradigm led the military regimes in Brazil and Argentina to violently evict settlers from their national parks, highlighting the complicated relationship between authoritarianism and conservation in the Southern Cone. By tracking almost one hundred years of national park history in Latin America's largest countries, *Nationalizing Nature* shows how conservation policy promoted national programs of frontier development and border control.

Frederico Freitas is an assistant professor of Digital and Latin American History and a core member of the Visual Narrative Initiative at North Carolina State University. He is the coeditor of *Big Water: The Making of the Borderlands between Brazil, Argentina, and Paraguay* and a recipient of an NEH fellowship.

CAMBRIDGE LATIN AMERICAN STUDIES

General Editors
KRIS LANE, Tulane University
MATTHEW RESTALL, Pennsylvania State University

Editor Emeritus
HERBERT S. KLEIN
Gouverneur Morris Emeritus Professor of History, Columbia University and Hoover
Research Fellow, Stanford University

Other Books in the Series

(*Continued after the Index*)

Nationalizing Nature

*Iguazu Falls and National Parks
at the Brazil–Argentina Border*

FREDERICO FREITAS
North Carolina State University

 CAMBRIDGE
UNIVERSITY PRESS

CAMBRIDGE
UNIVERSITY PRESS

University Printing House, Cambridge CB2 8BS, United Kingdom

One Liberty Plaza, 20th Floor, New York, NY 10006, USA

477 Williamstown Road, Port Melbourne, VIC 3207, Australia

314–321, 3rd Floor, Plot 3, Splendor Forum, Jasola District Centre, New Delhi – 110025, India

79 Anson Road, #06–04/06, Singapore 079906

Cambridge University Press is part of the University of Cambridge.

It furthers the University's mission by disseminating knowledge in the pursuit of education, learning, and research at the highest international levels of excellence.

www.cambridge.org
Information on this title: www.cambridge.org/9781108844833
DOI: 10.1017/9781108953733

© Frederico Freitas 2021

First published 2021

A catalogue record for this publication is available from the British Library.

ISBN 978-1-108-84483-3 Hardback

To Olívia and Aurora

Contents

Figures, Maps, and Tables

TABLES

Acknowledgments

Throughout the years, several organizations generously supported the research for and writing of this book. Research in Brazil was funded through the Graduate Research Opportunity Funds from the School of Humanities and Sciences at Stanford University and the Albert J. Beveridge Grant from the American Historical Association. Research in Argentina was made possible with the support of the Center for Spatial and Textual Analysis at Stanford and the John D. Wirth Fund at the Department of History at Stanford. The writing was supported by the Geballe Dissertation Prize Fellowship at the Stanford Humanities Center, the Department of History at North Carolina State University, and a National Endowment for the Humanities Fellowship.

This book is the result both of my personal effort and of the support of many individuals who offered me advice and friendship over the last decade. My highest debt is to my three mentors at Stanford University: Zephyr Frank, Richard White, and Mikael Wolfe. It is hard to find the proper words to acknowledge Zephyr for his guidance and exceptional generosity. Zephyr always played the right role at the right times: rigorous mentor, exceptional colleague, and true friend. Richard White was crucial in my development as a historian, offering precious advice on distilling chapters into their essential arguments and situating the research in the broader themes of environmental history. I am also indebted to Mikael Wolfe for his guidance and interest in my professional development.

I benefited from comments and suggestions from many colleagues who read different chapters of this book: Ryan Edwards, José Augusto Drummond, Richard W. Slatta, Mi Gyung Kim, and K. Steven Vincent. My special thanks go to Jacob Blanc, not only for offering insightful comments on rural Brazil but also for our friendship and partnership in different academic endeavors. I am also extremely grateful to those who provided feedback on the entire manuscript: my friend Andrea Rosenberg and the two readers selected by Cambridge University Press. Grateful thanks also go to the editors at Cambridge, who guided this book through the review, editing, and publication processes: Kris E. Lane, Matthew Restall, and Cecelia Cancellaro.

Throughout the years, numerous other people contributed to this project through conversations and feedback. I am grateful to colleagues and faculty I met during my time at Stanford, including J. P. Daughton, Ana Minian, Jon Connolly, Gabriel Lee, Rodrigo Pizarro, Victoria Saramago, George Phillip LeBourdais, Dylan J. Montanari, David Gilbert, Lena Tahmassian, Andrew Gerhart, Leonardo Barleta, and Mateo Carrillo. At Stanford, I had the privilege to engage with digital humanities researchers at the Spatial History Project and the Center for Spatial and Textual Analysis (CESTA): Matt Bryant, Celena Allen, Jake Coolidge, Nicholas Bauch, Ryan Heuser, Jason Heppler, and Maria dos Santos. I especially thank Erik Steiner for being an inspirational digital humanities scholar and a friend. I am particularly indebted to research assistants Eli Berg and Peter Salazar, who worked on some of the data used in Chapters 5 and 6.

At North Carolina State University, I found a welcoming interdisciplinary community of scholars. I am very grateful for the support I received from my colleagues here, including Matthew Booker, Todd Berreth, Arnav Jhala, Erin Sills, Daniel Burton-Rose, Adriana de Souza e Silva, Ross Bassett, Alicia McGill, Katherine Mellen Charron, David Ambaras, Megan Cherry, Xiaolin Duan, Sandy Freitag, Tammy Gordon, Nicholas Robins, Akram Khater, Verena Kasper-Marienberg, and David Zonderman. Thanks also go to Courtney Hamilton, Ingrid Hoffius, and Norene Miller, for their dedication and professionalism to faculty and students. Research in this book benefited from a partnership with the Program in Geospatial Information Science and Technology at NC State. Special thanks go to Eric Money and Juliana Quist, at the program, as well as Emily McNamar, who worked on some of the data used in Chapter 6. Within the greater North Carolina community of scholars, I am grateful to a few people for the opportunity to present on aspects of this book: John French, Christine Folch, and everybody else at Duke University's Global Brazil Lab; Cynthia Radding at UNC-Chapel Hill; and Jürgen Buchenau and Oscar de la Torre at UNC-Charlotte.

Numerous other colleagues have helped shape my scholarship in many ways through commentary on this book, guidance to sources, collaboration in panels, publications, and research projects, or conversations about history and methodology. In the United States, I would like to thank Emily Wakild, Thomas D. Rogers, Seth Garfield, Rafael Ioris, Myrna Santiago, Christopher Boyer, Matthew Vitz, Paul Katz, María de los Ángeles Picone, Daryle Williams, Zeb Tortorici, Patrick Iber, and especially Matt Spurlock for their support and friendship. In Ecuador, Nicolás Cuvi. In Colombia, Claudia Leal. In Argentina, Graciela Silvestri and Marina Miraglia. In Paraguay, Carlos Gómez Florentin. In Brazil, I am grateful to Luciano Figueiredo, Antonio Myskiw, Douglas Libby, Junia Furtado, Regina Horta Duarte, Yuri Gama, Martha Rebelatto, Sigrid Andersen, José Augusto Pádua, José Luiz de Andrade Franco, Lise Sedrez, Eunice Nodari, Sandro Dutra e Silva, Luis Ferla, Marcela Kropf, Eduardo Góes Neves, Gabriela Pellegrino Soares, Iris Kantor, Lincoln Secco, Carla Viviane Paulino, Leonardo Marques, and Daniel Strum. Special thanks go to my longtime friends outside academia, especially Ruy Fernando Cavalheiro, Tagori Mazzoni Vilela, André de Martini, André Mesquita, Lucas Monteiro de Oliveira, Daniela e Felipe Madureira, Luiz Menezes, Pedro Arcanjo Matos, Pedro Carvalho, Alexandre Fanucchi, Luciano Juliatto, Paulo Sérgio Sangiorgio Jr., and Tarcísio de Arantes Leite.

Many assisted me in my research in Brazil and Argentina. In Rio de Janeiro, thanks to Paulo Roberto Boechat at the CENDOC-Aeronáutica and Rosane Coutinho at the Arquivo Nacional. Special thanks go to Tereza Cristina Alves for helping me find my way in the maze of the Brazilian National Archives. Several people helped me in Curitiba, including Solange de Oliveira Rocha at the Arquivo Público do Paraná; Célia Carneiro at the DER-PR; Luiz Augusto Loyola Macedo at the IBGE office in Curitiba; Ronilson Campos, Rodrigo Asturian, and Fábio Pagliosa Ulkowski at the INCRA office in Curitiba; Arnaldo Alves de S. Junior at the Justiça Federal do Paraná; Gislene Lessa and Izaias Alves Pereira at the ITCG-PR; and Mauricio Savi. In Foz do Iguaçu, I want to thank Lara Luciana Leal Seixas, Aluízio Palmar, Lígia Basso, Alexandre Palmar, Adilson Borges, Pedro Berg, and Adilson Simão for their help in this project. My research at the Iguaçu National Park would not have been possible without the assistance of Ivan Batiston, Julio Gonchorowski, Antonia Monteiro, Apolonio Rodrigues, and Raphael Xavier. At the INCRA office in Cascavel, Emilio Stachowski was generous in sharing his time and resources. In Brasília, I am grateful for the help of Átila Ribeiro at IBAMA and Daianne Bezerra de Freitas and Marli dos Reis Alves Soares at ICMBio. I would also like to thank Maria Tereza Jorge Pádua for an enlightening interview.

In Puerto Iguazú, the people at the APN-NEA – Fernanda Fabbio, Guillermo Gil, Andrés Bosso, Fabián Gatti, and Marcelo Cavicchia – supported me in every way. Exceptional thanks go to Luciana Nicola, whose tenacity enabled me to conduct research at the Iguazú National Park archive. At the park, I enjoyed fruitful conversations with Daniel de la Torre, Justo Herrera, and Nancy Arizpe. In the town, Guillermina Hope, Osni Schreiner, and the late José Gorgues kindly shared their stories. In Buenos Aires, most of my research was carried out at the APN archives and library, and this was only possible thanks to the dedication of Sergio Silva, Laura Staropoli, and Catalina Coali. Sergio Pedernera at the Patrimonio e Instituto Histórico in Buenos Aires also offered valuable help.

I was lucky to have family support during the decade I spent researching and writing this book. I am grateful to Érica and her family – Luís, Thomas, and Maria Clara, and to Dulce and Joceli, for their support and for being part of what I am. A special thank-you to Heidi and Robert, whom I was lucky to encounter along this journey. I am also immensely thankful to my wife, Robin, a pillar of love, support, and companionship. Finally, I dedicate this book to Olívia and Aurora, who I hope will someday be inspired by this work.

Note on Terminology and Orthography

Iguazu is a term of Tupi-Guarani origin meaning "big water," "a great amount of water," or "abundance of water." In Spanish it is spelled *Iguazú*, with an acute accent on the final *u*. In Portuguese it was *Iguassú* until an orthographic reform in the 1950s changed it to its present form, *Iguaçu*. Iguazu was originally the name of the 1,300-kilometer-long river that serves as the boundary between Argentina and Brazil in its final 130 kilometers before flowing into the mighty Paraná River. It is also the name of the binational set of massive waterfalls that justified the creation of two national parks in the 1930s, which are the topic of this book. Here, I chose to keep the modern Portuguese spelling "Iguaçu" for the Brazilian park, Iguaçu National Park (Parque Nacional do Iguaçu); the Spanish spelling "Iguazú" for the Argentine park, Iguazú National Park (Parque Nacional Iguazú); and the English spelling "Iguazu" for geographical features such as the Iguazu River and Iguazu Falls.

I also use the word "settler" to refer to the farmers who moved into the Argentine–Brazilian borderland throughout the twentieth century. These farmers, the majority of whom were of European descent, identify themselves as *colonos* in Brazil, which can be roughly translated as "members of a colony" (i.e., a colonization project). In Argentina, to a lesser extent, a similar group of people is referred to as *pobladores* – "populators." In Brazil, they are also "colonos" for government agencies and in legislation, to such an extent that the Brazilian Congress even created a *dia do colono* (day of the settler) in 1968 to celebrate their role as frontier pioneers. The word "colono" acquires different meanings in other parts of Brazil, but in the Brazilian South, where Iguaçu National Park is located, it invariably refers to Brazilian migrants of European origin from other southern states who acquire land in frontier areas. Most "colonos" who moved to the area between the Iguazu and the Paraná rivers between the 1950s and 1970s trace their origin to the Italian and German immigrants who arrived in Brazil's southernmost state, Rio Grande do Sul, in the nineteenth century. "Poblador" has a similar meaning across the border in Argentina. To avoid switching back and forth between the Portuguese and Spanish versions of the term, I chose to refer to all of these migrants as "settlers."

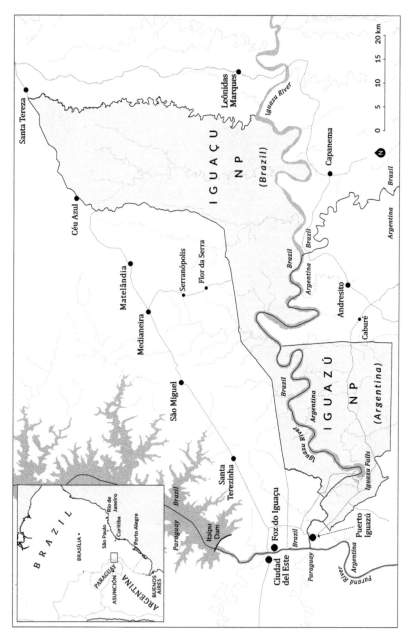

MAP 0.1 Iguazú National Park, Argentina, and Iguaçu National Park, Brazil, c. 2020. Map by Frederico Freitas

Introduction: Boundaries of Nature

Every year, the Iguazu Falls attract millions of tourists to the Argentine–Brazilian border. They arrive eager to see the complex system of cataracts that occupies a massive bend of the Iguazu River. Their magnitude makes the falls a unique geological feature. In its final stretch toward the Paraná River, the Iguazu abruptly turns backward into a gorge, plunging off an 80-meter-high plateau and crashing into a myriad of boulders, rocky ledges, and islets. The sight and sound of hundreds of powerful waterfalls spilling 1,750,000 liters of water per second into a narrow, steep canyon bewilder visitors. It is easy for newcomers to find themselves overwhelmed by the excesses of Iguazu Falls: it is too much water, too much noise, and too many different cascades. Networks of concrete and wooden pathways on the river's banks help visitors to make sense of their experience. They offer a vantage point from which tourists can assimilate the falls as a coherent landscape at different scales: as a massive, distant panorama formed by a 2.7-kilometer-wide staircase of water and rock; or through a series of close encounters with individual waterfalls. Visitors can get close enough to massive columns of falling water to be soaked in their dense spray, deafened by their constant roar, and saturated by their thick, earthy smell. A lush subtropical rainforest, complete with flying toucans, frolicking coatis, and colorful butterflies, encroaches on the walls of water and mist, providing for an Edenic backdrop. The experience of witnessing firsthand the sheer force of Iguazu Falls leaves a lasting impression on most people.

To fully experience Iguazu, visitors have to traverse a series of borders, as the cascades that form the falls are divided by the international boundary between Brazil and Argentina. Most tourists choose to see the falls

FIGURE O.I   Iguazu Falls, as seen from Brazil. Photo by Frederico Freitas, 2014

from both sides, believing they complement each other. From the Brazilian banks of the Iguazu, they can witness the falls as a massive, wide-angle spectacle (see Figure 0.1). In Argentina, they walk to see dozens of individual cataracts close at hand. National parks protect each side of the falls, introducing another set of boundaries to be crossed. The Brazilian side of Iguazu Falls is guarded by *Iguaçu* National Park (*Parque Nacional do Iguaçu* in Portuguese). Across the border, *Iguazú* National Park (*Parque Nacional Iguazú* in Spanish) harbors the Argentine side of the falls. Seeing Iguazu Falls in its entirety requires shuttling back and forth through a series of checkpoints. There are the gates and fences controlling the entry and movement of tourists inside each national park. Outside the parks, immigration and customs control offices for Brazil and Argentina regulate border crossings on the highway connecting the two countries. Depending on their nationalities, tourists may have to obtain a visa before entering or reentering either country.

Outside visitors expecting to encounter an unencumbered wilderness adventure at the falls may be surprised by the conspicuous nature of the borders encompassing Iguazu. In place of the unclaimed waterfalls lost in the jungle depicted in countless media, tourists find at Iguazu a landscape bisected by ever-present human-made boundaries, an intricate waterscape disputed between Brazil and Argentina. Barriers to the unobstructed circulation of people are expected at most international borders. At Iguazu Falls, however, they are even more salient, revealing the countries' attempts to assert rights over the forests, rivers, and waterfalls at the borderland. The national parks encompassing the falls on each side, Iguazú in Argentina and Iguaçu in Brazil, are the instruments each country wielded to nationalize nature at the border. This book examines how Argentina and Brazil utilized national parks to stake a claim to a piece of nature straddling their shared border, from the 1930s, when the parks were first created, until the 1980s, when they took their present shape.

As a unique geological feature, Iguazu Falls offered plenty of justification for establishing national parks at this particular spot on the international border separating Argentina and Brazil. The magnificent falls were a magnet for a few moneyed adventurers in the early 1900s. By the late twentieth century, Iguazu had evolved into a mass tourist attraction. For years, Iguazu Falls topped the lists of South America's most visited destinations.[1] The cataracts made Iguazú and Iguaçu the crown jewels of the national park systems in Argentina and Brazil.[2]

Iguazu Falls attracted so many because, among other things, they avoided the level of engineering intervention of their famous transnational North American counterpart, the Canadian–American Niagara Falls.[3] There are no nearby hydroelectric power plants, adjacent urban developments, or other types of heavy-handed interventions to spoil Iguazu's scenery.[4] Listing Iguazu Falls and their banks as national parks in the

---

[1] In 2018 alone, 1,520,743 tourists visited the Argentine side of the falls. Another 1,895,628 visitors saw the falls from across the river in Brazil. These numbers make Iguazu Falls one of the top destinations for tourists in the two countries. Source: Administración de Parques Nacionales and Instituto Chico Mendes de Conservação da Biodiversidade.

[2] Argentina and Brazil have other important border national parks adjacent to parks in other nations. In Patagonia, Argentina established several national parks bordering Chilean ones: Lanin, Nahuel Huapi, and Los Glaciares. Further north, in the Amazon rainforest, Brazil created the Pico da Neblina National Park, adjacent to a Venezuelan park, to protect its highest mountain. However, none of these parks houses an internationally famous binational landmark such as Iguazu Falls.

[3] Daniel Macfarlane, "Saving Niagara from Itself: The Campaign to Preserve and Enhance the American Falls, 1965–1975," *Environment and History* 25 (2019): 489–520; Daniel Macfarlane, "'A Completely Man-Made and Artificial Cataract': The Transnational Manipulation of Niagara Falls," *Environmental History* 18, no. 4 (2013): 759–84.

[4] Outside the parks, other sections of the Iguazu River were not lucky enough to avoid large engineering works. By 2020, the river flowed through six hydroelectric dams, all inside Brazilian territory, before arriving at Iguaçu National Park's eastern limits. The closest and last dam, built in 2019, was located just 160 kilometers upriver from the falls.

1930s prevented such developments. The area under protection, however, was not limited to the falls. Argentina's Iguazú National Park, for its part, encompasses over 56,000 hectares of protected, mostly forested, territory. The Brazilian Iguaçu National Park is even larger, expanding eastward and northward, protecting over 162,000 hectares (see Map 0.1). The area open to tourists is rather small in these two national parks: only about 0.2 percent of the total territory of Iguaçu, Brazil, and not more than 1 percent in Iguazú, Argentina.[5] Anyone who is not a scientist with a research permit or a park employee will be barred from setting foot beyond the falls area. Putting the two parks together, a vast territory of over 200,000 hectares is off-limits to ordinary visitors. This expanded area of preserved forest was established in the 1940s, but it has gained particular importance since the 1970s as much of the borderland area outside the parks became farmland. Why did the Iguaçu and Iguazú national parks end up protecting not only the waterfalls, but also expanses of forests along the Argentine–Brazilian border? How did the parks withstand the advance of settlement in this border area? To answer these questions, one needs to examine the role of geopolitics and nationalism in conservation. At the Argentine–Brazilian border, competing visions for the national parks ended up preserving the forest.

THE GEOPOLITICS OF NATURE PROTECTION

Official documents and the discourse of park administrators on the two sides of the border justify their policy of excluding visitors from most of the territory of the two parks based on the need to preserve biodiversity. The 2018 management plan of Brazil's Iguaçu National Park, for example, uses the word *biodiversidade* (biodiversity) eighteen times in fifty pages in the context of justifying its existence as a protected area. The plan argues the park is necessary as one of the few remaining continuous stretches of Atlantic forest in Brazil, and is a crucial instrument in preserving the

---

[5] In 2018 the administration of Iguaçu National Park opened new areas of "extensive use" for visitation by local communities at the park boundaries. These amount to about 7 percent of the area of the Brazilian park. Instituto Chico Mendes de Conservação da Biodiversidade [ICMBio], "Plano de manejo do Parque Nacional do Iguaçu" (Instituto Chico Mendes de Conservação da Biodiversidade, 2018), www.icmbio.gov.br/portal/images/stories/plano-de-manejo/plano_de_manejo_do_parna_do_iguacu_fevereiro_2018.pdf; Intendencia Parque Nacional Iguazú, "Plan de gestión – Parque Nacional Iguazú, período 2017–2023" (Administración de Parques Nacionales, 2017), https://sib.gob.ar/archivos/ANEXO_I_PGIguazu.pdf.

biodiversity of this threatened biome.[6] The two Iguazu parks are not alone in using the language of biodiversity conservation to justify their existence and territorial policies – most nature preserves today adopt the same language. The use of this rationale, however, conceals a glaring anachronism. The exclusion of visitors from most areas of the two parks preceded their adoption of biodiversity conservation as a guiding principle.

Biodiversity as a concept was coined in the mid-1980s and was only adopted in conservation policy in the 1990s.[7] In Latin America, a pivotal moment in the popularization of biodiversity was the 1992 United Nations Conference on Environment and Development in Rio de Janeiro, which opened the Convention on Biological Diversity for signature.[8] The establishment of the two national parks, however, occurred fifty years before the adoption of biodiversity as a subject of conservation policy. Argentina first created Iguazú National Park on its banks of Iguazu Falls in 1934, as part of a legislative push that included another national park, Nahuel Huapi in Patagonia, as well as a dedicated national park agency – the first in Latin America. Brazil followed suit in 1939, establishing Iguaçu National Park across the border – the second national park gazetted in the country after the creation of Itatiaia in 1937. Throughout the years, different concepts were invoked by the government agencies running the parks to justify their conservationist mission: preserving the natural scenery around the falls; preventing deforestation and conserving natural resources; protecting keystone animal species and their habitats; preserving "national" phytogeographic regions. Biodiversity appeared in park documents only in the 2000s. Had the 1930s-era parks been created with biodiversity in mind, they would have different boundaries today (see Map 0.1). Instead, they were the result of political, social, and

---

[6] ICMBio, "Plano de manejo do Parque Nacional do Iguaçu," 2018. In the case of Iguazú National Park in Argentina, its 2017 management plan is even more skewed toward using "biodiversity" (*biodiversidad*) as a justification, with over fifty occurrences of the word throughout almost 300 pages. Intendencia Parque Nacional Iguazú, "Plan de gestión," 2017.

[7] Timothy Farnham, *Saving Nature's Legacy: Origins of the Idea of Biological Diversity* (New Haven: Yale University Press, 2007); Libby Robin, "The Rise of the Idea of Biodiversity: Crises, Responses and Expertise," *Quaderni* 76 (Fall 2011): 25–37; José Luiz de Andrade Franco and José Augusto Drummond, "História das preocupações com o mundo natural no Brasil: Da proteção à natureza à conservação da biodiversidade," in *História ambiental: Fronteira, recursos naturais e conservação da natureza*, ed. José Luiz de Andrade Franco, et al. (Rio de Janeiro: Garamond, 2012); José Luiz de Andrade Franco, "The Concept of Biodiversity and the History of Conservation Biology: From Wilderness Preservation to Biodiversity Conservation," *História (São Paulo)* 32, no. 2 (2013): 21–47.

[8] Argentina and Brazil ratified the convention in 1994.

technical processes that produced oddly shaped territories that cannot be easily justified by modern conservation criteria.[9] What explains, then, the creation of these two parks? What are the origins of their restrictive territorial policies? To answer these questions, it is first necessary to understand the unique position of Iguazú and Iguaçu as boundary parks in a disputed borderland. Argentina and Brazil each established their own national park in the 1930s in the area known today as the "Triple Frontier," the strategic tri-border region they shared with Paraguay.[10] The Spanish and Portuguese crowns competed for dominance in the region during colonial times, and Argentina, Brazil, and Paraguay inherited the dispute in the nineteenth century. In the aftermath of the War of the Triple Alliance (1864–70), Argentina and Brazil emerged as the two regional powers of South America and the Triple Frontier regained importance as a locus of geopolitical contention. It is in the context of this competition between Argentina and Brazil that the creation of the national parks at Iguazu Falls must be understood.

Geopolitics provided the initial reasoning underlying the creation of the two parks in the 1930s. Policymakers on either side of the border deemed the nationalization of their respective sections of Iguazu Falls to be a matter of national interest. By establishing a federally controlled protected area at the falls, they planted a flag at a border seen as suspiciously porous to foreign influences. A national park is, after all, national. By 1940, both Argentina and Brazil had a gazetted national park in the area. They proved, at least on paper, that a piece of the magnificent falls, and of the border on which they stood, belonged in the body of each nation. To gazette is to make an ordinance official through its publication in a government journal. Gazetting nature reserves is low-hanging fruit – it requires only the passage of a law or the enactment of a decree.[11]

---

[9] Iguaçu National Park in Brazil, for example, is shaped like the letter "L" turned 90 degrees sideways. It has a narrow southwest band squeezed between the meanders of the Iguazu River and an abandoned highway. In this area, the park has sections as narrow as 2.5 kilometers wide. This section of the park was never conceived of as a wildlife corridor as per modern biodiversity conservation design.

[10] *Triple Frontera* in Spanish, or *Tríplice Fronteira* in Portuguese. For a deeper discussion on the importance of the Triple Frontier area for the three countries, see the anthology I coedited with Jacob Blanc, *Big Water: The Making of the Borderland Between Brazil, Argentina, and Paraguay* (Tucson: University of Arizona Press, 2018). Of particular importance is the conclusion, by Graciela Silvestri, on the uniqueness of this tri-border area for each of the three countries. See "Space, National, and Frontier in the Rioplatense Discourse," in that same volume.

[11] As Kelly et al. have discussed, national parks are a low-stakes form of modern state-building accessible to even small and poor states. Matthew Kelly et al., "Introduction," in

Implementation, on the other hand, demands the engagement of the state and the investment of its resources in transforming a nondescript piece of national territory into a special zone reserved for the seemingly opposed uses of preservation and tourism. The central state must, at a minimum, nationalize the land, hire employees, create a national park bureaucracy to manage the reserve, carry out surveys and scientific studies, and develop infrastructure such as roads and trails to allow visitation by tourists and surveillance by park wardens. In many instances throughout Latin America, national governments stopped at the first stage – gazetting the parks – and for decades the region was littered with "paper parks" with little implementation. Establishing protected areas only on paper made sense, as national governments could reap the benefits of a token of twentieth-century modernity – the national park – without incurring the political and economic costs of implementing it.

Iguazú National Park in Argentina and Iguaçu National Park in Brazil, however, were never paper parks. From the beginning, the two countries' governments have secured resources to make the two preserves functioning national parks. They invested public funds in building infrastructure and hiring personnel for the two parks at a scale rarely seen elsewhere in Latin America before the 1970s.[12] As national parks located at the border between South America's leading competing powers, Iguazú and Iguaçu were too important not to be implemented. Argentines and Brazilians saw them as bridgeheads for border nationalization. Moreover, policymakers at the federal and local levels seized on the establishment of the parks as an opportunity to bring development to the borderland. They used park funds to build roads, airfields, hydroelectric plants, schools, hospitals, and even urban settlements. In their first decades, the national parks at Iguazu Falls functioned as vectors of territorial development, funneling federal investment into creating an infrastructure designed to not only serve outside tourists

---

The Nature State: Rethinking the History of Conservation, Routledge Environmental Humanities (Oxford: Routledge, 2017), 9.

[12] The Mexican national parks established in the 1940s provide another example of early public investment in nature preserves in the region. Emily Wakild, *Revolutionary Parks: Conservation, Social Justice, and Mexico's National Parks, 1910–1940* (Tucson: University of Arizona Press, 2011). For a brief discussion of conservation in Latin America, see John Soluri, Claudia Leal, and José Augusto Pádua, "Introduction: Finding the 'Latin American' in Latin American Environmental History," in *A Living Past: Environmental Histories of Modern Latin America*, ed. John Soluri, Claudia Leal, and José Augusto Pádua (Oxford, New York: Berghahn Books, 2018), 1–22.

but also attract settlers to the border's main urban centers – Foz do Iguaçu in Brazil and Puerto Iguazú in Argentina.[13]

Competition between Argentina and Brazil led the two countries to use the parks as instruments for border nationalization.[14] National parks, which are rhetorically conceived as checks on development, were used in Iguazu to promote the development of the borderland. And yet, the tension between preservation and development was evident for most people working on implementing these two national parks. While some reasoned the ultimate goal of the parks was to bring progress to the border, others contended that the parks' raison d'etre was to protect nature from the incoming waves of migrants moving to the area. Initially, the champions of development had the upper hand – after all, they counted among their ranks those who had proposed creating the parks in the first place. But soon a cadre of agricultural and life scientists, working inside and outside state agencies, managed to steer the narrative around the two parks toward a stricter vision of forest protection. It was a parallel movement, happening at the same time on the two sides of the border and influenced by transboundary exchanges and the growing international importance of nature conservation. As a result, vast expanses of subtropical forests adjacent to Iguazu Falls were incorporated into the territories of the two parks. Eighty years later, they stand as islands of continuous Atlantic forest surrounded by a sea of small farms.

When Iguaçu and Iguazú were created in the 1930s, the Triple Frontier was still sparsely populated and covered by forests. The parks withstood the colonization of their surrounding areas as waves of migrants arrived in the borderland in subsequent years. The coming of settlers and the establishment of farms outside the parks represented a radical transformation in the landscape of this border region, especially on the Brazilian side. What was a carpet of forested expanses in the 1930s became one of

---

[13] Viewing national parks as vectors of economic development was nothing new. Railroad companies in North America had facilitated the creation of the first US national parks. What was new in Iguazú and Iguaçu was the commitment to attract not only tourists but settlers to the frontier. Richard West Sellars, *Preserving Nature in the National Parks: A History* (New Haven and London: Yale University Press, 1997), 8–11.

[14] Throughout the Americas, however, local officials could as well reject proposals to establish border parks. That was the case of Mexico, whose officials refused to establish a transboundary park with the United States in the 1930s because many saw the proposal as an imposition of US ideas. The asymmetry between Mexico and the United States defined the former's refusal to create border parks. Emily Wakild, "Border Chasm: International Boundary Parks and Mexican Conservation 1935–1945," *Environmental History* 14, no. 3 (July 2009): 453–475.

Brazil's breadbaskets in the 1970s. The parks, however, were already in place when these transformations occurred. Created in the 1930s to promote the development and colonization of the borderland, Iguazú and Iguaçu National Parks ended up becoming the last contiguous expanse of old-growth forest in a landscape dominated by agriculture, forestry, and energy production. Even as development arrived at the borderland at last, it was accompanied by increasingly restrictive land use policies inside the parks that sought to insulate whole sections from human interference.

How did Iguaçu National Park, for example, a park that is among the top five tourist destinations in Brazil, end up with extremely restrictive tourism policies? Such changes in policy and enforcement occurred mostly during the military dictatorships in Argentina and Brazil between the 1960s and 1970s. They benefited from a series of tools – legal, institutional, military, and even extrajudicial – developed by the two countries' military regimes to deal with internal dissent and reshape their countrysides. Reconstructing the historical evolution of national park policy in Argentina and Brazil offers a window into changes in the two countries' territorial policies. It shows how the rise of authoritarian regimes informed the conditions for implementing forceful territorial interventions, including shielding the space of the two parks from human interference.[15]

The creation and implementation of Iguazú and Iguaçu national parks (1930s–80s) coincided with a period in which both Argentina and Brazil were consolidating their capacity to exert power in the Triple Frontier borderland. Throughout the nineteenth and twentieth centuries, the political and military classes of Argentina and Brazil saw the other country as a potential rival. In establishing national parks at their shared international border, the two countries strove to demonstrate territorial control in areas where state power had chronically displayed its weaknesses to its international rivals. In subsequent decades, the two countries invested in creating transportation and energy infrastructure at the borderland and jockeyed to bring Paraguay into their spheres of influence. The two

---

[15] Ironically, for parks that started as projects to attract settlers to the borderland, Iguazú and Iguaçu evolved throughout the years into a transboundary zone emptied of people, acting as a buffer between the two competing powers of South America. On parks as buffers between warring nations see Greg Bankoff, "Making Parks out of Making Wars: Transnational Nature Conservation and Environmental Diplomacy in the Twenty-First Century," in *Nation-States and the Global Environment: New Approaches to International Environmental History*, ed. Erika Marie Bsumek, David Kinkela, and Mark Atwood Lawrence (New York: Oxford University Press, 2013), 76–96.

national parks played essential roles as initial steps in projecting state territorial power over the borderland. They reproduced the legal and administrative structures, economic processes, and ideological mindsets found in programs of frontier occupation put forward in the two countries. By putting together projects of border development and nature conservation, the two parks became powerful instruments for nationalizing the border for both Argentina and Brazil.[16]

CONSERVATION AND DEVELOPMENT

In the Americas, national park creation has relied on a myth of pristine nature. According to this mythology, in the beginning there was nature, replete with impressive forests, charismatic animal species, and magnificent mountains (or, in our case, waterfalls).[17] *Homo sapiens* was nowhere to be found in this primeval state of nature – it was the Garden of Eden without Adam and Eve. As the myth goes on, humans appeared in the story as disruptors, bringing civilization and progress, which spoils and destroys nature. Luckily, national park visionaries stepped up to turn civilization on its head. They used the tools of the modern nation-state to propose and implement protected areas. They aimed to preserve what was left of nature and, when possible, to revert landscapes to a pristine state.[18] As a myth, the trope of pristine nature

[16] Like other national parks, Iguazú and Iguaçu exemplify the kind of territorial power wielded by modern nation-states. They reproduce the processes of "mapping, bounding and containing nature and citizenry" that "make a state a state" (as argued by Neumann), and demonstrate how a "nature state" claims the right to protect nature from its very citizens (according to Kelly et al.). Roderick P. Neumann, "Nature-State-Territory: Toward a Critical Theorization of Conservation Enclosures," in *Liberation Ecologies: Environment, Development, Social Movements*, ed. Richard Peet and Michael Watts (London: Routledge, 2004), 195–217; Kelly et al., "Introduction," 5. See also Bernhard Gißibl, Sabine Höhler, and Patrick Kupper, "Introduction: Towards a Global History of National Parks," in *Civilizing Nature: National Parks in Global Historical Perspective* (Oxford: Berghahn Books, 2012), 1–27.

[17] In more recent versions of this origin myth, nature is filled with "biodiversity" – that is, a complex web of life forms and the relationships between them on a range of scales, from ecosystems to species to genes.

[18] The first US national parks such as Yellowstone (1872) aimed to preserve what was seen as "untouched" nature. Early national parks in Europe, on the other hand, recognized that landscapes on the continent had been occupied by humans for millennia, but insisted on recreating a primeval state of nature by banning visitors from their territories. See Patrick Kupper, *Creating Wilderness: A Transnational History of the Swiss National Park*, The Environment in History: International Perspectives 4 (New York: Berghahn Books, 2015).

saved by national parks says more about aspirations of modernity and progress – after all, parks were first envisioned as a civilized nation's heritage – than about nature itself. In fact, there is no such thing as pristine nature. Not, at least, where humans have chosen to establish their national parks.[19]

Historical scholarship has contested the pristine-nature mythologies underlying the creation of national parks and related protected areas. The work of environmental historians and paleoecologists, for example, has revealed the anthropogenic origins of the ecosystems found inside national parks, which are commonly gazetted in areas that previously harbored human populations, in some cases for millennia. Ancient human societies have managed the forests, savannas, and deserts chosen by modern conservationists for protection. Scholars also have shown how the implementation of nature preserves was carried out by displacing the recent human groups previously inhabiting those areas. In the Americas, these are usually indigenous and peasant communities, which one day woke up to find their land encroached on by a national park demanding their removal. Parks can also mean alienating surrounding communities from precious natural resources and sites with cultural and religious significance.[20] Not all nature preserves, however, adhere to the myth of pristine nature. The national parks established in Mexico in the 1930s, for example, were envisioned as spaces of both nature *and* humanity.[21] More recently, with the rise of the concept of "sustainable development" and

---

[19] William Cronon, "The Trouble with Wilderness; Or, Getting Back to the Wrong Nature," in *Uncommon Ground: Rethinking the Human Place in Nature*, ed. William Cronon (New York: W. W. Norton & Co., 1996); Antônio Carlos Sant'Ana Diegues, *O mito moderno da natureza intocada*, 6th ed. (São Paulo: Hucitec, 2008).

[20] Roderick Neumann, *Imposing Wilderness: Struggles over Livelihood and Nature Preservation in Africa* (Berkeley: University of California Press, 1988); Dan Brockington, *Fortress Conservation: The Preservation of the Mkomazi Game Preserve* (Bloomington: Indiana University Press, 2002); Jonathan S. Adams and Thomas O. McShane, *The Myth of Wild Africa: Conservation without Illusion* (Berkeley: University of California Press, 1997); Mark Spence, *Dispossessing the Wilderness: Indian Removal and the Making of the National Parks* (New York: Oxford University Press, 1997).

[21] Postrevolutinary Mexico established dozens of national parks in the 1930s during the Lázaro Cárdenas administration. Following the spirit of the 1917 revolutionary constitution, the Mexican parks had, by design, the goal of accommodating peasant demands for natural resource use. See Wakild, *Revolutionary Parks*. See also Lane Simonian, *Defending the Land of the Jaguar: A History of Conservation in Mexico* (Austin: University of Texas Press, 1995), 91–101, 107–108; and Christopher R. Boyer, *Political Landscapes: Forests, Conservation, and Community in Mexico* (Durham: Duke University Press, 2015), 94–95.

the recognition that local communities have a stake in the conservation of the lands where they live and work, there is a proliferation of new categories of protected areas that allow human settlement and low-intensity economic activities, particularly in Latin America. Among new, more inclusive, conservation directives are the "extractive reserves" introduced in Brazil in the 1980s and the "Parks with People" policy of Colombia in the 1990s.[22]

Back in the 1930s, Iguazú and Iguaçu National Parks carved a path that diverged from their counterparts in other regions of the Americas, for they were initially established to promote borderland settlement and development. Instead of reproducing the unpopulated landscapes found in US parks or creating inclusive spaces for traditional communities as in the Mexican example, policymakers in Argentina and Brazil designed their national parks to attract settlers to "nationalize" border zones.[23] They hoped to use parks to populate sparsely inhabited borderlands with migrants from their densely populated Atlantic seaboards. The border parks would provide for innovative ways of promoting territorial occupation, leading to protected areas that diverged from the other national park examples at the time.

In the case of Argentina, national park proponents consciously deviated from their initial inspiration in the US national park system. They conceived of Argentine parks in the 1930s as tools for colonizing and occupying borderlands and gazetted them alongside the country's international boundaries with Brazil and Chile for this very purpose. Among Argentine parks, the goal was to develop population centers. The

---

[22] Stephan Amend and Thora Amend, eds., *National Parks without People? The South American Experience* (Quito: IUCN/Parques Nacionales y Conservación Ambiental, 1995); Kathryn Hochstetler and Margaret E. Keck, *Greening Brazil: Environmental Activism in State and Society* (Durham: Duke University Press, 2007); Emily Wakild, "Environmental Justice, Environmentalism, and Environmental History in Twentieth-Century Latin America," *History Compass* 11, no. 2 (2013): 163–76; Mary Allegretti, Mauro W. Barbosa de Almeida, and Augusto Postigo, "O legado de Chico Mendes: Êxitos e entraves das reservas extrativistas," *Desenvolvimento e meio ambiente* 48 (November 2018): 25–49; Eve Z. Bratman, *Governing the Rainforest: Sustainable Development Politics in the Brazilian Amazon* (New York, NY: Oxford University Press, 2019); Claudia Leal, "National Parks in Colombia," *Oxford Research Encyclopedia of Latin American History* (March 2019).

[23] In Chile, the central government also used conservation, as well as forestry, to extend its control over frontier territory. However, the Chilean government never used parks as settlement tools in the way of its Argentine neighbors. Thomas M. Klubock, *La Frontera: Forests and Ecological Conflict in Chile's Frontier Territory* (Durham: Duke University Press, 2014).

Argentine national park system was unique, therefore, in its mandate to sell lots of national park land to, exclusively, Argentine citizens. The Argentine national parks of the 1930s also provided essential services such as schools and hospitals for a growing community of migrants settling in park lands. Brazil followed Argentina in funneling national park funds into developing its side of the border, but it refrained from using national park lands to create settlements. On the Brazilian side of the border, colonization was carried out mostly by local governments and private colonization companies. Iguaçu National Park was designed to support the advance of colonization in the surrounding area, but things did not go as planned, and thousands of white Brazilian farmers ended up also settling inside the territory of the Brazilian park. In this way, both Iguazú National Park and Iguaçu National Park reached the 1960s harboring large populations of settlers. The two parks had entire zones with hundreds of families living on farms and in villages and towns. At the same time, they also had vast expanses of old-growth forest spread through other parts of their territories.

Things changed over the course of the decade when the rise of a transnational consensus that defined national parks as unpopulated spaces compelled administrators in each country to rethink the nature of the two parks. This shift happened at a variety of levels.[24] At the international level, the late 1960s witnessed the consolidation of a concept of national park that excluded human dwelling and agricultural or extractive uses. This change took place in international bodies such as the Food and Agriculture Organization of the United Nations (FAO) and the International Union for Conservation of Nature (IUCN).[25] At the national level, a group of agricultural and life scientists employed by the

[24] Environmental history, as Richard White has suggested, offers historians the chance of understanding complex issues on multiple scales. See Richard White, "The Nationalization of Nature," *The Journal of American History* 86, no. 3 (1999): 976–986.
[25] The new 1960s paradigm updated and systematized the "Yellowstone model" of national parks for international adoption. The model was based on, among other things, government protection of natural landscapes through the eviction of the local population. Stan Stevens, "The Legacy of Yellowstone," in *Conservation through Cultural Survival: Indigenous Peoples and Protected Areas* (Washington, DC: Island Press, 1997); John Schelhas, "The U.S. National Parks in International Perspective: The Yellowstone Model or Conservation Syncretism?," in *National Parks: Vegetation, Wildlife and Threats*, ed. Grazia Polisciano and Olmo Farina (New York: Nova Science Publishers, 2010); Karen Jones, "Unpacking Yellowstone: The American National Park in Global Perspective," in *Civilizing Nature: National Parks in Global Historical Perspective*, ed. Bernhard Gißibl, Sabine Höhler, and Patrick Kupper (New York: Berghahn Books, 2012); Claudia Leal, "Behind the Scenes and out in the Open: Making Colombian National Parks

state, which had, from the parks' beginning, advocated a strict policy
banning the presence of humans, gained the upper hand as they gradually
replaced the retiring older generation of national park administrators.[26]
Finally, at the border level, the presence of settlers inside the parks
increasingly became a minor point of geopolitical contention between
the two countries, as settlers from one park repeatedly crossed the international border to hunt in the neighboring park.

This shift in the meaning of "national park" created the conditions for
the removal of park settlers from Iguazú and Iguaçu in the 1960s and early
1970s and the reforestation of previously occupied areas. The removal
occurred at the height of the military dictatorships in Argentina and
Brazil, and it was enmeshed in the politics of national security and the
policies of frontier intervention of the time. The eviction was also a spatial
process, in the sense that the political disputes between state agents and
settlers revolved around different interpretations of space and place. In
Argentina, the national park agency, working in concert with the federal
and provincial governments, decided to redraw the boundaries of Iguazú
National Park to exclude the areas already occupied by settlers. This
included Puerto Iguazú, a town of 3,000 created in the 1930s by
Argentina's national park agency inside the park territory. Across the
border in Brazil, the military government opted for a more radical solution, forcibly removing 2,500 settlers to keep the boundaries of Iguaçu
National Park intact. On both sides of the border, the threat of state
violence, of classifying those who resisted as "subversives" or internal
enemies, was always present.

The evictions bring to light the complex relationship between authoritarian regimes, conservation, and land policy in South America.[27] They also

---

in the 1960s and 1970s," in *The Nature State: Rethinking the History of Conservation*, ed.
Claudia Leal et al., Routledge Environmental Humanities (Oxford: Routledge, 2017).

[26] Twentieth-century Latin America provides several examples of technocrats determined to
intervene in the relationship between society and the environment. For recent examples in
the literature, see Mark Carey, *In the Shadow of Melting Glaciers: Climate Change and
Andean Society* (New York: Oxford University Press, 2010); Gregory T. Cushman,
Guano and the Opening of the Pacific World: A Global Ecological History (Cambridge:
Cambridge University Press, 2013); Regina Horta Duarte, *Activist Biology: The National
Museum, Politics, and Nation Building in Brazil* (Tucson: University of Arizona Press,
2016); Eve E. Buckley, *Technocrats and the Politics of Drought and Development in
Twentieth-Century Brazil* (Chapel Hill: University of North Carolina Press, 2017);
Mikael Wolfe, *Watering the Revolution: An Environmental and Technological History
of Agrarian Reform in Mexico* (Durham: Duke University Press, 2017).

[27] Authoritarianism and conservation are not necessarily situated on opposite poles, as a vast
literature on fascism suggests. The 1970s were a different period, but as David Harvey

complicate the claim that national parks in Latin America have done a better job integrating local populations and nature conservation.[28] Iguaçu and Iguazú national parks offer clear examples of Latin American states taking coercive measures, including human rights violations, to rid protected areas of their inhabitants. Ultimately, the 1960s reorientation of Argentine and Brazilian environmental policy and the 1970s forcible removal of settlers endowed the borderlands with enduring patches of subtropical forests. By the 1980s, mentions of the recent presence of settlers inside the parks had disappeared from the parks' official communications, and each park was named a United Nations Educational, Scientific and Cultural Organization (UNESCO) World Heritage Site as a nature preserve with "no permanent human population."[29]

CONSTRUCTING PARK BOUNDARIES

How do borders make a stretch of land into a national park? Twentieth-century protected areas are, at their most basic level, an imaginary polygon projected on a landscape. The edges of said polygon, its boundaries, separate the land, rivers, rocks, plants, humans, and other animals inside them from that which exists outside via a distinct legal system. Outside the boundaries of the park, one can own land, grow crops, and move freely. Inside, the state owns the land and subjects its space to different and more restrictive rules of resource and land use. The borders of a national park are designed to regulate the movements and behavior of people who find themselves within its area. At Iguazu, for example, hunters become poachers after they cross national park boundaries.

points out, a number of ecologists in that decade argued that authoritarian solutions might offer the only way out of the contemporary ecological crisis. David Harvey, *Justice, Nature, and the Geography of Difference* (Cambridge, MA: Blackwell Publishers, 1996), 177.

[28] Mark Carey, "The Trouble with Climate Change and National Parks," in *National Parks Beyond the Nation: Global Perspectives on "America's Best Idea,"* ed. Adrian Howkins, Jared Orsi, and Mark Fiege (Norman: University of Oklahoma Press, 2016), 267.

[29] IUCN, "Advisory Body Evaluation – Nomination to the World Heritage List No. 303 – Iguazú National Park" (UNESCO, December 31, 1983), UNESCO, http://whc.unesco.org /en/list/303/documents/; IUCN, "Advisory Body Evaluation – Nomination to the World Heritage List No. 355 – Iguaçu National Park" (UNESCO, December 27, 1984), UNESCO, http://whc.unesco.org/en/list/355/documents/. In its early days, the World Heritage Convention favored a view that equated natural heritage with pristine areas devoid of human intervention. See Christina Cameron and Mechtild Rössler, *Many Voices, One Vision: The Early Years of the World Heritage Convention* (Farnham, Surrey; Burlington, VT: Ashgate, 2013), 59–63.

Parks and other types of reserves are constituted through a multilevel process of enforcement and contestation of boundaries. Like other types of borders, national park boundaries are spatial phenomena, for they occur in space and produce specific places. Moreover, national parks are historical, in that their territories continue to be produced by social and political practices years after being established in law. My goal here, therefore, is threefold: to historicize the national parks at the Argentine–Brazilian border through the spatial practices that put together different groups in such particular spaces, to understand how changes in national park paradigms affected these spatial practices, and to assess the type of landscape produced by these national parks at the Triple Frontier. By establishing a bounded territory with distinct rules of land use, national parks, and the ecosystems inside them, are as much the result of human spatial processes as a farm or a city is, regardless of how "untouched" the nature inside the parks might be considered to be.[30]

A commonsense understanding of borders assumes they are able to be impenetrable, an idea betrayed by the term "porous border." One can only call a border porous if one presumes the existence of impervious ones. My analysis of the two Iguazu parks starts from the premise that all borders are porous and that permeability is not a defect but a constitutive feature of them. In Iguazu, park boundaries work as a filter, allowing some flows of people, animals, resources, and information to pass while barring others. They also work as a funnel, concentrating movement in checkpoints for ease of control, as in the present-day case of tourists who are directed to the parks' main gates and from there to the waterfalls.[31] Poaching is another example: the enforcement of park boundaries reoriented hunting to other areas, at times leading hunters to cross the international border between the two countries.[32]

In the 1930s, geopolitical competition between Argentina and Brazil, coupled with disputes between local and federal governments on either side

---

[30] Henri Lefebvre's idea of space as the product of social processes provides the main inspiration here. See Henri Lefebvre, *The Production of Space* (Oxford, UK: Blackwell, 1991). On how modern states produce nature through protected areas, see Kelly et al., *The Nature State.*

[31] For a detailed discussion on borders as technologies that divert and redirect movement, see Thomas Nail, *Theory of the Border* (New York: Oxford University Press, 2016).

[32] As we will see in Chapter 5, park boundaries would also mediate the exchange of information between park rangers and hunters through a game of surveillance and evasion. For a discussion on borders and communication in a different context, see Paul Carter, *The Road to Botany Bay: An Exploration of Landscape and History* (Minneapolis: University of Minnesota Press, 2010), 154–65.

of the border, contributed to the creation and expansion of Iguazú and Iguaçu. The following decades witnessed the beginning of the enforcement of park borders as well as changes in their very nature. Argentina experienced the most radical change, with boundaries that had initially allowed the presence of settlers in park lands redrawn to exclude dwellers after a paradigm shift in the 1960s. The boundaries of the national parks at Iguazu were also enforced by wardens and rangers working in the backcountry. To fight poaching, logging, heart-of-palm theft, squatting, and land grabbing, each park deployed employees along its outer boundaries, launching surveillance expeditions to search for signs of trespassing. Movement, therefore, is a key aspect of the construction of Iguazú and Iguaçu. The national parks established their boundaries to control movement of people and natural resources inside and outside of their territories and employed movement as a surveillance tactic to enforce those boundaries.[33]

An examination of the park administrations' attempts to control the movements of tourists, settlers, hunters, scientists, and park rangers reveals a series of disputes over space.[34] Power, therefore, is another useful category for understanding the two national parks. Among other things, it is through competition between different groups for the right to access specific spaces, or the resources inside them, that an institution like a national park is established in the first place. Borders constitute an easy way to control people's behavior by determining who and what is allowed within a bounded space. In a national park, boundaries act as a universal and impersonal tool for projecting the power of national park administrators, government agencies, and, ultimately, the state itself over everything and everyone inside and in the immediate surroundings of

---

[33] Historians have proposed movement as the key human phenomenon for understanding spatial practices. Indeed, movement is a crucial dimension in history, as humans shape the world in which they live by moving their bodies in space. Richard White, "What Is Spatial History?," *The Spatial History Project*, February 1, 2010, accessed on June 15, 2015, https://web.stanford.edu/group/spatialhistory/cgi-bin/site/pub.php?id=29.

[34] Some authors compared the establishment of parks to the process of encroaching on commons and primitive accumulation in England described by Marx. I believe, however, that such an analogy does not work for parks such as Iguazú and Iguaçu, since much of their area is off-limits to tourists and just a small section of the parks is commodified for tourism. See Nancy Lee Peluso and Christian Lund, "Introduction," and Alice B. Kelly, "Conservation Practice as Primitive Accumulation," both chapters in *New Frontiers of Land Control* (London: Routledge, 2013); James Fairhead, Melissa Leach, and Ian Scoones, "Green Grabbing: A New Appropriation of Nature?," *The Journal of Peasant Studies* 39, no. 2 (October 2011): 237–261; and Catherine Corson, "Territorialization, Enclosure and Neoliberalism: Non-State Influence in Struggles over Madagascar's Forests," *Journal of Peasant Studies* 38, vol. IV (2011): 703–26.

a demarcated area.[35] At the Argentine–Brazilian border, federal agencies worked for years to control the types of behaviors allowed in the national parks by drawing boundaries, parceling out land, zoning, and, later, displacing settlers. Each park in its way eventually prohibited settlers from logging and hunting, banned them from planting crops, and finally removed them altogether. At the same time, the two parks allowed the presence of visitors in areas set aside for tourism, such as around Iguazu Falls. By controlling the types of human behavior inside the national parks through establishing park boundaries, the state was able to test policies of territorial intervention that would soon be applied at a large scale in other contexts. In the case of Iguaçu National Park, for example, the Brazilian military dictatorship tested a newly developed framework of top-down agrarian reform to remove settlers from the park area in the early 1970s.[36] Soon after, the dictatorship employed the same agencies and legislation used in the Iguaçu eviction in its program of territorial intervention in Amazonia.

POCKETS OF ATLANTIC FOREST

My initial interest in studying Iguazú and Iguaçu national parks stemmed from their statuses as two of the most extensive remaining patches of Atlantic forest. The biome originally stretched along a large portion of the eastern coast of South America, from a strip of tropical rainforest near the Equator in northeastern Brazil to subtropical expanses in southern Brazil, northeastern Argentina, and eastern Paraguay. When the Portuguese arrived at the coast of present-day Bahia in 1500, the Atlantic forest occupied an area of about 1.2 million square kilometers and was home to several indigenous peoples who spoke Tupi-Guarani and Macro-Gê languages.[37] The Atlantic forest was the landscape that received the brunt

---

[35] Geographer Robert Sack defined the deployment of power through space as *territoriality*. Robert David Sack, *Human Territoriality: Its Theory and History* (Cambridge, UK: Cambridge University Press, 1986).

[36] Here, Brazil was not unique. In the 1960s, countries as diverse as Chile, Peru, and Costa Rica began employing agrarian reform tools to implement conservation policy and establish protected areas. New legislation and agencies allowed governments to expropriate land and relocate people to promote land reform, frontier colonization, and conservation. See Klubock, *La Frontera*; Sterling Evans, *The Green Republic: A Conservation History of Costa Rica* (Austin: University of Texas Press, 1999); Mary L. Barker, "National Parks, Conservation, and Agrarian Reform in Peru," *Geographical Review* 70, no. 1 (1980): 1–18.

[37] Hereafter, area numbers for the Atlantic forest are calculated based on GIS data from World Wildlife Fund, "Terrestrial Ecoregions of the World | Publications | WWF," World

of Portuguese colonization in South America between the sixteenth and nineteenth centuries, providing the biomass, water, and soil that enabled the development of sugar and coffee plantations in colonial and nineteenth-century Brazil.[38] Today, São Paulo and Rio de Janeiro, Brazil's two largest metropolitan areas and the country's industrial core, as well as about 70 percent of the Brazilian population, are located in areas previously occupied by this type of forest. Less than 10 percent of the biome exists today as standing forest.

Given its importance as the locus of much of Brazil's economic development, it is fair to say that the creation of Brazil as a modern nation-state resulted from the exploitation of Atlantic forest. Denunciations of the destruction of the forest via widespread practices such as slash-and-burn agriculture have been a fixture of the discourse of local and foreign elites since the nineteenth century.[39] Such accusations gained scholarly depth in Warren Dean's *With Broadax and Firebrand*, a robust examination of five centuries of "destruction" of Atlantic forest in Brazil.[40] Dean's work remains a core text for anyone seeking to understand the history of the forest and of the society it helped to build in the *longue durée*. Later authors criticized Dean's attempt to explain the destruction of the forest as resulting from the attitudes and mentalities of Portuguese and Brazilian historical agents, arguing that the ravaging of natural resources was a rational response to the institutional and legal frameworks of the time.[41] Others, trying to avoid Dean's excessive declensionism – his fixation on telling histories of decline and destruction – have focused on the role played by nonhuman species in shaping human history.[42]

This book uses the history of Iguazú and Iguaçu national parks as a lens for examining the transformations of the Atlantic forest from a different angle. By centering the historical narrative on the creation of the two

Wildlife Fund, August 1, 2012, www.worldwildlife.org/publications/terrestrial-ecoregions-of-the-world.

[38] Rogério Ribeiro de Oliveira and Verena Winiwarter, "Toiling in Paradise: Knowledge Acquisition in the Context of Colonial Agriculture in Brazil's Atlantic Forest," *Environment and History* 16 (2010): 483–508.

[39] José Augusto Pádua, *Um sopro de destruição: Pensamento político e crítica ambiental no Brasil escravista, 1786–1888* (Rio de Janeiro: Jorge Zahar Editor, 2002).

[40] Warren Dean, *With Broadax and Firebrand: The Destruction of the Brazilian Atlantic Forest* (Berkeley: University of California Press, 1997).

[41] Shawn William Miller, *Fruitless Trees: Portuguese Conservation and Brazil's Colonial Timber* (Stanford: Stanford University Press, 2000).

[42] Diogo de Carvalho Cabral, *Na presença da floresta: Mata Atlântica e história colonial* (Rio de Janeiro: Garamond, 2014).

borderland parks, it steers the history of the Atlantic forest away from Brazil's industrial and populational core. The works of Dean and his interlocutors share a focus on Brazil's eastern seaboard, crafting a history that is confined in its geographical scope to the heavily populated areas around Rio de Janeiro, São Paulo, and northeastern Brazil. This geographical bias stems from a focus on the early modern period,[43] as these were the regions that received the largest share of newly arrived Portuguese settlers and enslaved Africans at the time.[44] However, Atlantic forest also covered Brazil's present-day states of Rio Grande do Sul, Santa Catarina, and Paraná as well as neighboring countries.[45] Indeed, two-fifths of the biome's total area in the precolonial period was found in southern Brazil, northeastern Argentina, and eastern Paraguay.[46] There, in the interior highlands and riverine valleys of the Paraná River basin, a traveler accustomed to the rainforests of coastal Brazil would find a somewhat different Atlantic forest: subtropical, marked by short cold winters, abundant with deciduous trees, and home to the coveted Paraná pine (*Araucaria angustifolia*), one of the few conifers native to eastern South America.

Looking at the Atlantic forest from the borderland opens a window onto a different history of the forest. At the border, the biome can no longer be considered inherently Brazilian, as is tacitly assumed in much of the historiography. From an Argentine (or Paraguayan) standpoint, even its name, "Atlantic forest," could be a misnomer, for their share of the biome is located far from the ocean. The term is a translation from the Portuguese *Mata Atlântica,* of Brazilian coinage, and reflects the fact that in Brazil, this

[43] Dean's *With Broadax and Firebrand* covers the nineteenth and twentieth centuries, but its geographical scope is determined in its colonial chapters.
[44] Stands of Atlantic forest in present-day eastern Minas Gerais, however, remained off-limits to settlement during the colonial period through a combination of crown policy and indigenous resistance. See Hal Langfur, *The Forbidden Lands: Colonial Identity, Frontier Violence, and the Persistence of Brazil's Eastern Indians, 1750–1830* (Stanford: Stanford University Press, 2006).
[45] There is a growing literature on the environmental history of Atlantic forest in southern Brazil. Recent works include Sílvio Marcus de Souza Correa and Juliana Bublitz, *Terra de promissão: Uma introdução à eco-história da colonização do Rio Grande do Sul* (Santa Cruz do Sul: EDUNISC/UPF, 2006); Eunice Sueli Nodari and João Klug, eds., *História ambiental e migrações* (São Leopoldo: Oikos, 2012); Jó Klanovicz, Gilmar Arruda, and Ely Bergo de Carvalho, eds., *História ambiental no sul do Brasil: Apropriações do mundo natural* (São Paulo: Alameda Editorial, 2012); and Eunice Sueli Nodari, Miguel Mundstock Xavier de Carvalho, and Paulo Afonso Zarth, eds., *Fronteiras fluidas: Floresta com araucárias na América Meridional* (São Leopoldo: Oikos, 2018).
[46] The Brazilian South harbors about 31 percent of the original area of the Atlantic forest, Argentina about 2 percent, and Paraguay 7 percent. Data extracted from World Wildlife Fund, "Terrestrial Ecoregions."

complex of forests covered most of the country's Atlantic eastern seaboard. A rather new concept, *Mata Atlântica* gained its modern meaning only in the 1980s, in the context of the rise of new environmental groups in southeastern Brazil fighting to preserve what was left of the *mata* around São Paulo and Rio de Janeiro.[47] Soon it entered the Brazilian scientific and popular lexicon, becoming common currency among Brazilian policymakers.[48] For geographical and cultural reasons, it took longer for the term to be adopted in neighboring Argentina and Paraguay.[49] Argentine policymakers and scientists have historically referred to the forest in the Misiones Province as *Selva Misionera* (Misiones Jungle), a name that presents it not only as part of the political boundaries of Argentina but also as an exotic and distance place.[50] In fact, Argentine sources, especially those from the Pampas region, tend to depict the borderland forests with romantic or tragic undertones, as a *selva* (jungle) that is overdetermined by inscrutable natural forces and human exploitation[51]

---

[47] A search for the term "Mata Atlântica" in digitized Brazilian newspapers at the Hemeroteca Digital and in the *Folha de São Paulo* database found uses of the term from as early as 1939, but in the sense of specific types of forest formations, not as a biome or ecological region encompassing the entire Brazilian eastern seaboard. The first instance of using "Mata Atlântica" to refer to a region appears in a 1971 op-ed written by environmentalists. By the 1980s, the term was commonly used in the press. Roberto Macedo, "Riqueza que se esvae," *Correio da manhã*, July 30, 1939; Alcione T. Silva, "A natureza violentada dá-nos em troca uma atmosfera irrespirável," *Folha de São Paulo*, May 24, 1971. See also Ibsen de Gusmão Câmara, "Breve história da conservação da Mata Atlântica," in *Mata Atlântica: Biodiversidade, ameaças e perspectivas*, ed. Carlos Galindo-Leal and Ibsen de Gusmão Câmara (Belo Horizonte: Fundação SOS Mata Atlântica and Conservação Internacional, 2005).

[48] In 1988, the "Atlantic forest" was included in the new Brazilian constitution as a biome to be protected. See Chapter 14, "Getting It off the Paper," in Dean, *With Broadax and Firebrand*.

[49] Eventually, the term was adopted in Argentina and Paraguay in response to a biome and ecoregion classification proposed by international organizations such as the World Wildlife Fund and Nature Conservancy. The aforementioned volume *Mata Atlântica: Biodiversidade, ameaças e perspectivas* (2005) marks an attempt by Brazilian scientists to include Argentines and Paraguayans in the discussion of the Atlantic forest. See also David M. Olson et al., "Terrestrial Ecoregions of the World: A New Map of Life on Earth: A New Global Map of Terrestrial Ecoregions Provides an Innovative Tool for Conserving Biodiversity," *BioScience* 51, no. 11 (2001): 933–38; David M. Olson and Eric Dinerstein, "The Global 200: Priority Ecoregions for Global Conservation," *Annals of the Missouri Botanical Garden* 89, no. 2 (2002): 199–224.

[50] Justo Herrera (ranger at Iguazú National Park), in discussion with the author, August 2014.

[51] Misiones inspired an entire genre of novels and movies set in the "jungle" in Argentina. Across the border, in Brazil, there was nothing close to this. The classic Argentine example is Alfredo Varela's *El río oscuro*, first published in 1943, which denounced the exploitation of workers on the yerba mate farms in Misiones. It was made into a 1952 movie directed by Hugo del Carril, titled *Las aguas bajan turbias*.

For many twentieth-century Brazilians, on the other hand, the forests they encountered on their side of the border were just *mata* (forest), not too different from the ones their ancestors exploited in coastal areas.

Examining the fate of the Atlantic forest as a result of the establishment of Iguazú and Iguaçu national parks also allows for an examination of a crucial time in the environmental history of the borderland – the period between the 1950s and 1970s, when hundreds of thousands of incoming settlers transformed the forest into crop fields, highways, and towns. The stretches of Atlantic forest at the borderland had long withstood human intervention – indigenous people have used the forest for millennia and, more recently, the area of the two parks was selectively logged less than a decade before the parks were established. Even so, the mostly white settlers who arrived from the 1950s on introduced a more radical, permanent transformation to the borderland landscape, pushing out Guarani communities and mixed-race peasants, clearing trees, and putting the land to work producing crops. I believe this book is essential for showing how, through a series of spatial and boundary practices, a section of the border landscape was transformed by the Argentine and Brazilian states into spaces of protected nature during this critical conjuncture. The parks show how conservation policy works to create and preserve spaces of nature when a potent extraneous motivator for state engagement is in place. Today, the Brazilian government employs a nationalist discourse to defund its environmental agencies and resuscitate presumptuous dreams of frontier expansion in forested landscapes from their 1980s graveyard. It is enlightening, therefore, to learn how nationalism was wielded in the past to promote the opposite goal of conserving nature.

I

Nationalizing the Border

Argentina, 1898–1944

It promised to be an exciting day for Carlos Burmeister. The Argentine naturalist had persuaded Jordan Hummel, the captain of the steamship *Cometa*, to have the boat wait for him an entire morning while he made the trek to the massive falls of the Iguazu River, on the border between Argentina and Brazil. At thirty-two, Burmeister was an experienced traveler. He had accompanied his late father, the German-Argentine naturalist Hermann Burmeister, in many of his field explorations and had recently traveled to Patagonia on his own to collect birds. Now Carlos was spending the months of June and July 1899 surveying the status of yerba mate production in the northeastern Argentine territory of Misiones on behalf of the country's Ministry of Agriculture. Heretofore, his daily routine had consisted mostly of perfunctory observations of yerba mate operations, but now he would finally have a chance to see something different – the quasi-mythical falls.

At the time, Iguazu Falls attracted very few visitors. To reach them, it was necessary to disembark at a yerba mate port on the Brazilian banks of the Iguazu River and walk or ride mules through swamps and forests for several hours. The only existing land route to the falls cut across Brazilian territory. After spending the first hours of the morning traversing the forest, Burmeister and his guide arrived at the trailhead leading to the falls. At the entrance of the footpath, he was surprised to discover a sign nailed to a large tree: "National Park, March 1897, Edimundo Barros [*sic*]." Asking his local guide, a Frenchman named Puyade, what the sign meant, Burmeister was informed that it had been posted by Barros, a young Brazilian army captain stationed at the border military outpost twenty kilometers away. Burmeister concluded that Barros intended "to reserve the zone surrounding the falls for [the creation of] a national park, like those of the United States of North America [*sic*]."[1] To Burmeister, this might have been an alarming development, as it was a sign of Brazil taking steps to claim its side of a natural monument shared by the two countries.

Argentina, not Brazil, was the pioneer in establishing a national park to protect Iguazu Falls, and this chapter focuses on the creation of Iguazú National Park in 1934. Some of the themes informing the creation of the Argentine park were already present in Burmeister's reaction to the Brazilian "national park" invented by Barros in 1897. The rivalry between the two countries, for example, informed Argentine policy-makers' desire to take material and symbolic possession of their side of the falls. Furthermore, park proponents drew inspiration from the protection of natural landscapes in North America (and to a lesser extent in Europe) and saw national parks as perfect instruments to "Argentinize" the falls and, by extension, the nation's border with Brazil.

The establishment of Iguazú National Park was part of a 1930s boom of protected areas in Latin America that included five other national parks gazetted by Argentina and three by Brazil.[2] This upsurge in national park creation is best understood as part of the general expansion of the state in Latin America after 1929. The Great Depression had dealt a severe blow to most Latin American economies, and the response of country after country was to shift away from the largely laissez-faire policies of the previous decades. The reaction to the crisis included the adoption of new forms of economic nationalism and a renewed focus on expanding the institutional capacity of the state.[3] In the case of Argentina, public

[1] Carlos Burmeister, *Memoria sobre el territorio de Misiones, por el naturalista viajero* (Buenos Aires: Impr. de J. Peuser, 1899), 21–22.

[2] On the creation of national parks in other Latin American countries in the 1930s, see Wakild, *Revolutionary Parks*; Wallace W. Atwood and Instituto Panamericano de Geografía y Historia, *Publicación Núm. 50: The Protection of Nature in the Americas* (México, DF: Antigua Imprenta de E. Murguia, 1940); Rodrigo Pizarro, "The Global Diffusion of Conservation Policy: An Institutional Analysis" (PhD diss., Stanford University, 2012).

[3] On the question of Latin American modernization and state expansion in the 1930s, see Stephen Haber, "The Political Economy of Industrialization," in *The Cambridge Economic History of Latin America*, ed. V. Bulmer-Thomas, John H. Coatsworth, and Roberto Cortés Conde, vol. II (Cambridge: Cambridge University Press, 2006); Lawrence Whitehead, "Latin America as a 'Mausoleum of Modernities,'" in *Latin America: A New Interpretation*, Studies of the Americas (New York: Palgrave Macmillan, 2006); and Lawrence Whitehead, "State Organization in Latin America Since 1930," in *Latin America: Economy and Society Since 1930*, ed. Leslie Bethell (Cambridge: Cambridge University Press, 1998).

expenditure increased from 16 percent of GDP in 1925–29 to 21 percent in 1935–39 as the government of General Agustín Justo (1932–38) responded to the crisis by expanding the role of the state and entrusting several areas of governance to technocrats. It was during Justo's tenure that Argentina established its national park agency and started to develop the country's first national parks.[4]

Argentine policymakers were inspired by international examples of national parks, mainly from Europe and North America. The process of implementing those ideas was far from a reflexive adoption, however, as it involved negotiation between different government stakeholders and adaptation to perceived local needs. As the recent literature on protected areas has demonstrated, the national park model was transformed and adapted from its canonical form in most places, especially before the rise of global environmentalism in the 1970s.[5] Argentina was no different: The country devised national parks as geopolitical tools to "Argentinize" the country's northeastern and Patagonian borderlands through the promotion of tourism and settlement.

The lack of consensus on the tenets of national park policy was recognized by Exequiel Bustillo, the father of national parks in Argentina, as one of the main challenges to conservation. Writing in 1968, Bustillo explained that the absence of a unifying national park doctrine allowed adaptation to local "geographic, economic, and political needs" to occur.[6] In the 1930s, Bustillo and his colleagues understood national parks as drivers of economic development in peripheral areas. They were also cognizant of the geopolitical concerns of Argentine political elites, and they managed to reframe national park policy as an instrument for extending de facto sovereignty to sensitive border regions. Thus, park proponents in Argentina managed to create a national park model that combined their plans of fomenting a tourism industry with government and military officials' goal of promoting colonization at the border. This chapter explores the processes through which Argentine frontier boosters, loosely inspired by foreign examples of

---

[4] David Rock, "Argentina, 1930–46," in *The Cambridge History of Latin America*, ed. Leslie Bethell, vol. VIII (Cambridge: Cambridge University Press, 1991); Tulio Halperín Donghi, *La República Imposible, 1930–1945*, Biblioteca del Pensamento Argentino 5 (Buenos Aires: Emecé, 2007); Whitehead, "State Organization," 415–21.

[5] By canonical form I mean a model understood as being protectionist and exclusionary, which was purportedly drawn from the example of Yellowstone National Park. See Gißibl, Höhler, and Kupper, "Introduction"; Schelhas, "The U.S. National Parks in International Perspective."

[6] Exequiel Bustillo, *El despertar de Bariloche: Una estrategia patagónica* (Buenos Aires: Editorial y Librería Goncourt, 1968), 361–76.

national parks, worked to create the Argentine national park agency and
Iguazú National Park in 1934. It shows how they conceived parks in 1930s
Argentina as vehicles for the settlement and development of frontier regions
vis-à-vis competing neighboring countries.[7]

AN ARGENTINE RESPONSE TO THE BRAZILIAN "NATIONAL PARK"

Because of Iguazu Falls' scale, remote location, and uniqueness, many saw
them as a natural candidate for monumentalization, and thus as
a prominent location for a future national park. The "national park"
created on the Brazilian side of the falls by Captain Edmundo de Barros
was never more than a fabrication by an independent-minded army official deployed on the country's isolated frontier. Nevertheless, the effort he
put into publicizing the idea to visitors encouraged policymakers on the
other side of the border in Argentina to create their own national park.
One such visitor was Argentine politician Juan José Lanusse, the governor
of the Territory of Misiones between 1896 and 1905. In 1898, Lanusse
visited the falls with his family and friends as guests of the steamboat and
logging company Nuñez y Gibaja. Like Burmeister a year later, Lanusse
reached the falls after landing on the Brazilian banks of the Iguazu and
trekking through the forest. In this way, Lanusse ended up seeing the falls
from inside the "national park" established by Barros in Brazil.

Lanusse was amazed by the panoramic view of the magnificent falls and
began devising a plan to bring tourists from Buenos Aires, located 1,700
kilometers downriver. He first persuaded *Porteño* businessman Nicolás
Mihanovich, whose company operated more than 200 steamers in
Argentina, to initiate a regular service to the falls via the Paraná River.
The Mihanovich company started offering a twenty-day cruise (round
trip) in a luxurious steamboat from Buenos Aires to the falls that culminated with a visit to the "wonder of the Americas" that "put Niagara to

---

[7] Anthony Giddens's definition of sovereignty suggests that the gazetting of the Iguazú Park
could be construed as an attempt to employ at the borderlands a suite of powers typical of
a modern state (i.e., the ability to make laws, a monopoly on the means of violence, and
control over policy and economy). Establishing a national park means creating a space of
exception that supports a strengthened version of sovereignty – one in which the state has
extensive powers to control occupation patterns, the nature of labor, and the meaning of
the landscape. See Anthony Giddens, *A Contemporary Critique of Historical Materialism*,
vol. II, *The Nation-State and Violence* (Berkeley: University of California Press, 1987), 49,
119–21, 263–64, 282.

shame."[8] In 1901, the first Mihanovich ship arrived at the mouth of the Iguazu River, bringing a party of thirty tourists from Buenos Aires that included the crème de la crème of the Argentine elite. With 3,000 pesos donated by Victoria Aguirre, a Buenos Aires socialite who took part in the first 1901 excursion, Lanusse began building a road to the falls within Argentine territory, which would eliminate the embarrassing need for disembarking on the Brazilian side. Lanusse also started pressuring the Argentine government to create a real national park on the Argentine side of the falls. To this end, in 1902 he wrote a decree designating the lands around the falls for the creation of a park.[9]

As governor of a federal territory, Lanusse did not have the power to create a national park, but he persuaded the Argentine minister of the interior, Joaquín Víctor González, to support the initiative. The minister, in turn, commissioned the French-born landscape designer Charles Thays, one of Argentina's most renowned architects at the time, to design a plan for a national park in Iguazu. Since 1891, Thays had been the director of the Buenos Aires Office for Parks and Walkways, and as such was responsible for designing many of the city's Paris-inspired boulevards and plazas as well as the city's zoo and botanical garden.[10] In April 1902, Thays and his team of experts disembarked in Iguazu for a two-month stay, during which they surveyed the Argentine side of the falls and designed a plan for the future national park (see Figure 1.1). The architect was impressed not only by the falls but also by Avenida Aguirre, as he called the still unfinished road connecting the modest port at the mouth of the Iguazu to the cataracts upriver. In the plan he presented to the Ministry of the Interior, Thays expanded the twenty-meter-wide dirt road cutting through the dense forest into a manicured grid of walkways, roads, and gardens. The same principles of ordered and Cartesian nature found in the French-

---

[8] Manuel Bernárdez, *De Buenos Aires Al Iguazú: Crónicas de un viaje periodístico á Corrientes y Misiones*, ed. Luis de Boccard, P. Benjamín Serrano, and Francisco Feuilliand, 2nd ed. (Buenos Aires: Impr. de "La Nación," 1901), 17–18, 127–28.

[9] *Crónica de los gobernantes de Misiones* (Posadas, Argentina: Centro de Investigación y Promoción Científico-Cultural, Instituto Superior del Profesorado "Antonio Ruiz de Montoya," 1979); Emilio B. Morales, *Hacia el Iguazú, cataratas y ruinas* (Buenos Aires: J. Peuser, 1914), 44–45; Emilio B. Morales, *Iguazú, cataratas y ruinas* (Buenos Aires: Talleres Gráficos Argentinos L. J. Rosso, 1929), 111–15; Florencio de Basaldúa, *Pasado, presente, porvenir del Territorio Nacional de Misiones* (La Plata: n.p., 1901); Bernárdez, *De Buenos Aires Al Iguazú*; Santiago Pusso, *Viajes por mi tierra; al Iguazú, a Nahuel Huapí, por las costas del sur* (Barcelona: Casa Editorial Maucci, 1912).

[10] J. P. Daughton, "When Argentina Was 'French': Rethinking Cultural Politics and European Imperialism in Belle-Époque Buenos Aires," *Journal of Modern History* 80, no. 4 (2008): 831–64.

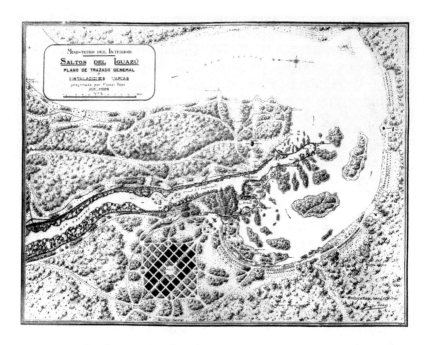

FIGURE I.I Plan for a national park on the Argentine bank of Iguazu Falls by
Charles Thays, 1902. Source: Charles Thays, "Saltos del Iguazú, plano de trazado
general e instalaciones varias, proyectado por Carlos Thays," map (Buenos Aires:
Ministerio del Interior, 1902), as collected in "Ciudad de Buenos Aires – Vistas de
algunos de sus paseos antiguos, 1870–1889." Archivo Thays, Archivo Histórico
de la Ciudad de Buenos Aires

inspired urban parks and plazas he had designed in Buenos Aires guided
his plan for a park in Iguazu.[11]

The push for national parks was gaining momentum in Argentina.
A year after Lanusse lobbied President Julio A. Roca for the establishment
of a national park in the northern tip of the country, in the south the famous
explorer Francisco P. Moreno returned 8,000 hectares of public land he

---

[11] Carlos Thays, "La excursión de Mr. Thays a Iguazú," *Caras y Caretas*, March 31, 1902;
"El Iguazú," *La Prensa*, September 10, 1902; Carlos Thays, "Saltos del Iguazú, plano de
trazado general e instalaciones varias, proyectado por Carlos Thays, 1902," in *Ciudad de
Buenos Aires – Vistas de algunos de sus paseos antiguos – 1870–1889*, DGPIH; Morales,
Hacia el Iguazú, 88–90; Sonia Berjman and Ramón Gutiérrez, *Patrimonio cultural
y patrimonio natural: La arquitectura en los Parques Nacionales Nahuel Huapi
e Iquazú (hasta 1950)* (Resistencia, Argentina: Editorial del Instituto Argentino de
Investigaciones de Historia de la Arquitectura y del Urbanismo, 1988).

had been granted around Lake Nahuel Huapi in Patagonia for the creation of a "natural park."[12] The Argentine government officially accepted the donation in 1904 in a presidential decree reserving the returned land for a future "national park." A decree issued by the Ministry of Agriculture and Livestock in January 1908 delimited the tract of land for the creation of the national park, and Congress passed the Territory Development Act in August of the same year, giving the national government greater powers to make use of public land and build railroads in Patagonia.[13] In 1909, a group of northern congressmen led by the representative Marcial Candioti and the senator Valentino Virasoro protested the exclusion of the Territory of Misiones from the 1908 Territory Development Act and drafted a bill for the development of the northern territory.[14] The new law, passed in September 1909, provided for the creation of a railroad connecting the falls to the rest of the country. More importantly, it also provided for the purchase – or, if necessary, the expropriation – of a 75,000-hectare tract of land at the border with Brazil. Making the land public would allow for the creation of a national park to facilitate tourism to the falls, the establishment of a military colony such as the one Brazil had established on its side twenty years before, and the construction of a hydroelectric power plant for the industrial exploitation of the falls. Provincial politicians already understood national parks as development tools on equal footing with transportation and energy infrastructure.[15]

The new 1909 law cited the military colony and national park on the border with Brazil as the backbone of the future development of Misiones.

[12] Argentina, Law 4192, "Acordando al Señor Francisco P. Moreno como recompensa por sus servicios veinticinco leguas de campos fiscales," August 11, 1903; Francisco P. Moreno to Wenceslao Escalante, "Carta de donación," November 6, 1903, in Administración de Parques Nacionales, *Documentos de la Biblioteca Francisco P. Moreno*, vol. II (Buenos Aires: APN, 2013), APN-B; Frederico Freitas, "As viagens de Francisco Moreno: Visões da natureza e construção da nação no extremo sul argentino – 1873–1903," *Angelus Novus* 1 (August 2010): 115–43.

[13] Ministerio de Agricultura y Ganaderia, Expediente 5-I-1908, "Decreto de reserva de lotes de Nahuel Huapi para parque nacional," January 17, 1908, *Documentos de la Biblioteca Francisco P. Moreno*, vol. II (Buenos Aires: APN, 2013), APN-B; Argentina, Law 5559, "Fomento de los territorios nacionales," September 11, 1908.

[14] "Fomento de Misiones – September 22, 1909," in *Diário de sesiones de la Cámara de los Diputados, Año 1909*, vol. II (Buenos Aires: Congreso Nacional, 1909), 771–72, BCN; "Fomento de Misiones – September 22, 1909," in *Diario de sesiones de la Cámara de los Senadores, Año 1909, sesiones ordinarias* (Buenos Aires: Congreso Nacional, 1909), 731–34, BCN.

[15] Argentina, Law 6712, "Comprendiendo en la ley número 5559 al territorio de Misiones," September 29, 1909; Morales, *Hacia el Iguazú*, 88–90; Graciela Silvestri, *El lugar común: Una historia de las figuras de paisaje en el Río de la Plata* (Buenos Aires: Edhasa, 2011), 360–61.

The plan Thays presented in 1902, which provided for a park along the lines of the urban parks he had designed in Buenos Aires, had to be redone to take into account the new demands of border colonization. In 1911, the Ministry of Agriculture commissioned Thays to update his project, and the architect presented his new plan along with a detailed explanation to Minister Adolfo Mujica in 1912 (see Figure 1.2). What Thays initially had envisioned as a French city park adjacent to the falls grew to the scale of a US national park, with an area of about 25,000 hectares. In his new project, Thays argued that the falls at Iguazu, unlike Niagara, were still surrounded by a beautiful, lush subtropical forest, and state intervention would be needed to avert a repetition of the rampant industrial and commercial development that had spoiled their North American counterpart.[16] This proposal was quite different from his 1902 vision of a manicured landscape, reflecting the influence of US ideas about national parks and the role of forests in the composition of natural scenery.

Thays was never an enemy of development, however, and his plan for the expanded reserve also provided for a panoply of border infrastructure including a railroad connecting Posadas, the capital of Misiones, to the park; an urban settlement; a military colony; highways; a forestry school; a government-run farm; hydroelectric power plants; hotels; and a casino. A closer look at Thays's 1909 national park blueprint makes clear his desire to translate Ebenezer Howard's increasingly popular idea of the *garden city* to a frontier setting. In the concentric rings of the projected town of "Iguazú," the new plan would combine conservation of nature with urban development and modernization.[17] For the architect, all this development

[16] Carlos Thays, "Parque Reserva del Iguazú – Plano de trazado general" (Buenos Aires: Ministerio de Agricultura, 1911), BNRA; Carlos Thays, "Parque Nacional del Iguazú, Informe elevado al Superior Gobierno Nacional," in *Carlos Thays: Sus escritos sobre jardines y paisajes*, ed. Sonia Berjman (Buenos Aires: Ciudad Argentina, 2002), 323–63; Carlos Thays, "Les forêts naturelles de la République Argentine: Project de parcs nationaux" (Congrès Forestier International de Paris, Paris: Touring-Club de France, 1913).

[17] Whereas Ebenezer Howard's original idea introduced garden cities as a solution for insalubrious and overpopulated Britain's industrial centers, Thays's own garden city at Iguazu would contribute to the occupation of a sparsely populated frontier. For the eclectic reception of Howard's ideas in Latin America, see Arturo Alamandoz, "The Garden City in Early Twentieth-Century Latin America," *Urban History* 31, no. 3 (2004): 437–51; Agustina Martire, "Waterfront Retrieved: Buenos Aires' Contrasting Leisure Experience," in *Enhancing the City: New Perspectives for Tourism and Leisure*, ed. Giovanni Maciocco and Silvia Serreli (Heidelberg: Springer, 2009), 245–73. To read Howard in his own words, see Ebenezer Howard, *Garden Cities of to-Morrow (Being the Second Edition of "To-Morrow: A Peaceful Path to Real Reform")* (London: S. Sonnenschein & Co., Ltd., 1902).

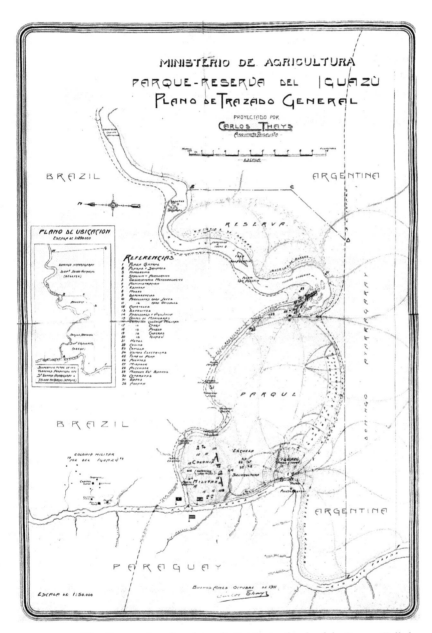

FIGURE 1.2 Plan for a national park on the Argentine bank of the Iguazu Falls by Charles Thays, 1911. Source: Charles Thays, "Parque-Reserva del Iguazú, Plano de Trazado General," Map (Buenos Aires: Ministerio de Agricultura, 1911). Biblioteca Nacional de la República Argentina

not only could be harmonized with the natural beauty of the falls and the surrounding forest but also, in fact, would improve it. As he saw it, the difference between his plan for Iguazu and the uncontrolled development at Niagara Falls was the mind of the planner, who was positioned to improve nature to better suit human needs without spoiling it.[18]

The tension between development and conservation did not go unnoticed by Thays's contemporaries. His harshest objector was Paul Groussac, a traveler, writer, and literary critic who, like Thays himself, was also a Frenchman living in Buenos Aires. After visiting the falls, Groussac contended that implementing Thays's plan would lead to a reproduction of the systematic degradation of the natural scenery created by tourism in places like Niagara Falls and the Swiss Alps. For Groussac, the project bore the "incongruity between the term 'virgin forest' and the barbarisms of [the proposed] boulevards, plazas, casinos, etc."[19] He believed some federal investment was necessary to keep the natural monuments public, but not at the gargantuan scale imagined by Thays – a simple but decent hotel and the renovation of the existing roads and port would suffice. Groussac criticized the excesses he had identified in Thays's 1911 project, pointing out that much of the planned infrastructure would be of more use elsewhere in the Territory of Misiones, in towns such as Posadas or Candelaria whose populations did not have yet access to necessary improvements such as a telegraph line. Where Groussac agreed with Thays was on the need for federal intervention with regard to the border landscape. Both men accepted the call for state action to preserve the falls and the legitimacy of the state claims to expropriate the lands adjacent to the natural monument.[20]

TURNING PRIVATE LAND INTO PUBLIC LAND

In the vast majority of cases, the national government owns a country's national parks. When the state designates private lands as parkland, it

---

[18] The belief in the capacity of the planner to improve nature was championed by others in Latin America at this time. One can think of Miguel Ángel de Quevedo in Mexico as the most prominent booster of the role of public parks, forests, and gardens in the modernization of a country. See Wakild, *Revolutionary Parks*; and Emily Wakild, "Naturalizing Modernity: Urban Parks, Public Gardens and Drainage Projects in Porfirian Mexico City," *Mexican Studies (Estudios Mexicanos)* 23, no. 1 (2007): 101–23.

[19] Paul Groussac, *El viaje intelectual: Impresiones de naturaleza y arte, segunda serie* (Buenos Aires: Simurg, 2005), 232–233.

[20] Ibid., 230–35.

demands their conversion into public land. In Argentina, the lands around Iguazu Falls were in private hands. Domingo Ayarragaray, a Uruguayan-born entrepreneur from Buenos Aires, had acquired the 75,000-hectare estate surrounding the falls in Argentina at auction in 1907. Although Law 6712 had provided for the federal purchase or expropriation of the estate in 1909, the Argentine government did nothing in the following decade. Ayarragaray, for his part, kept his new property idle and waited for the federal government to initiate the proceedings to acquire the estate. When the government in Buenos Aires made no move to purchase or expropriate the area, Ayarragaray decided to put his property to use.[21]

He first moved to profit from the increasing number of people arriving by river to see the cataracts, and in 1920 he hired Buenos Aires engineer Olaf Hansen to build a hotel in front of the falls. The new twenty-four-bedroom Iguazú Hotel was completed in 1922, as a substitute for the rustic wooden lodge that stood there previously. The engineer also built a new road connecting the falls to Puerto Aguirre, the port near the mouth of the Iguazu River where tourists disembarked, shortening by three kilometers the old route built by the territorial government. Hansen became partners with Ayarragaray in Iguazu, managing the hotel and starting an *obraje* on the estate in 1921.[22]

Obrajes (or *obrages* in Portuguese) were the most common type of enterprise in this border area before the 1930s. These companies employed temporary workers of indigenous or mixed descent, usually speakers of Guarani, in logging and yerba mate production. In many firms, the relationship between workers and bosses evolved into a situation of debt bondage analogous to the case of the rubber tappers in Amazonia.[23] In the upper Paraná River, it was common for entrepreneurs to receive land concessions from the governments of Argentina and Brazil of forested areas abundant in hardwood and wild yerba mate, which would be cut, processed, and sent downriver to consumer markets in and around Buenos Aires. At its height, the logging *obraje* on the Ayarragaray estate employed 1,000 seasonal workers and produced more than 6,000 eighteen-meter beams per month. The beams were transported on large timber rafts downriver to Posadas. For this logging

[21] Alberto Carlos Muello, *Misiones, las cataratas del Iguazú, el Alto Paraná y el cultivo de la yerba mate* (Buenos Aires: Talleres s.a. Casa Jacobo Peuser, 1930), 24–28.

[22] Ibid., 40–42, 59–64, 136–39.

[23] Ruy Christovam Wachowicz, *Obrageros, mensus e colonos: História do oeste paranaese* (Curitiba, Brazil: Gráfica Vicentina, 1987), 44–50.

TABLE I.I *Guests at the Iguazú*
Hotel

Year	Guests	Change
1924	525	–
1925	735	+40%
1928	950	+30%

Source: Morales, *Iguazú, cataratas*
y ruinas, 155

operation, Hansen had his workers blaze a series of trails penetrating deep into the woods, and a new port, called Puerto Iguazú, was established on the bank of the Paraná River, from which the rafts floated to Posadas. It was the first time since the late nineteenth century that the forests on the Argentine bank of the Iguazu were subjected to the pressure of human economic activity. Before the twentieth century, the area had been exploited as a source of wild yerba mate, but the activity had since moved northward to the richer forests of Brazil.[24]

Ayarragaray and Hansen's investment in the hotel improved the infrastructure to cater to the increasing stream of visitors coming from Buenos Aires through the Paraná River (see Table 1.1). The majority were members of the *Porteño* elite, but there were also many Europeans and North Americans who wanted to see the mythical cataracts that rivaled Niagara. The development of this nascent tourism industry rekindled in the Argentine government the desire to purchase the area. In 1926, the Ministry of Agriculture commissioned agriculture engineer Franco A. Devoto, along with forest technician Máximo Rothkugel, to survey the Ayarragaray estate and assess its market value in preparation for its nationalization or purchase by the state. Their report exposed the tension between conservation and colonization that dominated Argentine environmental policy up to the 1960s.

On the one hand, Devoto and Rothkugel criticized Thays's plans for a park modeled after the plazas of Buenos Aires, arguing that tourists arriving in the new national park were looking to experience a forest in its "natural state," not the "combed and perfumed" nature of urban parks.

---

[24] Morales, *Iguazú, cataratas y ruinas*, 117–19; Franco E. Devoto and Máximo Rothkugel, "Informe sobre los bosques del Parque Nacional del Iguazú," *Boletín del Ministerio de Agricultura de la Nación* 37, no. 1–4 (1935): 130; Muello, *Misiones*, 40–42, 59–64, 136–39.

All interventions should, therefore, be subtle, avoiding the introduction of nonnative species (the few existent should be extirpated), reforesting human-made clearings, and using rustic materials such as wood and stone in the buildings – thus mimicking the style of the hotel built by Olaf Hansen. On the other hand, the report emphasized, in geopolitical and racial terms, the need to create a military colony similar to the one existing in Brazil before 1910 that had eventually given rise to the town of Foz do Iguaçu. For the two engineers, establishing a military colony would create a vital hub for the "Argentinization" of the borderland.

Misiones already had colonies in other parts of the territory, but in some cases these harbored Brazilians who had moved in from across the border, and the lack of Argentines impeded the communities' cultural assimilation. Although they valued the "racial purity" of these settlers – the majority descended from Germans who had first immigrated to southern Brazil before moving on to Argentina – Devoto and Rothkugel despised their Brazilian "Creole culture" and their material poverty, which the two attributed to the loss of the work ethic that had characterized their German forefathers. Their close-knit communities were also a problem, keeping them isolated from the rest of Argentina. Using the Guarani and mixed-race population already present in this border region for a state-sponsored colony was out of the question for these two *Porteño* engineers. Colonization, like tourism, should focus on whites only. They believed a new colony should receive people from different European backgrounds to dilute group identity and facilitate assimilation. The colony's goal was to transform a heterogeneous influx of white immigrants into a homogenous group of Argentine citizens.[25]

The Argentine government finally purchased the 75,000-hectare estate, along with the hotel and other properties, through an agreement between the Ministries of Agriculture, Interior, War, and Finance on March 12, 1928, for which it paid the sum of 3,199,017.60 pesos to Ayarragaray's inheritors. Twenty years after the passage of Law 6712 in 1909, the Argentine side of the falls had finally become public land. The 1909 law had provided for the creation of a military colony and a national park, which replicated what Argentines perceived to have happened across the border, with a (real) military colony created by Brazil in 1889 in Foz do Iguaçu and a (made-up) national park on the Brazilian side of the falls. It also regulated the harnessing of the falls' hydroelectric power, a stricture that had been rejected since then. The Ministry of Public Works started

[25] Devoto and Rothkugel, "Informe sobre los bosques," 173–75, 177–91.

studying the hydroelectric potential of the falls in 1917. In 1928, a final report concluded that the building of a hydroelectric dam at Iguazu Falls was economically infeasible owing to the location's distance from the major centers of consumption in and around Buenos Aires. The project was dropped, which allowed the Argentine government to focus on border development through settlement and national park policies.[26]

The land was now public, but the creation of the Parque Nacional del Norte, as the project was called in the 1920s, would also require congressional approval and the establishment of a government agency charged with implementing it. The absence of the latter explained the initial failure in creating another national park, the Parque Nacional del Sud in Nahuel Huapi, and served as a cautionary tale for national park proponents in Argentina. This park was gazetted by a 1922 presidential decree, on the Patagonian lands donated by Francisco P. Moreno in 1903, but owing to the lack of institutional support, it existed only on paper until being re-gazetted in 1934.[27]

In the meantime, the Argentine Army would control the estate until a final decision was made. The military maintained a small garrison with sixteen soldiers and, through a concessionaire, exploited the groves of wild yerba mate on the property. The hotel by the falls, which now was state-owned, was also operating through a concessionaire, the Dodero Company. The army authorized the people living on the estate to temporarily plant fruit trees in existing clearings and to cut firewood for personal consumption, but commercial logging as it had been practiced during the Ayarragaray years was strictly prohibited. The military in charge intended to keep the estate free of any significant development until the definitive boundaries between the area of the military colony and the national park were set. The territory of the park was one step closer to becoming an area without extractive activities.[28]

[26] Muello, *Misiones*, 62–64, 136–39, 155; Humberto Gamberale and Francisco A. Mermoz, *Caídas del Iguazú, Salto Grande del río Uruguay y Rápidos de Apipé en el Alto Paraná: Estudio sobre su aprovechamiento hidroeléctrico*, ed. Argentina, Dirección General de Navegación y Puertos (Buenos Aires: Briozzo Hnos., 1928); Ministerio de Agricultura to Administración General de Parques Nacionales y Turismo, Expediente 4132, year 1952, with excerpts from Comisión Pro-Parque Nacional del Sud to Ministerio de Agricultura, Expediente 9758, year 1933, 61–66, APN.

[27] Argentina, Decree, "Creación del Parque Nacional del Sud," April 8, 1922, and Emilio Frey, "Parque Nacional del Sur: Reglamentación Provisória," January 1, 1928, both in APN, *Documentos de la Biblioteca Perito Moreno* 2 (January 2013): 7–9, APN-B.

[28] Ministerio de Agricultura to Administración General de Parques Nacionales y Turismo, Expediente 4132, year 1952, with excerpts from Comisión Pro-Parque Nacional del Sud to Ministerio de Agricultura, Expediente 9758, year 1933, APN.

THE NEW MODEL OF NATIONAL PARK MANAGEMENT

Argentina created Iguazú National Park in 1934, six years after the nationalization of the Ayarragaray estate. The law, which set apart a significant portion of the estate as a preserve, also created a national park agency and another park around Nahuel Huapi Lake in Patagonia, picking up where the early proponents of that southern national park had left off in the 1920s.[29] The 1934 national park act passed in the Argentine Congress with the help of two new lobbies; one from Misiones in the north and the other, more powerful and consequential, made up of a diverse group of Buenos Aires businessmen and politicians connected to the conservative politicians in power in the early 1930s. The Buenos Aires group was crucial to the crafting and passage of the national park act as well as to the establishment of the two parks the legislation gazetted, Iguazú and Nahuel Huapi.[30]

The group of national parks boosters from Buenos Aires included people from different backgrounds, ranging from natural scientists such as Ángel Gallardo to military officers such as General Alonso Baldrich. What they had in common was a connection to the Argentine government – many were employed in the highest echelons of the civil service – and an interest in Andean Patagonia. In 1931, they launched a campaign to reinstate a national park commission that had briefly existed in the 1920s. Initially led by Luis Ortiz Basualdo, the new commission was joined in 1933 by Exequiel Bustillo, who became a key figure in the establishment of a national park system in Argentina. Basualdo and Bustillo were both scions of patrician families from the Argentine capital with real estate interests in Patagonia. They intended to rekindle interest in the creation of a national park in Nahuel Huapi to promote infrastructure works in nearby Bariloche and develop the tourism industry in the Argentine Andes. They had limited knowledge of national parks and conservation – Basualdo introduced the topic to Bustillo as a strategy for reigniting stalled government investment in the region in an unlikely combination of conservation policy and real estate development. But as members of the *Porteño* elite, with family, friendship, and business ties to the conservative politicians in power during Agustín Justo's regime, the group now led by Exequiel Bustillo succeeded in convincing federal officials of the need for national parks in Patagonia.[31]

---

[29] Argentina, Law 12103, "Ley de Parques Nacionales," September 29, 1934.

[30] Bustillo, *El despertar de Bariloche*, 89.

[31] Bustillo, *El despertar de Bariloche*, 18–30, 87–89; Eduardo Miguel Bessera, "Políticas de Estado en la Norpatagonia Andina. Parques Nacionales, desarrollo turístico y consolidación

The Argentine government reinstated the Comisión Pró-Parque Nacional del Sud (Pro-Southern National Park Commission) in 1931, and in 1933 expanded it as a broader Comisión de Parques Nacionales (National Parks Commission), now with Bustillo at its head. More importantly, the commission, which initially focused only on Nahuel Huapi in Patagonia, now incorporated the creation of Iguazú National Park among its responsibilities. Led by Bustillo, the renamed commission gained momentum as it fervently started drafting a national park bill that would provide the legal basis for the creation of both Iguazú and Nahuel Huapi national parks as well as a national park agency.[32] Bustillo's concerns rested mainly on Nahuel Huapi and Patagonia in the south, and he was only nominally invested in Iguazú and the northern part of the country. However, he intended to ensure the commission would have a lasting legacy in the form of functioning national parks and saw the inclusion of Iguazú, a national park in an advanced stage of implementation on the opposite end of Argentina, as a way to institutionalize parks as a national policy. His goal was to avoid the fate of past isolated initiatives that had focused solely on the creation of Nahuel Huapi and had overlooked the establishment of an institutional structure in the form of a national park agency and specific legislation to support it. Including Iguazú in the responsibilities of the new commission was also a response to the general demand among politicians and the military that national parks be used as a tool for the development and nationalization of border zones. This idea was already present in the plans elaborated by Thays in the 1900s and 1910s for Iguazú and was quickly adopted by the group of park proponents led by Bustillo for the entire Argentine park system.[33] Geopolitical concerns were made clear in the 1933 presidential decree expanding the commission, whose seventh article stated that national parks located on international boundaries had the mission to "develop a policy of nationalization of borders."[34]

Bustillo spent months in 1933 drafting the national park bill with the help of other members of the commission – in particular, Antonio

de la frontera. El caso de San Carlos de Bariloche (1934–1955)" (Thesis, National University of Comahue, 2008), 46–47, APN-B; Eugenia Scarzanella, "Las bellezas naturales y la nación: Los parques nacionales en Argentina en la primera mitad del Siglo XX," *Revista europea de estudios latinoamericanos y del Caribe* 76 (2002): 5–21.

[32] Bustillo, *El despertar de Bariloche*, 88–89.   [33] Ibid., 90–91.

[34] Argentina, Decree 33192, "La Comisión Pro-Parque Nacional del Sud, se designará en adelante 'Comisión de Parques Nacionales,'" December 20, 1933, in Argentina, *Boletín Oficial* 2 (January 17, 1934): 580–81.

M. Lynch and Gustavo Eppens. Bustillo recognized that, initially, he had little knowledge of conservation and national parks, but he had an idea of how national park laws would serve to "occupy and nationalize a border where our sovereignty is only nominal."[35] The new legislation included as its backbone the creation of a powerful and semiautonomous national park agency charged with managing national parks and proposing new protected areas. The national park agency would be subordinated to the Ministry of Agriculture, but unlike other departments inside the ministry, it would enjoy greater financial and administrative autonomy to control land in designated areas.

The autonomy of the agency was a crucial point for the framers of the new law, and they closed ranks against attempts by other ministries (e.g., Finance, Interior) to subordinate the new agency to their own offices. Officials inside the Ministry of Agriculture, for example, raised questions about the autonomy of the new national park agency as defined by the new legislation. In his review of the draft of the bill, the head of the Dirección de Tierras (Directorate of Lands) complained that the new text granted excessive powers to the new national park agency, whose sovereignty over protected areas would be comparable to that of the national territories harboring the parks. Despite these criticisms, the commission finished the draft and the executive submitted the bill to the Argentine Congress in September 1934.[36]

National park commission members' ties to the conservative politicians ruling Argentina in the 1930s greased the process of passing the bill. The Senate commission designated to examine and approve the bill was not invested in advancing the matter, so Bustillo used his family and personal connections to set things in motion and collect a majority of signatures to put the bill to vote. One of the senators in the commission, Antonio Santamarina, was Bustillo's wife's uncle. His brother, José María, was a deputy in the lower chamber. Both politicians were members of the National Democratic Party, the conservative party that led the governing coalition and retained the largest number of senators and deputies in the Argentine Congress in 1934. Bustillo also used his contacts in the press to lobby for the passing of the national park act, asking

---

[35] Bustillo, *El despertar de Bariloche*, 91–92.
[36] Bustillo, *El despertar de Bariloche*, 091–097; Ministerio de Agricultura to Administración General de Parques Nacionales y Turismo, Expediente 4132, year 1952, with excerpts from Comisión Pro-Parque Nacional del Sud to Ministerio de Agricultura, Expediente 9758, year 1933, 19, 77–78, APN.

editor friends at *La Prensa* and *La Nación* to write editorials in support of the bill.[37]

The bill was put up for a vote at the end of September 1934. Socialist Senator Alfredo Lorenzo Palacios presented the only serious objection: to a clause requiring that all employees in border national parks be Argentine by birth. Palacios objected that not even senators like himself were required to be born Argentine to assume office. Cruz Vera, the conservative senator from Mendoza who had introduced the bill, explained that the planned national parks were located in border areas "flooded with foreigners," and the article was meant to "Argentinize" the border. Despite his frankness in explaining the geopolitical reasoning behind national park creation, the clause was removed and the bill was finally passed into law.[38] Law 12103, also known as the National Park Act, established the legal framework for an Argentine national park system. The 1934 act created not only the two first national parks in the country – Iguazú National Park in the north and Nahuel Huapi National Park in the south – but also established a national park agency, the Dirección de Parques Nacionales (Directorate of National Parks, DPN).[39]

The new agency enjoyed a great degree of autonomy, with a budget free from the constraints of the Ministry of Agriculture – to which it was formally subordinated – and with the power to create and enforce protected areas. It also had exclusive jurisdiction over the territories of the national parks, especially vis-à-vis other government agencies, a feature partially inspired by the US national park model. A strong, well-funded, and relatively autonomous national park agency like the one created in 1934 in Argentina was an oddity in South America. In neighboring countries like Brazil, national parks, when they were actually implemented, were usually

---

[37] Bustillo, *El despertar de Bariloche*, 107–8; Argentina, *El parlamento argentino, 1854–1951* (Buenos Aires: Congreso de la Nación, 1951), BCN; Argentina, *Nómina de diputados de la nación por distrito electoral: Período 1854–1991 (hasta el 31-5-1991)* (Buenos Aires: H. Cámara de Diputados de la Nación, Secretaría Parlamentaria, Dirección de Archivo, Publicaciones y Museo, Subdirección de Publicaciones e Investigaciones Históricas, 1991), 22; Argentine Senate, Buscador Histórico, accessed June 2019, www.senado.gov.ar/sena dores/Historico/Introduccion.

[38] "11—Creación de la 'Dirección de Parques Nacionales,'" *Diario de sesiones de la Cámara de Senadores—Período ordinario—Tomo II—1° a 30 de Septiembre 1934*, 53ª Reunión, cont. de la 26° Sesión ord. (Buenos Aires: Honorable Senado de La Nación, 1935), 722–30, BCN; "105 – Dirección de Parques Nacionales, Orden del día número 131," *Diario de sesiones de la Cámara de Diputados—Sesiones ordinarias—Tomo VI—Septiembre 21 a Septiembre 30*, Reunión num. 58 (Buenos Aires: Imprenta del Congreso Nacional, 1935), 1017, BCN.

[39] Argentina, Law 12103, "Ley de parques nacionales," September 29, 1934.

put under the supervision of forestry departments or botanical gardens, which lacked funds and specialized personnel.

In the case of Argentina, the new national park agency had the mandate to oversee all park-related issues, preserving the fauna, flora, and geological features of national parks; promoting tourism in the parks; and building infrastructure. On paper, this seems similar to the mission of contemporary national park agencies in North America and Europe.[40] The agency distanced itself from its foreign counterparts, however, in its commitment to nationalizing the border regions and developing settlements.[41] For this purpose, the national park act provided the DPN with the power to allocate public land within parks and reservations to unique uses. The Argentine agency could grant temporary permits for tenants or sell public land in areas reserved for real estate development inside national parks. National park administrators could set the location of new population centers, plan street grids, build urban infrastructure, and sell urban and rural lots of public land within a 5,000-hectare limit inside their territories. From its inception, national park policy in Argentina was designed to merge the potentially contradictory goals of conservation, public use, and urban development.[42]

DEALING WITH THE MILITARY

Argentine park proponents had managed to build a robust legal framework to support the establishment of the country's first national parks. At the heart of the new legislation lay the DPN, a powerful national park agency with the capacity, at least on paper, to act within Argentine territory. But as the DPN's mandate expanded onto other agencies'

[40] In the United States, conservation and providing the means of access were both goals of the National Park Service created in 1916. See Robin W. Winks, "The National Park Service Act of 1916: 'A Contradictory Mandate'?" *Denver University Law Review* 74, no. 3 (1997): 575–624.

[41] In the 1930s, Argentina's territorial nationalism was not limited to the discourse of far-right *nacionalistas*. The view that border areas needed to be "Argentinized" was shared by intellectuals, politicians, and policymakers at different points on the political spectrum and was also common currency within the top brass of the military. On Argentine territorial nationalism, see Carlos Escude, "Argentine Territorial Nationalism," *Journal of Latin American Studies* 20, no. 1 (1988): 139–65. On the fringe, but influential, far-right *nacionalistas*, see David Rock, *Authoritarian Argentina: The Nationalist Movement, Its History and Its Impact* (Berkeley: University of California Press, 1993); and Sandra McGee Deutsch, *Las Derechas: The Extreme Right in Argentina, Brazil, and Chile, 1890–1939* (Stanford: Stanford University Press, 1999).

[42] Argentina, Law 12103, "Ley de parques nacionales," September 29, 1934.

turfs, those agencies resisted transferring their functions to national park officials. For Bustillo and the other members of the national park commission, passing a national park law proved to be easier than convincing other sectors of the government to comply with the new legislation and recognize the DPN's powers and legitimacy. In the case of Iguazú, for example, this type of opposition came from the military.

The Argentine Army, which had assumed control of the Ayarragaray estate after its acquisition in 1928 and was required to hand over the area to the DPN in 1934, resisted for seven years before finally transferring the land to the national park agency in 1941. Anticipating this sort of resistance, in July 1935 Bustillo sent General Alonso Baldrich, then one of the directors of the DPN, to take official possession of the Campo Nacional del Iguazú (Iguazú National Camp), as the military called the estate after 1928. The army handed the hotel and other properties inside the estate over to the agency, but it did not give up the control of the land. In August a presidential decree established that of the estate's 75,000 hectares, 20,000 would be kept by the Argentine Army and 55,000 would be transferred to the DPN as a national park. The boundary between the two areas was to be defined by an agreement between the national park agency and the army.[43]

Setting this boundary proved difficult, as it required the armed forces to accept transferring their sovereignty over a sensitive border area to a new agency whose members had yet to prove their seriousness. The minister of war, General Manuel A. Rodríguez, purposefully delayed the demarcation as a way to postpone the transfer of the area to the DPN. Rodríguez believed the estate and its infrastructure were too important to be given to a "commission created by some politicians' whim" that "could disappear or be substituted by another commission with different ideas." In the following years, Rodríguez and his successors at the Ministry of War kept making vague promises to delimit the boundaries while doing little to advance the matter. In Argentina, in the 1930s, passing a new law did not result in immediate compliance, especially when it came to the perceived institutional interests of different entities that formed the state.[44]

---

[43] General Alonso Baldrich to Dirección de Parques Nacionales, Expediente 0535, year 1935, "Informe sobre toma de posesión del Parque Nacional del Iguazú," APN; Argentina, Decree 64974, August 8, 1935.

[44] Manuel A. Rodríguez to Carlos Acuña, February 14, 1935, Manuel A. Rodríguez to Exequiel Bustillo, March 7, 1935, and Carlos A. Gomez to Exequiel Bustillo, January 26, 1935, all letters in Fondo Exequiel Bustillo, Legajo 7, no. 3349, AGN.

The position of the military started to change by the end of the decade, mainly due to its own failure in bringing settlers to populate the border. A 1939 memo from General Martin Gras, the army chief of staff, to the minister of war, Carlos Márquez, brings to light the army's inability to establish a military colony "to settle an Argentine population in the region to cooperate with the armed forces deployed at the border." Reproducing a common perception among Buenos Aires–centered public officials, Gras blamed Misiones's subtropical forests for the army's failure to attract settlers from the temperate pampas to populate the area.[45] Also, five years after its creation, the DPN had already demonstrated its seriousness not only with the extensive infrastructure it had developed in Nahuel Huapi National Park but also by improving the properties in Iguazú. Since 1935, the agency had renovated the hotel, built pathways and trails by the falls, installed piers at three different points along the Iguazu River, initiated the construction of a 1,000-meter-long grass landing strip near the falls, and finished the park headquarters in Puerto Aguirre. It had become clear that the DPN's plan to develop the border through tourism and the urbanization of Puerto Aguirre could work where the military had failed.[46]

At the beginning of 1939 the Ministry of War, through its Engineering Department, finally agreed to demarcate the boundary between the national park and the military camp. But the process still dragged on for two more years as the two parties disagreed over the location of the boundary line between reserve and military area. National park engineer Ivan Romaro proposed boundaries that required the removal of all military settlements from Puerto Aguirre to the new area controlled by the Argentine Army. The engineer insisted that the area occupied by troops in Puerto Aguirre was essential for the expansion and "hygienization" of the town, as he envisioned a zone of small farms occupying the confluence of the Iguazu and Paraná.[47] The army, unsurprisingly, insisted on keeping the zone for national security reasons, as it was located right at the corner where Argentina, Brazil, and Paraguay met.

Bustillo intervened with the minister of agriculture to expedite a solution with the Ministry of War. After all, he argued, "the entire estate had been in

---

[45] Martin Grass to Carlos Marquez, May 5, 1939, in Dirección de Parques Nacionales, Expediente 0439, year 1939, "Mesura Puerto Aguirre/PNI," 13–15, APN.

[46] Dirección de Parques Nacionales, "Memoria correspondiente al año 1936" (1937), 51–52, "Memoria correspondiente al año 1937" (1938), 145, "Memoria correspondiente al año 1938" (1939), 104, "Memoria correspondiente al año 1939" (1940), 13, APN-B.

[47] Dirección de Parques Nacionales, Expediente 0434, year 1939, "Mesura Puerto Aguirre/PNI," 2–4, 16–43, APN.

the hands of the Army for five years, which had delayed the colonization and settlement of the area of Puerto Aguirre."[48] After two more years of negotiation, the two sides finally reached an agreement based on the DPN's proposed boundary. As a consolation prize, the army would receive lots in Puerto Aguirre along the Paraná River to establish vacation cottages for military officers deployed in the federal territory – an indication that the army's refusal to transfer the control of the area was as much the product of institutional inertia as it was of national security considerations.[49] With the boundaries defined, the Argentine Army passed over control of the estate to the DPN through a presidential decree in September 1941. The decree set the boundary line between army and national park lands and designated 500 hectares of public land in Puerto Aguirre to be sold to private parties for colonization with the rest of the land, both in the park and in the army area, remaining public. The agency could now begin the urbanization and colonization of Puerto Aguirre (see Map 1.1).[50]

THE POWER OF LOCAL PLAYERS

With Nahuel Huapi as the flagship of the new national park system, Iguazú occupied a secondary place. When crafting the national park law, Bustillo and his colleagues included the northern park in the draft legislation mainly to justify the creation of a robust national park agency, which they saw as crucial for the viability of Nahuel Huapi and the development of Patagonia in the south. What, then, explains Bustillo's later commitment to transferring Iguazú National Park's territory to the DPN in light of his lack of interest in anything outside Patagonia? Here, the same family and class connections that facilitated the passage of the national park bill in 1934, allowing him to create the Nahuel Huapi National Park, ended up working in the opposite direction in the early 1940s, pushing him toward a greater commitment to Iguazú. The most significant source of pressure was Carlos Acuña, Governor of Misiones (1930–35), whose lobbying proved to be crucial in preventing Iguazú from becoming a paper park. Acuña was a close friend of José Maria

---

[48] Ibid., 16–43.   [49] Ibid., 60.

[50] The GIS reconstruction of the park boundaries based on historical maps and the legislation indicates that the final area of the park was 44,000 hectares, not the 55,000 set by legislation. The Argentine park would eventually expand to more than 55,000 hectares when its boundaries were redrawn in the 1970s. Argentina, Decree 100133, "Fijándose los límites del Parque Nacional del Iguazú y excluyendo del dominio público 500 Hs., para el trazado del pueblo Puerto Aguirre," September 18, 1941.

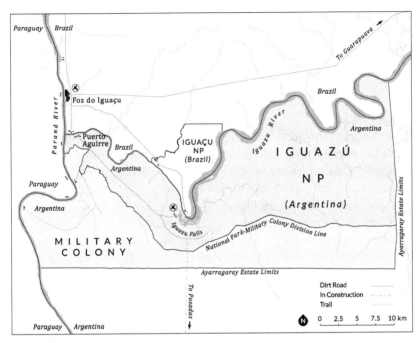

MAP 1.1 Iguazú National Park, Argentina, and Iguaçu National Park, Brazil, in 1941. Map by Frederico Freitas

Bustillo, the conservative federal deputy brother of Exequiel Bustillo who had worked in Congress for the passage of the 1934 national park bill, and thus had direct access to the head of the DPN.

Acuña was deeply invested in the creation of the national park in Iguazu and used his connection with the Bustillos to push the DPN to find a way out of the stalemate with the army. In the many letters Acuña exchanged with Exequiel Bustillo in 1935, he accused him – correctly, as it turned out – of favoring Nahuel Huapi National Park in Patagonia at the expense of Misiones and Iguazú National Park. For months Acuña pressed both Bustillo and the army to solve the imbroglio. Bustillo eventually grew tired of Acuña's pressure, as it steered his focus away from his main interests in Nahuel Huapi. Yet he maintained a conciliatory façade, pointing the finger at the minister of war for "making use of the most absurd and contradictory arguments" to delay transferring the estate. After a face-to-face meeting with Minister of War Rodríguez in June 1935, Exequiel Bustillo succeeded in gaining control of the hotel and other properties in Iguazu, but he fell short of seizing the land. But the renovation of the hotel and roads, the construction of park headquarters, and the assignment of Julio Amarante, Acuña's right-hand man, as Park Director in August 1935 were enough to placate the governor's anxiety.[51]

Julio Amarante was a high-profile federal official working for the government of the Territory of Misiones who had acted as interim governor between June and September 1935 before assuming the post of park director at Iguazú. Originally from Buenos Aires, Amarante had lived fifteen years in Misiones working for the federal government and had a vast knowledge of the federal territory. The first of many of Amarante's demands as park director was the swift construction of the park headquarters (and director's residence), which he required to be located not near the waterfalls, but in Puerto Aguirre. After all, it was the future location of "the most important urban settlement" of the region, to be created by the national park as part of its mission to occupy the border with Brazil. Upon moving in October from Posadas to Puerto Aguirre, Amarante was shocked by the destitution of the hamlet. Life in Puerto Aguirre proved to be almost unbearable thanks to the hot weather, mosquitoes, and lack of adequate accommodations for Amarante's family, who continued to live in Posadas during his tenure as park director. He complained that the rugged wooden house in Puerto Aguirre, where he lived in his first months in the park, lacked "a proper bathroom and shower," noting that guests "would have to make use of the nearby creek when answering the call of nature."[52]

Like Acuña, Amarante pressured Bustillo for more investment in the park and, especially, in Puerto Aguirre, which he classified as a "national disgrace." He found in Miguel Ángel Cárcano, Minister of Agriculture (1936–38), an unexpected ally. While visiting the falls in 1936, Cárcano

---

[51] Carlos Acuña to Exequiel Bustillo, January 29, 1935, and Carlos Acuña to Exequiel Bustillo, letters from November 13, 1934, February 14, 1935, April 11, 1935, April 28, 1935, and June 15, 1935, all in Fondo Exequiel Bustillo, Legajo 7, no. 3349, AGN; Exequiel Bustillo to Carlos Acuña, letters from April 2, 1935, April 22, 1935, June 12, 1935, August 8, 1935, September 19, 1935, October 3, 1935, November 11, 1935, and Exequiel Bustillo to Manuel A. Rodríguez, letters from November 11, 1934, January 7, 1935, April 4, 1935, May 6, 1935, June 21, 1935, all in Fondo Exequiel Bustillo, Legajo 9, no. 3351, AGN; Bustillo, *El despertar de Bariloche*, 429–35.

[52] Amarante insisted that mosquitoes and malaria must be eradicated to make the park a tourist attraction. To that end, he proposed having the area around Puerto Aguirre cleared of its "useless bush," which would be replaced by "valuable artificial hardwood." He suggested flamethrowers to eliminate insects, and draining the marshes near the waterfalls. Julio Amarante to Exequiel Bustillo, October 31, 1935, and Julio Amarante to Exequiel Bustillo, August 14, 1935, both in Fondo Exequiel Bustillo, Legajo 2, no. 3344, AGN.

expressed his support for the development of park infrastructure, which gave Amarante leverage to write Bustillo demanding these investments be made. Yet the head of the DPN turned a deaf ear to most of Amarante's requests, despite the support of Cárcano, who was nominally their boss. Echoing the opinion expressed by Paul Groussac almost three decades earlier, Bustillo emphasized that, unlike the lakes, mountains, and Swiss landscape of Patagonia in the south, Iguazu's only selling point was the waterfalls. After one or two days of visiting, tourists grew bored, as the subtropical forest lacked the same opportunities for leisure one encountered in an alpine setting like Nahuel Huapi. To Bustillo, it was foolish to sink funds into a park with only one main attraction, Iguazu Falls.[53]

Acuña and Amarante were right in complaining about the neglect of Iguazú vis-à-vis Nahuel Huapi, as Bustillo's initial interest in national parks came out of his commitment to developing Patagonia. He shared with others the view of the southern border with Chile, with its snowy peaks, sparse population, and boundary disputes, as a more important target than Misiones for a policy of borderland nationalization through national parks. In 1936 the DPN, through the Ministry of Agriculture, drafted a new bill for the creation of five new national parks, all of them in Patagonia. The new areas were decreed reserves for "future national parks" in 1937 and started receiving investments before being officially gazetted as national parks in 1949, an indication of the consensus around Patagonia as a priority.[54] In the period between 1935 and 1942, Nahuel Huapi alone received 86 percent of all DPN investment in national parks – Iguazú received only 6 percent (see Table 1.2). The national park agency built a 350-bed grand hotel in Patagonian Park and another thirteen smaller hotels, a ski resort, a golf course, more than 600 kilometers of roads, several public buildings in the town of Bariloche (including a city hall, a police station, a courtroom, a library, a market, and a hospital),

---

[53] Julio Amarante to Exequiel Bustillo, letters from October 13, 1936, and December 3, 1936, Fondo Exequiel Bustillo, Legajo 2, no. 3344, AGN; Exequiel Bustillo to Julio Amarante, October 27, 1936, Fondo Exequiel Bustillo, Legajo 9, no. 3351, AGN; Julio Amarante to Exequiel Bustillo, letters from March 28, 1937, March 11, 1938, and May 8, 1938, all in Fondo Exequiel Bustillo, Legajo 3, no. 3345, AGN; Bustillo, *El despertar de Bariloche*, 437–39, 442–48.

[54] These were the national parks of Lanín and Copahue in the Territory of Neuquén; Perito Francisco P. Moreno and Los Glaciares, both in the Territory of Santa Cruz; and Los Alerces in the Territory of Chubut. Argentina, Ministerio de Agricultura de la Nación, *Memoria correspondiente al ejercicio de 1936* (Buenos Aires: Ministerio de Agricultura, 1937), 433–38; Argentina, Decree 105433, May 11, 1937; Exequiel Bustillo to William Vogt, October 15, 1943, Fondo Exequiel Bustillo, Legajo 6, no. 3348, AGN.

TABLE 1.2 *Investment in national parks, 1935–42 (in peso moneda nacional)*

Year	Nahuel Huapi	Iguazú	Lanín*	Los Alerces*	Copahue*	Glaciares/Perito Moreno*	Total
1935	309,828	-	-	-	-	-	309,828
1936	2,868,586	172,354	-	-	-	-	3,040,940
1937	2,443,580	246,241	-	-	-	-	2,689,821
1938	2,383,853	80,389	4,379	5,596	-	-	2,474,217
1939	1,006,751	206,123	101,267	194,713	41,045	-	1,549,899
1940	2,022,678	46,188	84,517	57,736	1,079	-	2,212,198
1941	2,150,842	156,222	58,219	37,662	14,203	4,987	2,422,135
1942	2,300,833	290,967	257,126	138,625	70,160	53,400	3,111,111
Total	15,486,951	1,198,484	505,508	434,332	126,487	58,387	17,810,149

Source: Dirección de Parques Nacionales, "Memoria Correspondiente al Año 1941" (1942), 31, APN-B

* Established as national reserves for the creation of future national parks by the presidential decree 105433 of May 11, 1937. Law 13895 of September 20, 1949, transformed all the reserves into national parks, except for Copahue, which became a provincial park in 1963.

a zoo, and a game reserve stocked with imported Canadian moose and European deer.[55] Exequiel Bustillo's obsession with Nahuel Huapi was so flagrant that in its 1942 annual report, the DPN tried to justify it with a table using the area and population living in and around the parks to show that the agency had actually invested relatively more in Iguazú than in Nahuel Huapi (see Table 1.3). At first glance, the DPN seems reasonable in justifying more investment in Nahuel Huapi than in Iguazú, as the former park was home to 9,800 people (a figure that included the town of Bariloche), in contrast to the mere 431 individuals living at the border where Iguazú was created. Yet, if the goal was to establish a permanent settler population at the border, then parks in areas without established towns, as it was the case of Iguazú, should have been the ones receiving greater federal investment.

As a park, Iguazú was created in the same mold as Nahuel Huapi and the other Argentine national parks of the 1930s and 1940s. They were all conceptualized as instruments for the development and Argentinization of borderlands. Like Nahuel Huapi, Iguazú was devised to promote tourism and attract settlers to the border. The difference between the two parks was quantitative, not qualitative, as Bustillo's preference for Nahuel Huapi diverted resources from Iguazú. Still, this preference was somewhat mitigated by the pressure of local players such as Acuña and Amarante who insistently pushed the Argentine national park agency in Buenos Aires for more significant investments in the area. Bustillo's own view of Iguazú as a destination of minor importance revealed poor foresight, as Iguazú would grow to become the most visited national park in Argentina and would be designated a UNESCO natural heritage site, in 1984.

DEVELOPMENT VERSUS CONSERVATION

All the infrastructure developed by the DPN in Nahuel Huapi, and on a lesser scale in Iguazú, revealed a philosophy that subordinated conservation to tourism, nationalization, and colonization. Bustillo recognized that, internationally, national park policy lacked a clear doctrine, which freed him to embrace an "eclectic" view of protected areas as catalysts for border development. He understood that tourism would inevitably demand intervention in the form of infrastructure work in protected areas. He also doubted the existence of "unspoiled" natural spaces as

---

[55] This list was compiled by Eduardo Bessera based on the DPN annual reports. Bessera, "Políticas de Estado," 49–78, APN-B.

TABLE 1.3 *Investment in national parks by population and area, 1935–42*

Year	Area	Pop.	Annual increase in number of tourists 1938–1942	Investment (peso moneda nacional)	Investment per ha (peso moneda nacional)	Investment per capita (peso moneda nacional)
Nahuel Huapi	780,000 ha	9,800	22.11%	15,488,000.00	19.86	1,580.41
Iguazú	55,000 ha	431	5.04%	1,198,500.00	21.80	2,780.74
Lanín*	393,000 ha	2,917	–	505,510.90	1.28	173.00
Los Alerces*	263,000 ha	444	–	434,334.79	1.65	979.00
Copahue*	90,000 ha	500	–	127,500.00	1.42	255.00
Los Glaciares*	600,000 ha	179	–	58,400.00	.09	326.00
Perito Moreno*	115,000 ha	49	–	–	–	–

Source: Dirección de Parques Nacionales, "Memoria correspondiente al año 1941" (1942), 31, APN-B

* Created as national reserves for the creation of future national parks by presidential decree 105433 of May 11, 1937. Law 13895 of September 20, 1949, transformed all the reserves into national parks, except for Copahue, which became a provincial park in 1963.

defended by most national park proponents at the time. Therefore, in Bustillo's mind national park development, colonization, and conservation could and should all go together. He pointed out that even Yellowstone, a major inspiration for national parks in Argentina, had once yielded to the pressure of tourism, with its park officials putting up a "circus" with "indigenous camps" and "tamed bears" for visitors. He was not interested in such excesses, but as he saw it, there was no point in adopting a model of strict nature protection if such an approach posed a threat to a country's sovereignty or brought harm to its economy.[56]

Bustillo's opinion on the primacy of development over conservation was far from hegemonic. A small group of agricultural and life scientists, including Gustavo Eppens, the head of the DPN's Technical Division, believed national parks should prioritize protecting nature against human action. DPN scientists such as Eppens were conversant on international debates about conservation and preservation of nature. Bustillo, however, viewed them as an orthodox wing inside the national park agency. Clashes between conservationists and development boosters erupted several times early on in the DPN's existence. In 1935, for example, General Alonso Baldrich and Colonel Rómulo E. Butty, the two military members of the DPN's board of directors, proposed to set aside 48,000 of the 55,000 hectares assigned to the agency in Iguazú for settler colonization. They suggested dividing the area into twenty-five-hectare rural lots to be leased to tenants (according to the national park law, the land could not be legally sold). To Baldrich and Butty, there was no point in preserving a recently logged area lacking natural features if only a 2,000-hectare protective buffer around the falls was needed to maintain the park's aesthetic appeal for tourism. They believed the national park commission had recommended the purchase of the entire 75,000-hectare estate only to make the national park bill more appealing. They contested Gustavo Eppens's insistence that 50,000 hectares be designated as a protected national park.[57] Setting aside such a large part of the estate for conservation would be a mistake, the two military men argued, as it would create a "desert" of people in an area primed for colonization.[58]

---

[56] Bustillo, *El despertar de Bariloche*, 361–76.

[57] Alonso Baldrich to Exequiel Bustillo, September 4, 1935, and Alonso Baldrich and Rómulo E. Butty to Exequiel Bustillo, October 3, 1935, both in General Alonso Baldrich to Dirección de Parques Nacionales, Expediente 0535, year 1935, "Informe sobre toma de posesión del Parque Nacional del Iguazú," APN.

[58] In the nineteenth and early twentieth centuries the term *desierto* (desert) was continuously invoked to justify national expansion and federal intervention in frontier areas in

Despite his commitment to colonization, Bustillo was also a pragmatic man, and after consultation on the matter with the first park director, Julio Amarante, he decided to discard Baldrich and Butty's proposal. Amarante, who was not a conservationist himself, explained that the military's idea was nonsensical. Both army and state agents had for years tried to attract farmers to the region, with only partial success. He informed Bustillo that Iguazú was not an appropriate site for the type of colonization practiced in the rest of Argentina: the region had no natural pastures, and settlers would be unable to engage in cattle ranching as they did elsewhere in the country. Moreover, Amarante pointed out that the region's typical agriculture was based on permanent crops, which required a large investment in infrastructure and machinery. Finally, the estate was adjacent to vast expanses of public land, which were easily available to settlers for purchase, not leasing. Interested parties would prefer to settle in an area where they could acquire land instead of inside the park, where land tenure would be limited to temporary contracts. In sum, to Amarante, the two military men's plan was doomed to failure.[59]

The conflict resurfaced again with the suggestion, made at the end of 1939 by the park's second director, Balbino Brañas, of "rational exploitation" of the wild yerba mate groves located inside the park. Brañas was a journalist from Posadas who had acted as provisional director of the Nahuel Huapi (1936) and Lanín (1937) national parks before taking office at Iguazú.[60] In setting the definitive park boundaries, Brañas saw an opportunity for the national park agency to profit from the exploitation of the yerba mate groves. He planned to commission a third party to harvest yerba mate leaves deep in the forest. The director of the park believed that up to 150,000 kilograms of yerba mate could be processed annually, generating income for both the national park and the military colony.

Argentina. The term was used by Buenos Aires caudillo Juan Manuel de Rosas in his campaigns against natives (1833–34), was popularized during the Sarmiento administration (1868–74), was later used to name the military conquest of the southern Pampa and Patagonia (1878–85), and continued to be employed by politicians and the military in the discourse about border territories in the early twentieth century. For a detailed discussion on the concept, see Pedro Navarro Floria, "El *desierto* y la cuestión del territorio en el discurso político argentino sobre la frontera Sur," *Revista complutense de historia de América* 28 (2002): 139–68.

[59] Julio Amarante to Víctor Pinto, October 16, 1935, in General Alonso Baldrich to Dirección de Parques Nacionales, Expediente 0535, year 1935, "Informe sobre toma de posesión del Parque Nacional del Iguazú," APN; Julio Amarante to Exequiel Bustillo, October 31, 1935, Fondo Exequiel Bustillo, Legajo 2, no. 3344, AGN.

[60] Balbino Brañas, *Ayer: Mi tierra en el recuerdo* (n.p.: n.p., 1975).

At first, the head of the DPN and the military both liked the idea of exploiting yerba mate. Surprisingly, it fell to the regulatory agency in charge of the production and commerce of yerba mate, the Comisión Reguladora de la Producción y Comercio de la Yerba Mate (Regulatory Commission for the Production and Commerce of Yerba Mate), to criticize the proposal on conservationist grounds. Federico L. Ezcurra, the head of the agency, came forward to explain that granting a license for a yerba mate operation in the area would not only violate the extant ban on new yerba mate licenses (a ban that had been put in place to deal with an overproduction crisis) but also bring gangs of "reckless laborers" and "precarious encampments" to a national park whose mission was to keep the forest intact. There was also opposition to the proposal inside the DPN, with agency staff claiming that their mission was to preserve nature for tourism and science, not to exploit natural resources. As they saw it, having concessionaires operating in a protected area, however "rational" those commercial activities might be, meant a slippery slope toward allowing other less judicious agents in, which could radically alter the natural conditions of the park.[61]

The polarization on the nature of national parks in Argentina was stronger between outside environmentalists and the agency, with Bustillo calling the former "idiots" in his 1968 memoir.[62] In Argentina, the two most distinguished environmentalists during Bustillo's tenure as the head of the DPN were the French-Argentine physician Georges Dennler de la Tour and the German-Argentine physician Hugo Salomon. Both were members of the Comisión Nacional Protectora de la Fauna Sudamericana (National Commission for South American Fauna), which had Salomon as its president.[63] They believed parks should be created exclusively to preserve endangered species, particularly fauna, a model of conservation that soon became the new international paradigm for national parks after the creation, in 1948, of the International Union for the Protection of Nature, an organization Salomon helped found.[64]

---

[61] Intendencia Iguazú to Dirección de Parques Nacionales, Expediente 2135, year 1939, "Proponiendo explotación yerbales dentro de jurisdicción de dicho parque," APN.

[62] Bustillo, *El despertar de Bariloche*, 364–65.

[63] José Liebermann, "Breve ensayo sobre la historia de la protección a la naturaleza en la República Argentina," *Boletín del Ministerio de Agricultura de la Nación* 37, no. 1–4 (1935): 233.

[64] Georges Dennler de la Tour, "Introducción," and Hugo Salomon, "Nociones generales sobre la protección a la fauna y sugerencas para su preservación," both in *La protección de la naturaleza en el mundo: In memoriam doctoris Hugo Salomon*, ed. Georges Dennler de la Tour (Buenos Aires: Georges Dennler de la Tour, 1957), 23–25, 33–36.

In a 1943 article, Dennler de la Tour proposed the creation of new national parks in the north of Argentina, in the territories of Chaco and Formosa. The locations of these new parks, unlike those of the parks established by the DPN to that point, would be determined by biological criteria, with a focus on the protection of specific fauna and flora species instead of the conservation of natural monuments. Dennler de la Tour also proposed an eastward expansion of Iguazú National Park, which he thought to be too small to protect its fauna. The new park boundaries would encompass the entire area between its present eastern border and the international boundary with Brazil. Hunting had already been prohibited in the park thanks to the pressure of Dennler de la Tour and Salomon, who had managed to secure the passage of several laws banning hunting during that period.[65] In fact, if not for the pressure of those conservationists, the DPN under Bustillo would have continued to turn a blind eye to the sale of wild animal hides and dead butterflies in the park, and wildlife would still have been kept in cages for tourists in a mini-zoo at the park headquarters. Bustillo himself was oblivious to the conservationists' plea to protect native animal species and once gladly accepted the offer of two jaguar hides sent to him by park director Amarante.[66] For Dennler de la Tour the problem of the Argentine national parks went beyond hunting, as he vehemently opposed the DPN's policy of promoting urban development on park lands. He argued that the agency should evict all settlers living in Iguazú National Park, including those in Puerto Aguirre, and should shut down most of the roads and trails the park had inherited from the logging era, leaving just those necessary to serve tourists' access to the falls.[67]

Dennler de la Tour's proposal could not have come at a worse time. Not only had urban development been a key feature of Argentine national parks since their inception, but after 1940 it had become a source of

[65] The two parks proposed by Dennler de la Tour, to be created in the territories of Chaco and Formosa, had already been part of the 1936 plan that gave origin to the four Patagonian parks gazetted in 1949. However, these two northern parks were dropped from the plan in 1937. The parks proposed by Dennler de la Tour in the north were created in the 1950s as Río Picomayo National Park (1951) and Chaco National Park (1954). The expansion of Iguazú National Park, on the other hand, never came through. Georges Dennler de la Tour, "Protección y conservación de faunas de ambientes naturales: Parques nacionales y reservas del norte argentino," *Revista argentina de zoogeografía* 3, no. 1–2 (1943): 33–57.
[66] Exequiel Bustillo to Julio Amarante, letters from August 24, 1937, and September 29, 1937, both in Fondo Exequiel Bustillo, Legajo 9, no. 3351, AGN; Julio Amarante to Exequiel Bustillo, September 16, 1937, Fondo Exequiel Bustillo, Legajo 3, no. 3345, AGN.
[67] Dennler de la Tour, "Protección y conservación."

TABLE 1.4 *DPN's revenue share, 1935–42 (in* peso moneda nacional)

Period	Overseas Travel Tax	%	DPN's Own Revenue*	%	Total
1935	669,500.62	94	43,438.71	6	712,939.33
1936	935,512.48	86	155,820.24	14	1,091,332.72
1937	1,084,981.52	86	169,752.04	14	1,254,733.56
1938	1,219,301.95	87	184,450.77	13	1,403,752.72
1939	1,072,587.20	87	155,876.68	13	1,228,463.88
1940	425,176.30	49	433,811.98	51	858,988.28
1941	413,673.30	58	290,092.11	42	703,765.41
1942	176,162.29	41	420,373.23	59	1,362,535.52
Total	5,996,895.66	69	1,853,615.76	31	8,616,511.42

Source: Dirección de Parques Nacionales, "Memoria correspondiente al año 1935" (1936), 24–25, "Memoria correspondiente al año 1936" (1937), 14–15, "Memoria correspondiente al año 1937" (1938), 20–21, "Memoria correspondiente al año 1938" (1939), 21, "Memoria correspondiente al año 1939" (1940), 23, "Memoria del ejercicio de 1940" (1941), 9–10, "Memoria correspondiente al año 1941" (1942), 19, "Memoria correspondiente al año 1942" (1943), 10, APN-B

* The sources for DPN revenue were sale of public land; concessions for building, grazing, hunting, fishing, and operating services; sale of railroad tickets; leasing of land; land development services (land measurement, land registration, sale of plans); and fines.

revenue. A funding crisis that year forced the national park agency to sell lots inside the parks to balance its budget. The national park act of 1934 provided for the sale of public land inside a 5,000-hectare area inside national parks to develop urban settlements, which could generate some revenue for the agency. The DPN also profited from fishing and hunting permits, concessions to hotels and tourism agencies, and visitor fees. There was also 2,500,000 pesos in government bonds issued by the national park act to fund infrastructure projects in the parks. Yet the primary source of funding came from 50 percent of the tax on all the tickets for overseas trips sold in Argentina, which had been allocated by the national park act to fund the DPN.[68]

As we can see in Table 1.4, before 1940, income from the overseas tax represented about 87 percent of the agency's total revenue (excluding the bonds). But the war in Europe in 1939 put the agency in deep financial trouble: as Argentines stopped traveling to their preferred destinations in Europe, revenue from the overseas tax shrank to less than half. The DPN

[68] Argentina, Law 12103, "Ley de Parques Nacionales," Art. 18, h, September 29, 1934.

compensated for this loss of external tax income with an increase in revenue from entry fees, concessions, and the sale of land, especially in Nahuel Huapi.

Bustillo was, nevertheless, extremely unhappy with the situation and started lobbying the government and the Congress for an expansion in the DPN government bonds funding, from 2,500,000 to 4,000,000 pesos. To get the new funding approved by an increasingly recalcitrant Congress, he resorted to extreme maneuvers, such as delivering a resignation letter in 1942, which was refused by the Ministry of Agriculture. The bill with the new funding was voted into law, but his tenure as the head of the DPN was coming to a close. With the 1943 military coup, Bustillo became isolated politically and definitively resigned from his position as director of the DPN in 1944.[69]

A UNIQUELY ARGENTINE NATIONAL PARK

Bustillo's tenure as the head of the DPN coincided with the perception that Argentina was lagging behind its international rivals in the race to control territory and nationalize borders. The establishment of Iguazú National Park in 1934 was an attempt to reverse that trend and reassert Argentina's claim to its border with Brazil. Argentina created one of its first national parks both to control its side of the magnificent Iguazu Falls and as a response to the earlier creation of a military colony across the border in Brazil. The park was conceived as a means to take possession of and occupy a borderland that, in the eyes of Argentine leaders, was threatened by cross-border influences. For more than three decades this combination of conservation ideas and geopolitical thinking would guide the territorial policies employed in Iguazú National Park, helping to shape broader ideas of territory and nationhood throughout the country.

The Iguazu Falls, for its magnitude and beauty, comprised the fulcrum of the nationalization of the borderland. Argentine and foreign elites coming from Buenos Aires enjoyed easy river access to the falls, which contributed to a nascent tourism industry beginning in the early 1900s. Buenos Aires's direct access to the borderland gave Argentina an

---

[69] Dirección de Parques Nacionales, "Memoria correspondiente al año 1935" (1936), 8–9, "Memoria del ejercicio de 1940" (1941), 2–4, "Memoria correspondiente al año 1941" (1942), 1–2, "Memoria correspondiente al año 1942" (1943), 1–2, APN-B; "Los parques nacionales," *La Prensa*, May 26, 1942; "La dirección de Parques Nacionales," *La prensa*, September 25, 1942; Argentina, Law 11283, November 30, 1923; Bustillo, *El despertar de Bariloche*, 479–509.

advantage over Brazil, whose river connection to its own southwestern border was cut by the Iguazu and the Sete Quedas Falls (the latter on the Paraná River). Still, Argentine policymakers understood tourism as incapable of carrying out the desired Argentinization of a border area still sparsely populated. Only federally funded colonization projects, such as the one they saw across the border in Foz do Iguaçu, Brazil, could accomplish their vision of a frontier populated by Argentine nationals. In this sense, the demand for border control led to the development of a uniquely Argentine national park model that blended colonization and conservation in frontier areas.

Iguazú National Park fomented innovative ways of promoting territorial occupation. The 1934 national park law had provided for the parceling and sale of sections of national park land to encourage the development of border settlements. Thus, from the 1940s on, the Iguazú National Park administration promoted settlement inside the park, and by 1960, almost 3,000 people lived inside park boundaries.[70] Argentine national park proponents consciously distanced themselves from their North American and European counterparts, conceiving parks like Iguazú (adjacent to Brazil) and Nahuel Huapi (adjacent to Chile) as tools for colonizing and occupying borderlands. The colonization mission of Iguazú National Park was no accident, as it was already present in the second plan designed by Thays in 1911. From the beginning, national parks in Argentina included as part of their mission the development of population centers and the establishment of infrastructure for dwellers inside park boundaries.

The men in charge of the DPN, therefore, concurred with the military and with local politicians on the need to use the new national park policy to both preserve natural monuments and secure border zones via the development of tourism and settlements. In the 1940s, dissenting voices of conservationists such as Dennler de la Tour and Eppens, although important in curbing the extremes of the policy of border development, were still too weak to challenge the DPN's main tenets. Still, the near consensus around national park policy did little to harmonize the view of different institutional agents on the importance of a park that Exequiel Bustillo saw as secondary to his main focus on Patagonia.

In the end, the establishment of Iguazú National Park in Argentina owed much of its success to pressure from local players such as territorial governor Acuña and park director Amarante. Iguazú was conceptualized at the federal level as a geopolitical tool of national intervention in the

[70] Instituto Nacional de Estadística y Censos (INDEC).

country's borders with Brazil. But the park was implemented only after the involvement of locals who, in every step of the process, demanded from the central government a commitment to the creation of the park. Across the border, the state government in Brazil would also play a crucial role in lobbying the Brazilian federal government to gazette its Iguaçu National Park in 1939. The two largest countries in South America, therefore, went through similar processes of national park creation that were fueled by federal interest in borderland intervention but whose implementation depended on the active engagement of local elites.

2

Playing Catch-Up

Brazil, 1876–1944

In his 1937 book *Oéste paranaense*, Brazilian Army major José de Lima Figueiredo recalled the state of neglect he encountered while visiting the Brazilian side of the Triple Frontier in the early 1930s. After a few weeks traversing the state of Paraná in Brazil, from the Atlantic port city of Paranaguá to the Brazilian town of Foz do Iguaçu on the Paraná River, Figueiredo arrived at a border area entirely dominated by Argentine and Paraguayan nationals. In one of the logging companies operating in the Brazilian territory, for example, the owner and all the employees had been born in the neighboring countries. Brazilian children in the region spoke mostly Guarani or Spanish. A visit to Iguazu Falls served to confirm the impression that the central Brazilian government had abandoned the region. Bush covered the twenty-kilometer road opened by Edmundo de Barros in the 1890s that connected Foz do Iguaçu to the falls. At the falls, he found a "dirty" building that used to be a hotel but was abandoned. The situation in Brazil provided a stark contrast to what he saw across the border in Argentina, where tourists could stay in a "magnificent hotel" connected by an "excellent road" and a bus service to the hamlet of Puerto Aguirre, to which three Argentine companies brought visitors by river from Buenos Aires. Whereas in Argentina the state and private entrepreneurs acted together to provide tourists access to the falls with "absolute comfort," in Brazil there was no infrastructure for visitation, which reflected the Brazilian authorities' disregard for the border.[1]

---

[1] José de Lima Figueiredo, *Oéste paranaense, edição ilustrada* (São Paulo: Companhia Editora Nacional, 1937), 89–94, 104.

Figueiredo's book reproduced a recurrent trope of early twentieth-century Brazil: denunciations of border neglect by civil servants visiting frontier regions.[2] At the time they visited the border, the Iguazu Falls were not yet protected, but in 1939 the Brazilian government under Getúlio Vargas created the country's second national park on its side of the cataracts. Brazil gazetted Iguaçu National Park in the late 1930s along with two other national parks, Itatiaia (1937) and Serra dos Órgãos (1939). Iguaçu was unique among the first three national parks in Brazil because the rationale for it reproduced that of its Argentine counterpart across the border. The Itatiaia and Serra dos Órgãos national parks were established near the cities of Rio de Janeiro and São Paulo, in areas easily accessible to nature-loving urbanites with the means of transportation and leisure time for travel. Iguaçu, on the other hand, was set in a distant, sparsely populated, and backward frontier, lacking direct connections to the great Brazilian cities of the Atlantic seaboard. This chapter shows the factors that led the Vargas regime to gazette a park in such an isolated area – a location out of reach to the majority of prospective Brazilian visitors.

The choice of Iguaçu as a site for a national park can be understood as part of the Vargas regime's move to occupy Brazil's western hinterland, a campaign named "the March to the West." In the case of Iguaçu, by bringing economic development and territorial control over a sparsely populated border zone, the Brazilian government aimed to incorporate a peripheral region into the life of the nation. To politicians and high-ranking public officials in Brazil, national park policy fitted into their desire to promote the nationalization of a borderland population they saw as suspiciously foreign. A park would guarantee their share of control of a symbolic landmark, Iguazu Falls, and promote development through tourism.

Similar to the creation of the Iguazú Park in Argentina five years earlier, the establishment of Iguaçu in Brazil was also the result of the efforts of

[2] One of the first examples was Manuel Azevedo da Silveira Netto – a federal employee who, after a stint at the border, would tour literary salons in Rio de Janeiro and Curitiba promoting Iguazu Falls. Like Figueiredo, Silveira Netto would present the falls as a nature wonder and national monument neglected by the Brazilian authorities in a borderland dominated by foreigners. Manuel Azevedo da Silveira Netto, *Do Guairá aos saltos do Iguassú* (São Paulo: Companhia Editora Nacional, 1939); "Sabbados litera-rios: Os saltos do Iguassú, conferência de Silveira Netto," *A imprensa*, October 30, 1910; "Pequenos echos," *A notícia*, November 31, 1910; "O Alto do Paraná: A conferência de Silveira Netto – As cachoeiras do Iguassú e o salto das Sete Quedas – No Polytheama," *Diário da tarde*, July 12, 1912.

local agents, particularly state governors, to pressure the federal government into using national park policy as a means of controlling and developing the border. When pushing Rio de Janeiro to gazette the park, politicians in the state of Paraná followed an earlier tradition of locals and visitors who wielded their political clout to make a case for a Brazilian park at the Iguazu Falls. Uniting the two generations was a desire to counterbalance Argentina's initiatives to control its side of the falls. Distrust and rivalry toward Argentines became more salient among park proponents in Brazil after the creation of Iguazú National Park in 1934 in Argentina. Politicians in the state of Paraná began using the Argentine protected area across the border to justify their urgency in creating a Brazilian national park at the falls.

Vargas's first stint in power (1930–45) offered favorable conditions for the development of national park proposals. He nominally expanded the capacity of the central government to manage the life of the country, attempting to replace the loose federalist system with a centralized state equipped with new agencies and an expanded bureaucracy. The Vargas years saw the creation of agencies for mineral, water, and forest resources; a national institute of statistics; a national department of roads; and several other federal agencies whose responsibilities ranged from industrial to cultural policies. In many cases, the reach and intervention capabilities of these new agencies were greater on paper than in practice, as they were usually underfunded and geographically limited to the country's larger cities. In the case of protected areas, however, the creation of the Federal Forest Council and a revived Forest Service provided the Brazilian government with tools, albeit limited ones, to create and manage three national parks in the 1930s.[3]

The establishment of Iguaçu National Park in 1939 in Brazil mirrored some of the key features present in Argentina's creation of Iguazú National Park in 1934. Both parks, for example, were the result of a drive to use national park policy as a tool to occupy and develop a borderland. Their creation also depended on local pressure for national parks, which increased in times when federal initiatives stalled. Finally, developments across the border were used to justify a national park race

---

[3] Leslie Bethell, "Politics in Brazil under Vargas, 1930–1945," in *The Cambridge History of Latin America*, ed. Leslie Bethell, vol. IX (Cambridge, UK: Cambridge University Press, 2008); Dean, *With Broadax and Firebrand*, 256–64; Joel Wolfe, "The Faustian Bargain Not Made: Getúlio Vargas and Brazil's Industrial Workers, 1930–1945," *Luso-Brazilian Review* 31, no. 2 (1994): 77–95.

involving the two countries. Brazil took five years to follow in Argentina's footsteps and create its own park at Iguazu Falls, but the idea of a Brazilian park at the falls predated the first Argentine park proposals.

BRAZILIAN ANTECEDENTS

The creation of Yellowstone National Park by the United States in 1872 sparked the first proposal for a national park in Brazil. In 1876, Brazilian engineer, entrepreneur, and abolitionist André Rebouças (1838–98) pioneered a proposal to create national parks in the country, just four years after Yellowstone. In a manifesto addressed to Thomaz José Coelho de Almeida, imperial minister of agriculture, commerce, and public works, Rebouças argued for the establishment of two national parks in Brazil's vast and sparsely inhabited western hinterland. One of the parks, the Parque Nacional do Guayrá, would extend 200 kilometers along the Brazilian banks of the Paraná and Iguazu rivers, protecting two of the world's largest waterfalls – Sete Quedas and Iguazu.[4] Rebouças's proposal anticipated the 1939 creation of Iguaçu National Park by sixty-three years.[5]

Following the example of Yellowstone and the Northern Pacific Railway, Rebouças intended to establish the national park in conjunction with a railroad crossing the Paraná River near Sete Quedas Falls, which would connect Curitiba to Mato Grosso and Bolivia.[6] Rebouças was a great admirer of all things American, and his first contact with the idea

---

[4] André Rebouças and Francisco Antônio Monteiro Tourinho, *Provincia do Paraná: Caminhos de ferro para Mato Grosso e Bolivia. Salto do Guayra*, ed. Adolpho Lamenha Lins (Rio de Janeiro: Typographia Nacional, 1876).

[5] Present-day Iguaçu National Park harbors only Iguazu Falls. In 1961, the Brazilian government gazetted a second national park in the region, Sete Quedas National Park, which encompassed Sete Quedas. However, this park was never fully implemented or enforced, and was later squatted by settlers. It was finally degazetted in 1981 after Sete Quedas was destroyed by flooding to create the Itaipu reservoir.

[6] Rebouças's national park manifesto was an appendix to the proposal for a Curitiba–Mato Grosso–Bolivia railroad. The plan, the brainchild of engineer Francisco Antonio Monteiro Tourinho, drew from a previous railroad study done by the Lloyd company. Tourinho's plan also produced an on-site survey of the Sete Quedas carried out by Captain Nestor Borba, also included in the book. André Rebouças was chosen to comment on the plan because of his work with his late brother Antonio on a series of similar railroad proposals starting in the 1860s. Rebouças and Tourinho, *Provincia do Paraná*; André Rebouças, *Garantia de juros: Estudos para sua aplicação às emprezas de utilidade pública no Brazil* (Rio de Janeiro: Typographia Nacional, 1874), 477–87; Maria Alice Rezende de Carvalho, *O quinto século: André Rebouças e a construção do Brasil* (Rio de Janeiro: Editora Revan, 1998), 101–19.

of setting exquisite natural features as national monuments occurred in 1873, when he toured the United States for two weeks. Although he did not visit Yellowstone, he was captivated by Niagara Falls, its railroad line, the facilities built for visitors, and the progress tourism brought to the region. Inspired by his experience as a tourist at Niagara Falls, by the depictions of American natural monuments he encountered in books such as *Picturesque America* (1874), and by the text of the 1872 Yellowstone Act, Rebouças concluded that national parks were one of the greatest symbols of the progress and civilization of the United States – a policy to be emulated by the Brazilian Empire. He envisioned Brazil pursuing the path taken by the United States: using railroads to bring Brazilian settlers to the western frontier and tourists to national parks.[7]

Rebouças's manifesto fell on deaf ears. No national park was created in this sparsely inhabited area, and the planned railroad never came through. Other proposals for east–west lines crossing the state of Paraná would appear in the following years, but none was ever built. Yet, in 1889, the Brazilian Empire decided to establish in the region the Colônia Militar da Foz do Iguaçu (Military Colony of the Mouth of the Iguazu) – an agricultural colony formed by civilian settlers under the control of an army outpost. Since the late 1850s, Argentina and Brazil had been wrangling over ownership of a 3.5-million-hectare area located between the southern banks of the Iguazu River and the northern banks of the Uruguay River. The government in Rio de Janeiro chose to establish a military colony right outside this area, on the eastern bank of the Paraná River near the mouth of the Iguaçu River, but close enough to the disputed borderland to serve as a bridgehead for future colonization. The dispute over the area in question was resolved in 1895 with the arbitration of the US president Grover Cleveland, but the idea of taking control of the border continued to inform the actions of politicians, visitors, and the military in the two countries.[8]

---

[7] See André Pinto Rebouças, "O parque nacional: Notas e considerações geraes," in *Provincia do Paraná*, 63–73; André Pinto Rebouças, *Diário e notas autobiográficas; Texto escolhido e anotações*, ed. Anna Flora Verissimo and Inácio José Verissimo (Rio de Janeiro: José Olympio, 1938), 249–55, 270–73; Carvalho, *O quinto século*, 129; Pádua, *Um sopro de destruição*, 18, 271; William Cullen Bryant, *Picturesque America; or, The Land We Live In. A Delineation by Pen and Pencil of the Mountains, Rivers, Lakes, Forests, Water-Falls, Shores, Canyons, Valleys, Cities, and Other Picturesque Features of Our Country*, ed. Oliver Bell Bunce (New York: D. Appleton, [c. 1872–74]).

[8] From the Brazilian side, the dispute was negotiated by José Paranhos, Baron of Rio Branco, who later, as minister of external relations (1902–12) would lead Brazil's tacit alignment with US international interests. See Bradford Burns, *The Unwritten Alliance, Rio Branco*

Among these was Edmundo de Barros, the army captain stationed in the military colony of Foz do Iguaçu in the 1890s, who invented the "national park" visited by Argentine naturalist Carlos Burmeister in 1899 (see Chapter 1). According to border treaties between Brazil and Argentina, the thalweg of the Iguazu River defined their international boundary line. Interested in finding the point where the boundary crossed the falls, the Brazilian army officer had decided to survey the river. He claimed that several of the waterfalls that made up the 2.7-kilometer-wide wedge of Iguazu belonged to Brazil, and in an attempt to take possession of them, he named the larger falls after Brazilian historical figures.[9]

More importantly, Barros made plans for his "national park" on the Brazilian bank of the Iguazu Falls, which was to include a new urban settlement (see Figure 2.1). The park would be implemented and administered by the military colony, the owner of the lands at the time. Barros had his men cutting the twenty-kilometer trail through the dense subtropical forest to connect the military colony on the Paraná River to the falls on the Iguazu River. It was this pathway that allowed visitors coming in boats from Buenos Aires to see the cataracts safely from solid ground in the late 1890s. Barros's "national park" not only preceded the actual Brazilian national park by more than four decades but also influenced the creation of the Argentine one. It was after Barros's initiative that the Argentine governor of the Territory of Misiones, Juan José Lanusse, decided to act to

and Brazilian-American Relations (New York: Columbia University Press, 1966). See also Ing. Norberto B. Cobos, "Historia y demarcación del límite entre la República Argentina y Brasil, años 1454 a 1927," 1951, Caja AH0010, Documento 26, AHC; Ruy Christovam Wachowicz, *Paraná, sudoeste: Ocupação e colonização* (Curitiba: Instituto Histórico, Geográfico e Etnográfico Paranaense, 1985); José Cândido da Silva Muricy, *À Foz do Iguassu: Ligeira descripção de uma viagem feita de Guarapuava à Colônia da Foz do Iguassu em novembro de 1892* (Curitiba: Impressora Paranaense Jesuino Lopes & Ca., 1896); Silveira Netto, *Do Guairá aos saltos do Iguassú*, 78–79; Antonio Marcos Myskiw, "A fronteira como destino de viagem: A colônia militar de Foz do Iguaçu, 1888–1907" (PhD diss., Fluminense Federal University, 2011), 24–27, 114–82; Antonio Marcos Myskiw, "Ser colono na fronteira: A colônia militar de Foz do Iguaçu, 1888–1907," in *Campos em disputa: História agrária e companhia*, ed. Elione Silva Guimarães and Márcia Motta (São Paulo: Annablume, 2007), 381–88; Wachowicz, *Obrageros, mensus e colonos*, 13, 15–16, 21–24.
[9] The two countries agreed in 1903 that several of the individual waterfalls claimed by Barros in his 1897 national park plan belonged to Argentina. The agreement, signed in 1910, settled the dispute about the ownership of the hundreds of individual falls that comprised Iguazu and of the liquid border that separated the two countries. Argentina and Brazil, "Artigos declaratórios da demcarcação de fronteiras entre os Estados Unidos do Brasil e a República da Argentina," Rio de Janeiro, October 4, 1910, accessed at http://info.lncc.br /att1910.html.

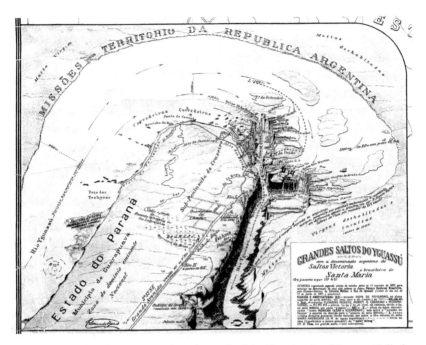

FIGURE 2.1 Plan for a national park on the Brazilian bank of Iguazu Falls by Edmundo de Barros, 1897. "Great Iguazu Falls . . . Plan organized according to the study made in the first semester of 1897 to be used in the demarcation of the urban area of the future Brazilian National Park by the interim director of the Military Colony of Foz do Iguaçu (July 11, 1897)." Source: Romario Martins, "Mapa do Estado do Paraná," map (São Paulo: Companhia Litographica Ypiranga, 1919). Arquivo Público do Paraná

create a national park in Argentina. The park also proved crucial for the model of Argentina's national parks, as its plan was the first to incorporate a settlement project inside its territory.[10]

PUBLIC LAND IN AN ISOLATED BORDERLAND

Similar to Rebouças's national park proposal in the 1870s, the "national park" put in place by Captain Edmundo de Barros in 1897 was ignored by

---

[10] Burmeister, *Memoria sobre el territorio de Misiones*, 21–22; Silveira Netto, *Do Guairá aos saltos do Iguassú*, 161–63, 171–75; Cezar Karpinski, "Navegação, cataratas e hidrelétricas discursos e representações sobre o Rio Iguaçu, 1853–1969" (PhD diss., Federal University of Santa Catarina, 2011), 166, 186.

the new Brazilian republican government even as the army's interest in keeping Foz do Iguaçu as a military colony waned. As settlers proved unable to secure subsistence through agricultural production and turned to logging and yerba mate harvesting, both extractive activities controlled by Argentinean entrepreneurs, the Brazilian Army began to see the military colony as a failure. The idea of a colony of self-sustaining Brazilian nationals rooted in the land and committed to working in the fields gave way to a reality of itinerant activities and dependence on the Argentine river trade to survive. By the 1910s, the colony, which was isolated from the rest of Brazil by geography, had become an appendage of Argentina through riverine chains of commerce. When this intimate relationship between Foz do Iguaçu and its neighbors downriver eventually became a source of anxiety for policymakers in Curitiba and Rio de Janeiro, a few of them ended up proposing a national park as an antidote to the excessive Argentine influence at the border.[11]

The region's remoteness derived from the lack of viable routes between Brazil's densely populated Atlantic shores and its western backdoor. The border town was isolated from the rest of Brazil not only by the thick carpet of forests still covering most of the western half of the state of Paraná during this period but also by two massive cataracts: Sete Quedas on the Paraná River and Iguazu Falls on the Iguazu River. Since colonial times, the two obstacles had barred north- and eastward river penetration coming from the Spanish Empire. As hurdles, however, the waterfalls worked both ways, preventing the Portuguese (and later the Brazilians) from controlling the region. Land routes offered little in the matter of alternatives to the blocked waterways, and the only portage option – a short narrow-gauge railway circumventing Sete Quedas – was controlled by a private company between 1917 and 1929, Companhia Mate Laranjeira, which used this option almost exclusively to transport its yerba mate production.

In 1920, the government of Paraná opened a highway connecting Guarapuava to Foz do Iguaçu that cut through vast tracts of forest.[12]

---

[11] Myskiw, "A fronteira como destino de viagem," 24–27, 114–82; Myskiw, "Ser colono na fronteira," 381–88; Wachowicz, *Obrageros, mensus e colonos*, 13, 15–16, 21–24, 28–32.
[12] Following the spirit of federalization of the first three decades of the new Brazilian republic, the Ministry of War in 1912 had handed control of the colony over to the government of Paraná, and in 1914 the then village of Foz do Iguaçu was promoted to a municipality. Paraná (Brazil), State Law 971, April 9, 1910; Paraná (Brazil), State Law 1383, March 14, 1914. On the opening of the 1920 road, see Paraná, "Mensagem dirigida

The 350-kilometer dirt road was ill-planned, however: Its route crossed too many waterbodies, which made it impassable during a significant portion of the year, especially in the rainy season.[13] In 1925, a Paraná government official traveling this road in a Ford truck described his challenging experience: The rough road demanded frequent stops to "have the car's parts disassembled to fix something," and the 400-kilometer trip took eight long days, during which they had "little sight of human beings."[14] The unreliable dirt road continued to be the primary land route connecting Foz do Iguaçu and the falls to the east of the country until the early 1950s, when a section of the new highway BR-277 opened.

It was much more difficult to visit the falls from Brazil than from Argentina. To reach Foz do Iguaçu from Rio de Janeiro by land and water before the 1950s, many Brazilians would take an ocean liner south to Buenos Aires (2,200 kilometers) and from there take another steamship upriver to Foz do Iguaçu (1,700 kilometers), the same route taken by the increasing number of elite tourists visiting the Argentine side of the falls (see Map 2.1). Traveling by land was shorter (1,500 kilometers) but more expensive and less reliable, and it required, for private parties, access to expensive automobiles. It was only in the 1940s that a bus line started connecting Guarapuava to Foz do Iguaçu, twice a month. Therefore, in the early twentieth century, the fate of the Brazilian border town was still tied to its water connection to Argentina.[15]

Before 1920, few Brazilians visited the border region. Only those who could afford the twenty-day river cruise from Buenos Aires could reach the Argentine–Brazilian border to see the falls. Among these was the famous Brazilian aviation pioneer Alberto Santos-Dumont, who visited the falls in 1916. On his return trip to São Paulo, Santos-Dumont stopped in Curitiba for a few nights, where he was received by state governor Afonso Camargo. There, Santos-Dumont convinced Camargo of the need

ao Congresso Legislativo pelo Dr. Caetano Munhoz da Rocha, Presidente do Estado, ao instalar-se a 2.ª Sessão da 15.ª Legislatura," February 1, 1921, 53–54, APP.

[13] Lima Figueiredo, *Oéste paranaense*, 42–43.

[14] Cesar Martinez, *Sertões do Iguassú* (São Paulo: Lobato, 1925), 27–92.

[15] Lima Figueiredo, *Oéste paranaense*; Silveira Netto, *Do Guairá aos saltos do Iguassú*, 33, 78–9; Theophilo de Andrade, *O rio Paraná no roteiro da Marcha para o Oeste* (Rio de Janeiro: Irmãos Pongetti, 1941); Américo R. Netto, "A marcha para o oeste em automovel: Ciclos evolutivos da rodovia para Foz do Iguaçu," in *Revista rodovia* 40 (May 1943), 9–12, 32, *Revista rodovia* 41 (June 1943), and *Revista Rodovia* 42 (July 1943), 3–7, DER-PR.

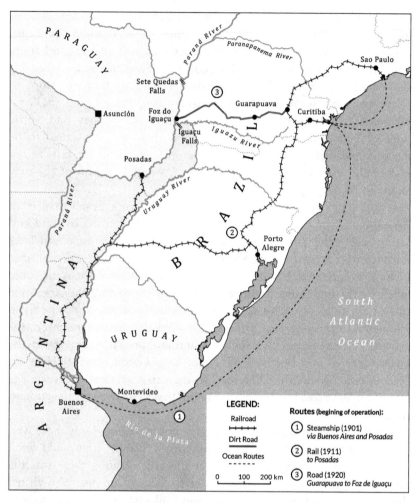

MAP 2.1 Most common routes to Foz do Iguaçu before the 1930s. Map by Frederico Freitas

to expropriate the falls to create a "national park" and develop tourism.[16] In 1907, the state of Paraná had passed a forest code, one of the first pieces of conservationist legislation enacted after the fall of the monarchy, and in

---

[16] "Santos Dumont em Curitiba," *Diário da tarde*, May 4, 1916; "Santos Dumont em Curitiba," *Diário da Tarde*, May 5, 1916; "Santos Dumont," *Diário da tarde*, May 6, 1916; "Santos Dumont," *Diário da tarde*, May 9, 1916; "Santos Dumont é entrevistado," *Diário da tarde*, May 11, 1916.

1913 the state government granted itself the power to expropriate land in the public interest. Paraná had put in place the legal instruments to expropriate the Brazilian bank of Iguazu Falls. Similarly to in neighboring Argentina, the creation of the national park in Brazil was the culmination of a legal process of transformation of private into public land initiated by local governments.[17]

The land was then owned by Jesús Val, a Spaniard who had acquired the 1,000-hectare estate surrounding the falls in 1910 from the military colony. Val became one of the first landowners in the state to be subjected to an expropriation process when in 1916 the state of Paraná issued decree 653, expropriating his lands. The decree transformed the allotment at the Brazilian margins of the falls into an area of public interest to receive a "village and a park," as set out by Edmundo Barros in his 1897 plan. Val sued to maintain his rights to exploit the Brazilian side of the falls. Before the expropriation, he had profited from the rent paid by Frederico Engels, who operated a rustic lodge on Val's land that catered to tourists coming from Argentina to see the falls from Brazil. In 1919, after three costly years of paying for attorneys in Curitiba, the distant state capital, Val agreed to settle the dispute and accepted the compensation offered by the state of Paraná. It was the first time that land around Iguazu Falls was made public for the specific reason of creating a protected area, preceding by twelve years the Argentine government's purchase of the Ayarragaray estate across the border.[18]

THE BORDER AS A PROBLEM

The lack of viable routes to Foz do Iguaçu posed a hurdle for prospective Brazilian visitors to Iguazu Falls. To public officials in Rio and Curitiba, however, a more pressing issue was the complete dominance of Argentines and Paraguayans in the borderlands economy and society. This concern soon matured into a discourse that posited the border as a problem to be solved by federal intervention. As a result, national park policy came to

---

[17] Paraná (Brazil), State Law 706, "Código florestal," April 1, 1907; Paraná (Brazil), State Law 1260, "Desapropriação de terras," March 10, 1913; Paraná (Brazil), State Decree 460, "Regulamento sobre desapropriações por necessidade ou utilidade publica estadual ou municipal," June 19, 1913.

[18] Jesús Val received 298,716,322 réis, of which 297,900,000 was paid in state bonds. Paraná (Brazil), State Decree 653, July 31, 1916; Exército Brasileiro, "Medição de terreno de Jesús Val," 1910, APP; "Procuração bastante que faz Jesús Val ao Dr. Antonio Joaquim Alves de Farias," Curitiba, January 26, 1917, INCRA-Cascavel; "Escritura pública de venda que faz Jesús Val ao Estado do Paraná," Curitiba, July 10, 1919, INCRA-Cascavel.

be seen as one of the antidotes for the excessive foreign influence at the border.

Brazilians who arrived at Foz do Iguaçu in the early 1920s saw a town of almost 1,500 inhabitants in which many were foreigners. Its economy relied on the *obrajes* headed by the Argentine entrepreneurs to whom past state governments had granted land concessions to exploit the wild yerba mate groves found in the subtropical Atlantic forest of the Triple Frontier region. The *obrajes* were concentrated in a 180-kilometer swath along the Brazilian bank of the Paraná River, from Foz do Iguaçu to Sete Quedas Falls. At the Iguazu River, the falls were separated from the mouth of the river by twenty-three kilometers of rapids, impeding serious navigation. With no portage options at Iguazu Falls, goods could not travel downriver from the upper banks of the Iguazu, which explains the absence of river ports in the area of the future national park (see Figure 2.2).

A sudden event in 1924 would put the preoccupation with the exposure and vulnerability of the border at the center of Brazilian politics. In that year, a column of rebel military officers from São Paulo occupied Foz do Iguaçu for months while resisting the incursions of the Brazilian Army. In his 1928 memoir, João Cabanas, one of the leaders of the rebel *tenentista* column, described his experience at the border. Cabanas argued that Argentines completely dominated the Brazilian side of the border: They owned most of the obrajes and oppressed local workers under a system of bonded labor. More importantly, the tenentista months-long occupation exposed the border area's incapacity to resist an invasion from Argentina. Cabana's group of rebel lieutenants from São Paulo, with no previous knowledge of the terrain, had managed to quickly take control of the entire region and resist the Brazilian Army for eight months. In the case of a war against Argentina, he argued, better-equipped enemy forces could swiftly reach the area via railroad and river. The foreign-owned obrajes, the vast majority of Argentine capital, would happily cede their fleet to the Argentine Army, collaborating to transport enemy troops into Brazilian territory. Brazilian forces, on the other hand, would take weeks to reach the area. Cabanas believed that by the time the Brazilian Army arrived in the region, it would encounter a foreign aggressor already entrenched and in complete domination of the terrain. Cabanas was part of the movement that brought Getúlio Vargas to power six years later, and his analysis would contribute to the view of the border as a problem.[19]

---

[19] João Cabanas, *A Columna da Morte sob o commando do tenente Cabanas* (Rio de Janeiro: Almeida & Torres, 1928), 245–52, 353–67.

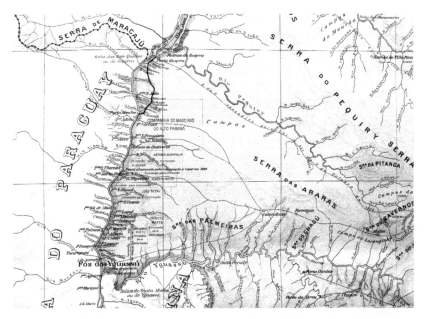

FIGURE 2.2 Land concessions and ports on the Paraná River, 1919. This excerpt from a 1919 map shows the concentration of concessions and ports on the Brazilian bank of the Paraná River between Foz do Iguaçu and Sete Quedas Falls ("Porto Guayra"). On the banks of the Iguazu ("Rio Yguassú"), on the other hand, ports are absent. Source: Romario Martins, "Mapa do Estado do Paraná," map (São Paulo: Companhia Litographica Ypiranga, 1919). Arquivo Público do Paraná

By the time Vargas rose to power in 1930, obrajes continued to dominate the banks of the Paraná River, which they used to export the yerba mate extracted in Brazil to the downriver consumer markets in Argentina. The continued criticism of the obrajes by Brazilian government officials and visitors to the region stemmed from two related reasons: Argentine entrepreneurs owned the firms, boats, and ports that made the border economy work; and they employed mostly transient, debt-bonded Guarani-speaking workers, many members of indigenous communities, whom the Brazilians treated indistinguishably as "Paraguayan." Officials feared that dependence on Argentina and the massive presence of foreigners in Brazilian territory could compromise Brazil's grip on the area. Things were changing, however. In the 1930s, the development of yerba mate plantations in Argentina and the increasing restrictions on foreign-owned companies in Brazil led many Argentine businessmen to leave the area. Guarani workers also out-migrated the Brazilian border zone, pushed by the decline of the obrajes and by the violence brought by the military clashes between the tenentistas and the Brazilian Army in the mid 1920s. Nevertheless, many Guarani remained, finding work in the new Brazilian logging companies that began operating in the region in the 1940s (I discuss the role of Guarani in logging in detail in Chapter 6). Therefore, the need to "nationalize" the Brazilian border against the excessive influence of Argentines and Paraguayans continued to frame the way politicians saw the region during the Vargas regime. Such geopolitical concerns came to play an essential role in the creation of the Brazilian Iguaçu National Park in 1939.[20]

This vision of the border as a problem, for example, informed the federal reaction to a proposal put forward by politicians from border towns to create a new state at the borderlands. In the early 1930s, local groups from western Santa Catarina and southern and southwestern Paraná joined forces to lobby the new provisional government of Getúlio Vargas for statehood. The proposed state of Iguaçu would comprise a large section of the border with Argentina that included Foz do Iguaçu and the falls. The new state would also mean partitioning the states of Santa Catarina and Paraná, whose governments opposed the measure. Despite that, in 1931 the federal government established a commission led by Zeno Silva, an employee of the Ministry of Transportation and member of the Comitê Central Pró-Estado do

---

[20] I studied the discourse on the "problem" of the Foz do Iguaçu border in greater detail in Frederico Freitas, "A Park for the Borderlands: The Creation of the Iguaçu National Park in Southern Brazil, 1880–1940," *HIB: Revista de Historia Iberoamericana* 7, no. 2 (2014). See also Silveira Netto, *Do Guairá aos saltos do Iguassú*, 45–47; Manuel Carrão, *Impressões de viagem à Fóz do Iguassú e Rio Paraná* (Curitiba: Lith. Progresso, R. S. Francisco, 1928); "Cuidemos do oeste do Paraná," *O dia*, April 1, 1936, 3; Comissão Especial de Revisão das Concessões de Terras na Faixa de Fronteiras, "Relatório apresentado pelo engenheiro civil Dulphe Pinheiro Machado, inspeção realizada no sul do Estado de Mato Grosso e no oeste do Estado do Paraná," November 1940, Comissão Especial da Faixa de Fronteiras, Conselho de Segurança Nacional – Presidência da CEFF, Lata 252, Pasta 1: 1941-1944/1947-1948, 172–74, AN-RJ; IBAMA, "Encarte 6," *Plano de manejo do Parque Nacional do Iguaçu* (Brasília: IBAMA, 1999); Wachowicz, *Obrageros, mensus e colonos*; Liliane da Costa Freitag, *Fronteiras perigosas: Migração e brasilidade no extremo-oeste paranaense (1937–1954)* (Cascavel, Brazil: Edunioeste, 2001); Luciana A. Mendonça, "Parques Nacionais do Iguaçu e Iguazú: Uma fronteira ambientalista entre Brasil e Argentina," in *Argentinos e Brasileiros: Encontros, imagens e estereótipos*, ed. Alejandro Frigerio and Gustavo Lins Ribeiro (Petrópolis: Vozes, 2002).

Iguassu (Central Committee for the Iguassu State), to visit Foz do Iguaçu and assess the matter. The commission painted a dire picture of the border in its 1931 report, counting only about 500 Brazilians in a population of 10,000 living in western Paraná. To them, the hegemony of Argentines and Paraguayans in the area was bound to trigger a border dispute with the neighboring countries. Silva accused Paraná's government of failing to settle the border zone and recommended sectioning off the western part of the state and making it a federal territory directly controlled by Rio de Janeiro. As expected, this idea displeased the elites of Curitiba, who in turn accused the federal government of neglecting the region after the 1910 closure of the military colony in Foz do Iguaçu. Vargas eventually called off the creation of the new federal territory to avoid alienating the political elites of Paraná who had supported his 1930 coup. However, the idea of creating a new constituent subdivision of Brazil on the borderlands continued to be a fixation for him, and the partition of Paraná was briefly implemented in the 1940s.[21]

Born and raised in São Borja in the state of Rio Grande do Sul, on the border with Argentina, Vargas was no stranger to the borderlands, hence his preoccupation with nationalizing Brazil's frontiers.[22] The topic featured prominently in the Vargas years and was one of the concerns of Mário Tourinho, the first Vargas-appointed federal *interventor* (non-elected governor) for Paraná (1930–31).[23] Tourinho was not only a member of

---

[21] Comité Pró-Estado do Iguassú, "Memorial: A autonomia do antigo território contestado entre Paraná e Santa Catarina – Comité Pró-Estado do Iguassú," c. 1930, Gabinete Civil da Presidência, Lata 99, Pasta Paraná: 1934/1936–1939, AN-RJ; "Estado do Iguassu ou território federal," *O dia*, April 16, 1931, 2; "A nacionalização do Oeste," *O dia*, July 22, 1931; "O Territorio Federal do Iguassú," *O dia*, July 24, 1931, 1, 8; "A primeira reunião da comissão nomeada para examinar a questão das fronteiras," *O dia*, July 30, 1931, 1; Ermelindo A. de Leão, "O problema das fronteiras: O Território Federal do Iguaçu," *Gazeta do Povo*, September 9, 1931; "Grande comissão nacional de redivisão territorial e localização da capital federal," *Revista da Sociedade de Geographia do Rio de Janeiro* 38 (1933): 132; Valdir Gregory, *Os eurobrasileiros e o espaço colonial: Migrações no oeste do Paraná, 1940–1970* (Cascavel, Brazil: Edunioeste, 2002), 91; Wachowicz, *Obrageros, mensus e colonos*, 141–42, 147–48.

[22] Vargas's hometown, São Borja, was occupied by the Paraguayan army in 1865, and Vargas grew up with stories about his father's participation in battles against the Spanish-speaking enemy. Lira Neto, *Getúlio: Dos anos de formação à conquista do poder (1882–1930)* (São Paulo: Companhia das Letras, 2012), 1: 30–32.

[23] Likewise, nationalism was a constant theme throughout the Vargas years. In December 1930 Vargas issued decree 19482, which obligated Brazilian companies to have a minimum of two-thirds of Brazilian employees. This dealt a death blow to the Argentine-led firms still operating in western Paraná. The same decree also increased the

a traditional family from Curitiba but also an army general and a veteran of the Contestado War. He was appointed interventor in recognition of his leadership of the pro-Vargas faction's seizing control of the state in the 1930 coup. In his years as interventor, Tourinho took a few measures to increase the presence of the Brazilian government at the borderland, and in September 1931 he requested the return of a military company to Foz do Iguaçu to prevent the "incursion of foreign elements" from neighboring countries. In 1932, nineteen years after the dissolution of the military colony in Foz do Iguaçu, the town received the First Independent Border Company to protect the Brazilian territory against an unlikely Argentine and Paraguayan invasion.[24]

More important here, in October 1931 Tourinho decided to expand the original one thousand hectares of public lands around Iguazu Falls to five thousand hectares. The state of Paraná "reserved" the new expanded area for the federal government for the creation of a "settlement and a national park," as well as for the future "industrial exploitation" of the waterfalls. With this decree, Tourinho intended to make clear his commitment to the development of western Paraná in the face of the looming threat of state partition by the federal government. It was the first time the term "national park" appeared in Brazilian legislation, and it was used in a state decree.[25] The old, decentralized federal system in place in Brazil before Vargas's rise to power in 1930 would continue to shape crucial aspects of Brazilian environmental policy in the 1930s and 1940s, despite the increasing centralization of executive power during that period.

obstacles to the entry and legal presence of foreigners in Brazil and made it harder for them to acquire real estate. Brazil, Decree 19482, December 12, 1930.

[24] Tourinho also took other measures to promote the nationalization of the border, such as by appointing a high-profile government employee, Othon Mäeder, Mayor of Foz do Iguaçu; making mandatory the use of Portuguese in commerce; and prohibiting the payment of taxes with foreign currency. See Governo do Estado do Paraná, *Mensagem dirigida pelo Interventor Federal do Paraná, General Mário Tourinho, ao Chefe do Governo Provisório da República Dr. Getúlio Vargas* (Curitiba: Tipografia do Diário Oficial, 1931); Cables from Mário Tourinho to Oswaldo Aranha, July 9 and 30, 1931, Série Correspondência Política, Rolo 7 fot. 422, CPDOC; Ricardo Costa de Oliveira, "Notas sobre a política paranaense no período de 1930 a 1945," in *A construção do Paraná moderno: Políticos e política no governo do Paraná de 1930 a 1980*, ed. Ricardo Costa de Oliveira (Curitiba: Secretaria da Ciência, Tecnologia e Ensino Superior; Imprensa Oficial do Paraná, 2004), 15–18.

[25] Other protected areas had been gazetted before by the states and the federal government in Brazil, including a federal "forest reserve" in the Amazonian territory of Acre in 1911. But prior to the 1931 state decree, the term "national park" had never been used. Paraná, "Decreto 2153, de 20 de outubro de 1931," in *Diário oficial*, Curitiba, October 23, 1931; Brazil, Decree 8843, "Crêa a Reserva Florestal do Territorio do Acre," July 26, 1911.

The Iguazu Falls state decree enacted by Tourinho in 1931 was also a response to developments across the border, as it reproduced the analogous Argentine national law from 1909 that had created a special zone at the Argentine side of the falls.[26] Similar to the Argentine law, the decree of the state of Paraná provided for a national park, a hydroelectric plant at the falls, and even an urban settlement – ignoring the fact that the town of Foz do Iguaçu already existed twenty kilometers away.[27] Politicians in Curitiba were well aware of the steps taken by the Argentine government to create its national park. In 1928 Manuel Carrão, the director of the department of hygiene of the state of Paraná, had brought attention to Argentina's purchase of the Ayarragaray estate, advising the Brazilian government to mimic its neighbor and develop its side of the border.[28]

Tourinho's military style and political ineptitude eventually put him at odds with local elite groups, ending his career as interventor prematurely – he was substituted in January 1932 by the much more apt career politician Manoel Ribas (1932–45). Yet his dire warnings about the excessive number of foreigners in Foz do Iguaçu continued to inform Vargas's view of the region. In a letter to the minister of war, General João Gomes Ribeiro, Vargas revealed Tourinho as his primary source on the vulnerability of the international border in Paraná. Vargas characterized the region as

a zone populated and explored by foreign elements, where a cosmopolitan society of newcomers is being formed, without a national spirit, without the feeling of Brazilianness and love for the fatherland, one which could become a dangerous epicenter of disorder, one capable of provoking incidents that would be unpleasant to our interests.[29]

Geopolitical concerns about border sovereignty led Paraná to give the lands surrounding Iguazu Falls in concession to the federal government in 1931. This concession was a necessary step for the creation of a national park in Brazil because the federal government lacked the legal mandate to manage untitled public land, known as *terra devoluta*, or to carry out

---

[26] Argentina, Law 6712, "Comprendiendo en la ley número 5559 al territorio de Misiones," September 29, 1909.

[27] Paraná, Decree 2153, October 20, 1931.

[28] Carrão, *Impressões de viagem*, 86–88; Cecília Maria Westphalen, *História documental do Paraná: Primórdios da colonização moderna da região de Itaipu* (Curitiba: SBPH-PR, 1987); Wachowicz, *Paraná, Sudoeste*, 140–41.

[29] Letter from Getúlio Vargas to João Gomes Ribeiro, May 20, 1933, Série Correspondência, Rolo 3 fot. 0403 to 0408, CPDOC. I believe the letter is misdated because Vargas's request in the letter – the deployment of a military company to Foz do Iguaçu – occurred in 1932.

eminent domain in lands under state jurisdiction. Such limitations of the
federal government to control public land in Brazil preceded the Vargas
regime – they had originated with the republican constitution of 1891,
when control of most untitled public land was passed down with the
stroke of a pen from the recently created federal government to the
states. Since then, the new republican regime was virtually powerless
to manage most untitled public land in the country, a category that
comprised the vast majority of land in western and northern Brazil.
Despite the centralization of power and the two new constitutions written during his first administration (1934 and 1937), Vargas never acted
to regain ownership of untitled public lands from the states. If the federal
government in Brazil were to create national parks on untitled public
lands, it would have to override the states' mandate to control such
lands, which rarely happened in the 1930s and 1940s. Therefore, by
expropriating the land from its private owners and ceding it for federal
use, the state of Paraná gave Rio de Janeiro a means to creating
a national park in Iguazu without incurring in the cost of purchasing
the land as had been the case with the Argentine government across the
border.

PARANÁ PUSHES FOR THE CREATION OF THE PARK

Even after providing Rio de Janeiro with the means (i.e., public lands) to
gazette the national park, the Paraná government continued to be the
driving force behind the establishment of the protected area. Initially,
federal officials seemed uninterested in transforming the 1931 land concession into a national park. Their plans for the border area did not yet
include the creation of a nature preserve around the falls, an idea pushed
mainly by a local Paraná lobby attuned to developments in the region.
This explains the new interventor for the state of Paraná, Manoel Ribas,
evoking Argentina's gazetting of Iguazú National Park in 1934 to push the
federal government into installing a similar park in Brazil, as revealed by
a few memos sent by the government of Paraná to the presidential office
between 1936 and 1938.

In a 1938 letter to Getúlio Vargas, Ribas asked for funds to rebuild the
precarious highway connecting Guarapuava to Foz do Iguaçu.[30] He

---

[30] The old road built in the 1920s remained impassable during the rainy season – sixteen
bridges were washed away by flash floods in 1938 alone. Thus, a change of route was
badly needed to circumvent the many water courses on the path of the old road. Letters

presented the renovation of the highway as strategic and "extraordinary leverage for the progress" of western Paraná. Ribas was a pragmatic career politician who, much like his predecessor Tourinho, believed investment in infrastructure would attract Brazilian settlers and help counter federal accusations of state neglect of the borderlands and the threat of state partition. In the same letter, Ribas presented the recently created Argentine Iguazú National Park as a sign that Brazil was lagging in borderland infrastructure. He stated, "[G]iven the fact that Argentina is planning to expand the area of its park right at the other side of the border, I think it is time for us to think about the organization of our park, to avoid remaining in a position of inferiority." [31] Ribas argued the Brazilian park was half ready, as the government of Paraná had already expropriated land and even built a "luxurious hotel" near the falls.[32] Ribas added that "if the federal government does not intend to create the national park in the near future," it should allow the state government to do so, thus preventing Brazil from lagging "far behind its friends and neighbors." As he saw it, the recently created Argentine national park would bring rail and paved roads to the other side, and the logical step for Brazilians was to emulate it.[33]

Six decades later, Ribas returned to the idea first proposed by André Rebouças in the 1870s of using national parks and railroads to boost development at the border. He crafted a plan for a 600-kilometer railroad from Foz do Iguaçu to Ourinhos, in the state of São Paulo, connecting the border town and Iguazu Falls to Brazil's rail network. In his proposal, Ribas included the gazetting of the national park in Foz do Iguaçu "to protect the region's forests and fauna" and tap into the falls' "touristic potential." Ribas planned to launch an era of mass visitation to the Brazilian side of Iguazu Falls with the proposed Foz–Ourinhos railroad and national park. In April 1938, the state interventor traveled to Rio to present his project to

---

from Manoel Ribas to Getúlio Vargas, October 10 and 12, 1938, Gabinete Civil da Presidência, Lata 99, Pasta Paraná, 1934, 1936–39, AN-RJ.

[31] Letter from Manoel Ribas to Getúlio Vargas, October 12, 1938, Gabinete Civil da Presidência, Lata 99, Pasta Paraná, 1934, 1936–39, AN-RJ.

[32] Actually, the hotel, called "Hotel Cassino," had not yet been finished. It was also located not on the falls, but in Foz do Iguaçu, twenty kilometers away.

[33] Letter from Manoel Ribas to Getúlio Vargas, March 31, 1936, Gabinete Civil da Presidência, Lata 23, Pasta Paraná, 1934–37, 1939, AN-RJ; Letters from Manoel Ribas to Getúlio Vargas, October 10 and 12, 1938, Gabinete Civil da Presidência, Lata 99, Pasta Paraná, 1934, 1936–39, AN-RJ; Osny Duarte Pereira, *Direito florestal brasileiro; Ensaio* (Rio de Janeiro: Borsoi, 1950), 538; Oliveira, "Notas sobre a política paranaense no período de 1930 a 1945."

the minister of agriculture, Fernando Costa. After showing footage of the falls, Ribas convinced Costa of the need to create a Brazilian national park to catch up to the Argentine development across the river.[34]

In December 1938, following a visit to the state of Paraná, Costa presented Vargas with a bill for the creation of Iguaçu National Park that contemplated using the area ceded by Paraná nine years before. After 1937, with the Congress dissolved, all bills were submitted by cabinet members directly to Getúlio Vargas for approval. In the introduction to the bill, Costa presented to Vargas the concept of national parks, framing them as tokens of modernity adopted by the United States and advanced European nations. Costa also conjured the context of transboundary competition with Argentina, explaining that the neighboring nation already had its own park on the other side of the falls. He stressed the existence of an "Argentine national park of similar name and purpose" across the border, suggesting a Brazilian park might help to "narrow the gap existing in the relations" between the two countries.[35]

On January 10, 1939, the laconic decree 1035 created Iguaçu National Park. The legislation contained seven articles that failed to stipulate the actual area of the park, which would be established after a survey. Also, unlike in Costa's project, the text did not set out the purpose of the national park, referring back to articles in the 1937 Constitution and 1934 Forest Code that rendered the state the custodian of "old-growth forests" (*florestas remanescentes*) and "natural monuments."[36] This conservationist justification implicit in the 1939 Iguaçu National Park Act conceals the role of the state of Paraná in the creation of the park. State officials in Paraná expropriated the lands around the falls in 1916, expanded the area and ceded it to the federal government in 1931, and continued pressuring Rio de Janeiro for the creation of the park by playing up Brazil's rivalry with Argentina. In all this, policymakers continually framed the park both as an initiative to conserve forests and waterfalls and as a tool to bring development to the borderlands. They were, thus,

---

[34] "Preciosa iniciativa," *O jornal*, April 10, 1938, 6; "Um grande plano da administração Manoel Ribas," *O dia*, April 12, 1938, 1; "A exploração da Foz do Iguassú," *O Jornal*, April 14, 1938, 5; "Parque de Iguassú," *Correio da manhã*, April 15, 1838, 1.

[35] Fernando Costa to Getúlio Vargas, December 27, 1938, G. M. 1036, AN-RJ.

[36] Brazil, Decree 23793, "Código florestal," January 23, 1934; Brazil, "Parque Nacional de Itatiaia," Decree 1713, June 14, 1937; Brazil, "Parque Nacional do Iguassú," Decree-Law 1035, January 10, 1939; "Vai ser construído um parque nacional na Foz do Iguassú," *Correio da manhã*, December 28, 1938; "A fundação do Parque Nacional do Iguassú," *Correio da manhã*, June 6, 1939.

successful in aligning the park with a federal policy geared toward the colonization of Brazil's sparsely inhabited western frontier.

All in all, the idea of colonizing and integrating Brazil's western hinterland guided much of Vargas's actions during his years in power, especially during the Estado Novo (New State), the period between 1937 and 1945 when he shut down the Congress and assumed dictatorial powers. In 1937, in a radio broadcast on New Year's Eve, Vargas introduced the new spirit of the Estado Novo by announcing that the "true sense of Brazilianness" was the integration of the country's hinterland to its economic core, a campaign baptized "the March to the West." On the radio show, Vargas presented the Brazilian people with their mission: To create a unique civilization in the New World. To accomplish such goal, it would be necessary to integrate the entire territory into a harmonious whole, one in which the rational exploitation of natural resources under the guidance of the federal government replaced backward subsistence endeavors such as slash-and-burn agriculture.[37] Vargas's mission was to dissolve local economic particularities into an organic internal market that channeled western resources to eastern industrialization. The March to the West was a state-sponsored ideology of manifest destiny inspired by positivist and fascist visions of an organic society free of class or regional tensions. To promote this ideal, the Brazilian state needed to drive a colonization process and control the country's natural resources.[38]

The creation of Iguaçu National Park in 1939 fit well into the Vargas mindset of controlling and nationalizing the country's western hinterland.[39] In 1939 the government adopted new regulations that put into practice the provisions of the 1934 and 1937 constitutions increasing federal control over a 150-kilometer security band along Brazil's international borders, including the area of Iguazu Falls.[40] The new legislation

---

[37] Getúlio Vargas, "Marcha Para Oeste – Rio de Janeiro, 31 de Dezembro de 1937," in *Getúlio Vargas*, Série Perfis Parlamentares no. 62 (Brasília: Câmara dos Deputados/ Edições Câmara, 2011), 368–73.

[38] Getúlio Vargas, *A nova política do Brasil*, vol. V (Rio de Janeiro: J. Olympio, 1938), 163–66; Getúlio Vargas, *A nova política do Brasil*, vol. VIII (Rio de Janeiro: J. Olympio, 1938), 23–24, 32–33; Cassiano Ricardo, *Marcha para Oeste: A influência da "bandeira" na formação social e política do Brasil* (Rio de Janeiro: José Olympio, 1940).

[39] As a federal institution, Iguaçu could also serve to undermine the power of local oligarchies over frontier territories, another goal of the March to the West. For a detailed discussion on the March, see Seth Garfield, *Indigenous Struggle at the Heart of Brazil: State Policy, Frontier Expansion, and Xavante Indians, 1937–1988* (Durham: Duke University Press, 2001), 26–31.

[40] *Annaes da Assembléa Nacional Constituinte*, vol. IX, 22 vols. (Rio de Janeiro: Impr. Nacional, 1934–37), 350–51; Brazil, Constitution of 1934, Article 166; Brazil,

stopped short from transferring ownership of untitled public lands from the states to the federal government, but it introduced federal checks on the states' ability to freely distribute public land at the border. State governments now had to go through a federally appointed commission for approval of land transactions within 150 kilometers of an international boundary. It constituted a considerable expansion in federal governance, but it affected the country unevenly. Away from international boundaries, the Vargas government still lacked the power to manage untitled public lands, as they continued to be owned and controlled by state governments.[41]

THE DEVELOPMENT OF CONSERVATION LEGISLATION

The limitations of the Brazilian federal government in controlling public land partially explains the moderate scale of its conservationist actions, especially when compared to national park implementation in Argentina, where the central government used public lands or expropriated land directly to create parks inside federal territories controlled by Buenos Aires. But dominion over public land was not the only element setting the two countries apart, for they also differed in the role that geopolitical concerns played in building the national park systems. In Argentina, preoccupation with the border allowed park proponents to create a powerful national park agency, to pass extensive legislation, and to guarantee adequate funding to support all of the country's new protected areas. Brazil fell short in its attempt to follow Argentine initiatives.

In Argentina, all the national parks created in the 1930s and 1940s fit into the model of borderland occupation, which explains the resources and initial coherence of the country's national park system. The national park act of 1934 established the first two Argentine parks, a new agency, and a legal framework, all of which were based on the idea of using parks as development tools in border areas. It helped that the country's most majestic mountains and waterfalls lay alongside its borders. In Brazil, on

Constitution of 1937, Article 165; Brazil, Decree-Law 1164, May 18, 1939; Brazil, Decree-Law 1968, January 17, 1940; Brazil, Decree-Law 4783, November 5, 1942.

[41] Ministério da Agricultura, Divisão de Terras e Colonização, Internal Memo, June 3, 1939, AN-RJ; "Histórico," Comissão Especial da Faixa de Fronteiras: 1940–1962, Fundo 1G, SDE-008, AN-RJ; Sérgio Lopes, *O território do Iguaçu no contexto da Marcha para Oeste* (Cascavel: Edunioeste, 2002), 52–53; Vanderlei Vazelesk Ribeiro, *Cuestiones agrarias en el varguismo y el peronismo: Una mirada histórica* (Bernal, Argentina: Universidad Nacional de Quilmes Editorial, 2008), 66–67.

the other hand, the establishment of parks was eclectic. Unlike Argentina, Brazil also harbored monumental landscapes close to its capital, Rio de Janeiro, which generated demands for national park creation at its populated Atlantic seaboard. Iguaçu National Park in the distant Paraná borderland came to be the only protected area created for geopolitical reasons in Brazil in the 1930s. Institutionally, the environmental agencies and federal legislation that supported the creation of the first Brazilian national parks owed little to border concerns. They were the fruit of a different process, one driven by conservationists lobbying for environmental legislation in Rio de Janeiro.

The new environmental legislation and institutions created during the Vargas years had their roots in a new phenomenon: The appearance on the national stage of a cadre of conservationists, several of them scientists. They managed to align US and European ideas of conservation with a nationalist discourse similar to that promoted by ideologues of the regime.[42] The case for national parks was put forward at the beginning of the decade by scientists such as Alberto José de Sampaio, Director of Botany at the National Museum (1912–37). In March 1931, Sampaio used his Sunday column in *Correio da Manhã* to propose the creation of over two dozen national parks, including one around Iguazu Falls, to be modeled after North American and European examples. The new

[42] This generation of scientists has been studied in extensive detail in recent years. See José Luiz de Andrade Franco and José Augusto Drummond, "Wilderness and the Brazilian Mind (II): The First Brazilian Conference on Nature Protection (Rio de Janeiro, 1934)," *Environmental History* 14, no. 1 (2009): 82–102; José Luiz de Andrade Franco and José Augusto Drummond, "Wilderness and the Brazilian Mind (I): Nation and Nature in Brazil from the 1920s to the 1940s," *Environmental History* 13, no. 4 (2008): 724–50; José Augusto Pádua, "Natureza e projeto nacional: As origens da ecologia política no Brasil," in *Ecologia e Política no Brasil* (Rio de Janeiro: Editora Espaço e Tempo, 1987); Franco and Drummond, "História das preocupações com o mundo natural no Brasil"; José Luiz de Andrade Franco, "A primeira Conferência Brasileira de Proteção à Natureza e a questão da identidade nacional," *Varia Historia* 26 (January 2002): 77–96; Regina Horta Duarte, "Pássaros e cientistas no Brasil: Em busca de proteção, 1894–1938," *Latin American Research Review* 41, no. 1 (2006): 3–26; Duarte, *Activist Biology*; José Augusto Drummond, "A visão conservacionista (1920 a 1970)," in *Ambientalismo no Brasil: Passado, presente e futuro*, ed. Enrique Svirsky and João Paulo R. Capobianco (São Paulo: Instituto Socioambiental/Secretaria do Meio Ambiente do Estado de São Paulo, 1997) 19–26; Carolina Marotta Capanema, "A natureza no projeto de construção de um Brasil moderno e a obra de Alberto José Sampaio" (MA thesis, Federal University of Minas Gerais, 2006); Natascha Stefania Carvalho Ostos, "Terra adorada, mãe gentil: Representações do feminino e da natureza no Brasil da era Vargas (1930–1945)" (MA thesis, Federal University of Minas Gerais, 2009); Dean, *With Broadax and Firebrand*, 256–64.

Brazilian parks would offer flora protection and allow visitation and scientific research.[43] At the time, environmental concerns started to penetrate the higher echelons of the Brazilian government, a process facilitated by Vargas's growing interest in conserving the forests in the mountain range surrounding the city of Rio de Janeiro.[44]

The topic gained momentum in 1934 with the issuance of a forest code and the federal sponsorship of Brazil's first Conference for the Protection of Nature. The main goal of the new forest code was to promote the "rational use" of the country's forests, but it also included articles on in situ conservation measures such as national parks. Unlike neighboring Argentina, 1930s Brazil did not draft legislation specific to national parks, but the new law offered at least a minimal institutional framework for the creation of the country's first protected areas. The new code also created a Federal Forest Council with members appointed by the executive from scientific and tourism institutions. The council was placed under the umbrella of the Ministry of Agriculture and had as its mission to advise the government on forestry and conservation issues and to draft new legislation.[45] After 1934, the proponents of a park surrounding Iguazu

---

[43] Alberto José de Sampaio, "Parques nacionaes," *Jornal do commercio*, March 1, 1931.

[44] On April 25, 1933, an 80-kilogram boulder fell on Vargas's car as he was traveling from Rio de Janeiro to Petrópolis. The boulder killed one passenger, and Vargas suffered a broken leg. The accident exposed Vargas to the increasing deforestation of the mountains outside Rio de Janeiro. In 1938 Vargas signed a decree creating forest reserves along the road connecting Rio and Petropolis, and at the end of 1939 he created Brazil's third national park in the area, Serra dos Órgãos National Park. "Um accidente com o automovel em que viajava para Petropolis o chefe do governo," *Correio da manhã*, April 26, 1933; "O doloroso accidente de ante-hontem, na rodovia Rio Petropolis," *Correio da manhã*, April 27, 1933; "Reuniu-se o Conselho Florestal Federal: A formação de parques nacionais," *Correio da Manhã*, May 22, 1937; "Para fundação, no país, dos primeiros parques florestais: O CFF cogita da desapropriação de matas na Serra de Petrópolis," *Correio da manhã*, May 29, 1937; "A conservação das florestas na estrada Rio-Petrópolis: A directoria da baixada fluminense dirige-se ao Conselho Florestal," *Correio da manhã*, July 4, 1937; "Impedindo a devastação das matas que marginam a Rio-Petrópolis: Uma reunião do Conselho Florestal Federal," *Correio da manhã*, February 11, 1938; "A fundação do Parque Nacional do Iguassú," *Correio da manhã*, June 6, 1939; "Constituirão um parque nacional: As terras desapropriadas à margem da estrada Rio-Petrópolis," *Correio da manhã*, November 17, 1939; Brazil, Decree 2398, February 16, 1938; Brazil, Decree-Law 1822, "Parque Nacional da Serra dos Orgãos," December 30, 1939. See also Lira Neto's reconstruction of the accident in Lira Neto, *Getúlio: Do governo provisório à ditadura do Estado Novo (1930–1945)* (São Paulo: Companhia das Letras, 2013), 2:131–37.

[45] Paulo Ferreira de Souza to Alberto José de Sampaio, June 24, 1933, in Fundo Alberto José de Sampaio, Pasta "Sobre o Código Florestal, DB-28," Envelope "Sobre o Código Florestal, 1933–1937," MN-A; Brazil, Decree 23793, "Código florestal," January 23, 1934.

Falls in Paraná could count on the new conservationist framework to support their goal.[46]

Park proponents such as Sampaio took inspiration from national parks in Europe, Canada, the United States, and, after 1934, Argentina. Nahuel Huapi for example, influenced the establishment of the first Brazilian national park in 1937 in Itatiaia, a mountainous area between Rio de Janeiro and São Paulo where the Botanical Garden of Rio de Janeiro had operated a scientific station since 1914. A year before the creation of the park, the director of the Botanical Garden and member of the Federal Forest Council, Paulo Campos Porto, visited Nahuel Huapi. Porto was impressed with the park's "hydro-biological stations" and botanical laboratory, calling it "one of the greatest feats of contemporary Argentina."[47] Porto's report after returning from Buenos Aires convinced the Federal Forest Council of the viability of transforming the scientific station in Itatiaia and the public lands around it into a national park. The area contained one of the few examples of public lands already controlled by the federal government in the 1930s. Odilon Braga, the minister of agriculture, broached the matter with Getúlio Vargas, emphasizing that a park would promote development in the region through tourism. The 11,000-hectare protected area was gazetted in July 1937, becoming the first national park in the country. Unlike Argentina, however, no national park agency was created, and the Botanical Garden remained the institution in charge of managing the area.[48]

---

[46] Environmental legislation already had been passed in several states. In Paraná, besides the expropriation of the lands around Iguazu Falls in 1916 and 1931, the state government had already passed a forest code in 1907 and another decree in 1908 reserving the lands around Sete Quedas Falls for the creation of a "city and a park." Sete Quedas Falls were located near Iguazu Falls but at the border with Paraguay. As early as 1908, Brazil was following the Argentine idea of creating parks and cities as settlement tools for geopolitical purposes. State of Paraná, Law 706, "Código florestal," April 1, 1907; State of Paraná, Law 815, May 5, 1908.

[47] "Noticiario e actividades varias," *Rodriguesia* 2, no. 7 (1936): 346–52; Paulo Campos Porto, "As orchideas brasileiras em Buenos Aires: Impressões de um scientista brasileiro, depois de algumas semanas de permanencia na capital e no interior da Argentina," *Correio da Manhã*, December 10, 1936; Paulo Campos Porto to Exequiel Bustillo and Victor Pinto, April 1937, Fondo Exequiel Bustillo, Legajo 7, no. 3349, AGN; Ingrid Fonseca Casazza, "Ciência e proteção à natureza: A trajetória do botânico Paulo Campos Porto (1914–1939)," in *Anais* (presented at the 13° Seminário Nacional de História da Ciência e da Tecnologia, University of São Paulo, Sociedade Brasileira de História da Ciência, 2012).

[48] "A exposição permanente de exemplares da nossa flora: Vai ser criado o primeiro parque florestal da união," *Correio da manhã*, April 20, 1937; "Parque Nacional de Itatiaia," Decree 1713, July 14, 1937; "Foi criado o Parque Nacional de Itatiaia: O que representa

This situation changed at the end of 1938, twenty days before the gazetting of Iguaçu National Park on January 10, 1939, when the Brazilian government created a Forest Service subordinated to the Ministry of Agriculture to protect Brazil's forests, foment silviculture, and organize national parks, national forests, and other reserves.[49] Brazil had already had a previous iteration of the Forest Service (1925–33) that never existed except on paper. In the words of historian Warren Dean, the first Forest Service "lacked a budget or a code to enforce, or even forests to maintain, because the Republican constitution had devolved all public land to the states."[50] At the moment of its refoundation, on the eve of 1939, the second Forest Service would have, at the very least, two national parks and a few woodland reserves around Rio de Janeiro to manage.

The new agency encompassed goals that were, at times, contradictory. On the one hand, the office was in charge of implementing and supervising the country's protected areas, including the recently created national parks of Itatiaia and Iguaçu, which were soon to be joined by Serra dos Órgãos, created in November 1939, as well as a few forest preserves in the state of Rio de Janeiro. Likewise, the Forest Service was responsible for promoting scientific research on Brazilian flora through the Botanical Garden in Rio de Janeiro. On the other hand, the agency was also responsible for advancing the rational use of natural resources. This included managing Rio's Forest Nursery, which produced seedlings for reforestation purposes; fostering forestry and developing technology for the logging industry in the country; ensuring the rational use of forests for firewood and charcoal; and enforcing the new Forest Code, which, reflecting the limited federal power to manage land, had to be done in "agreement with the states."[51]

Despite its mission to enforce the Forest Code throughout Brazil, the Forest Service had most of its personnel concentrated in Rio de Janeiro. In

o magnífico reservatório botânico das Agulhas Negras," *Correio da manhã*, June 16, 1937.
[49] Brazil. Decree-Law 982, December 23, 1938; Brazil, Decree 4439, July 26, 1939; Brazil, Decree 16677, September 29, 1944; Brazil, Arquivo Nacional, "Serviço Florestal," in *MAPA-Memória da Administração*, accessed January 5, 2014, www.an.gov.br/sian/Ma pa/Exibe_Pesquisa .asp?v_tela=ver_consulta_orgao_consulta.asp&pesquisa_mapa=1&v_Orgao_ID=7912.
[50] Brazil, Decree 4421, "Crêa o Serviço Florestal do Brasil," December 28, 1921; Brazil, Decree 17042, "Dá regulamento ao Serviço Florestal do Brasil," September 16, 1925; Dean, *With Broadax and Firebrand*, 257.
[51] Serviço Florestal, *Regimento do Serviço Florestal* (Rio de Janeiro: Ministério da Agricultura, 1944).

other states, the agency relied on the goodwill of local state governments and its delegates and rangers worked on a voluntary basis. In the state of Paraná, besides the officials working at the recently created Iguaçu National Park, the Forest Service employed only one voluntary official. The precariousness of the agency affected even its own salaried personnel – until the 1960s, it was common for employees of Iguaçu National Park to be hired through the Instituto Nacional do Pinho (National Pine Institute), a separate, bigger, and better-funded forestry agency that focused on the rational exploitation of Paraná pine (*Araucaria angustifolia*) in southern Brazil.[52] The lack of enforcement made the new Forest Code a dead letter in most of Brazil. In Paraná, Manoel Ribas publicly admitted the state government's inability to apply the "draconian punishment" prescribed in the new environmental legislation, which led officials to simply ignore it. Instead, the government had decided to "educate" the population on the need to "defend the forest" and reforest the regions "criminally and unconsciously" devastated by loggers and farmers.[53]

In contrast to Argentina, Brazil lacked a powerful national park agency, specific national park legislation, and resources to implement protected areas (including access to public land). The Brazilian national parks created in the 1930s were managed by a suboffice within the Forest Service, which in turn was primarily a forestry agency. Whereas Iguazú National Park in Argentina was part of a structure put in place to use national parks as a means to occupy the borderlands, Iguaçu National Park in Brazil, despite its similar developmentalist mission, had to make do with a nonspecialized and underfunded agency.

GEOPOLITICAL CONCERNS INSIDE THE FOREST SERVICE

During the Estado Novo, conservation initiatives such as national parks took a backseat vis-à-vis management and regulation of resources for production. Whereas national parks received limited funding and

---

[52] Fernando Costa, *As realizações do Presidente Getúlio Vargas no Ministério da Agricultura: Conferência realizada no Palácio Tiradentes, em 20 de dezembro de 1940* (Rio de Janeiro: Departamento de Imprensa e Propaganda, 1941), 66–67; Apolônio Salles, *As atividades do Ministério da Agricultura em 1942* (Rio de Janeiro: Ministério da Agricultura, 1943), 2:91; João Augusto Falcão, *O Serviço Florestal no biênio 1943–1944* (Rio de Janeiro: Ministério da Agricultura, 1945), 73–84; Instituto Nacional do Pinho, Registration Card of Albino Monteiro Berg, Foz do Iguaçu, 1946, c. 1970, in Pedro Berg Personal Archive.

[53] Manuel Ribas, *Mensagem apresentada pelo Exmo. Snr. Governador Manoel Ribas à Assembléia Legislativa do Estado* (Curitiba: Empresa Gráfica Paranaense, 1936), 112.

attention, initiatives to promote logging of Paraná pine and exploitation of yerba mate attracted substantial support from the state. Still, the federal government did invest something in the newly created national parks, and because of its role as a catalyst for border development, Iguaçu was the primary recipient of funding among the three Brazilian parks. That Iguaçu occupied a special place among its counterparts was the avowed opinion of Francisco de Assis Iglesias, the first director of the Forest Service. Iglesias was an agronomist by profession and a career employee of the Ministry of Agriculture who had worked with the famous scientist Vital Brasil at the Butantan Institute in his home state of São Paulo. He drafted the decree creating the first Forest Service and had been its director until 1932. With the refounding of the agency in 1938, Iglesias resumed his role as the director of the Forest Service, where he stayed until 1942.[54]

After leading a commission of Ministry of Agriculture employees to survey the area of Iguazu Falls in 1939, Iglesias claimed Iguaçu was unique among the new parks, for it responded to border demands that were absent in the other protected areas. In his survey report to the Minister of Agriculture, the head of the Forest Service made explicit the geopolitical motivations behind the creation of the park. It was Iguaçu National Park's location on an isolated frontier dominated by Argentina that made its creation, in the words of Iglesias, a "manly endeavor" that symbolized the entirety of the March to the West. In his view, the park would serve to integrate a "bastard and cosmopolitan" borderland population that was, at that time, "dominated" by a foreign language (Spanish), a foreign currency (the Argentine peso), and foreign customs. Iglesias pointed out that the region was "disconnected, unknown, and untapped" owing to its isolation and the lack of viable transportation routes. Establishing the park would help funnel federal resources to fight these problems.[55]

Iglesias proposed a plan for the establishment of the park that included several interventions aimed at providing the Brazilian borderlands with transportation infrastructure. Among the planned projects were the building of two new highways connecting Foz do Iguaçu and the national park to Curitiba to the east and Guaíra to the north. He also planned the

[54] "Noticiario e actividades varias," *Rodriguesia* 4, no. 15 (1942): 95–96.

[55] Comissão Especial de Revisão das Concessões de Terras na Faixa de Fronteiras, "Relatório apresentado pelo engenheiro civil Dulphe Pinheiro Machado," 129–35, AN-RJ. The same report was later republished in Francisco de Assis Iglesias, "Os parques nacionais existentes: Descrição e relevância" in *Anais, IX Congresso Brasileiro de Geografia*, ed. Bernardino José de Souza, Cristovão Leite de Castro, and Alexandre Emílio Sommler, vol. III (Rio de Janeiro: Conselho Nacional de Geografia, 1944), MA.

construction of an airport and a new river port on the Paraná (both in the town, outside the park), a park headquarters, a new highway connecting Foz do Iguaçu to the falls, a grand hotel, a hydroelectric power plant, and houses for park employees. In sum, the head of the Forest Service planned to use Iguaçu's strategic position as a border park as leverage for launching extensive investment in the frontier zone.[56]

Even when conservationist concerns came to the forefront, they were framed in geopolitical terms in Iglesias's report. He characterized the current area ceded by the state of Paraná in 1931 as "exiguous" compared to the Argentine park. At only 5,000 hectares, Iguaçu National Park's territory could prove to be insufficient to preserve the fauna and flora of the region against an impending future of frontier settlement and encroachment pressures. Expanding the park to "at least 100,000 hectares" would elevate Iguaçu to the same tier as its Argentine counterpart and, at the same time, protect a larger section of forests.[57] Iglesias's report encapsulates the tension between the need to promote the settlement of the border and the mandate to take preventive measures to protect forests and natural monuments. Not only would the park serve as a catalyst for the development of the region – "the best propaganda for the March to the West," in the words of Octávio Silveira Mello, head of the National Park Section of the Forest Service – but it would also act as a preventive measure against the destruction caused by this very development.[58]

IMPLEMENTING THE PARK

Construction of park infrastructure began in 1940. Ângelo Murgel, the Brazilian architect commissioned by the Forest Service to design the buildings in Iguaçu and the two other Brazilian national parks, was in contact with the US National Park Service, from which he obtained a model to implement in Brazil.[59] Iguaçu National Park would have as its centerpiece a luxurious hotel, to be constructed close to the falls, to

---

[56] Comissão Especial de Revisão das Concessões de Terras na Faixa de Fronteiras, "Relatório apresentado pelo engenheiro civil Dulphe Pinheiro Machado," 129–35, AN-RJ.

[57] Ibid.

[58] Octávio Silveira Mello, "Protecção à natureza," *Rodriguesia* 4, no. 13 (Summer 1940): 151–53.

[59] Ângelo Murgel, *Parques nacionais: Conferência pronunciada na Exposição de Edifícios Públicos do Departamento Administrativo do Serviço Público em 1944, pelo Engenheiro Ângelo Murgel* (Rio de Janeiro: Imprensa Nacional, 1945).

cater to moneyed tourists. It would mimic grand park hotels in the United States such as the Ahwahnee Hotel (Yosemite National Park) and the Old Faithful Inn (Yellowstone National Park), and put the old Argentine hotel across the river to shame.

A small wooden hotel had been built on the Brazilian side of the falls in 1915 by a local entrepreneur, Jorge Schimmelpfeng, who obtained permission from the property owner, Jesús Val, to cater to tourists willing to cross from Argentina for the Brazilian view of the falls. The hotel continued to exist after Val's estate was expropriated in 1916, but it was abandoned in 1924 when the tenentista column occupied Foz do Iguaçu. What remained of the old hotel after the occupation continued to function as a restaurant until 1937, when a fire destroyed it.[60]

The building of the new grand hotel was initiated in 1941, but already in 1942 construction had paused. Construction resumed, very slowly, in 1944, but stopped again in 1947. This pattern of stopping and resuming construction would continue until 1958, when the Hotel das Cataratas was finally inaugurated with the presence of presidents Juscelino Kubitschek (Brazil) and Alfredo Stroessner (Paraguay). These frequent interruptions were mainly due to budget cuts and payment delays. Another factor, suggested by Mário Câmara Canto, the first director of Iguaçu National Park (1941–49), was the difficulty in finding specialized tradespersons in the region. Local workers, of mostly Guarani descent, were skilled loggers but knew little of masonry and other similar crafts. Park administrators had to hire construction workers far away in São Paulo, Paraná, and Minas Gerais; gather them in Guarapuava; and haul them by truck to Foz do Iguaçu "with great difficulties, given the poor conditions of the highway," as reported by the engineer Dulphe Pinheiro Machado.[61]

---

[60] Otília Schimmelpfeng, "Pioneiros do turismo iguaçuense II," *O jornal de Foz,* July 12, 1970, 2; Otília Schimmelpfeng, "Pioneiros do turismo iguaçuense VII," *O jornal de Foz,* August 23, 1970, 2; Otília Schimmelpfeng, "Pioneiros do turismo iguaçuense X," *O jornal de Foz,* August 30, 1970, 2; Carrão, *Impressões de viagem,* 55; José E. Rodríguez, *A través del Iguazú y del Guayrá* (Buenos Aires: Talleres Gráficos del Estado Mayor del Ejército, 1917), 26; Jayme Ballão, *A Foz do Iguassu e as cataratas do Iguassu e Paraná: Descripção de viagem 1920* (Curitiba: Typographia da República, 1921), 30; Lima Figueiredo, *Oéste paranaense,* 88–93; Maria Luiza Nogueira Paes, "A paisagem emoldurada, do Éden imaginado à razão do mercado: Um estudo sobre os parques nacionais do Vulcão Poás, na Costa Rica, e do Iguaçu, no Brasil" (PhD diss., University of Brasília, 2003), 83–84; Wachowicz, *Obrageros, mensus e colonos,* 36–38.
[61] Comissão Especial de Revisão das Concessões de Terras na Faixa de Fronteiras, "Relatório apresentado pelo engenheiro civil Dulphe Pinheiro Machado," 131, AN-RJ;

Interestingly, the Forest Service managed to finish many of the other proposed infrastructure works between 1942 and 1944, including the hydroelectric power plant, which would supply energy to the park and Foz do Iguaçu, and the airport. The new airport had a grass landing strip and included a "beautiful passenger terminal in colonial style," in the words of a visitor.[62] It replaced the runway built by the Brazilian Army in 1935 for its airmail service. Since 1936 Pan Am had, through its subsidiary Panair do Brasil, operated a Rio–Asunción–Buenos Aires route with a stop in Foz do Iguaçu, but the inauguration of the new terminal in 1942 allowed the town to accommodate more tourists. Brazilian visitors who could afford to fly to see the falls no longer had to depend on unreliable land and water connections.[63]

All this investment meant Iguaçu was positioned to attract most of the meager funding designated to national parks in Brazil. A comparison of the investment in infrastructure made by the Brazilian government in its three parks reveals the importance of Iguaçu and territorial concerns for the Vargas regime's conservation policy. In the period between 1939 and 1945, Iguaçu National Park absorbed about 66 percent of the budget designated for infrastructure

Mário Câmara Canto, "Relatório que apresenta o administrador do Parque Nacional do Iguassú, referente ao período de abril, maio e junho de 1942" (1942), "Relatório que apresenta o administrador do Parque Nacional do Iguassú, referente ao 1° semestre do corrente ano" (1944), and "Relatório que apresenta o administrador do Parque Nacional do Iguaçu, referente ao ano de 1947" (1947), PNIB-A; Mário Pimentel de Camargo, "Relatório anual de 1959," (1959), 5–6, "Relatório do 1° semestre do exercício de 1959" (1959), 1, PNIB-A; "Foz do Iguaçu faz história: Quarto encontro dos presidentes do Paraguai e do Brasil," *A notícia*, November 30, 1958.

[62] Mário Câmara Canto, "Relatório que apresenta o administrador do Parque Nacional do Iguassú, referente ao período de abril, maio e junho de 1942" (1942), "Relatório que apresenta o administrador do Parque Nacional do Iguassú, referente ao 1° semestre do corrente ano, bem como sugestões para 1944" (1943), "Relatório que apresenta o administrador do Parque Nacional do Iguassú, referente ao período de janeiro, fevereiro e março de 1943" (1943), "Relatório que apresenta o administrador do Parque Nacional do Iguassú, referente ao 1° semestre do corrente ano" (1944), PNIB-A; Cândido de Mello Leitão, *A vida na selva* (São Paulo: Companhia Editora Nacional, 1940), 175–94.

[63] See Otília Schimmelpfeng, "Campo de aviação I," *O jornal de Foz*, November 1, 1970, 2; Otília Schimmelpfeng, "Campo de aviação V," *O jornal de Foz*, November 29, 1970, 2; João Gomes Ribeiro Filho, *Relatório apresentado ao Presidente da República dos Estados Unidos do Brasil pelo general de divisão João Gomes Ribeiro Filho, ministro de estado da guerra, em maio de 1936* (Rio de Janeiro: Imprensa do Estado Maior do Exército, 1936), 20, 67–69; Daniel Leb Sasaki, *Pouso forçado: A história por trás da destruição da Panair do Brasil pelo regime militar* (Rio de Janeiro: Editora Record, 2005), 73–74; William A. M. Burden, *The Struggle for Airways in Latin America* (New York: Council on Foreign Relations, 1943).

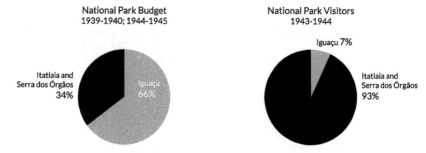

FIGURE 2.3 Budget and visitors in the Brazilian National Parks. With data compiled from João Augusto Falcão, *O Serviço Florestal no biênio 1943–1944*, 12, 14, 32–42; Fernando Costa, *As atividades agrícolas do Brasil em 1939* (Rio de Janeiro, Serviço de Informação Agrícola, Ministério da Agricultura, 1940), 1:353, 2:11; Fernando Costa, *As atividades do Ministério da Agricultura em 1940* (Rio de Janeiro: Serviço de Informação Agrícola, Ministério da Agricultura, 1941), 1:486

construction in the new national parks, despite garnering only 7 percent of national park visitation (see Figure 2.3).

In the first decades of Iguaçu, the Forest Service prioritized necessary transportation infrastructure and used the park budget on public works such as the airport, roads, and a hydroelectric dam, allowing the federal government to invest in the development of the frontier region. Brazil invested more in Iguaçu than Argentina did in Iguazú. In 1939, the Brazilian Ministry of Agriculture stipulated an annual budget of 2,500 contos de réis for park implementation, or 2.8 million US dollars in 2020 values. The same year, the Argentine national park service expended 206,123.45 pesos on the Argentine Iguazú National Park, or about 1.1 million US dollars in 2020 values. Indeed, Iguaçu National Park was one of the leading recipients of investment in South America in this period, second only to Argentina's Nahuel Huapi National Park.[64]

In its first five years of existence, Iguaçu National Park was restricted to the 5,000 hectares ceded by the state of Paraná in 1931. Compared to the

[64] Fernando Costa, *As atividades agrícolas do Brasil em 1939* (Rio de Janeiro: Serviço de Informação Agrícola, Ministério da Agricultura, 1940), 1:353; Dirección de Parques Nacionales, *Memoria correspondiente al año 1941* (Buenos Aires: Dirección de Parques Nacionales, 1942), 31; Samuel H. Williamson, "Seven Ways to Compute the Relative Value of a US Dollar Amount, 1774 to present," *Measuring Worth*, 2020, accessed at www.measuringworth.com/uscompare/; Federal Reserve, *Twenty-Fifth Annual Report Federal Reserve Bank of New York for the Year Ended December 31, 1939* (New York: Second Federal Reserve District, 1940), 32, accessed at fraser.stlouisfed.org.

44,000 hectares of the Argentine park across the border, the relatively small area of the Brazilian park continued to be an embarrassment for Forest Service officials after Iglesias suggested expanding the park in his 1939 report. An opportunity to expand the park appeared in 1940, when the Brazilian government nationalized the Companhia Estrada de Ferro São Paulo-Rio Grande (CEFSPRG), a bankrupt railroad company that had been granted large expanses of untitled public land in western Paraná for a railroad connecting Curitiba to Foz do Iguaçu that was never built. In 1942, Octávio Silveira Mello suggested using CEFSPRG lands east of the park to increase its area. Mello concurred with Iglesias that the park's modest size made it unworthy of "Brazil's territorial greatness." Like Iglesias, Mello also thought that increasing the area of the park was crucial for protecting the forest from the waves of Brazilian settlers foreseen by the March to the West campaign. He aimed to save the groves of Paraná pine located in the highlands of the former CEFSPRG estates from destruction. The logging of the native conifer corresponded to a significant share of Paraná's economy, but many observers, including employees at the National Pine Institute, had started to worry about the pace of deforestation and imminent demise of the pine tree. The new park boundaries planned by Mello would use rivers (Gonçalves Dias to the east, Iguazu to the south) and the highway to Foz do Iguaçu as the "natural boundaries" delimiting the park, allegedly encompassing expanses of old-growth Paraná pine in the expanded area. In the next years, other Forest Service employees such as Mário Câmara Canto, the director of Iguaçu, would return to the comparison with the neighboring country, insisting on park expansion by claiming incorrectly that the Argentine park was twenty-nine times larger than the park in Brazil (see Map 2.2).[65]

The boosters of Iguaçu expansion were all trained agronomists working for the federal government with professional or academic experience in forestry. By employing a conservation rationale to justify the addition of new lands to the parks' territory, they inserted themselves into the growing debate about Brazil's indiscriminate deforestation problem, which in the state of Paraná focused mostly on the waste of the coveted Paraná pine.[66]

[65] Francisco Iglesias, "Parques nacionais existentes, descrição e relevância"; Octávio Silveira Mello, "Parque Nacional do Iguaçu: Área a ser pleiteada," June 3, 1942, Fundo Parque Nacional do Iguaçu, ICMBio; Mário Câmara Canto, "Relatório que apresenta o administrador do Parque Nacional do Iguassú, referente ao corrente ano, bem como sugestões para 1944," December 22, 1943, Pasta "Relatórios de atividades," PNIB-A.
[66] Frederico Carlos Hoehne, *Araucarilândia* (São Paulo: Secretaria da Agricultura, Indústria e Commercio do Estado de São Paulo, 1930); Reinhard Maack, "As consequências da

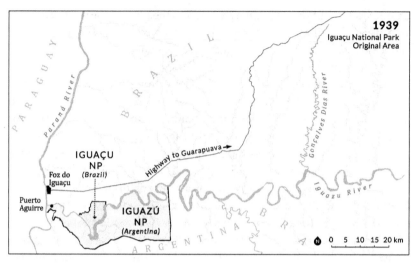

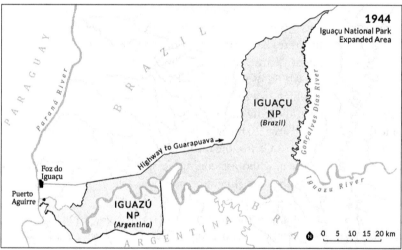

MAP 2.2 Iguaçu National Park expansion, 1939–44. Maps by Frederico Freitas

As mediators between ideas of forest conservation and frontier development, they also employed transborder envy to justify the enlargement of
Iguaçu National Park. However, expansion only took place through the
creation of a federal territory in the borderlands. As seen before, Vargas

devastação das matas no Estado do Paraná," *Arquivos de biologia e tecnologia, Curitiba* 8
(1953): 437–57.

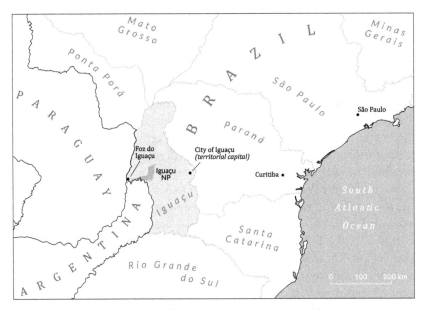

MAP 2.3 Territory of Iguaçu, 1943–46. Map by Frederico Freitas

had considered creating a federal territory in the western portions of Paraná and Santa Catarina in 1931 but caved in to opposition from elites in Curitiba and Florianópolis. The idea made a comeback in the context of the centralization of power during the Estado Novo and Brazil's entry into the Second World War, and Vargas embarked on the project of creating federal territories directly controlled by Rio de Janeiro. In 1943 the government in Rio created five new federal territories along strategic swaths of Brazil's international boundaries.[67] In the Brazilian south, a third of the states of Paraná and Santa Catarina was lopped off and combined into the new Territory of Iguaçu (see Map 2.3). With Rio controlling the territory, the government was able to expand Iguaçu National Park with part of the CEFSPRG estates, small stretches of private lands, and at least one large estate previously owned by the state of Paraná. With the new federal territory in place, in 1944 Vargas signed a series of decrees authorizing expansion in the area of the park. From a conservation standpoint, the expansion fell short of significantly preserving native Paraná pine groves,

---

[67] The new federal territories were Amapá, Rio Branco, Guaporé, Ponta Porã, and Iguaçu. Brazil, Decree-Law 5812, September 13, 1943.

as the new areas contained only a small number of those trees. But the expansion succeeded in making Iguaçu larger than its Argentine neighbor, giving the Brazilian park a thirtyfold increase in area – from less than 5,000 hectares to more than 160,000 hectares.[68]

With a stroke of Getúlio Vargas's pen, Iguaçu National Park became almost four times larger than its Argentine counterpart. By framing their discourse within the context of competition with Argentina, officials at the Forest Service managed to use the new Territory of Iguaçu, and the temporary incorporation of land by the federal government its creation entailed, to increase Iguaçu National Park. The Territory of Iguaçu failed to outlive Vargas's resignation in October 1945, and the new 1946 constitution terminated it, returning the territory's assets, including untitled public lands, to the original states of Paraná and Santa Catarina. Still, Iguaçu National Park kept its expanded boundaries after 1946. The need to utilize the creation of the short-lived federal territory to augment the park shows that the ability to control land was a necessary predicate for the successful implementation of national parks in Brazil. The federal government first created Iguaçu in an area ceded by the state of Paraná and expanded the park after federalizing the border region and gaining control of its public land. Something similar occurred in Argentina, which gazetted its first national parks inside federal territories directly controlled by Buenos Aires such as Misiones (Iguazú National Park) and Neuquén and Río Negro (Nahuel Huapi National Park).

COMMONALITIES AND DIFFERENCES

The history of the creation of Iguazú National Park in Argentina and Iguaçu National Park in Brazil reveals a few commonalities. Politicians and policymakers in both countries were concerned with the occupation of what they saw as a contested borderland, located Iguazu Falls at the center of this dispute, and understood the creation of a national park at the falls as a way to bring development and settlers to the region. Thus, the

---

[68] João Augusto Falcão, "O engrandecimento do Parque Nacional do Iguaçu," July 6, 1944, in O *Serviço Florestal no biênio 1943–1944*, 119–20, MA; "Ministério da Agricultura: Revigoramento da política florestal," *Correio da manhã*, March 7, 1945; Brazil, Decree-Law 2073, March 8, 1940; Brazil, Decree-Law 2436, July 22, 1940; Brazil, Decree-Law 5812, September 13, 1943; Brazil, Decree-Law 6506, May 17, 1944; Brazil, Decree-Law 6587, June 14, 1944; Brazil, Decree-Law 6664, July 7, 1944.

establishment of these parks cannot be dissociated from their geopolitical function.

Still, there were substantial variations on either side of the border. Whereas in Argentina the central preoccupation of the political elite lay in the border shared with Chile, while the Triple Frontier was relegated to a second plane of geopolitical concerns, in Brazil, the Vargas regime went to great lengths to nationalize what they called the "Guarani border," with actions that included the creation of two federal territories in the area: Iguaçu and Ponta Porã, the latter dismembered from the state of Mato Grosso (see Map 2.3).[69] Different attitudes were based on geography to some extent: Brazil lacked the unobstructed river connection to the Triple Frontier borderland available to Argentina. And yet, despite these differences, the establishment of the two parks in Iguazu reflected a shared language straddling the border, one that put international ideas of conservation in dialogue with local concerns about developing and nationalizing borderlands. The parks, then, had the potentially contradictory mission of promoting development and colonization and acting as buffers to preserve nature from the very processes they were about to ignite.

Another common trait was the crucial role of local politicians and other intermediary agents in creating these parks. The interference and pressure of governors (e.g., Acuña in Argentina) and state interventors (e.g., Tourinho and Ribas in Brazil) proved decisive in the establishment of these parks. The dialogue between these provincial actors and the seats of power in Rio de Janeiro and Buenos Aires reveals how the processes of territorialization are not the exclusive realm of central governments. In Brazil, local park proponents were also attuned to developments across the border and utilized their privileged access to this knowledge as leverage for pushing forward the case for a park at the falls.

Brazil also differed significantly in the power and tools at its disposal to manage land and control territory through national park policy. Whereas Argentina would consistently use national parks to intervene directly on the country's borderlands, Brazil would lose, after the fall of Vargas, much of its capacity to employ conservation in territorial organization,

---

[69] On the immigration of Paraguayans into Mato Grosso, which would influence Vargas's decision to create the Territory of Ponta Porã, see Robert Wilcox, "Paraguayans and the Making of the Brazilian Far West, 1870–1935," *The Americas* 49, no. 4 (April 1993): 479–512.

only regaining such capacity in the 1970s.[70] The exception of the Estado Novo period, when conservationists within the government used the creation of the Territory of Iguaçu to expand the Brazilian park, did not offer a long-term solution for the creation of parks elsewhere in the country. Brazil's shortcomings would be revealed as threefold. First, its central government did not own the country's public land. Second, it lacked the legal infrastructure and funds to expropriate land expeditiously. Third, despite all the considerable investment the Ministry of Agriculture funneled into Iguaçu for border development, the country never came close to create a robust national park agency in the vein of the Argentine DPN. The national parks section of the Brazilian Forest Service was underfunded and understaffed. It was just a small desk with half a dozen employees in some corner of the Ministry of Agriculture in Rio.

As a result, the Brazilian government in the 1940s and 1950s would come up short of mustering the necessary resources to enforce land tenure in the country's new protected areas. This institutional handicap was reflected in the difficulty park administrators faced to control Iguaçu National Park's newly enlarged territory after the dissolution of the Territory of Iguaçu in 1946. The federal government continued claiming the expanded park boundaries but faced competition from the state of Paraná and private parties. This state of affairs would dominate the life of the Brazilian park in the following decades, as the implementation of Iguaçu National Park, with all the investment in infrastructure it entailed, initially fell short in shaping the borderland as park proponents desired.

---

[70] An example of Brazil's regained capacity to use conservation policy to reshape frontier areas is the series of national parks the country established in Amazon in the 1970s and 1980s. Ronald A. Foresta, *Amazon Conservation in the Age of Development: The Limits of Providence* (Gainesville: University of Florida Press, 1991); Frederico Freitas, "Conservation Frontier: The Creation of Protected Areas in the Brazilian Amazonia," in *Frontiers of Development in the Amazon: Riches, Risks, and Resistances*, ed. Antonio Ioris et al. (Lanham, MD: Lexington Books, 2020), 51–79.

3

A Park and a Town

Argentina, 1945–1979

Two years into the Argentine Dirty War, the violence of the military regime came to Iguazú National Park when unidentified security agents stormed the guesthouse and campgrounds operated by Juan Hoppe, located inside the Argentine park, on the night of February 21, 1978. The plainclothes operatives dragged Hoppe and his guests out of their rooms and tents, beat them, and, after an entire night of psychological torture, threw them blindfolded and handcuffed into an unmarked truck. From there the agents took Hoppe and his guests to an undisclosed location near Posadas, where the detainees were continually tortured for several days. At the moment of his liberation, Hoppe was left blindfolded and alone in an open field in the town of Candelaria, 300 kilometers away from the park, and told to wait fifteen minutes before removing his blindfold. When he arrived home the next day, the fifty-seven-year-old settler looked like a different person: bearded, emaciated, and broken. The torture session Hoppe endured while in captivity left him partially paralyzed and with a hernia. According to his daughter Guillermina, he was never the same again.[1]

Hoppe continued living in Iguazú with his family after his release until national park authorities finally evicted them in September of the following year. They bluntly informed Hoppe of his two choices: to stay

---

[1] Juan Hoppe to Administración de Parques Nacionales, Expediente 0796, year 1987, APN; Corral Family to Comisión Nacional sobre Desaparición de Personas, May 28, 1984, accessed April 2, 2015, manueljaviercorral.blogspot.com.ar; "Manuel Javier Corral Detenido-Desaparecido, Datos, Cronología," May 28, 1984, accessed on April 2, 2015, manueljaviercorral.blogspot.com.ar; Guillermina Hoppe, "Ahora en que puedo sacar afuera tanto dolor, empiezo a sentir un poco de paz," in *Misiones: Historias con nombres propios*, ed. Amelia Báez (Posadas: Ministerio de Derechos Humanos de Misiones, 2011), 399–401.

in the border area and be killed by security forces or to leave the country and survive. Fearing for his family's life, Hoppe moved to Paraguay soon after, returning to Argentina only in 1983, after the end of the dictatorship.[2] Hoppe was a Polish national who had moved into the park in 1953. He had been invited by former park director Balbino Brañas to live in a lot formerly occupied by another settler, Juan Herrera, who had lived in the park area between 1944 and 1953. Over the course of his twenty-five years inside Iguazú National Park, Hoppe built a life there, working for the park administration performing a series of odd jobs such as maintaining an airstrip that existed inside the park and repairing the pathways leading to the waterfalls. He also raised eleven children in the park, many of whom helped him in the guesthouse he had opened to cater to campers and backpackers visiting the falls. Yet, the roots he had established in the park did not help to prevent his removal. All seems to indicate the imprisonment of Hoppe and his guests was "collateral damage" resulting from the presence of a *montonero* militant, Manuel Javier Corral, in Hoppe's guesthouse.[3] Nevertheless, park authorities took the opportunity to scare Hoppe and drive him out of Iguazú.

The ordeals of Juan Hoppe were unique, for he was the only settler living in Iguazú National Park to be arrested and tortured during the last military dictatorship in Argentina (1976–83). However, Hoppe's case was also part of a decade-long process of removal of dwellers living inside the park. He was the last settler pushed out of the park in 1979, and his history epitomizes the changes in national park policy occurring in Argentina between the 1950s and the 1970s. Hoppe arrived in Iguazú in the early 1950s, at a time when entrepreneurial settlers were welcomed by park authorities. He lived for many years undisturbed, working for the park as a contractor in informal arrangements that benefited both parties. As park administrators redefined Iguazú as a space devoid of dwellers in the late 1960s, they started pressuring Hoppe to leave the park. His arrest in the late 1970s and subsequent flight to Paraguay marked the beginning of the modern era of Iguazú National Park in Argentina.

Hoppe, like many others, found himself living inside Iguazú National Park because the protected area, like other parks in Argentina, was first

---

[2] Guillermina Hoppe (daughter of Juan Hoppe) in discussion with the author, August 2014.
[3] Mariana Corral, "Espero, Mariana, que tu generación sepa levantar nuestras banderas …," in *Misiones: Historias con nombres propios*, ed. Amelia Báez, 403–7; Sebastián Hacher Rivera, *Cómo enterrar a un padre desaparecido* (Buenos Aires: Editorial Marea, 2012), 113–18.

devised to attract settlers to the country's borderlands. Border colonization was a crucial feature of Argentine park policy well into the 1960s. However, it was not the only one; Conservation was another declared mission of the Argentine national park system from its inception, and it gained greater importance after Exequiel Bustillo stepped down from his position as the director of the Argentine national park agency in 1944.[4] Slowly the agency moved away from the "eclecticism" that characterized the Bustillo years to a more orthodox stance on protection and management of nature. In the following years, the agency adopted stricter conservation criteria and started zoning parks according to scientific and environmental parameters. Eventually, the contradictions between conservation, tourism, and border colonization became untenable, and park officials abandoned the last in favor of a national park model centered on preserving natural landscapes and providing visitation infrastructure.

This change was the result of three interrelated processes. First, civil servants trained in life and agricultural sciences started to replace the businessmen and politicians who initially occupied the ranks of the Argentine national park agency in the 1930s and 1940s. Second, the rise of these experts strengthened the connections between the national park agency in Argentina and international nongovernmental organizations (NGOs) such as the International Union for Conservation of Nature (IUCN) and intergovernmental bodies such as the Food and Agriculture Organization of the United Nations (FAO) and the United Nations Educational, Scientific and Cultural Organization (UNESCO).

---

[4] After Bustillo's resignation in 1944, the Argentine national park agency changed its name and institutional umbrella several times. These changes reflect the absence of a coherent view of national park policy among Argentina's highest echelons. They are also a testimony to the many institutional ruptures the country experienced in the twentieth century. Under this rough surface, a steady current powered by the solid legal framework established in 1934 and institutional inertia allowed the Argentine national park agency to maintain its coherence and high profile throughout the years. In this and the following chapters, I will refer to the former DPN simply as the "Argentine national park agency." For a detailed account of the changes in the name and institutional affiliation of the Argentine national park agency in Argentina, see *Documentos de la Biblioteca Perito Francisco Moreno* 1 (2013): 5–6, http://issuu.com/bibliotecaperitomoreno/docs/documentos_de_la_bibliote ca_n__1. See also Jack W. Hopkins, *Policymaking for Conservation in Latin America: National Parks, Reserves, and the Environment* (Westport, CT: Praeger, 1995), 10–12, 129–30, 181–18; Argentina, Decree 9504, April 28, 1945; Argentina, Decree 12054, April 30, 1946; Argentina, Decree-Law 6325, April 11, 1956; Enrique M. Sívori to Presidencia de La Nación, Carpeta "Plan de Gobierno," Iniciativa 2196, "Considere conveniencia de mantener los parques nacionales bajo la dependencia del M° de Agr y Ganad," April 1953, in Fondo Secretaría Técnica, 1ᵃ y 2ᵃ Presidencia del Teniente General Juan Domingo Perón (1946–1966), Legajo 395, AGN.

Third, in the period between the 1940s and the 1970s, the international paradigm for national parks changed from the conservation of natural monuments to the preservation of species and the environment, which helped sideline the older Argentine model of national parks as border development tools.

As crucial as these processes were in shaping a new Argentine national park policy, they did not happen overnight. In fact, they were accompanied by the parallel implementation of the policy of border development initiated in the 1930s. In the 1950s and 1960s, at a time when life and agricultural science experts at the national park agency increasingly pushed for a new focus on the conservation of fauna and flora species, the agency also continued to foster settlement and development in designated areas within national parks. The continuation of such a policy well into the 1960s had as much to do with institutional and legal inertia as with the need to justify national park policy to other branches of the Argentine government less receptive to conservation.

The history of Iguazú National Park is a story of change – from the idiosyncrasies of 1940s Argentine conservationism to the standardization of 1970s environmentalism. It shows how processes connecting the local to the international produced the space of a national park. This phenomenon reproduced changes happening elsewhere as national parks, and other types of environmental policies became more standardized.[5] In the end, the 1970s park would be unrecognizable to the users, residents, and workers who had helped create the space of the park thirty years earlier. Ultimately, a new international regime of protected areas supplanted the old Argentine idea of national parks as border colonization tools. After a few decades, Argentine environmental policy veered away from the support of government-sponsored settlement in national parks, transforming the paradigm of protected areas, with direct consequences for the people settled inside Iguazú.

NATIONAL PARKS UNDER PERONISM

Exequiel Bustillo remained the head of the Argentine national park agency between its creation in 1934 and his resignation in May 1944. He was succeeded as president of the agency by a series of military officers whose

---

[5] Here, I thank Rodrigo Pizarro for the insight of seeing national parks as a type of universalist policy that is adopted by developing countries as a token of modernity. Pizarro, "The Global Diffusion of Conservation Policy."

tenure coincided with the years of Juan Domingo Perón in power.[6] During his first presidential term (1946–52), Perón launched a campaign to promote mass tourism that aimed, among other things, to bring the Argentine working class to the country's parks. This focus on popular tourism had originated prior to Perón's election in 1946 when, after the military coup of 1943, the new regime devised plans to put the national park agency in charge of Argentina's entire tourism industry. The shift toward the popularization of national parks and the expansion of the agency's scope added to recent financial cuts that greatly displeased Bustillo, contributing to his decision to resign in 1944.[7]

With Bustillo's resignation, new national park legislation was introduced in 1945 and 1946 that incorporated the role of fomenting tourism both within and outside protected areas into the attributions of the national park agency.[8] The new legislation contained provisions aimed at developing a mass tourism industry, with the agency supporting "trips, cruises, and excursions" for the working class as well as sponsoring affordable tourism options for workers in association with private and public companies and unions.[9] The Argentine state aimed to expand its role in tourism by the way of introducing the urban working classes to a world of annual vacations in scenic landscapes that before Perón had been accessible only to the moneyed urban elite.[10]

---

[6] They were the retired army colonels Napoleón Irusta (1945–51) and Agustin Ramirez (1951–52) as well as Commodore Heraldo G. Borgonovo (1952–53).

[7] Exequiel Bustillo to Diego I. Mason, Minister of Agriculture, May 17, 1944, and Diego I. Mason to Exequiel Bustillo, June 16, 1944, both in Fondo Exequiel Bustillo, Legajo 1, no. 3343, AGN; Bessera, "Políticas de estado," 80–81, APN-B; Melina Piglia, "En torno a los parques nacionales: Primeras experiencias de una política turística nacional centralizada en la Argentina (1934–1950)," *Pasos: Revista de Turismo y Patrimonio Cultural* 10, no. 1 (2012): 61–73; Ximena A. Carreras Doallo, "Parques nacionales y peronismo: La patria mediante la naturaleza," in *Historia, política y gestión ambiental: Perspectivas y debates*, ed. Alejandra Salomón and Adrian Zarrilli (Buenos Aires: Imago Mundi, 2012); Argentina, Decree 9504, "Disponiendo que Parques Nacionales funcionará como Administración General de Parques Nacionales y Turismo, con carácter autárquico," April 28, 1945.

[8] Argentina, Decree 9504, April 28, 1945; Argentina, Decree 12054, "Atribuciones y deberes de la Administración General de Parques Nacionales y Turismo," Art. 14, April 30, 1946; Inspección General to Dirección de Parques Nacionales, Expediente 3171, year 1945, 2, APN.

[9] Ministerio de Obras Públicas, "Proyecto de decreto reglamentario de la Administración General de Parques Nacionales y Turismo," in División Inspección to Dirección de Parques Nacionales y Turismo, Expediente 0279, year 1945, 4, APN; Ministerio de Obras Públicas, "Aprobando el ordenamiento de la ley 12.103 y los Decretos-Leyes 9.504-45 y 2.524-46, que se denominará 'Ley 12.103 T.O.,'" Expediente 3215, year 1946, APN.

[10] Eduardo Elena, *Dignifying Argentina: Peronism, Citizenship, and Mass Consumption* (Pittsburgh: University of Pittsburgh Press, 2011), 122–23, 132–34.

The new emphasis on popular tourism was epitomized by the second Peronist five-year plan of 1952, which declared it a duty of the Argentine state to "give the people, whatever their social condition, access to the benefits of tourism, which would provide for their needed mental and physical rest, their direct knowledge of the country's natural monuments and economic realities, and the enrichment of their cultural background." The phrase "Conocer la patria es un deber" (Knowing the fatherland is one's duty) became the official motto of the Argentine national park agency at this time.[11] The promotion of this civic duty also benefited from the broader economic and social reforms introduced by the Peronist government, which included price controls in the tourism industry (e.g., the freezing of both government fees such as national park entrances and private prices such as hotel rates).[12] Furthermore, the new labor legislation expanded access to paid vacations, and the extra free time, coupled with new resources to travel, made vacation trips a social reality for Argentine workers. Unions such as the Confederación General del Trabajo (General Confederation of Labor, CGT), which formed the backbone of the new regime, established a network of popular beach and mountain resorts, which, along with the national parks, helped create new vacation locales touted as "paradises of the humble."[13]

However, this expansion of social tourism overburdened the Argentine national park agency with a task that had little to do with its original missions (i.e., the conservation of natural features and the occupation of the country's borderlands). When national park officials protested, the government agreed in 1951 to separate tourism from national park management. The Argentine government upgraded the agency's tourism section to a ministerial office under Transportation and transferred the rest of the national park agency back to Agriculture (the two had been together under Public Works between 1945 and 1951). The six-year period during which the national park agency under Perón was in charge of all the

---

[11] Administración de Parques Nacionales y Turismo, "Memoria correspondiente al año 1948" (1949), 14, 23, "Memoria correspondiente al año 1947" (1948), 9–15, APN-B.

[12] Argentina, Presidencia de la Nación, "2° plan quinquenal: Objetivos del plan de turismo" (Buenos Aires: Consejo Nacional de Planificación, 1952), Fondo Secretaría Técnica, 1ª y 2ª Presidencia del Teniente General Juan Domingo Perón (1946–1955), Legajo 395, AGN.

[13] Scarzanella, "Las bellezas naturales," 5–21; Elisa Pastoriza, "El turismo social en la Argentina durante el primer peronismo: Mar del Plata, la conquista de las vacaciones y los nuevos rituales obreros, 1943–1955," *Nuevo mundo mundos nuevos* (2008), http://nuevomundo.revues.org/36472?lang=pt; Pizarro, "The Global Diffusion of Conservation Policy," 261–71.

country's tourism industry marked a critical move away from the excessive focus on Nahuel Huapi, which had been the agency's previous trademark during Bustillo years. It was in this new period that more significant resources were channeled into the urbanization of Puerto Aguirre and toward the implementation of civil infrastructure for the settlers inside Iguazú National Park.[14]

BUILDING A NATIONAL PARK TOWN

The plan to transform the humble hamlet of Puerto Aguirre into a thriving frontier town was part of the national park agency's program from the time the park was gazetted in 1934. Even so, apart from a couple of infrastructure projects initiated before 1944, much of the investment in Iguazú was hindered by Bustillo's engagement in Patagonia. With Bustillo out of office, Puerto Aguirre, which had been renamed Puerto Iguazú in 1943, became the site of several new infrastructure projects.[15]

To the national park planners in Buenos Aires, colonizing this subtropical border area presented three main issues demanding immediate intervention. First, the zone suffered from recurrent outbreaks of malaria, and the national park agency needed to eradicate the disease to attract settlers and visitors. On top of that, the Argentine national park was heavily dependent on foodstuffs imported from Brazil, and park authorities believed that creating farms on the Argentine side of the border was the best way to address this problem. Finally, construction projects required building materials, which were abundant in the region but required processing. Relying exclusively on the bountiful timber found in local forests in constructing houses and public buildings was out of the question, as the policy of border settlement was limited by the park's conservation mission. But the solution they found, using a combination of dead wood timber and clay-based brick masonry, presented challenges of its own to the conservationist mission of the park.

The Perón government invested heavily in sanitation in the border area. In 1945, the Argentine national park agency started building a hospital in Iguazú and sent a physician to deal with the malaria problem in the region. The disease posed a significant complication for development of the border

---

[14] Decree-Law 6325, April 11, 1956.
[15] The town, which originally was called Puerto Aguirre, was renamed Puerto Iguazú in 1943, but between 1951 and 1955 its name was changed to Puerto Eva Perón. After 1955, it went back to being named Puerto Iguazú.

zone, and building a hospital in Puerto Iguazú inside the national park would serve to treat not only tourists and park personnel but also the entire population of northern Misiones. In 1946, reports by the national park agency declared the malaria outbreak to have been successfully contained at the Argentine side of the border thanks to the actions of park adminis- trators and army doctors with help from Paraguayan and Brazilian phys- icians. It was an overstatement, to be sure, as malaria is a tricky disease and it ended up taking a few more years of DDT spraying in areas of *Anopheles* incidence to reach a point where not a single new case was registered. Still, the campaign shows that the national park administration acted as the de facto government of the border area, coordinating a response to the out- break, providing doctors with transportation to distant areas, and estab- lishing a temporary clinic to tend to the local population. The new hospital would prevent Argentine nationals living at the border from procuring medical treatment in Foz do Iguaçu, dispelling the concerns of many in the Argentine federal government about excessive dependence on neigh- boring countries. The hospital was finished on October 1, 1946, and occupied a two-story building with thirty beds, an operating room, a laboratory, and a pharmacy (see Figure 3.1).[16]

Another problem posed to the national park agency in Iguazú was providing foodstuffs to a booming population of over 400 people. More than a decade had passed since the creation of the park in 1934, but people in Puerto Iguazú still depended on Posadas (300 kilometers downriver) and Foz do Iguaçu (Brazil) for most of their supplies. To address this issue, the national park agency proposed in 1945 the implementation of farms inside the national park area, both within and outside the 5,000-hectare perimeter designated for the development of Puerto Iguazú. The initial step was creating a national park-run farm to supply settlers, park employees, and visitors with vegetables, eggs, and dairy. Park authorities sought to ease the burden of the high cost of living at the border to make it more attractive to prospective settlers. They were also concerned, at least nominally, with improving nutrition among park dwellers, as a poor diet was viewed as one of the causes of the high mortality rate in the region. In keeping with Peronist social welfare, the national park agency sold the produce at cost to settlers. The farm, founded on an eight-hectare forested

---

[16] Administración de Parques Nacionales y Turismo, "Memoria correspondiente al año 1945" (1946), 5–9, "Memoria correspondiente al año 1946" (1947), 13, 101, "Memoria correspondiente al año 1947" (1948), 75, "Memoria correspondiente al año 1948" (1949), 21–22, APN-B.

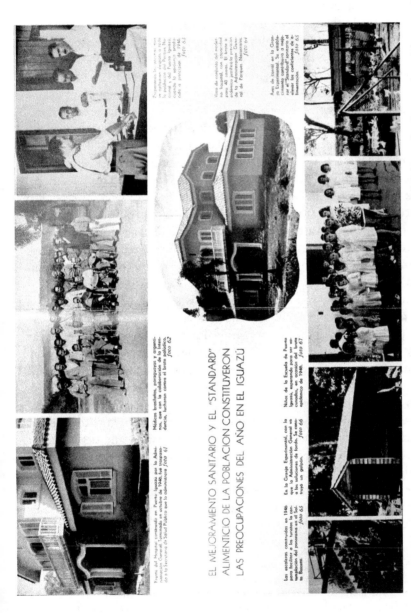

FIGURE 3.1 Iguazú National Park Hospital, 1947. "The improvement of sanitary and food standards constituted last year's main concerns in Iguazú." Source: Administración de Parques Nacionales y Turismo, "Memoria correspondiente al año 1946" (1947). Biblioteca Francisco P. Moreno, Administración de Parques Nacionales

EL MEJORAMIENTO SANITARIO Y EL "STANDARD" ALIMENTICIO DE LA POBLACION CONSTITUYERON LAS PREOCUPACIONES DEL AÑO EN EL IGUAZÚ

stretch near Puerto Iguazú, was a failure, but the preoccupation with procuring local food sources continued to guide park administrators, and it was one of the reasons for accepting prospective farmers such as Juan Hoppe in the park. By undertaking the task of providing the local population with access to health care and affordable produce, the administration of Iguazú National Park carried out the mandate of the Argentine welfare state at the border region.[17]

The national park was also responsible for implementing the physical structure that supported the presence of the Argentine state at the borderland. It included the building of houses for park personnel, administrative buildings, a water treatment plant, a power plant, a hospital, a post office, and two schools. All this activity substantially increased the demand for construction materials, which was met in part by a brickyard established by the national park administration in Puerto Iguazú. Soon the need for bricks necessitated the commission of new private brickyards, which would be located outside the 5,000-hectare area designated by law for development inside the protected area of the park. The construction boom required bricks, and park technicians had to come to terms with the fact that they could find locations with good clay only outside the zone initially slated for development.[18]

Another essential construction material was timber, demand for which put extra pressure on the forest and created animosity between settlers and park officials. Initially, the national park agency intended to allow only the use of dead wood gathered from the town area for construction. Demand for timber eventually grew to the point where the national park sawmill could no longer avoid resorting to traditional logging. Settlers who had acquired property in Puerto Iguazú also pressured the national park administration for permission to clear their lots and use the timber, which generated another clash between conservation and development goals. In the national park authorities' 1950 annual report, even as they cited environmental reasons to justify the ban on timber extraction (farms were exempt, as proprietors were allowed to clear land for cultivation), they also recognized that prohibiting settlers from logging in their new lots could undermine settlement goals.

[17] Administración de Parques Nacionales y Turismo, "Memoria correspondiente al año 1945" (1946), 5–9, "Memoria correspondiente al año 1946" (1947), 13, 16, 103–4, "Memoria correspondiente al año 1948" (1948), 21–22, APN-B.
[18] José Gorgues (retired Iguazú National Park employee), in discussion with the author, August 2014; Administración de Parques Nacionales y Turismo, "Memoria correspondiente al año 1945" (1946), 5–9, "Memoria correspondiente al año 1949" (1950), 113, 118–19, APN-B.

However significant, the demand for timber to be used in construction paled in comparison to the demand for firewood, especially for brick-yards. In 1949, for example, firewood comprised about 96 percent of the 4,121 m³ of timber legally extracted from the park. Brick production put considerable pressure on the forest, and the option for masonry was not as friendly to conservation as some national park employees might have initially thought. Still, colonization of border areas was one of the core missions of the Argentine national park system, and a total ban on logging would have jeopardized the development of Puerto Iguazú. To mitigate the impact of timber extraction, Iguazú National Park engaged in modest reforestation efforts in areas that had previously been cleared, planting both alien species (pine) and native species such as angico (*Parapiptadenia rigida*) and some types of Argentine cedar (*Cedrela fissilis* and *Cabralea oblongifoliola*). Most introduced pine trees, however, failed to survive, as ants attacked them.[19]

MODEL CITIZENS AT THE ARGENTINE FRONTIER

Much of the national park authorities' impulse to control the use of land and natural resources within park territory was also reflected in their relationship with settlers and workers. Park directors sought to control minute details of settlers' lives and customs, and the national park assumed the role of the Argentine state in transforming the border population into model Argentine citizens: An essential tool was educa-tion. Continuing with a policy of universal schooling inaugurated in Argentina in the 1870s by Domingo Faustino Sarmiento, the national park agency established a primary school in the 1930s in Puerto Iguazú and added a second one in the late 1940s near the falls. The schools provided children with not only education but also meals, clothes, shoes, and books. Besides requiring that all children attend school, park authorities also pressured settlers in Puerto Iguazú to formalize cohabitation through civil marriage – a civil registry office was estab-lished by the national park agency in 1945.[20]

Settlers interested in moving to Puerto Iguazú had to apply and be approved by the national park agency before purchasing a lot. Initially, the requirements for new applicants were strict; and of the seventy-two

---

[19] Ibid.
[20] Administración de Parques Nacionales y Turismo, "Memoria correspondiente al año 1946" (1947), 14–15, "Memoria correspondiente al año 1948" (1949), 23, APN-B.

requests filed in 1947, fifty-three were rejected. The agency intended to occupy the border with a population of entrepreneurial Argentine-born settlers, but many applicants failed to meet such criteria, whether they were foreigners, or poor, or did not constitute a legally sanctioned nuclear family. Nevertheless, these were the types of people attracted to Puerto Iguazú and the job opportunities it offered in tourism and construction, and their lack of legal access to land did not deter them from occupying the many unsupervised stretches of woodland still available around the town. Concerned with the growing problem of "undesired settlers and squatters," the agency initially threatened to resort to "judicial action and the use of force" to evict them, but ultimately the chronic labor shortage went a long way toward convincing park authorities to find a place in Puerto Iguazú for these unqualified migrants.[21]

By 1950, construction work had attracted hundreds of transient laborers, who settled with their families in shacks on empty lots on the outskirts of the town. The lack of oversight of the settlement process was a serious problem for an institution whose goal was to promote control of park landscape, and in 1950, the park opened a new area for settlement in the western section of Puerto Iguazú, in tract 43, to solve the squatting problem (see Map 3.1). The new lots encompassed a forested area previously designated as a woodland reserve for the town. Park administrators viewed the appearance of makeshift dwellings on squatted land as a "problem of transient workers," who did not fit the national park model for border settlers. Permanently resettling these workers in an area managed by the park would give administrators a greater amount of control over their life and labor. Park director Romeo Esteban Cafferata consciously equated settlement with labor control by stating that "this habit of periodic migrations, acquired in past years by the working population of the Territory of Misiones, has grave consequences and serious inconveniences in times of greater demand for labor, as it

---

[21] Similar to in Brazil, one of the biggest challenges faced by national park administrators in Argentina was finding skilled labor in the region. First, the workers had to be taught how to use wheelbarrows, shovels, helmets, and explosives. Accidents were frequent, and on two occasions, workers had to be treated by the Brazilian doctor from Foz do Iguaçu. José Gorgues (retired Iguazú National Park employee), in discussion with the author, August 2014; Ivan Romaro to Dirección de Parques Nacionales, "E/Informe de obras ejecutadas en el Parque Nacional de Iguazú en el mes de noviembre y diciembre de 1938," Expediente 0712, year 1939, APN; Administración de Parques Nacionales y Turismo, "Memoria correspondiente al año 1945" (1946), 43, 54–55, "Memoria correspondiente al año 1946" (1947), 109, "Memoria correspondiente al año 1947" (1948), 71, APN-B.

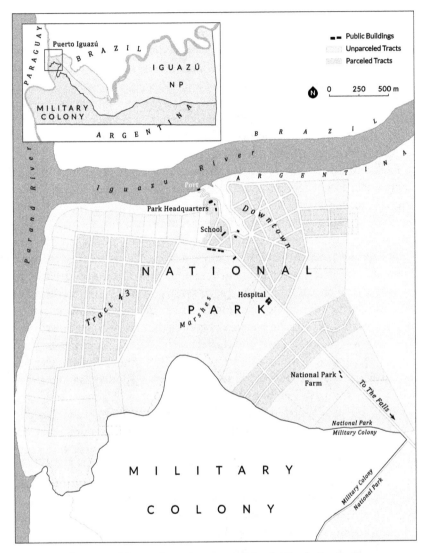

MAP 3.1 Planning of Puerto Iguazú, c. 1950. Map by Frederico Freitas

makes labor scarce when needed."[22] The new lots opened for settlement in tract 43 would be cheaper than the normal lots in Puerto Iguazú.

[22] Intendencia Iguazú to Administración General de Parques Nacionales, "Sol/la subdivisión de la chacra n° 43 Pto. Iguazú p/ formar lote de t ...," Expediente 8386, year 1950, 1–2, APN.

Cafferatta reasoned that the usual price of lots in Puerto Iguazú had made it impossible for impoverished transient workers to buy land. Subsidized lots sold under less restrictive conditions would confirm both a Peronist narrative of labor control through welfare and the original design of parks as tools for border development. After all, Cafferatta reasoned, one of the reasons for developing the town was to settle Argentine nationals on a "border zone with a high number of foreigners."[23] Hence, it was crucial to create the proper conditions for the settlement of the transient Argentine workers attracted by job opportunities in the park.

Park authorities also presented the parceling of tract 43 into lots for impoverished workers as a way to offer "comfortable and hygienic houses" to new arrivals.[24] Indeed, the administration of Iguazú commonly called out aesthetic and sanitary violations to control who occupied the land. Eviction, for example, was usually justified by the existence of inappropriate constructions at improper places. Such was the case with Angel Buiatti, who operated a boarding house and restaurant catering to construction workers for Puerto Iguazú's new power plant. After the plant was finished in 1949, park director Cafferata demanded that Buiatti be evicted and his facilities demolished, blaming the establishment's proximity to the new plant building and the technicians' quarters as justification for the decision. According to Cafferata, the restaurant's "characteristics and utilization" – it catered to menial laborers – spoiled the "aesthetic setting" of the new buildings.[25] Another example of someone evicted because of unauthorized construction was Anselmo Fruet Candia, whose new annex, built for a small dry goods and liquor store, drew the attention of park authorities. In 1956, the park demanded that Fruet Candia raze the annex, constructed on an occupied piece of land along the main avenue of Puerto Iguazú. The location was good for Fruet Candia's clientele but bad for visitors, the national park agency claimed, because officials considered the shack an eyesore for tourism. The park administration eventually evicted Fruet Candia after forcing him to tear down the facility.[26]

---

[23] Ibid.   [24] Ibid.

[25] Intendencia Iguazú to Administración General de Parques Nacionales, Expediente 9499, year 1949, APN; Procuración del Tesoro de la Nación to Dirección de Parques Nacionales, Expediente 4057, year 1957, APN.

[26] Parques Nacionales Direc. to Ministerio de Agricultura y Ganadería, "Se inicien acciones judiciales para desalojar a Anselmo Fruet Candia de las tierras fiscales que ocupa en el pueblo Puerto Iguazú y cobro de $ 1,200," Expediente 4065, year 1956, APN.

Decisions based on aesthetic and sanitary claims depended on who was affected by the perceived environmental nuisances. Whereas park visitors should be spared from visually unappealing buildings on their way to the falls, impoverished workers who had settled on the outskirts of Puerto Iguazú would have to cope with pollution from newly established businesses. This was precisely what happened when Balbino Brañas, who had returned to his post as Iguazú National Park director in 1951, suggested setting aside a portion of tract 43 for the establishment of new industries. The new location, isolated from the main thoroughfare in Puerto Iguazú, would spare park officials and tourists from the noise and pollution caused by industrial activities and the coming and going of trucks. It would also put jobs closer to labor. Conveniently, Brañas overlooked the possibility that industrial activities could become a nuisance for the very workers the park initially planned to settle in tract 43.[27]

The late 1960s saw the emergence of voices within the national park agency and the local government criticizing the urban development of Puerto Iguazú.[28] Between 1944 and 1970 the national park registered 494 transactions of sale, purchase, or donation of lots in Puerto Iguazú.[29] All of this activity, however, failed to produce the model border town planned

[27] Balbino Brañas to Departamento de Parques y Reservas, August 9, 1951, in Intendencia Iguazú to Administración General de Parques Nacionales, "Sol/la subdivisión de la chacra n° 43 Pto. Iguazú p/ formar lote de t ...," Expediente 8386, year 1950, APN.

[28] Although I agree with Berjman and Gutiérrez that, in practice, the national park agency in Puerto Aguirre acted to give order to a somewhat autonomous process of occupation promoted by individuals, I understand that classic colonization was always the ultimate goal of national park administrators, despite their failures in promoting it. See Berjman and Gutiérrez, *Patrimonio cultural y patrimonio natural*, 87–91; and Piglia, "En torno a los parques nacionales," 61–73.

[29] "Fichas Lotes: Iguazú-Puerto Iguazú," Programa Pobladores y Comunidades, APN-P. At the office for settlers and communities (Programa Pobladores y Comunidades) at APN, Laura Starópoli produced an extensive survey of the documents related to settlers in Argentine national parks in the APN archives. These parks were Nahuel Huapi, Lanín, Laguna Blanca, Los Glaciares, Tierra del Fuego, El Rey, and Iguazú. See Laura Liliana Starópoli, "Los documentos históricos de los pobladores y comunidades vinculados a los parques nacionales en el archivo de la APN, PPC cartilla de Difusión" (2011), and "Proyecto de sistematización de la documentación histórica relacionada a pobladores y comunidades vinculadas a los parques nacionales" (2009), APN-P. See also Laura Méndez, *Estado, frontera y turismo: Historia de San Carlos de Bariloche* (Buenos Aires: Prometeo, 2010). In the case of Iguazú, the majority of the "expedientes" (case files) of individual settlers in Puerto Iguazú were transferred to the government of Misiones in 1970, when the town passed into provincial control. See Administración Nacional de Parques Nacionales, "33—Elev. proyecto de mensaje y ley modificación actuales de límites del P. N. Iguazú transfiriendo a la Pcia. de Misiones aproximadamente 5,000 hectáreas," Expediente 150, year 1969, APN.

by the national park agency. In fact, by the late 1960s, the development of Puerto Iguazú had become a burden for the national park, which seemed unable to catch up with the growth of the town as plots of land were continuously squatted on by newcomers. Jorge R. Barroso, head of the agency's architecture office, revealed his disappointment in an assessment of thirty-five years of national park control of Puerto Iguazú. He argued that, given the environmental regulations in place, the town should have developed into a community "suitable for a national park." Instead, he contended, it had produced a community aesthetically worse than its counterparts in the province of Misiones. According to him, the town had a *"Villa Tacuara* [shanty town], insufficient drinking water and electricity provision, and a limited development dynamic."[30]

Another critic was Pedro Segovia, Puerto Iguazú's mayor, who in 1968 denounced the erection of "makeshift dwellings lacking minimal conditions of health, hygiene, and urbanism" in new occupied areas. The government of Misiones, in turn, demanded the construction of a grid of streets in the neighborhoods "occupied by squatters" and urged park administrators to allow the town government to implement the necessary infrastructure independently. It argued that such precarious neighborhoods had a deleterious effect on tourism and posed a threat to public safety and health. This growing criticism of local and provincial governments toward Iguazú National Park also stemmed from changes in the political geography of the region. The Argentine federal government granted the territory of Misiones provincial status in 1953, and in 1961, the new province elevated the town of Puerto Iguazú, still part of park territory, to the level of a municipality. The establishment of municipal and provincial powers in what had been until then exclusively a federal domain led to increased scrutiny of the national park agency's ability to manage the town.[31]

Officials within the national park agency and from the municipality and province directed their criticism at Iguazú National Park's failure in promoting development of the border zone. Critics cited the agency's inability to foment self-sufficient agricultural production to supply the town and the tourism industry. They also blamed the agency for failing to foster the urbanization of the booming town. Yet though people such

[30] Jorge R. Barroso to Italo Costantino, "Comisión Parque Nacional del Iguazú del 16/8 al 22/8/1970," Expediente 2755, year 1970, APN.
[31] Hugo Jorge Montiel to Alberto E. Mendonça Paz, July 31, 1968, in Expediente 4154, year 1968, APN.

as Segovia and Barroso believed the agency had fallen short in its duty to develop Puerto Iguazú, absent from their critiques was any challenge to the national park border colonization program. Since the Bustillo years, many national park officials had shared strict preservationist views that rejected most types of development in favor of protecting fauna and flora species, but a rejection of using the national parks as development tools was far from consensual in the 1940s and 1950s. This changed in the 1960s.

A GENERATIONAL CHANGE IN THE 1950S

In the period between the early 1940s and the mid-1960s, the consensus that national park policy should advance settlement in border areas steadily eroded in Argentina. This process was caused in large part by a generational change within the national park agency. Officials trained in agricultural or life sciences had been part of the national park agency since the establishment of a national park committee in 1931, and they were more likely to defend the use of conservationist criteria for establishing protected areas. The upper echelons of the national park agency, however, were initially occupied by businessmen, politicians, and military officers who, despite their differences, agreed that geopolitical concerns should take precedence over preservation. Over the years, this earlier contingent slowly retired and was replaced by technically trained officials with connections to international scientific and intergovernmental bodies, where much of the discussion on the nature of national parks was taking place. The Argentine officials now in charge of the national park agency not only drew from these international debates on conservation but also participated in them, helping to define the new international standards of national parks of the 1970s.

The 1940s started auspiciously for the Argentine proponents of "inviolable sanctuaries," as protected areas were characterized by environmentalist Georges Dennler de la Tour. In May 1941, thanks to the lobbying of the likes of Dennler de la Tour, Argentina signed the Convention on Nature Protection and Wildlife Preservation in the Western Hemisphere and, in May 1946, ratified it. For its part, Brazil signed the convention even before Argentina, in 1940, but only ratified it in June 1965. The ratification by Argentina just five years after the signature of the convention reflected the increasing role of technically trained officials in shaping the country's conservation policy. The convention put great emphasis on species conservation by committing signatories to "protect[ing] and preserv[ing] in their natural habitat representatives of all species and genera of [the signatories'] native flora and fauna, including migratory birds, in sufficient numbers and over areas extensive enough to assure them from becoming extinct through any agency within man's control." In Argentina, this marked the beginning of a shift in the rationale of protected areas, as the defining criterion began moving from the conservation of scenic landscapes to the preservation of species habitats.[32]

Following the new convention, future Iguazú National Park director Romeo E. Cafferata proposed a new paradigm for the country's national parks in a lecture to the Argentine Scientific Society in October 1946, just a few months after its ratification. Cafferata was an agricultural engineer hired by the national park agency in 1945 and two years later was appointed director of Iguazú National Park, where he stayed until 1950.[33] In his 1946 talk, Cafferata made a case for the creation of national parks to protect specific forest formations, like the groves of Paraná pine (*Araucaria angustifolia*) in the territory of Misiones. He insisted the government establish national parks in other areas of Argentina, especially in the forested subtropical north, a region that, except for Iguazú, had been neglected by the national park agency. To be sure, Caferatta's valorization of forests did not have a place for transcendental values, for to him their worthiness stemmed from utilitarian and scientific reasons. Yet his insistence on protecting subtropical forests was a departure from the obsession with natural monuments and border zones that marked 1930s park policy. He argued that the national park system ought to include all of Argentina's "indigenous

---

[32] The idea of protecting natural monuments was also cited as a reason to establish protected areas, as it continued to appear in the body of several late documents and laws, but the convention gave much more prominence to species conservation. Milan Jorge Dimitri, "La protección de la naturaleza en la República Argentina," *Natura: Órgano de la Administración General de Parques Nacionales* 1, no. 1 (1954): 21–41; Instituto Panamericano de Geografía e Historia, *Publicación Num. 61: Tercera Asamblea General* (Mexico, D.F.: Editorial Stylo, 1941); Organization of American States, "Convention on Nature Protection and Wildlife Preservation in the Western Hemisphere," accessed February 10, 2015, www.oas.org/juridico/english/treaties/c-8.html.

[33] Later Cafferata was also director of the Nahuel Huapi, Lanín, and Los Alerces parks, and after that he occupied many other positions in the national park agency. In 1983, he retired from the agency but continued working with environmental NGOs such as the Association of the Friends of National Parks. Argentine Senate, "Proyecto de resolución rindiendo homenaje al Ing. Romeo Cafferata por su trayectoria en Parques Nacionales," Expediente 127, year 2003, www.senado.gov.ar/web/proyectos/numexpe.php?cOrigen=S&cTipo=PR&cPostExp=03&cPreExp=127&cAction=1.

forest formations," protecting them for the "enjoyment and study of future generations."[34]

Cafferata's proposal was put forward two years after Bustillo's resignation in 1944, but the military officers who headed the national park agency until the early 1950s were not interested in prioritizing conservation over border development. The appointment of Lucas Tortorelli in 1953, during Juan Perón's second term, launched a new phase in Argentine conservation, as it was the first time the government put the agency under the leadership of a civil servant trained in life sciences. Tortorelli was a French-trained agricultural engineer who had previously headed Argentina's national forest service. His appointment as the head of the national park agency was indicative of the higher profile achieved by life and agricultural scientists within the agency.[35]

Like Cafferata, Tortorelli was greatly informed by forestry, making a case for the rational management of forest resources and the importance of native tree formations. He helped to shift the focus away from scenic landscapes, which had marked Bustillo's tenure at the agency, without veering too much toward charismatic animal species – the obsession of international conservation in the 1950s. Instead, Tortorelli focused on forests, arguing national parks had a "primordially protectionist orientation" and were necessary to preserve in situ certain forest formations. It was a shift that had slowly started before his appointment, as between 1948 and 1954 Argentina created four new national parks, all in the northern region of the Chaco, away from geological monuments. Tortorelli recognized a forest could have value beyond its scenic potential or rational exploitation, as was the case with the subtropical rainforest in Iguazú National Park, which boasted a biological phenomenon "unique in the context of Argentina," where a single hectare harbored more than "ninety different species of tree."[36]

[34] Romeo E. Cafferata, *Conservación de los bosques: Conferencia dictada en la Sociedad Científica Argentina el 15 de octubre de 1946* (Buenos Aires: Administración General de Parques Nacionales y Turismo, 1947), APN-B.

[35] Argentina, Ministerio de Agricultura, Ganadería y Pesca, "Ing. agr. Lucas A. Tortorelli" (2008), accessed May 2015, www.minagri.gob.ar/new/o-o/forestacion/biblos/homenaje/tortorelli.pdf.

[36] Lucas A. Tortorelli, "La lucha por la vida en los bosques argentinos," *Natura: Órgano de la Administración General de Parques Nacionales* 1, no. 1 (1954): 5–20; Lucas A. Tortorelli, "Lo biológico y lo económico en Parques Nacionales," *Natura: Órgano de la Administración General de Parques Nacionales* 1, no. 2 (1955): 235–55.

A map produced in 1954 by Milan Jorge Dimitri, head of the department of nature protection in the national park agency, encapsulates the changes in ideas about national parks that were taking place in Argentina in the 1950s. In it, the author plotted proposed parks on a map of Argentina apportioned according to different "phytogeographical formations." The parks would no longer serve primarily the geopolitical purpose of guaranteeing state sovereignty in border areas. Rather, they would serve as in situ living archives of biological "formations," understood as repositories of stable flora and fauna complexes. Protected areas were to serve a national function by preserving the formations unique to Argentina. New national parks would serve to preserve and present to a domestic public a collection of different "phytogeographies" that, ultimately, formed the body of the nation (see Figure 3.2).[37]

The change in the ideas about national parks reached Iguazú in 1954 when Alberto F. Anziano surveyed the park and proposed it be expanded on conservation grounds. His proposal was based on the view that the *Selva Misionera* (Misionero Jungle), the stretch of Atlantic forest encompassed by the Argentine territory of Misiones, was one of the phytogeographical units that formed a patchwork of biological areas constituting the nation, all of which needed to be preserved by at least one protected area. In the case of Iguazú National Park, Anziano proposed annexing the unspoiled Errecaborde estate, adjacent to the southern boundary of the park, based on a previous study produced by the agency's agricultural engineer Vsevolod Koutché in 1948. The expansion never took place, but the proposal introduced the vision of a country made up of a collection of discrete biological units that needed protection.[38]

Despite advancing new proposals for protected areas on conservation grounds, technicians at the national park agency had yet to question where the colonization projects carried out by the agency in parks such as Iguazú fit into the new paradigm. Institutional inertia was partly responsible for the lack of criticism within the national park agency regarding its unique development mission. This was clear in a 1956 leaflet published by the agency in which conservation and development were presented jointly as frictionless endeavors. The text explained that, besides conserving unspoiled nature for future generations, the agency was also in charge of "promoting the development of national parks

[37] Dimitri, "La protección de la naturaleza," 21–41.
[38] Alberto Anziano, "Informe Comisión Técnica al Parque Nacional Iguazú—Resolución 566/53," January 12, 1954, Carpeta 17, APN-B.

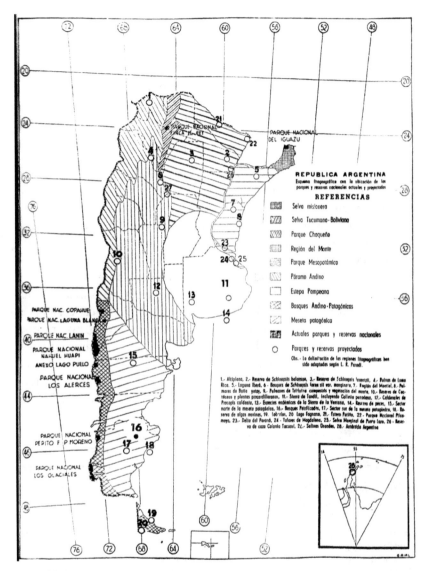

FIGURE 3.2 Proposed national parks and Argentine phytogeography. Source: Milan Jorge Dimitri, "La protección de la naturaleza en la República Argentina," *Natura: Órgano de la Administración General de Parques Nacionales* 1, no. 1 (1954): 41. Biblioteca Francisco P. Moreno, Administración de Parques Nacionales

through the construction of roads, bridges, airports, schools, telegraph and telephone lines, piers, sanitary works, ... set locations for the establishment of local industrial endeavors and to regulating them ... [and] tracing new population centers." Any possible tension between the two goals seemed to go unnoticed in the agency's official discourse.[39]

AN INTERNATIONAL NATIONAL PARK PARADIGM TAKES SHAPE IN THE 1960S

A reevaluation of the role of national parks as colonization tools was soon to come. It came in part as a result of the ever-increasing collaboration between Argentine national park officials and international organizations working to define new standards for protected areas.[40] Since the 1950s, a series of international meetings offered a forum for discussing the precepts behind national park policy. The First World Conference on National Parks in 1962, held in Seattle, was one of these meetings. The conference was sponsored by a wide range of organizations that included IUCN, UNESCO, FAO, the United States National Park Service, and the Natural Resources Council of America. Argentina sent a five-member delegation, including Milan Jorge Dimitri; Italo N. Costantino, who was then Vice Director of the Argentine Forest Service; and Maria Buchinger, a forestry advisor at the Institute for Forest Research under the Argentine Forest Service.[41] The conference was important, as Buchinger recalled it in 1965, for the pressure it placed on Latin American countries – Brazil included – to ratify the 1940 Convention on Nature Protection and Wildlife Preservation in the Western Hemisphere. Moreover, it also led to the creation of the Latin American Committee on National Parks (Comité Latinoamericano de Parques Nacionales, CLAPN) under the

---

[39] Eduardo Miguel Bessera argues that at Nahuel Huapi the contradiction between the new emphasis on protection and the needs of development manifested as early as 1952, when the national park agency withdrew from intervening in Bariloche. Bessera, "Políticas de Estado," 91, APN-B. See also, Dirección de Parques Nacionales, *Qué son los parques nacionales argentinos* (Buenos Aires: Dirección de Parques Nacionales, 1956), APN-B.

[40] Studying the cases of Costa Rica and Bolivia, Paul F. Steinberg introduced the concept of *bilateral activists* to describe domestic players who seamlessly circulated in national and international meetings and organizations, helping to shape conservation policy in developing countries. Paul F. Steinberg, *Environmental Leadership in Developing Countries: Transnational Relations and Biodiversity Policy in Costa Rica and Bolivia* (Cambridge, MA: MIT Press, 2001).

[41] United States National Park Service, *First World Conference on National Parks* (Washington, DC: United States Department of the Interior, 1962).

IUCN. Buchinger imagined the committee serving as a "clearing house" of information on national parks in the region: It would serve not only to lobby Latin American governments on creating national parks but also to establish common park standards across the hemisphere.[42]

Buchinger was a Hungarian-born biologist who moved to Argentina in 1948 after studying in Vienna. Like Georges Dennler de la Tour and Hugo Salomon before her, Buchinger was an European-born life scientist working to advance environmental policies in Argentina. Unlike them, however, she was not only a woman circulating in a technical world still dominated by men, but also someone able to move between government agencies and international organizations, which made her an important broker in the reception of international ideas on conservation in Argentina and the rest of Spanish America.[43] With the creation of CLAPN in 1963, Buchinger moved to Washington, DC, to serve as the organization's secretary. Once there, she also began working as the head of the Latin American Desk for Nature Conservancy.[44]

Buchinger's views on national park policy sought to achieve a new compromise within Argentine national park agency. She stated that national parks had "cultural, scientific, economic, and recreational goals, as they were important centers of attraction for national and international tourism."[45] Parks should function as in situ laboratories for biologists to both "improve cultivated plants and domestic animal breeds" and study native species, but they could also play a role in preserving sovereignty in border areas.[46] She drew inspiration from the Waterton-Glacier national parks (at the US–Canada border) to propose the creation of other transboundary parks in Latin America, which she stressed should be jointly managed by bordering countries – an idea she extended to the two existent Iguazu parks. As a concrete step toward establishing a uniform conservation standard across the hemisphere, Buchinger organized a CLAPN meeting in Quito in 1964 and obtained the support of IUCN and the scientific department of the Organization of

---

[42] Maria Buchinger, "Conservation in Latin America," *BioScience* 15, no. 1 (1965): 32–37.

[43] Of course, Buchinger was not alone in the 1960s. Milan Jorge Dimitri, for example, had translated into Spanish for the organ of the Argentine national park agency a text introducing the IUCN. International Union for Conservation of Nature and Natural Resources, "Qué es la Unión Internacional para la Conservación de la Naturaleza y de los Recursos Naturales," trans. Milan Jorge Dimitri, *Anales de Parques Nacionales* 10 (1964): 99–105.

[44] Maria Buchinger, "El Comité Latinoamericano de Parques Nacionales," *Ciencia Interamericana* 5, no. 3 (1964): 12–16.

[45] Ibid., 12.   [46] Ibid., 12-13.

American States (OAS) to bring the Inter-American Conference on Renewable Natural Resources to Argentina. The conference was held in Mar del Plata, on the Argentine coast, in October 1965, and brought together delegates from nineteen countries in the hemisphere, including Argentina, Brazil, and the United States.

The challenges brought to conservation by the import-substitution-industrialization policy widely adopted in Latin America in the 1950s and 1960s set the tone of the meeting. Regarding national parks, the conference's final text concluded, rather explicitly, that the main threat faced by protected areas was the "demographic and economic pressures" to which they were subjected. The text continued in a more diplomatic tone, recognizing that although agriculture and industrial practices "could, or should, not always be prohibited inside national parks," they nevertheless led to the destruction of the "useful elements in nature." This statement was, among other things, a recognition of the tension between development and conservation and, in the case of Argentina, a partial acknowledgment of the criticism of national park development put forward by outside conservationists since the 1930s.[47]

Another important mediator between international organizations and Argentine policymaking was the aforementioned agricultural engineer Italo N. Costantino, who developed strong ties to the IUCN throughout his career. Besides being vice director of the Argentine Forest Service, he was also part of the IUCN executive board, vice chairman (and later chairman) of CLAPN, and vice chairman of IUCN's International Commission on National Parks (ICNP). In 1968, he organized IUCN's first Latin American Conference on the Conservation of Renewable Natural Resources in Bariloche, Argentina. Unlike the similarly themed OAS meeting in Mar del Plata three years before, the new conference was open to civil society organizations. The IUCN meeting was also sponsored by UNESCO, FAO, the International Council for Bird Preservation (ICBP), and the Argentine Ministry of Agriculture and Livestock, and was held at the Llao Llao Hotel, built by Nahuel Huapi National Park in Bariloche in the 1930s.[48]

[47] Organization of American States, *Conferencia Especializada Interamericana para Tratar Problemas Relacionados con La Conservación de Recursos Naturales Renovables del Continente—Informe Final*, OEA Documentos Oficiales Serie C Vi.9.2 (Washington, DC: Organization of American States, 1966), Microfiche-182, Green Library, SU.

[48] International Union for Conservation of Nature and Natural Resources, *Proceedings of the Latin American Conference on the Conservation of Renewable Natural Resources: San Carlos de Bariloche, Argentina*, IUCN Publications New Series 13 (Morges,

The conference's final resolution, known as the Nahuel Huapi Manifesto, dispensed with the diplomatic precautions utilized in the 1965 OAS text, thereby furthering the criticism of Latin American developmentalism. The text also exemplified the neo-Malthusian fears informing much of the new ecological movement in the 1960s. The manifesto stated that population growth and modernization had resulted in "heavier demands on renewable natural resources," and that "man's unwise use" of natural resources was compromising their availability to future generations. It proposed a commitment to the "correct application of science and technology, joint policies, and coordinated legislation" to safeguard natural resources.[49]

Conservation was the conference's main theme, and many participants saw national parks as playing a fundamental role in that effort. A crucial issue was the lack of clear international standards for national parks, a lack accentuated by the existence of urban development inside Argentine parks such as nearby Nahuel Huapi. The chairman of ICNP, Belgian Jean-Paul Harroy, for example, was both a promoter of the standardization of national parks according to scientific criteria and a long-time critic of the effects of colonization on the environment.[50] In his opening address at the Bariloche conference, Harroy presented the birth of national parks as a direct effect of humanity's overexploitation and pollution of natural resources. He conceded that, although this goal was not clear to the first park proponents, it was the threat posed by the overuse of natural resources that had led past generations to "set aside some portions of the national territory" and grant them a "strict and effective protective status."[51]

However anachronistic Harroy's account of the beginning of national parks might have been, it reflected the push toward an international redefinition of national parks that would soon affect national park policy in Argentina. Harroy argued that the main reason for the creation of ICNP

Switzerland: International Union for Conservation of Nature and Natural Resources; published with the assistance of UNESCO, 1968).

[49] "Nahuel Huapi Manifesto," in International Union for Conservation of Nature, *Proceedings of the Latin American Conference*, 13.

[50] Association pour l'Histoire de la Protection de la Nature et de l'Environnement, "HARROY Jean Paul (1909–1995)," accessed February 15, 2015, http://ahpne.fr/spip .php?article151; Roderick Nash, *Wilderness and the American Mind* (New Haven: Yale University Press, 2001), 363.

[51] Jean-Paul Harroy, "The International Commission on National Parks," in International Union for Conservation of Nature, *Proceedings of the Latin American Conference*, 62–67.

was to "place the national parks problem within the general framework of conservation of nature and natural resources." For him, the issue with national parks was the lack of clear parameters unifying the various national park policies and experiences adopted by different countries.[52] On this matter, the conference recommended the adoption of a coordinated system for planning and implementing Latin American national parks, which included a unified nomenclature and zoning system as well as standardized norms for tourism and scientific activities.[53] In fact, similar standards would eventually be put in place in the late 1970s with the adoption of "management plans" for national parks in Brazil and other Latin American countries. By and large, the international move to redefine national parks according to the contemporary environmental crisis added to a growing consensus in Argentina regarding the existence of an irreconcilable contradiction between conservation and development inside parks. The conference strengthened the position of those environmentalists within and outside the government who believed the national park agency's mission to be defending nature *from* colonization.[54]

Italo N. Costantino was appointed head of the Argentine National Park Agency in September 1969, and in November of that same year he traveled to New Delhi, India, as the only Argentine delegate to the IUCN's Tenth General Meeting.[55] The IUCN's International Commission on National Parks had been a force for the standardization of national parks across the globe since 1967, when, under the guidance of Jean-Paul Harroy, the organization started publishing a UN-sponsored "List of National Parks and Equivalent Reserves." The list helped establish a canon of national parks and lent ICPN/IUCN legitimacy to define national park parameters. More important, the Delhi conference issued as its first resolution a new definition of national parks, which was the result of three years of correspondence and international visits by Harroy.[56]

[52] Ibid.

[53] "Resolutions Adopted by the IUCN Latin-American Regional Conference on Conservation of Renewable Natural Resources," in International Union for Conservation of Nature, *Proceedings of the Latin American Conference*, 455.

[54] For an example of the position of conservationists with the Argentine national park agency, see Juan Daciuk, "Consideraciones acerca de los fundamentos de la protección y conservación de la fauna nativa," *Anales de Parques Nacionales* 11 (1966–67): 43–96.

[55] Harold J. Coolidge, IUCN to Secretaría de Estado de Agricultura y Ganadería, "Se ref. a Asamblea Gral. UICN en Nueva Delhi, India, y s/la concurrencia del Ing. Italo N. Costantino," Expediente 4471/4610, year 1969, APN.

[56] International Union for Conservation of Nature and Natural Resources, *Tenth General Assembly: Vigyan Bhavan, New Delhi, 24 November–1 December, 1969*, IUCN

The new definition crystallized the incompatibility between human occupation and national parks. It defined national parks as areas where "one or several ecosystems are not materially altered by human exploitation and occupation," and where the government "has taken steps to prevent or to eliminate as soon as possible exploitation or occupation in the whole area." Furthermore, it excluded from the category of national park any

> inhabited and exploited area where landscape planning and measures taken for the development of tourism have led to the setting up of "recreation areas" where industrialization and urbanization are controlled and where public outdoor recreation takes priority over the conservation of ecosystems. ... Areas of this description which may have been established as "National Parks" should be redesignated in due course.[57]

As an NGO recommendation, the definition lacked the binding force of an international treaty. Still, it was an "object to be aimed at," in the words of Harroy, and the ICNP/IUCN partnership with the United Nations gave weight to the new proposed standard. This was even more true in the case of the Argentine national park agency, now headed by Costantino, who was also the vice chairman of ICNP and probably coauthored the new definition. Despite all this, Argentina still presented one of the biggest challenges for the adoption of the new national park definition, as for more than thirty years its well-developed national park agency had promoted settlement and urban development within park boundaries. In the end, the new definition galvanized the idea of an incompatibility between human occupation and parks, a tension that had been the cornerstone of the Argentine national park system since its inception.[58]

Publications New Series 27 (Morges, Switzerland: International Union for Conservation of Nature and Natural Resources; published with the assistance of UNESCO, 1970), 2:116–19, 2:148.

[57] The model of national parks without people had been criticized by IUCN delegates, many of them from Africa, since the 1950s. This criticism gained momentum a mere six years after the Delhi national park resolution, when ICUN's General Assembly in Kinshasa approved Recommendation 12/05, which stressed the right of indigenous populations to remain inside parks. Unlike their African counterparts, however, Argentina and Brazil furthered a new policy of exclusion of dwellers in their two border parks. This was in some measure understandable, as the criticism of the Yellowstone model of "fortress parks" centered on the rights of indigenous and traditional populations. In Iguazú and Iguaçu, the evicted population in the 1960s and 1970s comprised mostly newly arrived settlers. International Union for Conservation of Nature, *Tenth General Assembly*, 156; Martin Holdgate, *The Green Web: A Union for World Conservation* (London: IUCN, Earthscan, 1999), 106–7, 124–25, 142.

[58] As a response to the 1960s environmental movement and the growth of militant organizations such as Greenpeace, IUCN officials decided in New Delhi to change the

In face of these challenges, Argentina reformed its national park legislation in 1970 in line with the new international standards. The new law redefined national parks as areas of integral protection with minimal tourism activity, prohibition of settlements, and a ban on hunting and commercial activities unrelated to visitation. A second category of protected area, "national reserve," was also redefined in the new law. These constituted zones of transition combining protection with limited economic activity, thereby allowing the existence of settlements, which would be limited to 10 percent of each reserve's area. Therefore, through a legal redefinition of the space of Argentine protected areas, the national park agency would maintain the power of promoting development inside *national reserves* at the same time that *national parks* would be free of development and able to gain international recognition.[59]

To adapt Iguazú National Park to the new legislation, the national park agency decided to sever the area containing Puerto Iguazú, the farms, and the landing strip from the rest of the park. In this way, the park would comprise an eastern 10,000-hectare area constituting a *national reserve*, which included the town of Puerto Iguazú, and a western 34,000-hectare *national park* area containing the hotel, the campgrounds, and the falls as well as the more extensive western stretches of forest. Iguazú National Park was the first to have its area legally divided into national reserve and national park in October 1970. A year later a new law defined the division between national reserve and national park for eight other Patagonian

organization's mandate. The union moved to a more assertive position in putting forward an environmental agenda, connecting governments and NGOs, and bridging developed and developing countries. Holdgate, *The Green Web*, 101–29.

[59] Although the category of *national reserve* had been first introduced in the original 1934 national park law, the text failed to lay out its defining features. Both *national reserves* and *national parks* were then defined as those "portions of the Nation's territory that, due to its extraordinary beauty, or for a particular scientific interest, were worthy of conservation for the utilization and enjoyment of the population of the Republic." In practice, *national reserve* was used as a transitional category of areas slated to be transformed into national parks. This was the case with the five Patagonian parks created in 1937, which, after a period as *national reserves,* became *national parks* in 1949. Prior to 1970, the category had never been utilized to define a different type of zone in the same protected area. Before that, the 5,000-hectare area set aside by law for development inside parks was known as the *exploitation zone* and was a constitutive part of the national park. Argentina, Law 12103, "Ley de Parques Nacionales," September 29, 1934; Argentina, Law 105433, May 11, 1937; Argentina, Law 13895, September 20, 1949; Argentina, Law 18594, February 6, 1970; Argentina, Decree 637, February 6, 1970; Argentina, Decree-Law 20161, February 15, 1973.

parks, including Nahuel Huapi.[60] Hence, through a legal sleight of hand, the Argentine national park agency adjusted conditions to gain international recognition for its older border national parks without having to cede the control of its developed assets (in the case of Iguazu, the town it had developed). However, local developments would very soon change this situation.

THE PROVINCIALIZATION OF PUERTO IGUAZÚ AND THE EXPANSION OF THE PARK

Today, Puerto Iguazú is independent of the national park. The town's emancipation from Iguazú National Park's control occurred just six months after the park was divided into national reserve and national park in October 1970. To understand this process, it is necessary not only to cast light on the role of environmentalists in advancing a preservationist agenda but also to investigate how local forces pushed for greater independence from federal oversight. It was the combined result of international, national, and local forces that created the conditions for the separation between the town and the park in 1971, ending almost four decades of a policy of border colonization through national parks in Misiones.

When the Argentine government gazetted Iguazú National Park in 1934, Misiones was a federal territory directly controlled by Buenos Aires. This was the case with all eight other parks created in that decade, including Nahuel Huapi, which straddled the border of the then territories of Neuquén and Rio Negro. For a federal republic such as Argentina, establishing national parks was, indeed, analogous to creating territories, as they were both central attempts to directly control frontier areas without the mediation of local power. Locals were unhappy with the lack of autonomy of their territories, and in the early decades of the twentieth century, they pushed unsuccessfully for various bills aimed to turn the territories into provinces. The original national territories law of 1884 mandated a 60,000-person population threshold for a given territory to become a province. Misiones surpassed this threshold in the 1920

---

[60] Argentina, Law 18801, "Establécese la delimitación del Parque Nacional y de la Reserva Nacional Iguazú," October 7, 1970; Argentina, Law 19292, "Límites de los distintos Parques y Reservas," October 11, 1971; Regina G. Schlüter, *Turismo y áreas protegidas en Argentina* (Buenos Aires: Centro de Investigaciones y Estudios Turísticos, 1990), 39–41.

census when it counted 63,176 inhabitants, fourteen years before the gazetting of Iguazú Park. It was only during Perón's second term (1952–55) that this provision was broadly enforced, with the provincialization of several territories between 1952 and 1955, including Misiones in 1953.[61]

The 1950s legislation eradicating the old territories provided for the transfer of all federal property (including public land) to the new provinces, creating a serious challenge to the sovereignty of the national park agency over its border parks.[62] The agency faced the risk of losing the country's national parks to the provinces. In 1958, a new law solved the conundrum and confirmed the national parks' exceptional status – despite provincialization, they would remain under federal control. The new law defined the Argentine federal government through the national park agency as the owner of the national parks located inside the old Argentine territories. It also established a commission to set new limits for the parks, excluding all areas that failed to meet the requirements of "extraordinary beauty or scientific interest" that defined those stretches of land deemed worthy of conservation efforts according to the national park law. It represented a victory for the sectors within the Argentine national park service that reviled the agency's involvement with colonization projects, as it meant the removal of towns like Puerto Iguazú from national park areas.[63]

The autonomy of the border towns located inside national parks was already an issue under debate among the drafters of the 1934 national park law. As historian Laura Méndez points out, the voting of the national park bill into law consolidated two positions on the matter. For Exequiel Bustillo's allies in Congress, municipalities within national parks should be placed under the authority of the new national park agency, which was designed by Bustillo to be the main institution in charge of nationalizing the borders. To opposition members, however, those municipalities should be autonomous and abide by national laws directly through the territory in which they were located. Although the latter position was victorious, Méndez points out that, in the case of the already existing San Carlos de Bariloche, the town became a de facto protectorate of the national park agency and Bustillo after the creation of the Nahuel

---

[61] Argentina, Law 1532, "Organización de los territorios nacionales," October 1, 1884; J. A. Maeder, *Misiones: Historia de la tierra prometida* (Buenos Aires: Eudeba, 2004).
[62] Argentina, Law 14294, Art. 11, December 10, 1953; Argentina, Law 14408, Art. 10, June 15, 1955.
[63] Argentina, Decree-Law 654, January 25, 1958.

Huapi National Park. The dependency of settlements such as Villa la Angostura, also in Nahuel Huapi, and Puerto Iguazú in Iguazú was even more extreme, as they were created *by* the national park agency *without* being granted the status of municipalities.[64]

As these settlements grew into towns, calls for increased autonomy mounted from the local population as well as from territorial, and later provincial, governments.[65] In the case of Puerto Iguazú, in the early 1950s the government of Misiones initiated the bureaucratic process of creating a municipality in Iguazú. The first step was setting up, in 1951, a formal "development committee" (*comisión de fomento*), which in Argentina acted as the legal body for community action in third-class municipalities. Although prominent members of the community composed much of the committee, it was still heavily influenced by national park administrators. Indeed, in its first term, the committee in Iguazú was headed by the national park director himself, Balbino Brañas, who acted as de facto mayor of the town. The committee functioned as the town government until Puerto Iguazú finally became a municipality in 1961, eight years after the provincialization of Misiones in 1953.[66]

The new 1958 national park law set the legal precedent for retracing national park boundaries sans urban settlements via the creation of a committee to reassess the limits of parks. Despite the already existing pressure of local communities and environmentalists for the separation of towns and parks, it took ten years for the Secretary of Agriculture and Livestock to finally form the committee. By 1968, the collaboration between conservationists within the national park agency and those in international bodies had laid the groundwork for the idea of settlement-free parks. It was a propitious environment for separating towns from

---

[64] Méndez, *Estado, frontera y turismo*, 240–43; Argentina, Law 12103, "Ley de parques nacionales," September 29, 1934.

[65] As settlements controlled by the Argentine national park agency, towns such as Puerto Iguazú in Misiones and Villa la Angostura in Neuquén became sites of dispute between overlapping federal and provincial/territorial jurisdictions. Mikael Wolfe describes a similar process occurring in Mexico in the 1940s, where the Mexican federal government established the settlement of El Palmito at the construction site of the Lázaro Cárdenas Dam in Durango. In this case, the local union of construction workers complained to the federal government about the increasing power that the state of Durango and the local municipality had over the federal site. Wolfe, *Watering the Revolution*, 145–51.

[66] Misiones, Resolution 870, August 1, 1951; Puerto Iguazú, Dirección Municipal de Cultura, *Breves reseñas de Puerto Iguazú* (Puerto Iguazú, Argentina: n.p., n.d.), BPI; Daniel de La Torre, "Reseña histórica de Pto. Iguazú y del Parque Nacional Iguazú," 2003, PNIA; Parque Nacional Iguazú, "Cataratas de historia," n.d., PNIA.

parks. The Secretary of Agriculture and Livestock formed the committee with members of the national park agency, the Forest Service (then headed by Costantino), the National Institute of Agricultural Technology, and other federal agencies.[67]

The resulting report by the committee was a victory for the critics of the development mission of national parks, as it established the primacy of "preservation over use" in these protected areas. It listed a series of threats to national parks, including not only poaching and other types of economic activities but also tourism and "social and land-ownership problems." The latter included Indian communities, rural settlements, and urban areas. Unsurprisingly, at a time when the drive to "de-Peronize" Argentina still loomed large in most sectors of the government, the report also denounced as incompatible with preservation the mass tourism and major infrastructure works promoted during the Perón years (1946–55).[68] More important, the report condemned the emphasis of past national park administrations on promoting urban development, arguing rather explicitly that "urban environments and their services should be excluded from the jurisdiction of a national park, as they obviously represent the opposite of the concept." Therefore, a new demarcation for national parks became necessary to separate urban areas and prospective spaces of development from their territories. In the case of Iguazú National Park, the commission recommended the excluding of the 5,000-hectare area of Puerto Iguazú from the national park. As Jorge Milan Dimitri suggested, the agency was to instead transfer the town to the province of Misiones.[69]

In January 1969, the Secretary of Agriculture and Livestock produced the first draft of the law transferring Puerto Iguazú to the control of the province of Misiones. The new law was enacted in April 1971 after two

[67] These included the National Bureau of Fish and Wildlife, the National Security Council, the National Development Council, and the National Council of Scientific Research. See Secretaría de Estado de Agricultura y Ganadería, Resolution 162, February 2, 1968, in Dirección General de Parques Nacionales to Secretaría de Estado de Agricultura y Ganadería, "Ref. Nota 331—Com. haber design. a los ings. agrs. Milan Jorge Dimitri y Lucio Debenedetti, como representantes de esa D. G. para integrar comisiones de trabajo a que se refiere la Resolución 162/68," Expediente 732, year 1968, APN.

[68] Dirección General de Parques Nacionales to Secretaría de Estado de Agricultura y Ganadería, "Ref. Nota 331—Com. haber design. a los Ings. Agrs. Milan Jorge Dimitri y Lucio Debenedetti, como representantes de esa D. G. para integrar comisiones de trabajo a que se refiere la Resolución 162/68," Expediente 732, year 1968, APN.

[69] Dirección General de Parques Nacionales to Secretaría de Estado de Agricultura y Ganadería, "Ref. Nota 331—Com. haber design.," Expediente 732, year 1968, APN.

years of negotiation between the national park agency and the provincial government over the fate of the remaining public land and over restrictions on development in a proposed buffer zone along the new boundary dividing park and town.[70] With the new law, the national park agency handed the control of Puerto Iguazú over to Misiones. As a result, not only did the town cease to be part of park territory, but also the national park administration no longer owned and managed urban infrastructure in Puerto Iguazú. The park ceded the ownership of most property and facilities, including the water treatment plant and the town's cemetery. It also shed its administrative duties, transferring to the provincial government all the files for more than thirty years of public land sales. Initially, the national park agency attempted to keep control over most of the remaining public land, but after pressure from the government of Misiones the park opted to maintain only a few dozen lots for the future expansion of housing for park personnel. The park did, however, continue to have a say in the town management to guarantee that new developments did not compromise Puerto Iguazú's aesthetic and environmental value as a gateway to the park.[71]

For thirty-five years, the national park agency was the main institution governing Puerto Iguazú. It transformed a hamlet of 100 inhabitants into

---

[70] Dirección General de Parques Nacionales to Secretaría de Gobierno, "Consideraciones—Ref. Ley n° 436 Relac. Prov. Misiones fijan límites de los ejidos municipales de diversos municipios entre ellos de Puerto Iguazu—adj. planos," Expediente 3427 (102576—Interior), year 1969, APN; Argentina, Law 18991, "Parques nacionales, Iguazú, modificación de límites," April 20, 1971; Argentina, Decree 431, April 20, 1971; Administración Nacional de Parques Nacionales, "33—Elev. proyecto de mensaje y ley modificación actuales de límites del P. N. Iguazú transfiriendo a la Pcia. de Misiones aproximadamente 5,000 hectáreas," Expediente 150, year 1969, APN. Around the same time the Argentine national park agency transferred control of other national park towns to the provinces; see Servicio Nacional de Parques Nacionales, "295—Elev. proyecto de mensaje y ley donde este serv. nacional propicia la transf. a la jurisdicc. da la Pca. Neuquén tierra que constituyen la Villa Angostura P. Nac. N. Huapi," Expediente 3151, year 1971, APN.

[71] The legal transfer of Puerto Iguazú to the province of Misiones initially exacerbated the contradiction between the town and the park. Local politicians believed the town now had a claim over the park, as the latter was located within the legal boundaries of the municipality of Puerto Iguazú. They also complained the park hindered the town's development by impeding new road construction and limiting the supply of land for colonization. According to the mayor of Puerto Iguazú, "border zones like Iguazú should be defended with settlements, bridges, and [paved] highways," not with empty areas. Ramón Víctor Pablo Elías to Clemente Durán, n° 2195, June 8, 1976, Caja 3.A 1/1, Carpeta "Notas despachadas ene 76 a sept 76," PNIA; Oscar A. Álvarez to Supervisor Regional, n° 4045, September 4, 1978, Caja 3.A 1/1, Carpeta "Notas despachadas 1/7/1976 a 29/03/1979," PNIA.

a town of 3,000 building park headquarters, customs building, port, hospital, school, police headquarters, hotel, power plant, water treatment plant, and housing for park personnel as well as tracing a street grid, building streets, and selling urban plots to settlers.[72] Ultimately, however, the environmentalist criticism of the parks' colonization mission coupled with pressure for greater municipal autonomy culminated in park and town being separated in 1971. An expansion of the park area in 1972 indicated the increased importance of the mission to preserve species and ecology. The expansion was proposed by national park agency officials Juan Daciuk, Milan Jorge Dimitri, and Hugo Correa Luna, who called for an increase in park area to protect unique tree species such as the Paraná pine (*Araucaria angustifolia*), the juçara palm (*Euterpe edulis*), and the peroba rosa (*Aspidosperma polyneuron*) as well as the many animal species in the park (e.g., jaguar, ocelot, tapir, howler monkey, and caiman). The total expansion swelled the park's size by almost 150 percent in 1972, more than compensating for the area lost with the emancipation of Puerto Iguazú (see Map 3.2).[73]

SETTLERS IN THE PROTECTED AREA

Between 1934 and 1971, the Argentine national park agency sold and leased land to settlers in Puerto Iguazú, which was part of Iguazú National Park. When government officials began planning the redrawing of park boundaries and the separation between town and national park, the

---

[72] I was not able to find a source for the actual number of residents in Puerto Aguirre in 1934, as most figures included the inhabitants of other settlements. However, I could infer it to be around 100 based on impressionistic descriptions of the hamlet by visitors, comparisons with Foz do Iguaçu, and the number of dwellings accounted for by the DPN in 1935: six houses and seven shacks. General Alonso Baldrich to Dirección de Parques Nacionales, "Informe sobre toma de posesión del Parque Nacional del Iguazú," Expediente 0535, year 1935, APN.

[73] Juan Daciuk, Hugo Correa Luna, and Milan Jorge Dimitri, "El Parque Nacional Iguazú: Fundamentos que avalan su creación como parque nacional," March 1969, Carpeta 5, APN-B; Milan Jorge Dimitri to Dirección General de Parques Nacionales, "S/N.º Elev. Inf. Ref. al P. Nac. Iguazú c/ motivo reciente viaje de estudio e inspección técnica," Expediente 1384, year 1969, 47–63, APN; Milan Jorge Dimitri to Italo Costantino, April 22, 1969, in Milan Jorge Dimitri to Dirección General de Parques Nacionales, "S/N.º Elev. Inf. Ref. al P. Nac. Iguazú c/ motivo reciente viaje de estudio e inspección técnica," Expediente 1384, year 1969, APN; Argentina, Decree 4982, August 19, 1968; Argentina, Law 19478, "Incorpórase al Parque Nacional Iguazú una fracción de campo," February 4, 1972; Argentina, Decree 374, February 14, 1977; Servicio Nacional de Parques Nacionales to Dirección de Remonta y Veterinaria, Expediente 2670, year 1977, APN.

MAP 3.2 Change in Iguazú National Park boundaries, c. 1950–80. Maps by Frederico Freitas

protected area had short of 3,000 official people living inside its territory, a figure that included those settled in Puerto Iguazú. The existence of official settlements in the park served to discourage squatting in most of the rest of Iguazú. The exception was the restricted zone near the waterfalls, where park administrators had encouraged informal settlements. This was the case for Juan Hoppe, who had been living for decades inside Iguazú National Park with the directors' acquiescence but without land ownership or any signed agreement. The establishment of other 300 settlers near Iguazu Falls, in the area visited by tourists, had not been foreseen by the original national park legislation. It was the result of pragmatic decisions by park directors, who initially understood the presence of workers near the park's attractions to be beneficial for settlers and park alike. In the late 1960s, however, the same change in national park paradigm that provoked the separation of Puerto Iguazú from the area of the park also made necessary the eviction of the settlers living around Iguazu Falls.

Initially, the Argentine national park law had defined 5,000-hectare zones for the establishment of "population centers" inside Iguazú and Nahuel Huapi national parks. These formed stretches of land that were, before the 1970s, technically part of their respective national park territories, but with special land regimes that allowed land to be sold and settled. In Iguazú, the 5,000-hectare zone set aside for development hosted Puerto Iguazú and was referred to as the "exploitation zone" in park parlance.

The area outside the exploitation zone, however, was technically off-limits to prospective dwellers. Another goal of the creators of Iguazú National Park, besides occupying borderlands, was to gain control of the increasing stream of visitors arriving at the falls every year. To the national park agency, reorganizing the use of the natural monument inevitably involved preventing people who saw tourism as a job opportunity from settling near the falls. But this de jure ban on settlements inside the protected area of the park existed alongside the de facto endorsement of dwellings by local park authorities. As a result, between the 1930s and the 1960s workers settled inside the protected area of the park, on multiple occasions with the blessing of local park authorities. As with transferring Puerto Iguazú to provincial control, removing settlers from the protected area took place in the 1960s and 1970s, a time of a growing consensus on the preservationist goals of national parks. Unsurprisingly, the removal of at least some of these settlers proved to be a difficult and contentious process.[74]

In 1939, even before the national park agency had officially gained control of the park area from the army, Park Director Balbino Brañas started offering lots for temporary settlement in the area surrounding the

---

[74] Argentina, Law 12103, "Ley de parques nacionales," Art. 22, September 29, 1934; Argentina, Decree 12054, "Atribuciones y deberes de la Administración General de Parques Nacionales y Turismo," Art. 23, April 30, 1946.

recently built airstrip, all with the permission of his superiors in Buenos Aires. The park had built the airstrip on a flat, marshy salt lick near the falls that attracted wild animals for its mineral deposits. Considerations on how building the airstrip would affect the fauna of the region were absent, as the conservationists within the agency still focused mostly on the aesthetic value of forests and saw marshes as wasteland.[75]

The national park agency needed to maintain the threshold cleared around the runway for the safe landing of airplanes. Labor was scarce in the region, so Brañas proposed settling farmers around the airstrip to guarantee that the area would be maintained without the expense and headache of hiring workers. The new residents would be free to grow crops but would have to keep their plots clear of tall trees, ensuring that the edges of the runaway were free of obstacles to takeoffs and landings. The deal was especially advantageous for the national park administration, as settlers would not only provide free labor but also pay to use the land.[76]

These settlers would also help solve the problem of the regional food supply. Permission for these farms was based on a provision of the 1934 national park law allowing for temporary settlement on inalienable national park land. Brañas initially parceled eighty-eight hectares of land surrounding the airstrip into nine lots and offered them to prospective settlers of Argentine citizenship. As previously seen, Brañas had also proposed a plan in 1939 to exploit the national park's wild yerba mate groves, and was invested mostly in promoting the development of the national park as a generator of non-tourism-related economic activity.[77]

Brañas's plan to settle families in the airstrip threshold was beset with problems. There was a lack of interested parties, an absence of basic infrastructure, and recurrent miscommunication between park authorities

---

[75] José Gorgues, who started working at Iguazú National Park in 1937, before the airstrip was built, described the area as "an ugly wetland, where animals would come to eat mud [salt]." According to him, the contractors cleared and graveled the area, and a "very large roller" finished the job. José Gorgues (retired Iguazú National Park employee), in discussion with the author, August 2014. See also Devoto and Rothkugel, "Informe sobre los bosques," 129–204; and Muello, *Misiones, las cataratas del Iguazú*.

[76] Initially settlers would pay five pesos per hectare per year for the land around the airstrip. Intendencia del Iguazú to Dirección de Parques Nacionales, "Eleva proyecto reglamento para concesiones de chacras en el campo de aterrizaje," Expediente 2128, year 1939, 1–11, APN.

[77] Intendencia del Iguazú to Dirección de Parques Nacionales, "Eleva proyecto reglamento," 1–11, APN; "Reglamento de ocupación de tierras en el Parque Nacional del Iguazú," in Dirección de Parques Nacionales, *Decreto reglamentario de la ley 12103 y recopilacion de reglamentos vigentes* (Buenos Aires: Ministerio de Agricultura, 1940), 151–52, APN-B.

and settlers. In its first year, the project attracted only four families, three of which consisted of Polish immigrants who had recently arrived in Argentina after fleeing the war in Europe. Invited by Brañas, they settled in the area in August 1940. As foreigners, they were less than ideal prospects for a settlement on a border zone, but the park director accepted them because of the lack of Argentine applicants. Soon enough, however, settlers became dissatisfied with the living conditions around the airstrip. They felt isolated and claimed it was impossible to sell produce or send their children to school without public transportation to the town.[78] The settlers also complained about the environmental restrictions imposed by the national park administration, especially the prohibition against planting trees in the new lots, which reduced their options as far as which crops they could cultivate.[79]

Two years later, in a 1941 memo to Antonio M. Lynch, Brañas revealed his disappointment with the outcome of the project. Instead of setting the stage for the development of a thriving community of prosperous frontier farmers, the settlement inside the protected area of the park "had devolved into a group of miserable dwellings." To the park director, despite their "work ethic," settlers were living in a shocking state of "extreme poverty," malnourished and wearing wretched garments. Settlers also had a hard time understanding the terms of the deal – the foreigners among them still had not mastered the Spanish language. They refused to pay the lease because they believed they were working for free in clearing the airstrip threshold. Brañas agreed to reduce their lots from ten to five hectares, which would cut their debt to the park in half, and requested a halt to the charging of annual fees. Things changed with Alejandro Cané, the new park director appointed in 1942, who opposed the idea of granting settlers debt amnesty. He blamed the settlers themselves, who he

---

[78] In 1940, the closest school was still located twenty kilometers away in Puerto Aguirre (later Puerto Iguazú), and a second school was not completed until 1946.

[79] Aleksander Sobestjaniuk to Dirección de Parques Nacionales, "Solicita se le conceda en ocupación a título precario superficie 10 has en la zona denominada 'zona granja campo aterrizaje,'" Expediente 5109, year 1940, APN; Basyle Zuk to Dirección de Parques Nacionales, "Sol. en ocupación a título precario superf. 10 hect. en la zona denominada 'zona granja campo aterrizaje,'" Expediente 5110, year 1940, APN; Joaquin Kot to Dirección de Parques Nacionales, "Sol. en ocupación a título precario superf. 10 hect. en la zona denominada 'zona granja campo aterrizaje,'" Expediente 5108, year 1940, APN; Gabino Irala to Dirección de Parques Nacionales, "Sol. en ocupación a título precario superf. 10 hect. en la zona denominada 'zona granja campo aterrizaje,'" Expediente 2959, year 1941, APN.

believed had failed to comply with the "minimal requirements set by the national park administration" (i.e., clearing the land surrounding the airstrip). To Cané, their foreign nationality lay at the root of their inability to abide by park rules. After all, he reasoned, they were "Polacks" with "little propensity to work and no attachment to the land." He warned that debt forgiveness meant free land distribution, which would only attract "the worst kind of people" to the park.[80]

Despite all the hurdles, at least two of the four original settlers stayed in the area, and in the following two decades they were followed by many others who, officially or without the sanction of the national park agency, settled inside the protected area of the park to take advantage of the proximity to Iguazu Falls and its tourists.[81] Few of these settlers had official temporary permits. Between 1940 and 1958, the national park agency granted only fifteen permits for temporary settlement outside the town of Puerto Iguazú. These permits, in general, were related to services needed by the national park administration, such as the clearing of the airstrip threshold or brick-making. The great majority of settlers who came to live inside the protected area, however, did so without official permits. Often enough they obtained oral permission from park directors, and over the years this became a preferred arrangement for settlers working at the hotel, at the airstrip, or as oarsmen at the falls.

The arrangement initially benefited both settlers and park directors. On the one hand, workers did not have to deal with bureaucracy, requirements, and costs of leasing the land from the national park agency. For park directors, on the other hand, it made it easier to attract laborers to the park by bypassing the scrutiny and approval of their superiors in Buenos Aires. By the late 1950s, the area of the falls inside the protected zone contained a small population of settlers who provided the park with a source of menial labor (see Map 3.3).

---

[80] Intendencia del Iguazú to Dirección de Parques Nacionales, "Eleva proyecto reglamento," 13–17.
[81] The case of Basyle Zuk exemplified the problem settlers faced with the debt they accrued during their national park adventure. Zuk, a thirty-two-year-old farmer from Poland, married and the father of two, leased a ten-hectare lot near the airstrip in 1940. In March 1944, after failing to thrive in the area, he moved to Buenos Aires and started working as a carpenter. He was tracked down by revenue authorities in 1947 and forced to pay his leasing debt with the national park authorities in installments. He finally finished paying in 1950. Basyle Zuk to Dirección de Parques Nacionales, "Sol. en ocupación a título precario."

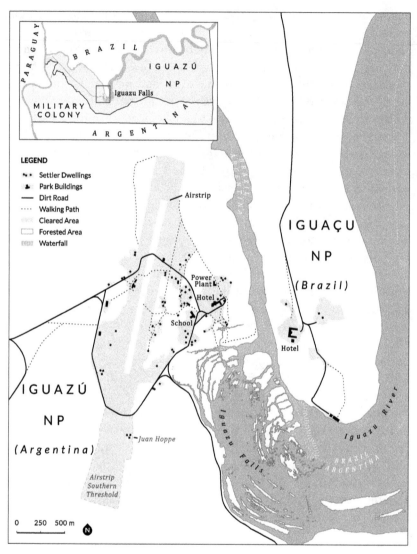

MAP 3.3 Dwellings around Iguazu Falls, c. 1960. Map by Frederico Freitas

A PARK WITHOUT INHABITANTS

The presence of settlers inside the protected area of Iguazú National Park inevitably became the target of criticism within the agency. A 1961 survey of the park's visitation zone painted a dire picture of the state of the fauna in the area. According to the report, signed by Agricultural

Engineer Juan Daciuk of the nature protection office, the population of mammals had decreased dramatically in the last decade. Daciuk blamed the proximity to the town, the circulation of cars, and the presence of dogs, owned by settlers, as the culprits for the disappearance of fauna. "Dogs are, indeed, the only abundant mammal in this area," quipped the agricultural engineer. Daciuk based his observations on interviews with settlers, who informed him of the abundance of fauna in previous years, a time when coatis, iguanas, cougars, and jaguars were a common sight in the area. As the wildlife was replaced by humans and their animals, the national park decided to reverse the situation with a gradual program of dog eradication.[82]

From dogs to dog owners was a small step, and Daciuk's follow-up report tackled the problem of settlers. The report made it clear that the presence of "settlers and squatters" inside the zone of strict protection was a source of the "biological imbalance" of animal species, especially small predators (e.g., opossum, oncilla, and ocelot), which preyed on chicken and were therefore killed by settlers. Daciuk also identified free-range cattle as a major cause of disturbance because they attracted large predators and impacted the forest. As implied in the first report, settlers' numerous dogs posed another serious problem, preying on small wild animals. As the last refuge of "Misionero fauna," Daciuk reasoned, Iguazú National Park should receive special attention from the national park agency, as protecting its fauna was a "patriotic goal of singular worth."[83]

Daciuk believed the existence of a "dense population" consisting of long-time residents and recent squatters also posed other problems for conservation. One was aesthetic, as settlers' "miserable houses" offered "an awful sight for tourists," especially foreign ones. He reproduced the same tropes utilized to condemn squatters in Puerto Iguazú. Daciuk depicted the settlers' "way of living" as being "indolent, indecorous, and a health hazard." Another problem was the introduction of alien plant species. As shown in Table 3.1, settlers grew various fruit trees inside the protected area. In conclusion, Daciuk feared population growth could lead to the creation of a second town inside the park close to the falls. He advised that the inhabitants be removed from this area and sent

---

[82] Juan Daciuk to Dirección General de Parques Nacionales, "Eleva informe técnico ref. viaje de estudios al Parque Nacional Iguazú mes de enero ppdo.," Expediente 1746, year 1961, APN.

[83] Juan Daciuk to Dirección General de Parques Nacionales, "Reactualización sistemática de las especies animales exhibidas en el Museo del Iguazú ...," Expediente 2372, year 1962, Carpeta 16, APN-B.

TABLE 3.1 Survey on the population of the recreational zone, Iguazú
National Park, 1961

Population		Livestock		Crops	
Age		Chickens	1,097	Individual Plants	
Adult	183	Ducks	61	Pineapple Plants	5,630
Minor	182	Dogs	43	Banana Trees	1,873
Gender		Cattle	42	Orange Trees	583
Male	176	Pigs	27	Pine Tress	514
Female	169	Horses	14	Tangerine Trees	283
Nationality		Goats	10	Peach Trees	129
Argentina	249	Geese	8	Grapefruit Trees	17
Paraguay	93	Cats	7	Avocado Trees	14
Brazil	18	Guinea Fowl	2	Grapevines	6
Poland	2			Fig Trees	3
Uruguay	1			Pear Trees	1
Austria	1			Cultivated Area (ha)	
Germany	1			Maize	17
Total Population	365			Manioc	15
				Beans	1

Source: Juan Daciuk to Dirección General de Parques Nacionales, "Reactualización
sistemática de las especies animales exhibidas en el Museo del Iguazú …," Expediente
2372, year 1962, Carpeta 16, APN-B

to the Villa Tacuara in Puerto Iguazú, the shanty town on the outskirts of
town. Once there, park dwellers could benefit from the town services:
"drinking water, electricity, hospital, and school."[84]
    The tension caused by the presence of settlers reached its climax in
June 1962, when news of the killing of a jaguar reached Hugo Correa
Luna, the new director of the nature protection office at the national park
agency. The animal had been prowling around the Villa Cataratas, as the
hamlet where most of the population inside the park's protected area lived
was known. By April the jaguar had eaten several domestic animals, and
the settlers started hunting the feline. A failed attempt to capture the
animal left one of the settlers, Benedito Garcia, maimed, which legitimized
the rangers' decision to kill the jaguar. According to ranger José Gorgues,
the animal's behavior in attacking people posed a threat to settlers,

[84] Ibid.

MATAN A UN TIGRE, LO ASAN Y LO COMEN: MEJOR QUE LECHON

E N la última quincena de abril y en diferentes lugares, entre las Cataratas del Iguazú y Puerto Iguazú, algunos tigre comenzaron a rondar los ranchos de los pobladores. A pocos metros del campo de aviación de Cataratas, en una pensión, ya habían comido más de veinte gallinas, hirieron también al perro que custodiaba la casa. Por estas razones un fotógrafo de apellido García y el agente policial Acosta montaron guardia en una pieza donde aquél se hospedaba. Dejaron semiabierta una ventana esperando que del lado más tupido del monte apareciera la fiera, suponiendo que el ladrido del perro los alertaría. Cansados de esperar se quedaron dormidos y a las 3 de la madrugada del 1° de mayo despertaron de improviso ante ruidos extraños. De pronto un tigre amenazante penetró en la habitación seguido del perro. García le disparó con el winchester sin dar en el blanco y fue derribado por la fiera. Perdió la linterna y quedaron en la oscuridad. El animal atacó al fotógrafo provocándole un desgarrón en el brazo izquierdo y mordiéndole una mano. García le aplicó varios culatazos y logró desprenderse, introduciéndose en la cocina, ya herido. Cerraron la puerta y el tigre abandonó la habitación saltando por la ventana.

Al día siguiente, en el kilómetro 11 entre el Puerto y Cataratas, el guardabosques José Gergues, quien hace cinco años mató a otro tigre que se encuentra embalsamado en el museo de Iguazú, subido a un árbol con un compañero, esperó la llegada de la fiera y al verla llegar le hizo un disparo con el winchester hiriéndola. Poco después descendieron y de dos tiros en la cabeza le dieron muerte. Por la noche, en casa del guardabosques, compañeros y vecinos prepararon al tigre, lo pusieron sobre un asador y se dieron un banquete. Aseguran que su carne es más exquisita que la del lechón. Ahora Gergues se dispone a eliminar otros tigres que siguen atacando terneros o lo que encuentran, impulsados por el hambre. El señor Adelaido Ifrán, domiciliado en Puerto Iguazú (Misiones) ha tenido la gentileza de enviarnos los datos de este suceso y las dos fotografías que acompañan la nota.

ARRIBA: *JUNTO AL TIGRE CAZADO, EL SEÑOR ADELAIDO IFRAN Y SU ESPOSA EN LA OTRA JUTO JOSE GERGUES (EL SEÑOR CALVO CON UN CORREAJE), UN VECINO, IFRAN Y SI SORA, JUNTO A LA FIERA A LA QUE SE DIO MUERTE, SIN VIENDO PARA UN BANQUETE EN CASA DEL GUARDABOSQUES.*

FIGURE 3.3 News of the death of a jaguar in Iguazú National Park, 1962. "They killed, roasted, and ate a jaguar: it tasted better than pork." Source: "Matan a un tigre, lo asan y lo comen: mejor que lechón," *Ahora*, May 15, 1962, in Protección de la Naturaleza to Dirección de Parques Nacionales, "Nota 119-Sol/instrucción sumarias con motivo de versiones, de haber matado un jaguar y dado muerte a otro en Par. Nac. Iguazú," Expediente 2026, year 1962, 2. Biblioteca Francisco P. Moreno, Administración de Parques Nacionales

especially "young children." Therefore, the park rangers opted for "the elimination of the beast … for security reasons and the settlers' peace of mind." Gorgues and another ranger, Enrique Miranda, ambushed and killed the jaguar without authorization from Correa Luna or another official at the national park agency. To make matters worse, Gorgues and a number of settlers roasted and ate the animal, and the story made it to the local news, with one of the settlers declaring that jaguar meat "tasted better than pork" (see Figure 3.3).

Gorgues himself had killed another jaguar five years earlier, which was used in the park museum exhibits, but this time he had acted of his own volition. The park director at the time, Ramón Víctor Pablo Elías, gave full support to the rangers' actions, but also emphasized that it was a symptom of the larger problem of settlers living inside the protected area. He advocated removing the settlers to Puerto Iguazú to solve the problem of encounters between domestic animals and predators. To proponents of species conservation such as Correa Luna, the killing of the jaguar by a park ranger illustrated the contradiction between the park missions of protecting nature and colonizing the border. As Correa Luna saw it, the presence of settlers living in the park, the vast majority of them workers employed in services related to the park's tourism infrastructure, threatened the local fauna. Park administrators started viewing settlers as intruders and jaguars as the rightful dwellers of the park.[85]

A decision was made to relocate settlers from the falls area to Puerto Iguazú. The park administrator designated lots for settlers in tract 43, which had been created in 1950 to receive workers squatting vacant lots elsewhere in the town (see Map 3.1). The park director, Elías, was critical of the new location in Puerto Iguazú, arguing it was a marshy terrain prone to flooding. Drainage works were not feasible due to excessive projected costs, which, Elías reasoned, made the area unsuitable for development. The response of Juan F. Carrevedo, subdirector of Parks and Reservations, attests to the change in priorities within the national park agency. Carrevedo contended that the new location had similar characteristics to the Villa Tacuara – a shantytown – which proved settlers from the protected area of the park could be relocated to the chosen location. He candidly explained that relocating working-class dwellers to "places that were the most unsuitable from a residential perspective" was indeed common practice in other areas of Argentina, such as Buenos Aires.[86]

Park Director Elías accepted the decision from Buenos Aires but insisted on granting those settlers "whose activities forced [them] to live in the Waterfalls Zone" temporary permits allowing them to remain in the area. Among these were school and hotel janitors, police officers – there was a police post by the falls – and those working at the airstrip. However, these comprised only a fraction of the people living in the area of strict protection, and they would be forced to get rid of their domestic animals. Unquestionably Elías wanted the removal to cause as little disruption as

[85] Protección de la Naturaleza to Dirección de Parques Nacionales, "Nota 119-Sol /instrucción sumarias con motivo de versiones, de haber matado un jaguar y dado muerte a otro en Par. Nac. Iguazú," Expediente 2026, year 1962, 1–5, APN.
[86] Ibid.

TABLE 3.2 *Residents in Iguazú National Park, inside the protected area, 1958–62*

Year	Residents
1958	354
1959	259
1960	354
1961	365
1962	240

Sources: Protección de la Naturaleza to Dirección de Parques Nacionales, "Nota 119-Sol/instrucción sumarias con motivo de versiones, de haber matado un jaguar y dado muerte a otro en Par. Nac. Iguazú," Expediente 2026, year 1962, 67, APN

possible to the services provided by settler labor inside the park.[87] In November 1962, resolution 444 enacted by the national park agency stipulated the "eradication" of most settlers from the protected areas of the park. Once they left, the park would be "destined exclusively to the free life of fauna, without the interference created by permanent dwellings."[88]

In February 1966, a few months before the coup that brought General Juan Carlos Onganía to power, Iguazú National Park's administration initiated the eviction of two dozen households located in Villa Cataratas, near the falls. The prospect of removal and the issues it generated laid bare the ground upon which the relationship between park and settlers was based. One of the issues park dwellers faced with removal was a longer commute for children studying in the park school. A few families decided to leave only after the end of the school year. Money was another problem, as settlers would have to purchase the lots in the new location in Puerto Iguazú. On average, the settlers at the Villa Cataratas had lived in the park for seventeen years, a period during which they had not had to pay occupation fees. Indeed, many settlers had been orally granted permission by previous park directors to live near their jobs in the park. Others had arrived in the area for temporary jobs and overstayed their contracts. People living in the park were tied, in one way or another, to the economy developed around visitation to the falls, and because of their

[87] Ibid., 67–76. [88] Ibid.

dependence on the park and their status as temporary dwellers, most settlers chose to accept removal.[89]

By 1970, Iguazú National Park had relocated most settlers from around the falls, but a few households remained in the park's protected area, including Miguel Benítez, a seventy-three-year-old fisherman who was too old to move to Puerto Iguazú. Benítez was one the settlers who had arrived in the area before the park's creation in 1934. The old fisherman had been living in the area since 1920, before the construction of the hotel, and had provided it with fish while his wife worked as a washerwoman. In 1972, the national park authorities obtained an eviction order for the last six inhabitants of the Villa Cataratas, including Benítez, which resulted in their removal from the park. The only settler left was Juan Hoppe living near the old airstrip, who consciously opted for resisting removal until being kidnapped by security forces in 1978 and evicted by the park administration in 1979 at the height of the Argentine Dirty War.[90]

The forced removal of Hoppe brought to a close a period of profound changes for Iguazú National Park. Beginning in 1962, successive redrawing of park boundaries redefined the park's mission in consonance with the new consensus on species and environment protection, steering it away from the original concern with borderland occupation. The change in priorities relied on the exclusion from park territory of a 3,000-person town, Puerto Iguazú, which had been created entirely by the national park agency. It also led to the adoption of stringent controls on the uses of the landscape within the park's protected section, especially at the falls area, where most visitors concentrated.

The history of settlers in Iguazú encapsulates the changes in Argentine national park policy after Perón. Arriving in the area in the 1940s and 1950s, settlers benefited from a policy of borderland occupation through national park development. Whereas most acquired or squatted land in the town of Puerto Iguazú, a few others seized the opportunity to settle inside the protected area near Iguazu Falls. As the 1960s came to a close, the context that allowed the establishment of settlers in Iguazú eventually changed with the consolidation of a new international park paradigm. The presence of settlements became anathema to the protection of plant

---

[89] Intendencia Iguazú to Dirección General de Parques Nacionales, Expediente 6174, year 1966, APN.
[90] Zenon Miño to Dirección General de Parques Nacionales, Expediente 6195, year 1967, APN.

and animal species, leading Argentina's national park agency to eliminate settlements from protected areas. On top of this, national, regional, and local processes all converged to make the presence of settlers inside Iguazú unacceptable.

Between the 1940s and the 1970s, Argentina faced political turmoil and many institutional ruptures (1955, 1962, 1966, and 1976). And yet, this overall pattern of instability was never crucial in defining the type of territorial policies carried out at Iguazú, for much of the park's policy maintained a consistency unaffected by political upheaval. Change happened, to be sure, but it followed the national park agency's own pace, influenced by both domestic and international discussions on the nature of conservation policies, and evolving from an attempt to combine settlement and conservation to a later option for the latter at the expense of the former. The history of Iguazú National Park also casts light on the increasing ability of the Argentine state to intervene at the border, as shown in its employment of territorial strategies to control the behavior of people and access to land and resources at the park. There were limitations to this power, demonstrated by the park's failure, in Puerto Iguazú, to implement the type of model town envisioned by its experts in the 1950s. But when the model of a park without people finally prevailed in the 1960s, the national park agency was able to successfully recreate the space of the park according to the new paradigm.

In the end, the removal of Puerto Iguazú and of settlers from within the national park boundaries foreshadowed the defining characteristics of present-day Iguazú National Park: A territory that bans individual settlements but accepts corporate ones in the form of big business hotel and touristic service operators. Likewise, across the border in Brazil, present-day Iguaçu National Park shares characteristics similar to those of its Argentine counterpart: The absence of individual settlers; the presence of large economic conglomerates operating its hotels and touristic services; and the enforcement, by the local national park agency, of strict control over most of its protected area. Much like the Argentine park, Iguaçu also underwent a pattern of settler occupation and displacement whose evolution reflects the entanglement of the local, regional, national, and international processes at play in national park implementation and border occupation. Still, despite similarities and transboundary connections, the Brazilian park offers a radically different example of border occupation through national parks. Thus, the contrast between the two divergent but interconnected paths of national park implementation opens a window from which one can obtain a better view of two polities subjected to concomitant international and regional pressures. Having analyzed the case of the national park in Argentina, we will now steer our focus to the history of land occupation and settler removal in Brazil's Iguaçu National Park.

4

Land Conflict

Brazil, 1944–1982

In the two decades after they were first gazetted, Iguaçu National Park in Brazil and Iguazú National Park in Argentina existed in isolation from each other. They shared Iguazu Falls and were separated only by the Iguazu River, but it was as if a vast ocean divided the administration of the two parks. Neither side's officials were ever willing to cross the border for a formal meeting to discuss shared issues. Geopolitics had informed the creation of the two parks, and the view of Iguaçu and Iguazú as tools for border nationalization implicitly precluded transboundary collaboration. Hunters and animals, however, did not observe the border, which made conservation a clearly binational issue, and fauna protection soon became a priority for park administrators. Agricultural engineer Juan Daciuk of the Argentine national park agency's nature protection office took the first step to end the estrangement on June 27, 1962, when he went to Brazil to meet with Mário Pimentel de Camargo, the director of Iguaçu, to discuss the joint management of the two parks. Shocking as it may seem, this was the first formal conversation between officials of the two national parks since the parks' establishment in the 1930s. On the surface, Daciuk's visit to the Brazilian park was inspired by conservationist goals and the "need to establish international norms to unify action toward the comprehensive protection of nature."[1] To the Argentine conservationists,

---

[1] Indeed, this was the title of a rejected paper sent by Daciuk and Alberto F. Anziano to the First World Congress of National Parks, which was being held in Seattle that same month. Juan Daciuk to Dirección General de Parques Nacionales, "Expone conveniencia de que se tramite un pedido a autoridades del Brasil, a fin de lograr desalojo de intrusos en un vasto sector del Par. Nac. País vecino a nuestro Parq. Nacional Iguazú," Expediente 2624, year 1962, APN-B; US National Park Service, *First World Conference on National Parks.*

administrators on both sides should conceive of the parks as a single "biogeographical unit," a geographical and biological continuum separated only by a river. Managerial integration was a desirable goal.[2]

Daciuk's trip to Brazil also had a further motivation related in part to geopolitical concerns. The Argentine national park officer intended to ask his colleagues across the river about the presence of settlers living on the Brazilian bank of the Iguazu. In the early 1960s, Argentine park officials were accusing Brazilian settlers of continually crossing the river to hunt in the Argentine national park. Daciuk and his colleagues believed it was in the interest of the Argentine national park agency to reach an agreement with Brazil regarding the "extension of the southern limit of Iguaçu National Park [in Brazil] to the shores of the Iguazu River, thus closing an enormous gap [in the Brazilian protected area]." During his stay in Brazil, Daciuk learned from Camargo that, in reality, the southern boundaries of the Brazilian park already reached the shores of the Iguazu, and that the few dozen families living in the area were, in fact, "squatters" who had entered the park after its creation in 1939 (see Map 4.1).[3]

For years, national park administrators in Brazil had demanded that the Brazilian Forest Service office remove these settlers – Camargo himself made this request twice at the beginning of 1962 – but the agency had yet to show any sign of carrying out the eviction. Camargo saw in Argentine discontent with hunters from across the river an opportunity to frame the settlements inside the Brazilian park as an international issue affecting both countries. He asked Daciuk to have the Argentine national park agency intervene. A few weeks later, the agency, through the Argentine Foreign Ministry, requested that the Brazilian government remove the settlers from Iguaçu National Park because of their involvement in transboundary poaching in Argentina. The Brazilian Foreign Ministry confirmed that the country was eager to collaborate, and park officials in Iguazú noticed a subsequent decrease in the cases of hunting along the

---

[2] The visit was a testament to the greater influence gained by Argentine conservationists inside the Argentine national park agency in the 1960s. Juan Daciuk to Dirección General de Parques Nacionales, "Expone conveniencia de que se tramite un pedido a autoridades del Brasil, a fin de lograr desalojo de intrusos en un vasto sector del Par. Nac. País vecino a nuestro Parq. Nacional Iguazú," Expediente 2624, year 1962, APN-B.

[3] Juan Daciuk to Dirección General de Parques Nacionales, ". . . III Viaje de interiorización al Parque Nac. do Iguassu, de la Rep. de Brasil . . . " Expediente 2372, year 1962, APN-B; Juan Daciuk to Dirección General de Parques Nacionales, "Expone conveniencia de que se tramite un pedido a autoridades del Brasil, a fin de lograr desalojo de intrusos en un vasto sector del Par. Nac. País vecino a nuestro Parq. Nacional Iguazú," Expediente 2624, year 1962, APN-B.

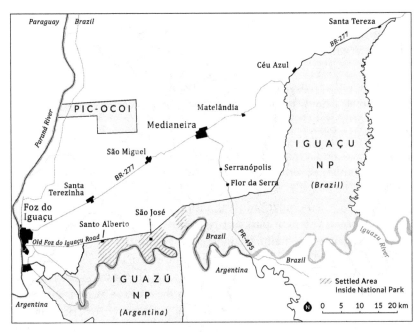

MAP 4.1 Iguaçu National Park, Paraná, Brazil, c. 1970. Map by Frederico Freitas

international border in 1963.[4] But the Brazilian actions were temporary and limited to repressing transboundary poaching; settlers remained living inside Iguaçu National Park. Argentine park officials would have to wait a decade before Brazilian authorities addressed the root of the problem.

It was only in the 1970s that Brazil acted to remove the hundreds of families living inside Iguaçu National Park. Similar to the park in Argentina, most settlers in Iguaçu entered the park after its creation in 1939. The first families arrived in the 1950s, but the bulk of farmers moved into the area in the 1960s. Inside the Brazilian park, settlers started farms and founded two villages, Santo Alberto and São José. By 1980, they were all gone: The Brazilian government had evicted around 2,500

---

[4] Juan Daciuk to Dirección General de Parques Nacionales, "Expone conveniencia de que se tramite un pedido a autoridades del Brasil, a fin de lograr desalojo de intrusos en un vasto sector del Par. Nac. País vecino a nuestro Parq. Nacional Iguazú," Expediente 2624, year 1962, APN-B; Parque Nacional do Iguaçu to Presidência da Comissão Especial da Faixa de Fronteiras, 1959, Comissão Especial da Faixa de Fronteiras, Conselho de Segurança Nacional – Presidência da CEFF, Lata 252, Pasta 2, 1951, 1955, 1957, 1959–61, AN-RJ.

people from Iguaçu National Park, razed their houses and other facilities, and let the forest encroach on their fields. The mass removal of settlers from a national park was a novelty in Brazilian environmental policy. Before 1970, the federal government had removed only a handful of dwellers in other national parks, and problems of land-grabbing, overlapping claims of land ownership, and lack of enforcement were still the norm in protected areas.

In Brazil, this was all true for Iguaçu National Park, and yet no other park in the 1970s presented such a challenge for regularization owing to the high number of settlers involved – in the end, about 450 families were removed. The Brazilian state engaged in the arduous process of evicting and resettling the population living inside Iguaçu, a policy rarely reproduced in other Brazilian parks at the time.[5] Why did Brazil choose to enforce its territorial mandate in Iguaçu National Park? For one, the removal followed, in many ways, the same international trend toward the standardization of protected areas that led Argentina to evict settlers and separate urban areas from its parks in the late 1960s. Moreover, the pressure to comply with an international consensus of parks without people also came directly from Argentina, whose officials continued to

---

[5] Iguaçu was unique, for the population living in the park was comprised mostly of white Brazilians who had arrived in the area years after it had been gazetted. This was not the case for the national parks and forest reserves created on the northern frontiers of Brazil between 1959 and 1961, as many harbored large indigenous populations. Some scholars argue they were deliberately designed to include native peoples to lend "authenticity" to the natural landscape. With the shift toward a strict model of parks without people in the 1970s, policymakers decided to nominally convert these areas into indigenous reservations, avoiding the cost of evicting the populations. Among the parks and forest reserves later converted into indigenous lands are Tumucumaque Forest Reserve, recreated as an indigenous reservation in 1968; Araguaia National Park, with two-thirds of its territory converted into indigenous lands in 1971; and Xingu National Park, reclassified as an indigenous reservation in 1978. See Henyo Trindade Barreto Filho, "Notas para uma história social das áreas de proteção integral no Brasil," in *Terras indígenas & unidades de conservação da natureza: O desafio das sobreposições*, ed. Fany Ricardo (São Paulo: Instituto Socioambiental, 2004), 57; José Luiz de Andrade Franco and José Augusto Drummond, "Nature Protection: The FBCN and Conservation Initiatives in Brazil, 1958–1992," *Historia ambiental latinoamericana y caribeña* 2, no. 2 (2013): 343; Gary B. Wetterberg and Maria Tereza Jorge Pádua, "Preservação da natureza na Amazônia Brasileira, situação em 1978," Technical Series (Brasília: UNDP/FAO/IBDF, 1978), 1; Instituto Brasileiro de Desenvolvimento Florestal, "Plano de ação" (Brasília: Ministério da Agricultura, 1975), 9; Brazil, Decrees 51024 to 51030, and 51042 to 51043, July 25, 1961; Brazil, Decree 50455, April 14, 1961; Brazil, Law 4771, "Novo código florestal," September 15, 1965; Brazil, Decree 62998, July 16, 1968; Brazil, Decree 68873, July 5, 1971; Brazil, Decree 71879, March 1, 1973; Brazil, Decree 82263, September 13, 1978.

complain about the transboundary poaching of hunters allegedly living in the Brazilian park. Still, the Brazilian state not only failed to remove settlers from Iguaçu after repeated Argentine requests but also proved incapable of preventing new families from settling inside Iguaçu. Only after 1970 did the Brazilian government manage to pour resources into and solve the problem of settlers living in the national park. What was behind the country's failure to enforce its national park regulations in the 1950s and 1960s? Why did the removal finally succeed in the 1970s?

To understand Brazil's failure to deal with the population living in Iguaçu before the 1970s, it is necessary to take into account the country's initial lack of tools of territorial intervention. Throughout the twentieth century, the states, not the federal government, controlled most public land in Brazil. There were a few instances where the federal government disputed such control, which was the case in the western half of the state of Paraná. In that area, a legal conflict pitting the federal and state governments against each other over ownership of public land set the stage for fraudulent land titling and the occupation of Iguaçu National Park by migrants from other Brazilian states. A weak federal mandate on public land was one of the problems that plagued the implementation of protected areas in Brazil. Another problem was the lack of a robust national park agency. Historically the agencies in charge of the national parks in Brazil lacked institutional support, funding, and focus on protected areas.

The lack of a dedicated national park agency and a well-regulated federal system for managing public land prevented park officials in Brazil from transforming the country's protected areas into what they had long desired – natural spaces devoid of inhabitants. The removal of settlers would have to wait for the development of a different set of tools: ones devised to deal with the problem of land tenure in Brazil at large, including new land legislation and an empowered agrarian reform agency. It was at the height of the Brazilian military dictatorship (1964–85) in the early 1970s that the infrastructure, funding, and mindset created by the military to control the countryside and solve the land problem were applied to the issue of residents inside the national park. The existence of settlers in Iguaçu provided the military regime with an opportunity to employ its newly developed land reform apparatus.

This chapter shows how, in the absence of a reliable national park agency and legislation, the Brazilian government utilized its newly minted agrarian reform provisions, the 1964 Land Statute, to relocate settlers from Iguaçu National Park to a nearby colonization project.[6] It was a conflictive process that generated the resistance of local politicians, left-wing militants, and the settlers themselves to the federal government's decision to enforce territorial control over Iguaçu. Similar to the eviction of settlers in Argentina, the process was carried out by a military regime. A significant difference, however, lies in the fact that western Paraná, where the Brazilian park is located, is a region with a long history of violent agrarian conflict. As a result, Brazilian authorities framed the removal of settlers from Iguaçu as a matter of national security in a way that Argentine authorities, for the most part, did not, despite the arrest and torture of Iguazú's last settler, Juan Hoppe. All in all, the case of Iguaçu National Park in the 1970s offers a clear example of an authoritarian state employing heavy-handed methods designed for territorial pacification and frontier development to realize a paradigm of unpopulated national parks.

GRILAGEM AT THE BRAZILIAN BORDERLAND

Like many other national parks in Latin America, Iguaçu presented a problem of uncertainty of land rights, and the occupation of the park demonstrates how weak control over public land can undermine a central government's conservation mandate. *Grilagem*, the appropriation of public land through forged property titles, is a recurrent phenomenon in Brazilian history and the source of many of the country's agrarian problems. In Iguaçu, shady land agents took advantage of a dispute between federal and state government over the ownership of the park's public land to forge land titles and sell parcels to incoming settlers.[7] The dispute originated in the way government officials expanded the park in the 1940s. As seen in Chapter 2, the Brazilian government established Iguaçu National Park in 1939 on lands ceded by the government of the

---

[6] As detailed in this chapter, Iguaçu complicates traditional narratives of green grabbing: its evicted dwellers, for the most part, avoided proletarization. The top-down agrarian reform tools employed by the military regime in Brazil guaranteed their access to new plots of land as part of the process of removal from the park. On the concept of green grabbing, see Fairhead, Leach, and Scoones, "Green Grabbing."

[7] In Brazil, disputes between states and the central government over control of public land have been at the center of many cases of *grilagem*. Uncertainty of public land ownership allowed claim jumpers, many times in cahoots with state government, to use fraud and violence to displace other claimants and privatize public land. Seth Garfield highlighted this phenomenon in his discussion of indigenous land encroachment in Mato Grosso in the 1950s. See Garfield, *Indigenous Struggle*, 89–102.

state of Paraná and located on the Brazilian banks of Iguazu Falls. From 1939 to 1944, the park was restricted to the 5,000-hectare area ceded by the state government, but in 1944 the federal government decided to incorporate new land into the park, expanding the park to thirty times its original size. The land used in the expansion had been granted by the Empire of Brazil to a railroad company in 1889 as part of a concession for the building of new east–west rail lines in southern Brazil. The railroads were never built, but the inheritor company, Companhia Estrada de Ferro São Paulo-Rio Grande (CEFSPRG), kept the lands until the company was nationalized by the regime of Getúlio Vargas in 1940. With the expropriation of the railroad company, officials at the National Park Section of the Brazilian Forest Service seized the opportunity to use a few of the renationalized land tracts to expand the park area and protect the groves of Paraná pine (*Araucaria angustifolia*) located in the hills adjacent to the park. Both Octavio Silveira Mello, head of the National Park Section, and Mário Câmara Canto, the first director of Iguaçu National Park, saw the incorporation of the new public lands into the park as a way of expanding its territory without incurring the expense of compensating previous owners for the value of the land.

Contrary to Canto and Mello's plans, adding these new lands to the park proved to be a convoluted and protracted process. The land tracts incorporated into the park by federal decree in 1944 had already been claimed by the state of Paraná, which had demarcated and transferred the lands to CEFSPRG in the 1920s. As the east–west rail lines were never built and the inheritor company had been nationalized, the land grants were set to return to public domain. However, nationalization generated disputes over which level of the government was the legitimate owner of the land. State officials believed the railroad land grants had originated in lands owned by the state of Paraná, as after the Republican Constitution of 1891, all public land passed from the hands of the central government to the states' control. The federal government, on the other hand, claimed that the original contract granting the lands to the railroad companies had been signed before the transfer of the country's public lands to the states in 1891, which meant they were part of the nationalized assets to be assimilated by the federal government in 1940.[8]

---

[8] Brazil, Decree 10432, November 9, 1889; Brazil, Decree 305, April 7, 1890; Brazil, Decree 920, October 24, 1890; Brazil, Decree 397, June 20, 1891; Brazil, Decree 968, August 1, 1892; Brazil, Decree 1386, May 6, 1893; Cecília Maria Westphalen, Brasil Pinheiro Machado, and Altiva Pilatti Balhana, "Nota prévia ao estudo da ocupação de terra no

After the fall of Getúlio Vargas in 1945, a legal dispute over the ownership of the railroad land put the government of the state of Paraná, where the park was located, in conflict with the Brazilian federal government.[9] The tracts in question included not only the area used to expand Iguaçu National Park but also much of the land in the western half of the state. These were areas covered by forests, soon to be rife with *grilagem* and agrarian conflict as settlers moved from other parts of Brazil in the 1950s. In western Paraná, the federal government would consistently fail to impose a territorial order owing to the behind-the-scenes maneuvering of local politicians, colonization companies, and local land notaries.[10] The matter of the ownership of the railroad land was legally settled with a 1963 Brazilian Supreme Court ruling in favor of the federal government. However, uncertainty about public land tenure persisted into the late 1960s and created the conditions for the systematic *grilagem* that characterized the region of Iguaçu National Park.[11]

The 1950s political class in the state of Paraná was steeped in land speculation and *grilagem*, influencing the state government to illegally title

Paraná moderno," *Boletim da Universidade Federal do Paraná – Departamento de História* 7 (1968); Antonio Marcos Myskiw, "Colonos, posseiros e grileiros: Conflitos de terra no oeste paranaense (1961/66)" (MA thesis, Fluminense Federal University, 2002), 148–55; Rubem Murilo Leão Rêgo, "Terra de violência: Estudo sobre a luta pela terra no sudoeste do Paraná" (MA thesis, University of São Paulo, 1979), 90–95, UFRRJ; Wachowicz, *Paraná, sudoeste*, 140–48, 177–81; Joe Foweraker, "Political Conflict on the Frontier: A Case Study of the Land Problem in the West of Paraná, Brazil" (PhD diss., University of Oxford, 1974), 103–5.

[9] A detailed study of the history of the public land used in the expansion of Iguaçu National Park can be found in Frederico Freitas, "Terras públicas e política de conservação da natureza: O caos fundiário na formação do Parque Nacional do Iguaçu," in *História ambiental 3: Natureza, sociedade, fronteiras*, ed. José Luiz de Andrade Franco, et al. (Rio de Janeiro: Garamond, 2020).

[10] In Brazil, land registry is performed by private agents, the *tabeliões*, who are empowered by public authorities to perform notarial activities.

[11] Supremo Tribunal Federal, Acórdão Apelação Cível 9621/63: Reconhece como Patrimônio da União imóveis da Cia. Estrada de Ferro SP-RS e Cia. Brasileira de Viação e Comércio (BRAVIACO) (Brazilian Supreme Court June 11, 1963), accessed on June 14, 2019 at www.direito.mppr.mp.br/arquivos/File/stfacordaobraviaco.pdf; Antonio Cordeiro de Jesus Espólio e outro v. INCRA, TRF-4 – APELAÇÃO CIVEL: AC 17258 PR 2004.04.01.017258-5, accessed on March 21, 2014 at http://trf-4.jusbrasil.com.br/jurisprudencia/8879247/apelacao-civel-ac-17258-pr-20040401017258-5-trf4; Leandro de Araújo Crestani and Erneldo Schallenberger, "Nas Fronteiras do Oeste do Paraná: Conflitos Agrários e Mercado de Terras (1843/1960)," *Revista Trilhas da História* 2, no. 4 (2012): 100–05; Joe Foweraker, "Political Conflict on the Frontier," 8–14, 114–18, 120–33; INCRA, *Livro Branco da Grilagem de Terras* (Brasília: INCRA, 2012), 17–19; Emílio Stachowski (INCRA Official) in discussion with the author, October 2013.

public land to cronies in the local business class.[12] Many, encouraged by the state government's reckless behavior, sold land parcels as if they were twice or three times their actual size to absentee speculators from São Paulo or Curitiba. The state government and local land notaries conveniently ignored the fact that many parcels already had titles. Claim jumpers in cahoots with corrupt government officials stacked fraudulent deeds like a house of cards. Land surveys made by the local department of land and colonization were purposely dubious, and many tracts were renamed in attempts to confound buyers and prevent future legal actions.[13]

All this *grilagem* provided land for the many migrants arriving in the region. They brought a small amount of capital and acquired parcels from land speculators or colonization companies deeply involved in the practice. Beginning in the late 1940s, western Paraná became a prime destination for German– and Italian–Brazilian settlers coming from the southern states of Santa Catarina and Rio Grande do Sul. In the 1950s, the opening of a new federal highway connecting Foz do Iguaçu to Curitiba, the BR-277, opened a previously isolated frontier to thousands of settlers in search of cheap and accessible land. Between 1950 and 1970, the population of western Paraná increased from about 16,000 to over 698,000 people.[14] In Brazil, settlers displaced the Guarani and mixed-raced population living on the border. Their arrival also radically affected the landscape of the borderland, which outside the Iguaçu National Park, was converted from forests into farmland. I discuss the environmental transformation unleashed by such a massive migration to the borderland

---

[12] A similar process was happening in the neighboring state of São Paulo, where governors such as Adhemar de Barros turned a blind eye to squatting on state public lands and the depletion of forest reserves in the western portion of the state. See Dean, *With Broadax and Firebrand*, 277–82.

[13] Joe Foweraker, "Political Conflict on the Frontier," 8–14, 116–18, 132–33; Myskiw, "Colonos, posseiros e grileiros;" Jefferson de Oliveira Salles, "A relação entre o poder estatal e as estratégias de formação de um grupo empresarial paranaense na década de 1940–1950: O caso do Grupo Lupion," in *A construção do Paraná moderno: Políticos e política no governo do Paraná de 1930 a 1980*, ed. Ricardo Costa de Oliveira (Curitiba, Paraná: Secretaria da Ciência, Tecnologia e Ensino Superior; Imprensa Oficial do Paraná, 2004); Processo n° 87.10.11573–0 – Ação de desapropriação/INCRA vs. Colonos do PNI, JFP-F.

[14] The arrival of hundreds of thousands of internal migrants profoundly changed the Brazilian side of the Triple Frontier. It was not mirrored by internal migratory movements at the same scale in Argentina (or Paraguay), despite all the efforts of the Argentine government to lure settlers to its side of the border, as documented in previous chapters. Population numbers for western Paraná compiled from census data from the Brazilian Institute of Geography and Statistics (IBGE). See Table 6.2 in Chapter 6.

in Chapters 5 and 6. In the present chapter, I focus on the overlapping territories of private and public land in a context of precarious enforcement of property rights.

For settlers arriving in western Paraná, the possession of a deed was not a guarantee of land ownership, as a piece of land could be claimed by other deeds. Land speculators would use competing deeds to justify evicting settlers with an army of henchmen before reselling the land to the next settler. In many cases, land agents and colonization companies employed extreme violence, making use of arson, beatings, rape, and murder against settlers who refused to recognize bogus claims to the land they had acquired in the region.[15] Inside Iguaçu, land agents thrived on similar legal uncertainty, selling public park land to migrants from Santa Catarina and Rio Grande do Sul in the 1960s. Much like elsewhere in western Paraná, inside the park, land was sold by individuals who knew how to navigate the complexities of local land bureaucracy and take advantage of the federal government's inability to enforce its claims over the area of the national park.[16]

FROM COMPROMISE TO INFLEXIBILITY

In Iguaçu, park administrators and state officials were not oblivious to the parceling and selling of what they deemed national park land. In 1949, Mário Câmara Canto recognized that the park expansion he had

---

[15] On violence on the Brazilian frontier, see Otávio Guilherme Velho, *Capitalismo autoritário e campesinato: Um estudo comparativo a partir da fronteira em movimento* (São Paulo: DIFEL, 1979); José de Souza Martins, *Fronteira: A degradação do outro nos confins do humano*, 2nd ed. (São Paulo: Editora Contexto, 2009).

[16] Processo n° 87.10.11573–0 – Ação de desapropriação/INCRA vs. Colonos do PNI – Pastas 12 and 13 (1987), JFP-F; Emílio Stachowski, INCRA, Memos OFÍCIO/AGU/PGF/PF-PR/NAGRA/59/2008, OFÍCIO/AGU/PGF/PF-PR/NAGRA/100/2008, November 20, 2008, and deeds for the Iguaçu National Park estates 1930, 1958, 1973, 1974, 1979, 1996, Fundo PIC-OCOI files, INCRA-Cascavel; Gaspar Peixoto Costa, "Relatório apresentado à Comissão Especial do Estudo da Faixa de Fronteiras do Paraná e Santa Catarina, pelo General Gaspar Peixoto Costa, diretor do DGTC, na qualidade de representante do Estado do Paraná, junto ao IBRA," Curitiba, 1966, AIPOPEC; Arnaldo Carlos Muller, "História cronológica do Parque Nacional do Iguaçu," Western and Southwestern Paraná, May 1998, AIPOPEC; "Anexo 6 – Histórico da região do parque," Fundo Parque Nacional do Iguaçu, ICMBio; Alvaro Loureiro Martins, "Levantamento do Parque Nacional do Iguaçu," IBRA, Cascavel (Paraná), August 9, 1968, Fundo Parque Nacional do Iguaçu, ICMBio; Adilson Simão (Iguaçu National Park director, 1974–86) in discussion with the author, October 2013; Lara Luciana Leal Seixas, "Memória dos desapropriados do Parque Nacional do Iguaçu: As fronteiras do cotidiano em terras (i)legais?" (MA thesis, State University of Western Paraná, 2012), 81.

proposed five years earlier would be harder to accomplish than previously thought. Land speculators in cahoots with state and municipal officials were already illegally transferring lots in the expanded area of the park to third parties. The land was, after all, still under dispute in a court battle between the federal and state governments. Canto requested that the Forest Service create a committee to initiate the expropriation of these private parcels for "public utility," the Brazilian equivalent to US eminent domain. In 1952, a year before the opening of Highway BR-277 connecting Foz do Iguaçu to the state capital Curitiba, the Forest Service conducted a survey and confirmed that settlers were acquiring land inside the park. Between 1953 and 1954, a series of telegrams and memoranda from park directors to the Forest Service insisted on the need for "titling" or "expropriating" the land in the expanded area of the park. Federal officials understood it would be easier to expropriate lots that had already been titled by private parties than to revert their fraudulent titling in court. In 1955, for the first time the federal government green-lighted the expropriation of the land tracts used for the 1944 park expansion. However, Forest Service officials lost track of the expropriation ordinance somewhere between the Office of Federal Assets and the Office of Public Works of the Ministry of Agriculture in Rio de Janeiro.[17]

The park administration in Foz do Iguaçu insisted on the urgency of the matter as the state government turned a blind eye to the titling of public land in the region based on an interpretation of the federal legislation that put national park lands under state control. The legal stalemate between state and federal government over CEFSPRG land contributed to the lack of action by federal officials, who were waiting for a final ruling on the matter. Still, park officials on the ground continued to witness park land being parceled and developed, and urged the federal government to at least declare the land in question subject to expropriation for public utility, which they hoped would bring legitimacy to national park claims over the area. They argued that it was important to put a stop to the "criminal devastation" occurring in those lands.[18]

By the time Juan Daciuk visited the Brazilian park in 1962, the population inside the expanded area was booming thanks to the constant influx

---

[17] Forest Service, Memo, 1959, Comissão Especial da Faixa de Fronteiras, Conselho de Segurança Nacional – Presidência da CEFF, Lata 252, Pasta 2, 1951/1955/1957/1959–61, AN-RJ; Mário Pimentel de Camargo to Forest Service, September 29, 1961, PNIB-A.
[18] Ibid.

of settlers arriving mainly from Rio Grande do Sul. The director of Iguaçu
National Park at the time, Mário Pimentel de Camargo, warned the Forest
Service that settlers had already established a village, and soon "it would
be too late or costly to remove [them]." The Brazilian government started
seriously tackling the land issue in the park only after the 1963 Supreme
Court ruling that confirmed federal ownership of the public land in the
region. It began with the easiest task: regularizing the uncolonized sections
of the park. The two federal land agencies, the Instituto Nacional de
Desenvolvimento Agrário (National Institute of Agrarian Development,
INDA) and the Instituto Brasileiro de Reforma Agrária (Brazilian Institute
of Agrarian Reform, IBRA), acquired and incorporated large sections of
uninhabited land in the expanded area of the park between 1966 and
1967. Still, it would be three more years until the government started
processing the settled portions of the park in 1970 – a crucial period
during which settlers continued to arrive in the park, increasing the
costs of the eviction considerably.[19]

It is true that Brazilian authorities had not always been convinced that
removal was the best solution for the settlers in Iguaçu. In early 1966, the
Ministry of Agriculture under the new military regime designated a
committee to assess the status of all the Brazilian national parks. The
committee, led by the agricultural engineer Harold Edgard Strang, traveled throughout Brazil to assess the parks' status in loco. This, the first
time officials from the Ministry of Agriculture had visited most national
parks, was part of the military government's larger initiative to organize
and restructure its environmental policy under a single national agency;
a year later, in February 1967, the government created a new environmental agency, the Instituto Brasileiro de Desenvolvimento Florestal
(Brazilian Institute for Forest Development, IBDF), the result of merging
several smaller agencies under the aegis of the Ministry of Agriculture.[20]

---

[19] Mário Pimentel de Camargo, "Relatório anual de 1959"; Mário Pimentel de Camargo,
"Relatório anual de 1962," Iguaçu National Park, December 7, 1962, PNIB-A; Peixoto
Costa, *Relatório apresentado à Comissão Especial do Estudo da Faixa de Fronteiras*,
AIPOPEC; Alvaro Loureiro Martins, "Levantamento do Parque Nacional do Iguaçu."
[20] The Forest Service, which had been reintroduced as an agency within the Ministry of
Agriculture in 1938, lasted until 1962, when it was substituted by the Departamento de
Recursos Naturais Renováveis (Department of Renewable Natural Resources, DRNR).
The creation of the IBDF in 1967 consolidated into a single agency the DRNR and three
other agencies created under Vargas: the Instituto Nacional do Pinho (National Pine
Institute, INP); the Instituto Nacional do Mate (National Yerba Mate Institute, INM);
and the Conselho Federal Florestal (Federal Forest Council, CFF). Brazil, Delegated-Law

FIGURE 4.1 "Routes of the National Park Committee," c.1966. Credit: IBDF and IBRA, *Parques nacionais e reservas equivalentes no Brasil: Relatório com vistas a uma revisão da política nacional nesse campo* (Brasília: Ministry of Agriculture, 1969), 5. IBAMA

The committee's creation in 1966 was in line with the move to regularize land markets in Brazil, one of the core issues for the military officers who took power in 1964. For this reason, the committee's membership also included technicians from IBRA. The committee traveled more than 30,000 kilometers by airplane, automobile, boat, and horse through isolated areas with poor transportation infrastructure (see Figure 4.1).

9, October 11, 1962; Brazil, Decree 52442, October 8, 1963; Brazil Decree-Law 289, February 28, 1967.

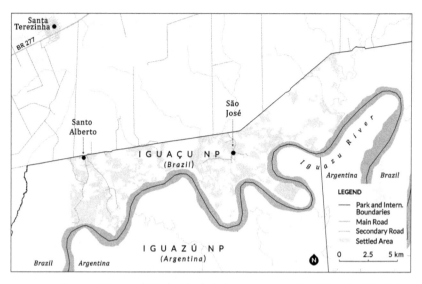

MAP 4.2 Iguaçu National Park, Settled Area c. 1975–80. Map by Frederico Freitas

In Iguaçu National Park the committee did not visit the settled area, but they were informed on the settlements by the park director, René Denizart Pockrandt. Before the committee's arrival, an attempt by Pockrandt to count the number of families living in the park area met with fierce opposition as settlers furiously chased him and his party away from the settled area. Nevertheless, Pockrandt reported to the IBDF on hundreds of families living in the area with farms, crop and grazing fields, houses, and a village complete with a church and a school. Pockrandt made a point of mentioning that many settlers had "deeds for their lands."[21]

Unsurprisingly, he was very pessimistic about the chances of successfully removing the families, which he presented as quite "stubborn and dangerous." Pockrandt believed removal would demand the use of force, probably by the army itself, with IBRA incurring the cost of offering the families new lands in other areas. Based on Pockrandt's assessment, the national park committee suggested in its 1969 report that the park should be sectioned into two parts, with the settled area excluded from the protected territory (see Map 4.2). The government should then build

[21] IBDF and IBRA, *Parques nacionais e reservas equivalentes no Brasil: Relatório com vistas a uma revisão da política nacional nesse campo* (Brasília: Ministry of Agriculture, 1969), IBAMA.

fences isolating the two separate sections of the park from the middle occupied zone, expropriating any remaining parcels within the new park boundaries and providing settlers with legal land titles. The park director believed the IBDF should prioritize the conservation of the old-growth subtropical forest in the eastern section of the national park instead of spending resources on expropriating an area that had already suffered considerable human impact. In spatial terms, this proposed retracing of the boundaries of the Brazilian park was a more radical intervention than removing Puerto Iguazú from the area of the neighboring Argentine park. It not only involved a population scattered across a larger area but also meant splitting the Brazilian park into two unconnected sections.[22]

The committee's reporting on the settlers living in Iguaçu National Park led the Serviço Nacional de Informações (National Information Service, SNI), the Brazilian intelligence agency headquartered in Brasília, to request from its local branch in Curitiba an inquiry on the sale of land inside the protected area. The request accused Antônio Ayres de Aguirra, the land notary in Foz do Iguaçu, of being complicit in the fraudulent registration of land inside the park. According to the report, it was public knowledge in the region that Aguirra had partnered with a land speculator, Tertuliano Nogueira Cabral, who laid claim to and sold vast expanses of land inside the park.[23] A year and a half later the local police officer in charge of the investigation, Captain Wilson de Almeida Garrett, turned in the result of his investigation in the form of an evasive report on Aguirra's and Cabral's activities. Garrett had been "unable to verify" whether the land sold by Aguirra and Cabral was located inside the national park. Yet he confirmed that Cabral claimed parcels in two large public land tracts that bisected the park territory. It is clear that speculators like Cabral bet on federal inaction in titling these lands to profit from their sale. To Cabral, the fact that the federal government "never attempted to expropriate the [park] area" constituted a carte blanche for him to claim and sell public land.[24]

---

[22] IBDF and IBRA, *Parques nacionais*, IBAMA; René Denizart Pockrandt, "Relatório das atividades e problemas do parque," Iguaçu National Park, October 12, 1967, PNIB-A; Parque Nacional do Iguaçu, "Relatório," 1976, PNIB-A.

[23] Serviço Nacional de Informações, "Pedido de busca no. 547/SNI/ACT/67," December 7, 1967, DOPS/PR – Pastas Temáticas – Delegacia de Polícia de Foz do Iguaçu – Número: 0499a, Topografia: 55, Data: 1942–81, APP. On the SNI, see Elio Gaspari, *A ditadura envergonhada* (São Paulo: Companhia das Letras, 2002), 168–71.

[24] Delegacia Regional de Foz do Iguaçu, "Problema de terras," March 14, 1969, DOPS/PR – Pastas Temáticas – Delegacia de Polícia de Foz do Iguaçu – Número: 0499a, Topografia: 55, Data: 1942–81, APP.

Meanwhile, members of the military were increasingly concerned about the land situation in the national park. While visiting the park in 1968, Army General João de Melo Morais stated that for the IBDF and IBRA to reach an agreement, it was crucial to monitor the activity of poachers and, especially, squatters inside the park. He suggested that the IBDF use the resources of the better-funded IBRA to do that. The IBRA had a helicopter at its offices in Cascavel, and Morais committed to personally intervening to coordinate cooperation between the two branches of the Ministry of Agriculture.[25] It seemed that, at last, the presence of settlers had ceased to be merely a local issue concerning park administrators as different branches of the federal government started to acknowledge it as a problem to be resolved. This shift was primarily the result of the changes brought about by the 1964 military coup, which introduced a new preoccupation with land disputes as a possible source of subversive activity.

What the federal government lacked, however, was a consensus on how to deal with the issue. By the end of the decade, experts had split into two camps on addressing the problem of settlers inside the park. On the one hand, the IBRA office for Paraná and Santa Catarina, headed by General Monteiro do Valle, agreed with Pockrandt that the best solution was to leave the settlers where they were and excise the occupied area from the national park territory. On the other hand, the newly appointed minister of agriculture, Luís Fernando Cirne Lima, was confident that completely removing the settlers was the only way of dealing with the issue. The new government of General Emílio Garrastazu Médici appointed Lima minister in October 1969 with the avowed mission of dealing with the land problem in Brazil. In keeping with federal momentum toward colonizing Amazonia, Lima saw the parceling of land in "inhabited" frontier areas as the best way to promote agrarian reform without actually touching the land of large landowners. For this purpose, one of his first measures was to merge the two federal land agencies, IBRA and INDA. The resulting entity, the new Instituto Nacional de Colonização e Reforma Agrária (National Institute for Colonization and Agrarian Reform, INCRA), put the words "colonization" and "agrarian reform" together in its official name. Agrarian reform through colonization was to be the formula applied to solving the problem of settlers inside Iguaçu National Park.[26]

[25] Eugênio Cichoviski, substitute director for Iguaçu National Park, "Report," November 5, 1968, PNIB-A.
[26] Parque Nacional do Iguaçu, "Relatório," 1976, PNIB-A; Ministério da Agricultura, Divisão de Segurança e Informações, "Pedido de busca n° 05/PSI/DSI/MA/75

THE NECESSARY CONDITIONS FOR EVICTION

A meeting between the presidents of the IBDF and INCRA, Newton Isaac da Silva Carneiro and José Francisco de Moura Cavalcanti, and their boss, Agriculture Minister Cirne Lima, decided the fate of the settlers living in Iguaçu: Their land would be confiscated and they would be relocated to another "frontier" area nearby. INCRA and the IBDF signed an agreement to carry out the resettlement plan on August 26, 1970, less than two months after the creation of the new land agency in July of that same year. In its first article, the document states its main goal: To restore the final function of national parks in consonance with the conservation agreements between Brazil and other countries (i.e., Argentina).[27] The agreement between the two agencies empowered the nature protection department within the IBDF, an agency whose goal of protecting nature was still secondary to forestry development.[28] Furthermore, besides the avowed goal of enforcing the IBDF's conservationist mandate, the agreement also offered an opportunity for the newly created INCRA to put its colonization mission into practice.

The resettlement of park dwellers offered a testing ground for two new pieces of legislation introduced during the first years of the military

Desenvolvimento do setor primário – Colonização OCOI – 5.1," February 28, 1975, Pasta 2.6, Fundo Parque Nacional do Iguaçu, ICMBio; Alvaro Loureiro Martins, "Levantamento do Parque Nacional do Iguaçu"; "Luis Fernando Cirne Lima," verbete biográfico, no date, CPDOC; Brazil, Decree-Law 1110, July 9, 1970; "No Congresso decreto-lei que criou INCRA," *Correio braziliense*, July 14, 1970. Another forceful voice against splitting up the park was Maria Tereza Jorge Pádua, the new head of the Department of Research and Nature Conservation within the IBDF. See Foresta, *Amazon Conservation*, 101.

[27] A year earlier, the final manifesto of an international meeting across the border in Iguazú National Park had demanded, among other things, the removal of settlers from the neighboring Brazilian park. Milan Jorge Dimitri to Dirección General de Parques Nacionales, "S/N.° Elev. Inf. Ref. al P. Nac. Iguazú c/ Motivo reciente viaje de estudio e inspección técnica," Expediente 1384, year 1969, APN; INCRA-IBDF agreement, August 26, 1970, Processo n° 87.10.11573–0 – Ação de desapropriação/INCRA vs. Colonos do PNI – Pasta 1 (1973), JFP-F.

[28] The late 1970s witnessed the further growth of the IBDF's conservationist mandate, with the agency becoming more active in fighting deforestation in the Amazon, gazetting dozens of new large national parks, and establishing a nationwide national park system. See Antoine Acker, *Volkswagen in the Amazon: The Tragedy of Global Development in Modern Brazil*, Global and International History (Cambridge, UK: Cambridge University Press, 2017), 130–35; José Augusto Drummond, "From Randomness to Planning: The 1979 Plan for Brazilian National Parks," in *National Parks beyond the Nation: Global Perspectives on "America's Best Idea,"* ed. Adrian Howkins, Jared Orsi, and Mark Fiege (Norman: University of Oklahoma Press, 2016); and Foresta, *Amazon Conservation*.

regime. The first was the 1964 Land Statute – implemented months after the military coup as a preventive measure against land conflicts and the emergence of rural political movements.[29] The second was the new Forest Code of 1965 – a revision of the old 1934 Forest Code passed by Getúlio Vargas.[30] Agitation in the countryside had provided a major justification for the overthrow of former president João Goulart, but after the coup, the military recognized that some form of agrarian reform was still badly needed.[31] The idea that access to land was a problem to be solved by the state was also a tenet of the US-supported Alliance for Progress, which saw agrarian reform as an antidote to the spread of communism in the Latin American countryside. The creation of INCRA offered the Brazilian generals a compromise: a program to solve the land question in Brazil through the colonization of public lands instead of the redistribution of idle, privately owned estates. Sending surplus rural population to frontier areas had already been tried by the Vargas administration, with the government sending northeastern rural laborers to Amazonia, and the new military regime rekindled this idea in the several colonization projects it implemented in the 1970s. The resettlement of farmers from Iguaçu National Park into a nearby forested area on the western Paraná frontier reproduced key features of the broader policy of massive settlement of Amazonia – a pet project of the military in the early 1970s.[32]

[29] Brazil, Law 4504, "Estatuto da terra," November 30, 1964.
[30] Brazil, Law 4771, "Novo código florestal," September 15, 1965.
[31] Mario Grynszpan, "O período Jango e a questão agrária: Luta política e afirmação de novos atores," in *João Goulart: Entre história e memória*, ed. Marieta de Moraes Ferreira (Rio de Janeiro: Fundação Getúlio Vargas, 2006); Lilia Moritz Schwarcz and Heloisa Murgel Starling, *Brasil: Uma biografia* (São Paulo: Companhia das Letras, 2015), 438–39; Marcos Napolitano, *1964: História do regime militar brasileiro* (São Paulo: Contexto, 2017), 75–77.
[32] Brazil, Decree 1106, June 16, 1970; Brazil, Decree-Law 1110, July 9, 1970; Brazil, Law 5727, November 4, 1971; Brazil, *I Plano nacional de desenvolvimento (PND) 1972/74* (Brasília: Imprensa Nacional, 1971); Foresta, *Amazon Conservation*; Otávio Guilherme Velho, *Frentes de expansão e estrutura agrária: Estudo do processo de penetração numa área da Transamazônica* (Rio de Janeiro: Zahar, 1972); Joe Foweraker, *The Struggle for Land: A Political Economy of the Pioneer Frontier in Brazil from 1930 to the Present Day* (Cambridge, UK: Cambridge University Press, 1981), 132–39; Philip M. Fearnside, "Projetos de colonização na Amazônia brasileira: Objetivos conflitantes e capacidade de suporte humano,"*Cadernos de geociências* 2 (1989): 7–25; Charles H. Wood and Marianne Schmink, "The Military and the Environment in the Brazilian Amazon, " *Journal of Political and Military Sociology* 21 (1993): 81–105; María Verónica Secreto, *Soldados da borracha: Trabalhadores entre o sertão e a Amazônia no governo Vargas* (São Paulo: Editora Fundação Perseu Abramo, 2006); Seth Garfield, *In Search of the Amazon: Brazil, the United States, and the Nature of a Region* (Durham: Duke University Press, 2013); Hochstetler and Keck, *Greening Brazil*, 25–30; Rodrigo Asturian and Cássia

In March of the following year, the national press highlighted the eviction of settlers from Iguaçu National Park, denouncing the way the Brazilian national park had been "occupied" and "devastated" by settlers. The story began with a public letter sent to President Emílio Garrastazu Médici and selected newspapers by two high-profile Brazilian conservationists, Johan Dalgas Frisch and Paulo Nogueira Neto – the latter a member of the IUCN's executive board.[33] In the letter, they argued that the IBDF controlled "only three percent of the park," an obvious exaggeration, and that the rest "had been invaded by settlers and farmers," endangering both the "environment and *national security*" (emphasis added). They knew which buttons to push to propel the military into action. Asked for clarification by the Air Force's intelligence service, Frisch painted a dire picture, depicting the park's territory as being completely controlled by farmers who had "built roads, cleared land, and installed mills," all financed by the state-owned Banco do Brasil. He contended that "the federal government had no control whatsoever over that border region," as the hundreds of clandestine farms in the park "allowed the free circulation of people to and from Argentina." During the apex of the repression against armed left-wing groups by the dictatorship, the denunciations of Frisch and Nogueira Neto helped galvanize the military's fear that losing control of the park could allow subversive activities to flourish at the border.[34]

To head up the eviction process, the military appointed one of its own, the retired army colonel Jayme de Paiva Bello, as the new park director in May 1971. Bello was the first military officer to serve as park director since its gazetting in 1939. As the former commander of the army's First Border Battalion in Foz do Iguaçu, Bello knew the region and the land conflicts in the area well, and his main mission was to carry

---

Morgana Faxina, *INCRA Paraná: Quatro décadas de história* (Curitiba: INCRA, 2011); Gerd Kohlhepp, "Tipos de colonização agrária dirigida nas florestas brasileiras: Exemplos históricos," *Fronteiras: Journal of Social, Technological and Environmental Science* 4, no. 3 (2015): 102–21.

[33] In 1974, the Brazilian military would appoint Nogueira Neto head of the newly created Special Secretariat for the Environment (SEMA), a chair he would occupy for twelve years.

[34] "Fazendas ilegais no Parque Iguaçu," *Folha de São Paulo*, March 3, 1971; "Nossa opinião: Parque Nacional do Iguaçu," *Diário do Paraná*, March 4, 1971; "IBDF verá hoje a devastação do parque," *Diário do Paraná*, March 18, 1971; "Assim se devastam as reservas florestais," *Diário do Paraná*, March 19, 1971; Centro de Informações de Segurança da Aeronáutica (CISA), "Parque Nacional do Iguaçu," May 1971, Serviço Nacional de Informações (BR AN BSB VAZ 037 0079), 1971, AN-DF; Andrade Franco and Drummond, "Nature Protection," 338–67; Holdgate, *The Green Web*, 246–47, 253.

out the eviction of settlers from the protected area. He faced his new task with a military disposition, much in the authoritarian spirit of post-AI-5 Brazil, which earned him the hatred of many in Iguaçu. Among settlers, Bello gained a reputation for intolerance by saying, for example, that "German-Brazilians were unfit to settle on the borderlands of Brazil for their lack of commitment with the nation, as demonstrated by the invasion of a national park."[35] German-Brazilians comprised the great majority of the population living in Iguaçu National Park. In his discourse about the settlers, Bello reproduced Vargas-era prejudices against German-Brazilians as forming an untrustworthy fifth column within Brazilian society.[36]

In internal documents, Bello singled out the Ministry of Agriculture's "twenty-seven years of inaction" as the cause of the *grilagem* inside the national park, but in public, he exculpated the federal government from any responsibility for allowing the development of settlements inside the park, blaming the state government and settlers instead. In an interview in 1976, Bello accused the state of Paraná of having promoted illegal colonization in federal lands since the 1960s. To him, the federal government had offered a show of good faith through its decision to expropriate the land and compensate farmers instead of simply nullifying the land titles. The settlers were the ones to blame for their own situation, as "those who bought land inside a national park must have known that they were illegally acquiring federal land. ... [T]hey bet on it and lost, it took a couple of years, but they lost."[37]

---

[35] Seixas, "Memória dos desapropriados do Parque Nacional do Iguaçu," 150; "Paraná: Proibido plantar," *Veja*, July 21, 1976; Adilson Simão (Iguaçu National Park director, 1974–86) in discussion with the author, October 2013.

[36] During the Vargas years, earlier commanders of the First Border Battalion carried out the Estado Novo program of "Brazilianization" of German and Polish settlers in the area. See Luiz Carlos Pereira Tourinho, *Toiro passante: Tempo de República Getuliana*, vol. IV, 5 vols. (Curitiba: Instituto Histórico, Geográfico e Etnográfico Paranaense, 1991), 499–500, 527–33. See also Taís Campelo Lucas, "Cortando as asas do nazismo: A DOPS-RS contra os 'súditos do eixo,'" in *Presos políticos e perseguidos estrangeiros na Era Vargas*, ed. Marly de Almeida Gomes Vianna, Érica Sarmiento da Silva, and Leandro Pereira Gonçalves (Rio de Janeiro: Mauad X/FAPERJ, 2014).

[37] Bello also had conservationist concerns and believed parks were valuable for their environmental services. To him, it was important to preserve stretches of forest to recycle carbon and clean the atmosphere. "They do what our lungs do for our breathing," declared Bello, repeating what was a cliché among Brazilian conservationists in the 1970s and 1980s. He conceded that some level of progress in the form of colonization and agriculture should exist, but averred that on his current path, "man would destroy the renewable resources before they have time to be replenished." In the end, he was convinced of his mission of preserving the national park territory's flora and fauna by

Foreseeing possible acts of resistance, in 1970, the IBDF signed an agreement with the state of Paraná to use the state police in Iguaçu National Park. Before that, it was impossible for the few wardens working in the park to evict settlers. The partnership provided the IBDF and INCRA with the manpower to enforce the new restricting environmental regulations put forward by Bello. The idea was to force settlers into accepting the eviction. Fifty state troopers from the new Polícia Florestal contingent were assigned to patrol the park with cars and boats, a great improvement on the sixteen poorly armed wardens originally employed by the IBDF.[38] Now the Brazilian government had all the elements necessary to carry out the removal of the thousands of settlers living inside Iguaçu: a claim to the land sanctioned by the 1963 Supreme Court ruling; new land and forest legislation as well as new agrarian reform (INCRA) and environmental (IBDF) agencies; the commitment of the military, with the appointment of Bello as head of the park; and manpower to enforce the eviction, in the form of the fifty state police troopers stationed at the park. In the following years, all these different elements would align to promote the complete evacuation of the settlers living inside Iguaçu National Park.

RESETTLING SETTLERS

In 1971, the Brazilian federal government started the process of expropriating the occupied section of Iguaçu National Park. At that time, the area contained hundreds of farms and two villages, Santo Alberto and São José (see Map 4.2). INCRA and IBDF officials informed community leaders that, "due to a decree by the president Emílio Garrastazu Médici," they would have to leave the area, since "the land where they lived had been part of the park since the 1940s." Settlers were astounded: some were unaware their lots comprised land claimed as a national park; others knew about the federal claims but assumed public lands to be fair game for

---

extirpating all "alien" elements from the area, which included interloping plants, animals, and people. "Os inquilinos do parque estão saindo," *Referência em planejamento* 1 (1976): 12–13; Jayme de Paiva Bello, "Parque Nacional do Iguaçu: Informação sobre o Parna," July 2, 1975, PNIB-A.

[38] Although they were called the Forest Police (*Polícia Florestal*), these were regular state police officers (*Polícia Militar do Paraná*) with little training in conservation issues. Instituto Brasileiro de Desenvolvimento Florestal, "Termo de acordo," May 7, 1970, Pasta "Termo de acordo de contrato IBDF com a Secretaria de Agricultura do Estado do Paraná," PNIB-A.

frontier settlement. Government officials justified the eviction through Brazil's "international agreements" with neighboring countries, particularly Argentina – officials at the Argentine Iguazú National Park continued to complain about Brazilians crossing the river to poach in their park (see more in Chapter 5). Launching the expropriation program at the federal level gave the park administration in Iguaçu National Park a reason to harden its stance toward settlers living inside the park area. Bello, the new park director, made it explicit that any further clearing of land inside the park area was now prohibited.[39]

The federal plan was never limited to eviction; it also included resettling farmers and their families into another area. Thus, the relocation of settlers in Iguaçu would closely follow contemporary Brazilian programs aimed to bring landless peasants to frontier areas in the north of the country. In 1971, INCRA began its first Integrated Colonization Projects, known as PICs, in frontier areas in Brazilian Amazonia as part of the ambitious Program of National Integration (PIN) launched by the military in power in Brazil. Down south in western Paraná, INCRA officials followed the same model developed for Amazonia to deal with settlers in Iguaçu. The agency established a "colonization project" for settlers from São José and Santo Alberto on the banks of the Ocoí River, thirty kilometers north of the park (see Map 4.1). INCRA chose to establish the PIC-OCOI (Ocoí Integrated Colonization Project) in a private 12,500-hectare tract that was, along with the national park itself, one of the few large stretches of forested terrain still intact in western Paraná. As a private estate, the area also had to be expropriated by INCRA, which would then parcel the tract into lots, implement the basic infrastructure of roads and electricity, establish agricultural villages, provide technical advice to settlers, and facilitate bank loans. INCRA officials wanted prospective small farmers to switch from staple crops such as corn and beans to soybeans, a more marketable one.[40]

---

[39] Brazil, Decree 69411, October 22, 1971; Brazil, Decree 69412, October 22, 1971; Seixas, "Memória dos desapropriados," 26–27, 127–28; Ministério da Agricultura, Divisão de Segurança e Informações, "Pedido de busca nº 05/PSI/DSI/MA/75 Desenvolvimento do setor primário – Colonização OCOI – 5.1," February 28, 1975, Pasta 2.6, Fundo Parque Nacional do Iguaçu, ICMBio; Eugênio Cichovski to Secretário Geral do IBDF, 299/68, October 15, 1968, Pasta "Parque Nacional do Iguaçu – Informações complementares," PNIB-A; "Colonos no parque," *Diário do Paraná*, July 3, 1971.

[40] The Ocoí estate had been owned by land speculators from Santa Catarina since the early 1950s. The expropriation of the estate was contested in court by its absentee owners, who attempted to increase the value of the compensation paid by INCRA. Graciela Maculan, "A questão agrária na faixa de fronteira: O conflito judicial da fazenda Ocoy" (MA thesis,

The location chosen for the colonization project, a forested "idle" area "empty" of people, was analogous to the type of landscape chosen by INCRA in its colonization efforts far away in Brazil's Amazonian frontier. The idea was to solve the land problem in the Brazilian countryside by relocating people to lightly populated areas where they would produce highly marketable crops for domestic and international markets. Unlike Amazonia, the area selected down south in Paraná was just thirty kilometers away from the place of origin of settlers, the Iguaçu National Park, but it presented similar challenges – it was home to indigenous people and faced competition from looming infrastructure projects.

Since the 1950s, the arrival of settlers from southern Brazil had pushed many Guarani out of western Paraná, including from the area of Iguaçu National Park (which I discuss in Chapter 6). However, there were still some communities scattered across the region. A group of Guarani, for example, lived at the confluence of the Ocoí and Paraná rivers, which created a significant problem for INCRA's plan of using the Ocoí estate to receive white settlers from Iguaçu. Recognizing these individuals as Guarani would trigger the involvement of the Fundação Nacional do Índio (National Indian Foundation, FUNAI), which threatened to delay INCRA's plans of using the estate for the Iguaçu settlers. INCRA, therefore, engaged in a series of tactics to delegitimize and harass the Guarani. In its initial survey, the agency classified the Guarani as squatters and denied they had indigenous heritage. Furthermore, the agency brought in henchmen to harass them, burning their houses and confiscating their fishing and agricultural tools. Many decided to flee to Paraguay or Argentina, but some resisted. Eventually, FUNAI was forced to get involved, and a (tiny) portion of the Ocoí estate was set apart as indigenous lands.[41]

State University of Western Paraná, 2015); Ataliba Ayres de Aguirra, Registro de Imóveis, "Imóvel Ocoi," Fls. 241/242, livro 3-P, Cartório de Registro de Imóveis de Foz do Iguaçu, June, 25, 2008, INCRA-Cascavel; Ministério da Agricultura, Divisão de Segurança e Informações, "Pedido de busca n° 05/PSI/DSI/MA/75 Desenvolvimento do setor primário – Colonização OCOI – 5.1," February 28, 1975, Pasta 2.6, Fundo Parque Nacional do Iguaçu, ICMBio; Brazil, *I plano nacional de desenvolvimento*; Fearnside, "Projetos de colonização na Amazônia brasileira;" Wood and Schmink, "The Military and the Environment;" Kohlhepp, "Tipos de colonização."

[41] I have discussed how the eviction of white Brazilian settlers from the park affected Guarani communities at PIC-OCOI in Frederico Freitas, "The Guarani and the Iguaçu National Park: An Environmental History," *ReVista: Harvard Review of Latin America* 14, no. 3 (2015): 18–22. Further details in Ministério da Agricultura, Divisão de Segurança e Informações, "Pedido de busca n° 05/PSI/DSI/MA/75 Desenvolvimento do setor primário – Colonização OCOI – 5.1," February 28, 1975, Pasta 2.6, Fundo Parque

Another issue was Itaipu Dam, a major hydroelectric plant still in the planning phase in the early 1970s. The dam was planned to be built on the Paraná River by Brazil and Paraguay and it was too distant to directly affect the Iguaçu National Park. However, its planned reservoir threatened to submerge part of the area chosen to receive settlers, kilometers away from the park (see Map 4.1). No one foresaw Itaipu being an issue, not even INCRA technicians, when the agency acquired the Ocoí estate in 1971. By the late 1970s, however, it had become clear for the Iguaçu farmers now settled by INCRA at PIC-OCOI that their new lands would be considerably affected by the gigantic reservoir of the new plant. At this point, they had already left their old lands in the national park and it was too late to reverse course. The looming threat of Itaipu finally became a reality in 1982, when its reservoir started filling, flooding two-thirds of PIC-OCOI and affecting Guarani and white settlers alike.[42]

COUNTING, SURVEYING, COMPENSATING

Back in the early 1970s, INCRA had designed a plan of action for relocating the occupants of the national park that divided settlers into two categories: those who held land titles certified by local land notaries and those without deeds. All small and medium landholders in possession of deeds would receive compensation for their land and improvements and be offered the option of buying a new lot in PIC-OCOI at subsidized prices.[43] INCRA would compensate for settlers' land with agrarian reform bonds, paid annually and fully redeemed in twenty years, and would pay in cash for land improvements – such as houses, barns, fences,

Nacional do Iguaçu, ICMBio; "Desapropriação de Terras no Sul Provoca Clima de Tensão," *Jornal do Brasil* (Rio de Janeiro) January 5, 1976; Carlos Alberto Luppi, "Itaipu acirra disputa por terras em litígio no Oeste do Paraná," *Jornal do Brasil,* January 25, 1976; Aristides de Oliveira Coelho, INCRA, "PIC-OCOI Estate Report," Cascavel, PR: December 1971, and Antônio Vanderli Moreira, "INCRA Queima Casas de Colonos," letter sent to the press, December 11, 1975, both in Dossiê PIC-OCOÍ, 1974–78, INCRA-Curitiba; Edgard de Assis Carvalho and Conselho Indigenista Missionário – Sul, *Avá-Guarani do Ocoí-Jacutingá: Município de Foz do Iguaçu – PR* (Curitiba: Conselho Indigenista Missionário/CIMI Regional Sul, 1981) MI.

[42] Jacob Blanc unearthed the history of displacement of farmers and indigenous people by the Itaipu reservoir, which happens right after the period discussed here. See Jacob Blanc, *Before the Flood: The Itaipu Dam and the Visibility of Rural Brazil* (Durham: Duke University Press, 2019).

[43] Ministério da Agricultura, Divisão de Segurança e Informações, "Pedido de busca n° 05/ PSI/DSI/MA/75 Desenvolvimento do setor primário – Colonização OCOI – 5.1," February 28, 1975, Pasta 2.6, Fundo Parque Nacional do Iguaçu, ICMBio.

and roads – depending on its assessment.[44] Despite the bonds' appreciation, in the short run possessing land titles did not offer settlers much of an advantage, as the land would take twenty years to be fully repaid. Also, farmers would have to restart their lives somewhere else without much capital – the payment for improvements would start only in July 1974. Nevertheless, by choosing to compensate deed-bearing settlers, government officials had accepted the claims to land ownership inside the park despite the questionable origin of most land titles. It was easier and cheaper to recognize the deeds and expropriate all lots by decree than to contest the legality of the claims in court on an individual basis.[45]

Settlers without deeds, however, would not receive any compensation for their land. What they did receive was indemnity for the improvements made on the land they lived on.[46] They were also eligible to buy parcels at the new site at subsidized prices. For squatters or tenants who had never paid for the land, this was a good opportunity to acquire land for cheap in the new location. However, for settlers who had mistakenly paid for land to a third party but failed to provide any notarized land titles – and Iguaçu housed a good number of them – the INCRA policy was terrible news. It meant the loss of the investment made in purchasing the land. This difference in treatment was the source of much discontentment among settlers, as many had acquired land from shady real estate agents who never provided them with deeds, just receipts for the purchase of land. They saw the federal government's refusal to recognize settlers' claims to land for which they had paid as being analogous to the harassment of

---

[44] Improvements were everything that an owner had built or introduced on the property that was not removable. It excluded things like agricultural machines, equipment, seeds, and any cultivation of hanging fruits, "because they were removable." By January 1975, 103 families had received compensation for improvements. INCRA-PR to Second District Court of Paraná, "Expropriation request of lands inside Iguaçu National Park," Curitiba, October 18, 1973, Processo n° 87.10.11573–0 – Ação de desapropriação/ INCRA vs. Colonos do PNI – Pasta 1 (1973), JFP – F.

[45] In the long run, payment in bonds was a good deal for settlers. Between 1971 and 1974, for example, bonds had a 678 percent gain in value – a better appreciation than the 173 percent cumulative inflation of the period. Humberto José Jusi, "Response to Process no. 01151-IBDF 6/3/75," March 11, 1975, Pasta 2.6, Fundo Parque Nacional do Iguaçu, ICMBio. On inflation in Brazil, see Dercio Garcia Munhoz, "Inflação brasileira: Os ensinamentos desde a crise dos anos 30" (paper presented at the First Brazilian Conference on Economic History, University of São Paulo, September 7–10, 1993), accessed June 12, 2015, www.ie.ufrj.br/images/pesquisa/publicacoes/rec/REC%20I/RE C_I.1_03_Inflacao_brasileira_os_ensinamentos_desde_a_crise_dos_anos_30.pdf.

[46] Studying the same region a few years later, Jacob Blanc identified an even sharper and racialized division in compensation between title-bearing and landless farmers among those displaced by the Itaipu reservoir in the early 1980s. Blanc, *Before the Flood*, 4–11.

land speculators who produced fraudulent land titles to push settlers off their land.[47]

How many settlers possessed land titles? How much land did they have inside the Brazilian national park? What was the average area of properties? To reclaim land inside Iguaçu, the Brazilian state used the same resources and institutional framework introduced by the military in 1964 to relocate migrants to frontier areas in Brazil. The entire process was well documented, not only by the new agencies carrying out the relocation but also in the legal challenges put forward by the affected population. The wealth of data produced allows for a quantitative assessment of the population living in the park at the beginning of the 1970s. In 1968, even before the creation of INCRA, IBRA technicians had taken a first census of the settler population living inside the national park.[48] With the 1970 agreement between INCRA and the IBDF, a second census was produced that year, and a third, more detailed one in 1971. The three censuses provide interesting detail on settlers' lives and the state of land ownership in the park.

The censuses recorded the number of families as counted by the head of household, who in the vast majority of cases were males. There is a considerable discrepancy in the total number of families among censuses (see Table 4.1), especially between 1970 and 1971. Between the two later censuses, the number of families increased 67 percent, with the overall number of inhabitants rising 34 percent. It is reasonable to think that the 1968 and 1970 censuses grossly underestimated the number of squatters, tenants, and settlers with precarious claims to land tenure already living in the area, focusing only on those with legal documents lending legitimacy to their claims to the land.

Indeed, the most significant difference between 1970 and 1971 lies in the number of families without deeds. In 1970, there were 115 families without deeds, a figure that jumped to 289 in 1971. What explains a 150 percent increase in the number of households without land titles in just one year? It seems likely that the first two censuses missed a large group of

---

[47] INCRA-PR to Second District Court of Paraná, "Expropriation request of lands inside Iguaçu National Park," Curitiba, October 18, 1973, Processo n° 87.10.11573–0 – Ação de desapropriação/INCRA vs. Colonos do PNI – Pasta 1 (1973), JFP-F; Ordinance 259, October 11, 1973, Ministry of Agriculture, Processo n° 87.10.11573–0 – Ação de desapropriação/INCRA vs. Colonos do PNI – Pasta 1 (1973), JFP-F.

[48] General Oliverio Monteiro do Valle, Instituto Brasileiro de Reforma Agrária, Distrito de Terras do Paraná e Santa Catarina, DFZ-01, Ordinance no. 3/68 – Parque Nacional do Iguaçu, Cascavel (Paraná), February 15, 1968, Fundo Parque Nacional do Iguaçu, ICMBio; Eugênio Cichovski to Secretário Geral do IBDF, January 29, 1968, Documentos diversos 1966 a 1979, 1, PNIB-A.

TABLE 4.1 *Comparison between censuses*

	1968	1970	1971
Families with Deeds	168	152	158
Families w/o Deeds	50	115	289
Total Families	218	267	447
Population	1,137	1,587	2,138
Cleared Area	2,124 ha	2,851 ha	4,164 ha
Forest Area	N/A	8,925 ha	7,836 ha
Total Area	N/A	11,776 ha*	12,000 ha**

Sources: Alvaro Loureiro Martins, "Levantamento do Parque Nacional do Iguaçu," IBRA, Cascavel (Paraná), August 9, 1968, Fundo Parque Nacional do Iguaçu, ioio; Aristides de Oliveira Coelho, Relatório, INCRA, DPZ-3 (C1), July 27, 1970, Pasta 2.6, Fundo Parque Nacional do Iguaçu, ICMBio; and INCRA, PIC-OCOI Internal Report, Cascavel, PR, 1975, Dossiê PIC-OCOI/1974–78, INCRA-Curitiba.
* Total area considered in the survey
** Total area expropriated

precarious occupants and that these figures, as well as the amount of land cleared by settlers, were corrected in 1971, when the final number of families subjected to resettlement was 447. A second explanation could be that families merely split into smaller units – a rational decision, as access to land in PIC-OCOI was granted on a household basis. The fact that the 1971 boom in the number of families without deeds (150 percent) was greater than the increase in the overall population (35 percent) could indicate that there was a – deliberate or unconscious – process of familial subdivision at play. Fragmentation would occur when marrying children became heads of new households.

Finally, a third explanation could lie in the allure the relocation process might have had for people living outside the park. Quickly squatting on land in the national park at the beginning of the eviction process made one eligible to acquire new land in PIC-OCOI through subsidized prices. As we will see in the following sections of this chapter, there are indications of settlers arriving in the area quite late in the game. It is hard to assess how common this was, however, as surveillance in the park increased with the new state troopers patrolling the park and preventing newcomers from settling inside it.[49] All in all, it is possible that all three of these factors – undercounting,

[49] According to a 1973 news story, state troopers had been deployed at the Colono highway, a dirt road bisecting the park that served as the gateway for southern migrants into the

splitting of families, and the arrival of newcomers – contributed to the overall increase in the number of people in the last census. But given the short interval between 1970 and 1971, it is reasonable to believe that the undercounting of those without deeds explains most of the difference in the last census.

In the end, INCRA identified 232 land parcels with deeds, which were owned by 227 individuals and one company, Aranha S/A Engenharia e Construções, from Matelândia. The company owned the Pinheirinho estate, an undeveloped piece of land located in the middle of the forest outside the colonized area of the park. Of the 227 individuals who owned parcels, a few were absentee landowners who lived in Rio Grande do Sul, as attested by the several class-action lawsuits that contested the expropriation. The existence of absentee claimants explains the difference between the 227 owners who had parcels expropriated in 1973 and the 158 families with deeds identified in the 1971 census. Some of these owners had acquired the land as an investment and kept tenants there. It was not uncommon for these tenants to be relatives who had moved to the area from Rio Grande do Sul. Other absentee landowners had recently bought the land but got caught up in the expropriation process before they had the chance to move to Paraná. It is also possible that some of the new owners had "produced" deeds in the two-year time span between the census and the expropriation process. The land market in the region was rife with fraud, and forging deeds was always a possibility.[50]

One group of absentee owners stands out for the size of their properties, which in general were twenty to seventy times larger than the average estate of the southern settler (twenty-one hectares). These were people such as Luiz Correa de Lara and Paulo Correa de Lara, justice department officials in the state of São Paulo, who owned about 800 hectares, and

region. Once there, police officers would interrogate prospective settlers crossing the Iguazu River by ferry and send them back if their final destination happened to be a location inside the park. "IBDF garante que Parque do Iguaçu não é invadido," *Diário do Paraná*, June 13, 1973, 3.

[50] Adilson Simão (Iguaçu National Park director, 1974–86) in discussion with the author, October 2013; Alberto Franco da Silva, "Trajetórias geográficas do pioneiro André Antônio Maggi na abertura da fronteira do oeste paranaense," *Geographia* 2, no. 4 (2000): 89–102; Ministério do Exército, "Informação no. 543-E/2–77 – Atividades subversivas no Parque Nacional do Iguaçu," April 20, 1977, Serviço Nacional de Informações (ACT ACE 2234/82), 1982, AN-DF; INCRA-PR to Second Federal Court of Paraná, "Pedido de expropriação de terras do Parque Nacional do Iguaçu," Curitiba, October 18, 1973, Processo n° 87.10.11573–0 – Ação de desapropriação/INCRA vs. Colonos do PNI – Pasta 1 (1973), JFP-F; Brazil, Decree 84653, April 23, 1980.

Maria Angélia Solivar Bawart, a widow from Curitiba who owned 1,410 hectares of land in São José. One unoccupied park tract was titled in the name of Alexandre Gutierrez Beltrão, a lawyer from Curitiba who had acquired the land in 1930 with the help of his brother, Francisco Beltrão, the secretary of agriculture, roads, and public works for the state of Paraná at the time, a transaction that aroused suspicions of corruption and nepotism in contemporary commentators.[51]

LAND STRUCTURE INSIDE IGUAÇU NATIONAL PARK

Despite some amount of absenteeism, the majority of landowners were settlers living in the area. Who were these settlers? What type of farms did they establish in the national park? What was their primary economic activity? The INCRA censuses reveal that, as with elsewhere in the region, small family farms constituted the majority of properties. Most settlers were from Rio Grande do Sul and of German descent: four-fifths of the 185 small landowners listed in the expropriation process bore at least a German surname.[52] Similar to the great majority of settlers in this frontier region, they grew soybeans, maize, wheat, rice, beans, and potatoes along with raising pigs and chickens. Some owned cattle but ranching was not their primary activity. The area where they had settled was relatively flat, and once the forest had been cleared, it was possible to use machines for harvesting. Mechanization was typical in the region, and settlers organized themselves into cooperatives to buy expensive machinery such as tractors.

Forest still covered a large part of the surveyed area in 1970, and six small lumber mills were still operating in the area of the park (see Map 4.2). These mills were supplied by the logging performed by settlers on their parcels, and produced timber primarily for settlers' own houses and furniture. A web of dirt roads linked to the old Guarapuava-Foz Road connected the villages of Santo Alberto and São José inside the park to the

---

[51] INCRA-PR to Second Federal Court of Paraná, "Expropriation request of lands inside Iguaçu National Park," Curitiba, October 18, 1973, Afonso Augusto Rohden et al. versus INCRA, Curitiba, May 5, 1974, and Germano de Rezende Foster and Geraldo Castellano Biscaia, INCRA, "Autos principais de desapropriação n° 87.1011573–0," First Federal Court in Curitiba, PR, March 29, 1974, and May 22, 1974, all documents in Processo n° 87.10.11573–0 – Ação de desapropriação/INCRA vs. Colonos do PNI – Pasta 1 (1973), JFP-F; Deeds for Fazenda Iguaçu, of Alexandre Gutierrez Beltrão, 1930, 1958, 1973, Fundo PIC-OCOI files, INCRA-Cascavel; INCRA-IBDF agreement, August 26, 1970.

[52] By small landowners I mean those who owned less than 100 hectares of land inside the national park. "Autos principais de desapropriação n° 87.1011573–0."

cities of Foz do Iguaçu and Cascavel. These roads were passable only during dry weather, which occurred in the winter from June to August, and required constant maintenance by the local municipalities.[53]

Despite the history of substantial land conflict in areas like western Paraná, land tenure in southern Brazil consisted mostly of small to medium-sized holdings, a pattern partially reproduced inside the national park.[54] Dividing the varied group of settlers with deeds into six different classes based on estate size casts light on the agrarian structure of settlements inside the park (see Figure 4.2). It also helps separate settlers from speculators – although by the time of the expropriation in 1973, some speculators had already parceled and sold most of their property. Gaspar Coitinho, for example, who had acquired 3,025 hectares inside the park in 1962 and was one of the principal land speculators there, had only 75 hectares left in 1973, having sold off the rest of the land to settlers in the 1960s.[55] Still, other large owners had all of their land expropriated. Maria Angélica Solivar Bawart – one of the few women who owned land inside the park – lost 1,410 hectares of land in 1973.[56]

Among all landowners whose property was seized, 91 percent owned less than 100 hectares of land, which added up to 3,901 hectares, or 32 percent of the total expropriated land. The largest class of owners consisted of those in the 10–20-hectare range, accounting for 59 percent of owners. At the other end of the spectrum, a small group of 12 owners possessing more than 200 hectares each controlled about 60 percent of the land. The numerical prevalence of small and medium holdings contrasts with the massive concentration of a few large ones, which resulted in part from the way expropriation froze the ongoing parceling of large estates. The process promoted by INCRA provides a snapshot of the evolution of

[53] "Desapropriação de terras no sul provoca clima de tensão," *Jornal do Brasil* (Rio de Janeiro), January 5, 1976, Habeas Corpus n° 00.00.27777-2 (PR), 1976, JFP-C; Aristides de Oliveira Coelho, Relatório, INCRA, DPZ-3 (C1), July 27, 1970, Pasta 2.6, Fundo Parque Nacional do Iguaçu, ICMBio.

[54] In the universe of titled properties in 1970, the average rural estate in Brazil was eighty-one hectares, whereas in the three states that comprise the Southern Region (Rio Grande do Sul, Santa Catarina, and Paraná) the average estate was forty-four hectares. IBGE, *Sinopse preliminar do censo agropecuário, VIII recenseamento geral 1970* (Rio de Janeiro: IBGE, 1970), 27.

[55] A detailed discussion on Gaspar Coitinho's role in attracting settlers to Iguaçu National Park can be found in Freitas, "Terras públicas." See also Joe Foweraker, *The Struggle for Land*, 83–93, 143–49.

[56] About 10 percent of the individuals claiming land ownership inside the park were female.

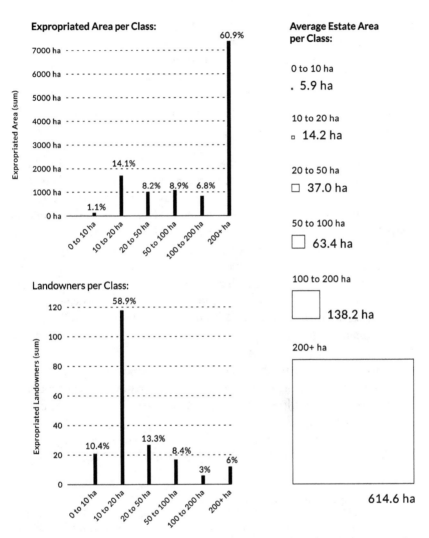

FIGURE 4.2 Expropriated estates in Iguaçu National Park, 1973. Figure by Frederico Freitas

land tenure in the region: with the help of local authorities, large and contested tracts of public land were subdivided into large estates by land agents and companies that, in turn, parceled their properties to incoming southern settlers. With her 1,410 hectares of unparceled forested land, Bawart was the prime example of the absentee speculator. The federal government's retaking of the park territory aborted the inevitable parceling process taking place both in the park's other occupied estates and outside it.[57]

Still, some of the largest landowners had operating farms on their properties. Among these were Amadeu Gava, Severino Bombarda, Júlio Tozzo, and Luiz Bonatto, who had been identified by INCRA in 1975 as the most resistant to expropriation and compensation. As INCRA officials saw it, these four individuals were setting the example for others to defy eviction. Amadeu Gava was the owner of a mechanized 798.6-hectare farm, which former park director Simão declared to be one the few "real farms" in the park.[58] Severino Bombarda and Júlio Tozzo, for their part, claimed a parcel of 2,420 hectares at the east end of the village of São José but failed to provide deeds for the area. The lack of legal documents prevented them from receiving compensation for the value of land. Still, despite this lack of clarity about the legitimacy of their claims, Bombarda, Tozzo, and many of their relatives were allowed to buy land at PIC-OCOI, which indicates they at least resided in the park. Another landowner, Luiz Bonatto, was the most recalcitrant and the last of the landowners whose land was seized through the 1973 decree to leave the park, in December 1978. Bonatto was a local politician and acted as appointed mayor of Medianeira from 1970 to 1982. He owned 17 parcels on an isolated peninsula surrounded by the Iguazu River that amounted to 484.4 hectares. Both his clout as a politician of the ruling party and the geographical isolation of his lands allowed him to extend his presence inside the park up to the end of 1978.[59]

Large landholders such as Bombarda and Tozzo were not the only individuals to have land compensation denied by INCRA. Adelino

[57] "Autos principais de desapropriação n° 87.1011573–0."

[58] In Simão's view, "real farms" were the few larger estates with capital to invest in machinery and the capacity to "produce" commercial crops. "Real farms" should also have several head of cattle, a marker of a budding landed aristocracy in a region marked by small family farms with few cattle. Adilson Simão (Iguaçu National Park director, 1974–86) in discussion with the author, October 2013.

[59] Geraldo Castellano Biscaia and Luiz Carlos Taulois do Rosário (INCRA) to the First Federal Court in Curitiba, March 5, 1975, Processo n° 87.10.11573–0 – Ação de desapropriação/INCRA vs. Colonos do PNI – Pasta 5 (1987), JFP-F; INCRA-PR, "Reintegração do Parque Nacional do Iguaçu," Memo, Curitiba, PR, June, 1975, Dossiê PIC-OCOÍ, 1974–78, INCRA-Curitiba; Humberto José Jusi to Celso Soares de Castro, DF no. 4221/78-DE-PR, December 22, 1978, Pasta 2.6, Fundo Parque Nacional do Iguaçu, ICMBio; Paulo Roberto Rompczynski to the First Federal Court in Curitiba, April 6, 1984, Processo n° 87.10.11573–0 – Ação de desapropriação/INCRA vs. Colonos do PNI – Pasta 14 (1987), JFP-F; Humberto José Jusi to Paulo Azevedo Berutti, DF no. 4222/78-DE-PR, December 22, 1978, Pasta 2.6, Fundo Parque Nacional do Iguaçu, ICMBio.

Brunner and Arlindo Back are two examples of small landholders who failed to obtain compensation because of their lack of knowledge of legal procedures. On March 17, 1969, through Gaspar Coitinho, Brunner bought a fifteen-hectare parcel carved out from the park lands claimed by an absentee speculator, Paulo da Cunha Mattos. Although he paid for the land, Brunner never registered it with the notary in Foz do Iguaçu, wrongly believing that the sale contract alone was enough to provide him with legal ownership. The same thing happened to Back, who bought a twenty-six-hectare parcel from Mattos. When the two settlers realized they needed actual deeds to receive monetary compensation for their land, it was too late, as INCRA had already expropriated the parcels under Mattos's name. The agency compensated Brunner and Back only for the improvements they had built, allowing them, like Bombarda and Tozzo, to purchase lots at subsidized prices at PIC-OCOI.[60]

Although a good share of the land in the occupied area of Iguaçu National Park was concentrated in a few hands, many who had their land expropriated through the agrarian reform legislation were, in fact, small landholders, which made the situation absurd, given the nature of the law. Indeed, a closer look at the legislation used to remove settlers from Iguaçu casts light on a ultimate goal of the relocation program. Instead of employing expropriation for public utility (*desapropriação por utilidade pública*), INCRA officials chose to use a new legal instrument introduced with the 1964 Land Statute: expropriation for social interest (*desapropriação por interesse social*).[61] The differences between the two approaches had to do not only with the types of compensation they provided to settlers but, more important, with the logic behind them. Expropriation for public utility in Brazil was similar to the US institution of eminent domain – expropriation for the purpose of building roads and dams or establishing parks for the common good. Expropriation for social interest, on the other hand, was designed to achieve agrarian reform goals, promoting access to land by putting idle properties to use. The latter was the legal instrument used by the Brazilian federal government to expropriate both the land of those who possessed deeds for lots inside Iguaçu National Park and the land at the relocation site, PIC-OCOI. The choice

---

[60] Paulo Roberto Rompczynski to the First Federal Court in Curitiba, April 6, 1984, Processo n° 87.10.11573-0 – Ação de desapropriação/INCRA vs. Colonos do PNI – Pasta 14 (1987), JFP-F; Freitas, "Terras públicas."
[61] Brazil, Decree-Law 3365, "Lei da desapropriação por utilidade pública," June 21, 1941; Brazil, Law 4504, "Estatuto da terra," November 30, 1964.

of agrarian reform legislation was a clear indication that top-level government officials viewed removing the settlers as a social and political problem rather than an environmental one.

SETTLERS' DECISIONS

Several settlers who acquired lots in Santo Alberto claimed to have been
unaware that they were buying land inside a national park. One of these
was José Olivo Kaefer, a southerner who had moved to Santo Alberto in
1965, when he was thirty-five years old and already an experienced
farmer. He followed a neighbor who was looking for a region where one
could buy a legal piece of land. "Everybody in Rio do Grande Sul knew
that properties in Paraná were frequently the result of *grilagem*," he
noted. Despite that, Kaefer and his neighbor each bought a twelve-hectare
plot in the park. He prospered and persuaded others in Rio Grande do Sul
to move to the area. In 1968, he heard the first rumors about the land
belonging to a national park, but, after confirming the "inaccuracy" of
such claims with local politicians, he did not take them seriously.[62]

Another settler, José Siebert, moved to the region in 1966, after he was
contacted by an agent from a colonization company that persuaded him to
buy land in the area. Knowing there was a risk of buying fraudulent deeds,
he consulted the notary office in Foz do Iguaçu before making up his mind
on the acquisition. As a double precaution, he made sure to complete the
land registration before moving to his new piece of land from Rio Grande
do Sul with his family of eight. The Sieberts cleared and cultivated twenty-
two of their twenty-seven hectares and eventually ended up well-off by
local standards, growing corn, soybeans, and cassava and raising pigs and
cows. In 1968, a neighbor told him IBRA officials were surveying the area,
which, they stated, belonged to Iguaçu National Park. According to
Siebert, the bureaucrats showed settlers an aerial picture of their properties, saying that "it was park area" and that their deeds therefore lacked
legal force.[63]

Otto Hendt, another southerner, bought his land in Iguaçu while he
was still in Rio Grande do Sul, in 1969. A colonization company offered
him the possibility of buying a piece of land in western Paraná. Like
Siebert, he investigated the legal status of the land and, after confirming

---

[62] *Jornal bi-nacional*, Foz do Iguaçu, September 18, 1974; "Em busca do Eldorado," *Estado
do Paraná*, May 5, 1975, Dossiê PIC-OCOÍ, 1974–78, Curitiba.
[63] Ibid.

its purported legitimacy with the land notary Aguirra in Foz do Iguaçu, decided to buy it. He knew the land market in Paraná was rife with fraud and *grilagem*, but the local notary dispelled enough of his doubts for him to move forward. Hendt claimed to have first learned about the status of the land in a meeting with local authorities in 1971, when settlers were informed they could no longer cut down trees on their estates. The authorities insisted that any attempt to contest the IBDF's mandate over the land would be in vain, as the reintegration of the park "was an issue of national security for both Brazil and Argentina." According to one rumor, the neighboring country was insisting that the settlers should be removed because they were invading the Argentine territory and park to hunt and log.[64]

Maurício Schossler was one of the last settlers to arrive in Santo Alberto, in 1970, when he was twenty-one years old. In that year, he decided to sell his lands in Rio Grande do Sul and pay a visit to his brothers who lived in the area, "where the land was famous for being extremely fertile." He acquired a parcel and obtained a lease with the bank for machinery. It was after paying the first installment that he started to hear rumors about the ban on felling trees and about park authorities seizing land.[65]

The stories of the Brunners, Backs, and Schosslers reveal that as late as 1970 people such as Coitinho, Mattos, and Aguirra, the land notary, were still selling land inside the park. The question is whether settlers were aware of this fact and took a chance, as park director Colonel Jayme de Paiva Bello suggested, or were defrauded by middlemen such as Gaspar Coitinho. The accounts of settlers suggest that both scenarios were at play. On the one hand, settlers knew that there might be already existing claims on the lands they were acquiring. Western Paraná was a region with a notorious history of *grilagem*, and incoming settlers actively sought information on the lots' legal status before deciding to purchase. Moreover, despite the claims of Schossler and other latecomers, by the end of the 1960s, it was common knowledge among settlers that federal authorities considered the area a national park, especially after the first IBRA survey in 1968.[66] Indeed, settlers complained about the survey to

---

[64] Ibid.   [65] Ibid.

[66] This timeline is confirmed by interviews with former park settlers conducted decades after the eviction. Until the mid-1960s most settlers were unaware of the park's existence. By the decade's end, however, the repeated visits by IBDF and IBRA agents had alerted settlers to the national park claims on their lands. Rudy Nick Vencatto, "Parque

local politicians, and the state assembly launched an inquiry into the land situation in the park that same year. It is unlikely that after that point most settlers were unaware of the federal claim on their properties.[67]

On the other hand, it was equally unlikely that a farmer in 1960s rural Brazil had a clear notion of what a national park entailed or how its existence could lead to people being removed from its territory. Brazil at the time still had few national parks, most of them only minimally implemented. Unlike Argentina, the country never had a campaign to popularize its national parks, and it is reasonable to think that few lay people had a clear picture, if any, of the implications for territorial policy. Even if there were some who knew that a national park encompassed lands they intended to acquire, there was a general perception among many in Brazil at the time that public lands were up for grabs and that the government would eventually grant amnesty to squatters, land grabbers, or seemingly bona fide purchasers. Indeed, amnesty was park administrators' original proposal – to divide the park in two with a settled area in between. Federal officials accepted eviction as a solution only in 1970, after the creation of INCRA and the push to establish colonization projects in frontier areas.[68] It is reasonable, therefore, to conclude that the settlers who acquired land in the park area did not possess all of the necessary information to weigh the risks involved in their decision.

Even after many accepted the legitimacy of the federal government's determination to evict them from the park, settlers still bristled. As noted earlier, some became dissatisfied with the expropriation process because of the differences in compensation the landholders received. Whereas those with deeds were eligible for compensation for both estate improvements and land value, the ones who failed to present land titles received indemnity only for improvements. Even those with deeds were sometimes unhappy about the twenty-year payment process involving government bonds. A number of settlers received twice the amount of land at PIC-OCOI, which helped assuage resistance to the expropriations. Meanwhile, some opted out of PIC-OCOI: about sixty families moved to Mato Grosso,

Nacional do Iguaçu: O processo de migração, ocupação e as marcas na paisagem natural," *Revista latino-americana de estudos avançados* 1, no. 2 (2017): 108–9.

[67] "Colonos ameaçados," *Diário do Paraná*, June 12, 1968, 3.

[68] The idea that park authorities should avoid splitting up the park to avert inbreeding and a decrease in genetic variability in animal species was largely absent from the conservation debates in 1970s Brazil. The territorial integrity of protected areas became important for policymakers and park advocates only when "biodiversity" became a value to be protected in the 1980s.

others crossed the border and emigrated to Paraguay, and still others moved to cities, mainly Foz do Iguaçu, abandoning farming altogether.

In 1976, there were ninety remaining landholders continuing to resist eviction from the park. They were dissatisfied with the new location at PIC-OCOI, contested INCRA's assessment of the value of their properties and improvements, and demanded payment in cash instead of bonds. They also demanded the right to eventually sell their PIC-OCOI land so they would be free to move somewhere else. Their lawyer summarized their situation in a 2010 interview, noting that they "were small farmers, with little capital, and should have received compensation in cash, especially because land was expropriated to be incorporated into the national park, not to promote agrarian reform."[69]

NATIONAL PARK AS LATIFUNDIA

In the winter of 1976, some of the remaining settlers in the villages of São José and Santo Alberto started being arrested for routine activities such as preparing the land for summer crops. At around 4:00 p.m. on June 30, Bruno Wagner, Urbano Diel, and Armindo Criveler Diel were arrested by state troopers for plowing their lands. They spent the night in the Federal Police jail in Foz do Iguaçu. In their testimony, they complained of having been subjected to ongoing harassment and assault by the state police, culminating with their imprisonment. A week later, police officials arrested two other settlers, Lucila Postai and Romeu Canicio Postai. According to the police report, the couple were also plowing their fields for summer crops, and Lucila Postai verbally and physically assaulted the officers during the arrest.[70]

Plowing fields was not the only reason settlers were being incarcerated in 1976. Around that time, Maurício Schossler was arrested at home by plainclothes officers who claimed he possessed subversive material. Officers accused him of having an audio tape of a manifesto inciting settlers to revolt. Schossler spent a night in the Federal Police headquarters in Foz do Iguaçu, where, according to him, he was forced to witness the torture session of an unknown prisoner before his own interrogation – a procedure used to break detainees' will, common in many police stations

---

[69] Seixas, "Memória dos desapropriados," 26–27, 138–43.
[70] Bruno Wagner, Urbano Diel, and Armindo Criveler Diel, "Notarized statement," July 1, 1976, and Forest Police of Paraná, "Report n° 31/76," Foz do Iguaçu, 1976, both in Habeas Corpus n° 00.00.27777-2 (PR), 1976, JFP-C; "Paraná: Proibido plantar."

during Brazil's military dictatorship. Arrests for planting crops and for subversive activities were a novelty for the settlers in Iguaçu National Park, who prior to 1976 had been prohibited only from clearing new patches of forest on their plots.[71]

These settlers were part of a substantial minority who had refused to accept INCRA's terms and leave the park to move to PIC-OCOI. As a way of pushing the remaining ninety families into leaving the park, in May 1976, the head of the IBDF in Paraná prohibited farmers who had already received compensation for their expropriated properties from planting new crops. Those who had yet to receive compensation were allowed to plant, but only winter crops such as wheat, barley, rye, and oats, which were grown mostly for subsistence purposes.[72]

On July 9, 1976, a local attorney, Antônio Vanderli Moreira, made a bold move when he petitioned for a preventive writ of habeas corpus at the Second Federal Court in Curitiba. He filed the petition on behalf of eighty of the remaining farmers from São José and Santo Alberto and against the director of Iguaçu National Park. In the petition, Moreira argued that settlers had suffered unlawful coercion and restrictions by the IBDF on their constitutional right to freedom of movement, and thus needed habeas corpus to move freely.[73] The substitute judge Silvio Dobrowlski swiftly denied the petition, arguing that the "expropriated parcels were part of Iguaçu National Park" and that "there was nothing strange in setting aside deforested areas for nature conservation," as such decisions were based on "ecological studies" conducted by the IBDF in the affected areas. The judge, however, failed to present such studies, as none were in fact produced during the entire eviction process. Removal had originated in a political decision, not a scientific one.[74]

Settlers' discontent was grounded in what they saw as an unjust resettlement process based on a faulty justification. They considered the 1971 expropriation act null and void because, as they explained in the petition, it decreed that the land be expropriated for nominally agrarian reform ends, when in fact the government's true intention had always been expropriation for "ecological preservation." To the settlers it was

---

[71] Seixas, "Memória dos desapropriados," 132–36.

[72] IBDF, Internal Memo no. 019/76/PR, April 19, 1976, Habeas Corpus n° 00.00.27777–2 (PR), 1976, JFP-C.

[73] "Freedom of movement" was a safe, apolitical choice, as until 1978 Brazil banned habeas corpus for political crimes.

[74] Silvio Dobrowlski, "Habeas corpus preventivo," autos no. 859/76, 2ª Vara, July 17, 1976, Habeas Corpus n° 00.00.27777–2 (PR), 1976, JFP-C.

clear that "agrarian reform" implied the expropriation and parceling of idle latifundia to be distributed to landless peasants and small farmers, or, as defined by the 1964 Land Statute, to promote "the better distribution of land through modifications in its ownership and occupancy regime in keeping with the principles of social justice and increased productivity." Expropriating small proprietors to cobble together idle latifundia was exactly the opposite of what the law defined as agrarian reform, and ultimately that was how settlers and their lawyer understood the national park – an enormous expanse of unused land that would be in better use if put into production.[75]

A second item in the list of complaints, however, reveals the settlers' ability to contest displacement not only under the letter of the law but also through its technical justifications. Settlers saw a basic contradiction in their forced removal from a cleared area to one, PIC-OCOI, which consisted of "virgin forest." The resettlement, they argued, entailed a second and unnecessary cycle of deforestation on a new site. They claimed that the agency, according to what was acceptable in the environmental ideas of the time, could very well compensate for the loss in the occupied area inside the national park by transforming the PIC-OCOI estate into a protected area of its own. After all, the chosen area was also forested, largely "empty," and even slightly bigger – 12,500 hectares compared to the 12,000 hectares occupied by settlers in the park.

The remaining complaints on their list all had to do with alleged failures during the removal and resettlement process. The actions of park wardens and police officers had become more punitive as they started arresting settlers for removing tree stumps from fields, a necessary step before plowing. Settlers also accused local municipal governments of ceasing to maintain the dirt roads leading to communities inside the park, thus impeding their access to local markets. By putting up hurdles to cultivation and circulation inside the park area, authorities hoped to strangle the remaining settlers economically. "We have to wait either for the court decision or for the living conditions inside the park to deteriorate – settlers will have to move out," confessed the head of the INCRA office for the State of Paraná, Aroldo José Moletta, in an interview.[76]

---

[75] Antônio Vanderli Moreira, "Pedido de habeas corpus preventivo," July 6, 1976, Habeas Corpus n° 00.00.27777-2 (PR), 1976, JFP-C; Brazil, Law 4504, "Estatuto da terra," Art. 1, November, 30, 1964.

[76] É proibido cortar árvores no parque," *Diário do Paraná*, May 15, 1974; "INCRA desmente coação," *Estado do Paraná*, July 14, 1976, Dossiê PIC-OCOÍ, 1974–78, INCRA-Curitiba; Antônio Vanderli Moreira, "Pedido de habeas corpus preventivo,"

AGITATORS AND SUBVERSIVES

Conflict in the countryside had been one of the justifications for the 1964 coup that brought the military into power. Recent history in western Paraná was dotted with examples of land conflict, sustaining the suspicion that a revolt was imminent among the settlers resisting eviction from Iguaçu National Park. Before 1964, the state of Paraná had seen major armed uprisings that pitted settlers against henchmen and state troopers carrying out evictions on behalf of land speculators. The first major conflict occurred between 1947 and 1951 in Porecatu, a town in the northern part of the state, where displaced settlers working with Brazilian Communist party operatives formed armed groups to resist land eviction.[77] A second and more successful uprising occurred in southwestern Paraná in 1957, adjacent to the southern border of the Iguaçu National Park. In that year, thousands of armed settlers besieged several cities and towns in the region, shunning local authorities in each of these places. They protested the violent encroachment of claim jumpers, successfully pushing federal and state governments to work together to solve the land problem in the region.[78] Following Porecatu and the Southwest, Medianeira, at the border of the park, had its own minor conflict in the winter of 1961, with exchanges of gunfire between settlers and land speculators' henchmen.[79] Contributing to the impression of a problematic borderland, after the 1964 coup the military began to view the park's forests as a potential haven for guerrilla groups fighting against the dictatorship.[80]

July 6, 1976, Proof of payment of Rural Property Land Tax in name of José Telmo Schneider, October 10, 1973, IBDF-PR, Logging Authorization, Foz do Iguaçu, May 24, 1976, and Alvino Baltazar, Emilio Leichtweis, Eugenio Hilario Leichtweis, José Antônio Postai, Notarized statement, June 1, 1976, all in Habeas Corpus n° 00.00.27777-2 (PR), 1976, JFP-C.

[77] Cliff Welch, *The Seed Was Planted: The São Paulo Roots of Brazil's Rural Labor Movement, 1924–1964* (University Park: Pennsylvania State University Press, 1999), 126–52.

[78] Lindomar W. Boneti, "O significado histórico do levante armado dos colonos do sudoeste do Paraná ocorrido em 1957," Porto Alegre, Federal University of Rio Grande do Sul, 1988, 1–16, UFRRJ; Westphalen, Machado, and Balhana, "Nota Prévia," 38–48.

[79] Secretaria de Estado de Segurança Pública; Divisão de Segurança e Informações, "Questões de Terras Gleba Silva Jardim," August 1961, DOPS/PR – Pastas Temáticas – Parque Nacional de Foz do Iguaçu – Número: 1659, Topografia: 199, Data: 1961, APP; Myskiw, "Colonos, posseiros e grileiros," 79–90; "Santa Terezinha, ontem, hoje," *Nosso tempo*, March 10, 1983.

[80] In March 1965, only a year after the military coup, the Brazilian Army occupied Foz do Iguaçu and adjacent municipalities in search of a group of rebel army officers who had

The history of land conflict in western Paraná coupled with the park's location at a sensitive international border framed the manner in which government officials saw the problem of settlers living inside Iguaçu National Park.[81] The removal of settlers from Iguaçu began in 1970, during the harshest period of political repression in Brazil, and continued after 1974, when the military announced "a process of slow, gradual, and secure decompression" that aimed, in the words of historian Marcos Napolitano, to "institutionalize the [dictatorial] regime" by reducing the direct violence that had prevailed until then.[82] Throughout that, government officials continued to understand settler relocation as a matter of national security and sometimes treated resistance to eviction as potentially threatening to the military regime's political order.[83]

taken up arms against the new regime. The small group of rebels, including four guerrillas hiding inside Iguaçu National Park, was soon arrested by the army. Almost a decade later, the Brazilian Army would use the park for clandestine killings. On the night of July 14, 1974, an undercover agent lured five left-wing militants (four Brazilians and one Argentine national) to the Colono Highway that bisected the park, where they were executed by an army commando unit. "Guerrilheiros acossados por patrulhas do exército tentam escapar para a Argentina," *Correio do povo*, March 28, 1965; "Exército prende chefe e 17 dos guerrilheiros," *Folha de São Paulo*, March 29, 1965; "Exército prende mais onze rebeldes," *Correio da manhã*, March 30, 1965; Comissão Nacional da Verdade, *Relatório*, vol. II (Brasília: Comissão Nacional da Verdade, 2014), 40; Aluízio Palmar, *Onde foi que enterraram nossos mortos?* (Curitiba: Travessa dos Editores, 2012); Comissão Nacional da Verdade, "Capítulo 13, Casos emblemáticos, 3 – A chacina do Parque Nacional do Iguaçu," in *Relatório*, vol. I (Brasília: Comissão Nacional da Verdade, 2014), 633–40.

[81] On the history of modern land conflict in Brazil, see Foweraker, "Political Conflict on the Frontier"; Foweraker, *The Struggle for Land*; José de Souza Martins, *A imigração e a crise do Brasil agrário* (São Paulo: Pioneira, 1973); Martins, *Fronteira: A degradação do outro nos confins do humano*; Velho, *Capitalismo autoritário e campesinato*; Velho, *Frentes de expansão*; Hermógenes Lazier, *Análise histórica da posse de terra no sudoeste paranaense* (Curitiba: Biblioteca Pública do Paraná, Secretaria de Estado da Cultura e do Esporte, 1986).

[82] Ernesto Geisel, "Discurso feito aos dirigentes da Arena, no Palácio da Alvorada, em 29 de agosto de 1974," in *Discursos, Volume I, 1974* (Brasília: Assessoria de Imprensa e Relações Públicas da Presidência da República, 1975); Napolitano, *1964: História do regime*, 234–35. See also Maria Helena Moreira Alves, *State and Opposition in Military Brazil*, Latin American Monographs 63 (Austin: University of Texas Press, 1990); Thomas E. Skidmore, *The Politics of Military Rule in Brazil, 1964–1985* (New York: Oxford University Press, 1988); Elio Gaspari, *A ditadura encurralada* (São Paulo: Companhia das Letras, 2004).

[83] This treatment extended to the entire border region. In June 1968 several municipalities in the area of Iguaçu National Park, including Foz do Iguaçu, were declared national security zones. As such, they lost their ability to elect local government; officials would now be directly appointed by the federal government. Brazil, Law 5449, June 4, 1968; "Paraná no esquema de segurança," *Diário do Paraná*, April 18, 1968, 1, 3.

The fear of settler radicalization was patent in an internal memo of May 7, 1975, in which the Assessoria de Segurança e Informações (Office for Security and Information) of the IBDF in Brasília reached out to the Departamento de Parques Nacionais e Reservas Equivalentes (Department of National Parks and Equivalent Reservations, DPNRE) to request information on the mounting tension inside the national park. In the 1970s, many Brazilian federal agencies and departments created their own "intelligence departments" that functioned mostly as a press clipping service. According to the IBDF's intelligence memo, "squatters" notified of their upcoming eviction had been encouraged by local opposition politicians to resist by force. The agents believed a manifesto was to be sent to newspapers and TV stations in Curitiba blaming the minister of agriculture, the head of the IBDF, and the park director for the eviction. Even more startling, they were convinced that there was an imminent threat to the life of park authorities.[84]

One of the immediate causes for the mounting tension among settlers, as identified by the head of the IBDF in Brasília, Paulo Azevedo Beirutti, was the stalemate that had arisen in the compensation process. Beirutti believed settlers would leave only after receiving full payment for their land and improvements, but payment had to wait for a court decision in Curitiba. In Beirutti's view, the delay in processing indemnity had galvanized the radicalization of the remaining settlers, who were defying the ban on crop cultivation inside the park and threatening to reoccupy areas already reclaimed by the national park administration. To Beirutti, it was a question of national security requiring the intervention of the Secretaria de Segurança Nacional (National Security Office), whose Comissão Especial da Faixa de Fronteira (Special Committee of the Border Strip, CEFF) would be able to expedite compensation payments and, consequently, the removal of the settlers. He also made a direct request to the Ministry of Agriculture for additional funds for compensation to mitigate settler dissatisfaction and accelerate the eviction process.[85]

A year later, additional funds had not yet been allocated and compensation was still enmeshed in the judicial morass in Curitiba. Clashes between the remaining settlers and the state police deployed in the park led government authorities to believe that a general uprising was

---

[84] "Pedido de busca n° 119/ASI/IBDF/76," Fundo Parque Nacional do Iguaçu, ICMBio.

[85] Paulo Azevedo Beirutti, IBDF director to Alysson Paulinelli, Minister of Agriculture, Of. no. 358/75-P, April 25, 1975, annexed to Arnaldo Carlos Muller, "Proposição de manejo para o Parque Nacional do Iguaçu" (MS thesis, Federal University of Paraná, 1978).

brewing. A letter from the director of the IBDF for Paraná, Humberto José Jusi, to the SNI details the imagined conspiracy. According to Jusi, park authorities in Foz do Iguaçu were convinced that malicious individuals were leading settlers to reject compensation and removal in an effort to sabotage the resettlement process. Meetings in Santo Alberto and São José featured "offensive signs attacking INCRA, the IBDF, and the 1964 revolution," which provocateurs called a "real April Fools' Day" – the 1964 military coup had occurred in the night between March 31 and April 1. Rumor had it that several "subversive activities" were being planned: the occupation of PIC-OCOI; the kidnapping of the PIC-OCOI director's son; the murder of the PIC-OCOI and Iguaçu National Park directors, one of whom, Jusi stressed, was an army colonel (Bello); and the murder of the two commanders of the state police platoon quartered inside the park. May Day, which is Labor Day in Brazil, was the chosen date of action.[86]

The SNI office in Curitiba sent at least one agent to the area to investigate the situation.[87] He singled out the settlers' lawyer, Antônio Vanderli Moreira, as the main provocateur working to radicalize settlers. The SNI report describes a meeting attended by "people with low education uttering slogans against the government and the 1964 revolution [sic]." The author was surprised that, despite its "low intellectual level," the audience was able to discuss complex issues such as Brazil's external debt, a recurrent object of criticism on the Brazilian left during the final years of the dictatorship. Local Federal Police agents, in turn, reported radicals going among the settlers and preaching a peasant revolution that would be ignited by the password *sol de maio* (May sun) in the ensuing month. Relatives of public officials at PIC-OCOI and Iguaçu National Park would then be kidnapped. Fearing for the safety of his family, the head of PIC-OCOI had already left the region. May Day eventually came, and nothing happened.[88]

The settlers' plight also attracted outside "agitators" such as Waldomiro de Deus Pereira, a left-wing journalist with a history of militancy with peasants in Amazonia. He settled in Foz do Iguaçu in 1974, where he published a single-issue newspaper featuring interviews with settlers from Santo Alberto. After an altercation with INCRA officials, Pereira was

---

[86] Humberto José Jusi to Aldyr Eduardo Martins, April 26, 1976, Serviço Nacional de Informações (ACT ACE 2234/82), 1982, AN-DF.

[87] "Atividades subversivas no Parque Nacional do Iguaçu," memo, April 28, 1976, Serviço Nacional de Informações (ACT ACE 2234/82), 1982, AN-DF.

[88] Serviço Nacional de Informações, "Pedido de busca no. 079/16/AC/76," June 9, 1976, Serviço Nacional de Informações (ACT ACE 2234/82), 1982, AN-DF.

denounced as a subversive and subsequently investigated by the Departamento de Ordem Política e Social (Department of Political and Social Order, DOPS), the state political police headquartered in Curitiba. The memo sent by INCRA to DOPS on September 29, 1974, depicted a defiant Pereira storming the INCRA office in Cascavel with three Santo Alberto settlers, José Siebert and two others, in tow. Pereira presented himself first as a journalist writing a piece on the evictions and then, after being asked for press credentials, as a lawyer acting on behalf of the three farmers. Pereira, who was no lawyer, wanted to show INCRA officials that the "humble farmers" had an attorney and the press backing them. However, as news of his activities reached the upper echelons of the political repression apparatus at the SNI in Brasília, his actions backfired. He was taken to the headquarters of the First Border Battalion in Foz do Iguaçu for questioning and, once there, ordered to leave the region, which he promptly did.[89]

Despite government officials and the military's view of a stubborn Iguaçu community ready to take up arms against the IBDF and INCRA, other members of the political establishment demonstrated their support to the settlers' cause. These included several politicians in the Movimento Democrático Brasileiro (Brazilian Democratic Movement, MDB), the only opposition party of the military regime. The lawyer Antônio Vanderli Moreira, for example, was the head of the local MDB chapter in Foz do Iguaçu. In May 1975, a group of settlers from Santo Alberto led by Schossler held a meeting at the Foz do Iguaçu town hall with MDB senators and federal deputies who expressed their support for the settlers' decision to resist eviction.[90] Around that same time, in Brasília, an MDB politician from Paraná, Federal Deputy Paulo Marques, spoke multiple times in Congress on behalf of the expropriated settlers. He described settlers being arrested and cuffed, put in trucks, and transported to PIC-OCOI, which he depicted as a "concentration camp" with barbed wire and iron gates.[91] Settlers also sought the help of MDB politicians in their

---

[89] INCRA, "Agitação entre Colonos do Parque Nacional do Iguaçu," September 9, 1974, DOPS/PR – Pastas Temáticas – Parque Nacional de Foz do Iguaçu – Número: 1461. Topografia: 171. Data: 1974, APP; Aluízio Palmar, "Jornal fechado e seu diretor expulso de Foz," *Documentos revelados*, January 9, 2011, www.documentosrevelados.com.br/g eral/jornal-fechado-e-seu-diretor-expulso-de-foz-2/

[90] National Archives of Brazil, Brasília, Serviço Nacional de Informações (AC ACE 85634/75), 1975.

[91] Paulo Marques, Speeches at the Brazilian Federal Congress, *Diário do Congresso Nacional*, Brasília, March 21, 1975, 693–94, April 28, 1976, 2809, and May 6, 1976, 3285–86.

home state, Rio Grande do Sul, and the MDB Federal Deputy Antônio Bresolin proposed a federal bill canceling the expropriation, which never passed.[92]

Even members of the local chapter of the Aliança Renovadora Nacional (National Renewal Alliance, ARENA), the official party of the military regime, felt the need to voice criticism of the resettlement process. Cleodon Alberto de Albuquerque, who was president of the Rural Union in Foz do Iguaçu and vice president of the local ARENA chapter, believed INCRA had used questionable methods to force people to accept its conditions and that attempts to persuade higher echelons to intervene in the matter had not been effective. Despite his criticism, Albuquerque avoided addressing crucial issues such as settlers' right to own land in the park. He summarized the problem as being simply a matter of indemnity, stating that INCRA "should not expropriate land for social interest where the compensation is insufficient, but instead should do it for public utility," which provided better compensation.[93]

Albuquerque hinted at one of the core issues in the removal process: the way an agrarian reform law conceived to improve production had been made into a tool to create a preserved natural space. INCRA's choice to use expropriation for social interest – an agrarian reform law devised to put idle land to use – makes it clear that in the eyes of government officials, the removal of settlers was as much a social and political problem as an environmental one. Among the aims of the military that took power in 1964 was to resolve land conflicts and achieve a top-down pacification of the countryside. Since the Contestado War (1912–16), western Paraná had been a hotspot of violent land disputes that conflated uncertainty of land tenure with the excessive power of local potentates and the weak presence of the federal government. Therefore, the use of newly minted agrarian reform tools seemed an obvious choice to a national government interested in imposing a territorial order on this turbulent borderland.

---

[92] Antonio Bresolin, "Justificativa," Brasília, May 1975, and Antônio Vanderli Moreira to Antônio Brezolin, June 23, 1975, both in Habeas Corpus n° 00.00.27777-2 (PR), 1976, JFP-C.

[93] As noble as it might appear, Albuquerque's concern with the settlers' situation stemmed from a pragmatic realization: As he himself admitted, the "negative social effects" sparked by the expropriation process would inform voters' choices in the next local election. The official party of the military regime would inevitably be associated with the unjust displacement of constituents from their lands. As he put it, the local ARENA chapter could "consider itself defeated in the next elections, all because of this land problem." "Desapropriação de terras no sul provoca clima de tensão."

Ultimately the federal government's approach paid off. Despite being contested by a few different class-action lawsuits, related to both the expropriation itself and the compensation offered, expropriation was never overturned in the courts. By 1982 most settlers had reached amicable agreements with INCRA regarding land value and compensation, and all had left the park. With removal complete, the park territory returned to the control of the federal government.[94]

THE INSTRUMENTS OF EVICTION

When government officials created Iguaçu National Park in 1939, they intended to use it to channel resources to develop their side of the border. Unlike Argentina's, however, the Brazilian park system never provided for the use of national park land for settlement purposes. The exclusion of settlers from national parks, although not initially codified in Brazilian law, was a staple of the discourse of national park officials beginning with the establishment of the first parks in the 1930s. The legal basis of these designations was the forest code of 1934, which did not offer a precise definition of Brazil's putative national parks but prohibited "the exercise of any activity against the flora and fauna of the parks." A revision of the code in 1965 rephrased the prohibition in terms of a ban on "natural resource exploitation." Despite the lack of precision of the legal text, it was the widespread view among park officials that inhabitants should be excluded from future parks.[95] Still, problems of land demarcation, squatting, *grilagem*, and settlement inside park areas were common across the country. In 1978, an IBDF report revealed that 40 percent of the 1,457,518 hectares of protected areas gazetted before 1972 still needed to be regularized and incorporated by the federal government.[96] In this

---

[94] José Alfredo Dewes et al. versus INCRA, Amicable Agreement, Curitiba, May 3, 1982, Processo n° 87.10.11573–0 – Ação de desapropriação/INCRA vs. Colonos do PNI – Pasta 5 (1987), JFP-F; Humberto José Jusi to Aldyr Eduardo Martins, April 26, 1976, Serviço Nacional de Informações (ACT ACE 2234/82), 1982, AN-DF.

[95] Brazil, Law 23793, "Código florestal," January 23, 1934; Brazil, Law 4771, "Novo código florestal," September 15, 1965; Clóvis Cavalcanti, "Economic Growth and Environmental Protection in Brazil: An Unfavorable Trade-Off," in *Environmental Governance and Decentralisation*, ed. Albert Breton, Giorgio Brosio, Silvana Dalmazzone, and Giovanna Garrone (Northampton, MA: Edward Elgar Publishing, 2008), 52.

[96] Carlos Manes Bandeira, "Proteção e preservação nos Parques Nacionais,"*Anais do 2° Congresso Brasileiro de Florestas Tropicais* 2 (Viçosa: UF de Viçosa, 1974), MA; Eduardo de Freitas Machado, COPLAN, and IBDF, *Diagnóstico do subsistema de conservação e preservação de recursos naturais* (Brasília: IBDF/COPLAN, 1978), MA.

context, the removal of 2,500 people from Iguaçu National Park in the 1970s stands out as an exceptional event, the first time the Brazilian government acted to pursue a long-standing consensus policy of parks without people. Why did Brazil take so long to remove inhabitants from a national park? Why choose Iguaçu over the other national parks to first implement such a policy?

To effectively establish a national park according to what could be called in very broad strokes the "Yellowstone model" – that is, excluding inhabitants through territorial control – two essential elements are necessary: federal land control and strong national park agencies. Compared to neighboring Argentina, Brazil initially lacked both of these elements. In the case of Iguaçu, the legal uncertainty over the origin of the park land prevented federal action for almost two decades, from the park expansion in 1944 until the Supreme Court ruling in 1963. Territorial power demands justification, usually on the basis of a legal mandate over space (in this case, the land). The absence of an indisputable decision on the land's status not only allowed settlers to enter the national park in the first place but also prevented the Brazilian federal government from developing a strategy to claim its mandate over park territory before the late 1960s.

Even if the origin of the public land in Iguaçu was indisputably federal, however, enforcing national park policy depended on the existence of a robust national park agency, and Brazil lacked one. Unlike in Argentina, where a functional national park service had been established in 1934, in Brazil national parks were under the authority of an understaffed and underfunded national park section within the Forest Service agency. The agency itself had forestry as its primary goal, not conservation. The creation of the IBDF in 1967 did not change much, as the national park section became a subsection of the Department of Nature Protection within the IBDF, an agency whose main focus was, again, forestry and the extraction of forest resources. As José Luiz de Andrade Franco and José Augusto Drummond have noted, "caring for national parks was only one of [the IBDF's] sixteen statutory duties ... [F]or several years protected areas remained a definitely secondary concern of the agency."[97]

---

[97] Franco and Drummond, "Nature Protection," 338–67; Teresa Urban, *Saudade do Matão: Relembrando a história da conservação da natureza no Brasil* (Curitiba, Brazil: Editora da UFPR, 1998), 127, 145–47; Hochstetler and Keck, *Greening Brazil*, 23–31; "Serviço Florestal," "Departamento de Recursos Renováveis," and "Instituto Brasileiro de Desenvolvimento Florestal," MAPA/SIAN, accessed June 2015, www.an.gov.br/sian/inicial.asp.

Removing settlers from Iguaçu was much more the work of INCRA, as the land and colonization agency had the institutional profile and access to resources to carry out the eviction and relocation.[98] By tapping the resources made available to INCRA by the military regime to promote agrarian reform in frontier areas, government officials at the IBDF managed to achieve their historical goal of removing dwellers from a national park.

Another question demands an answer: Why Iguaçu? Only Iguaçu was a national park in a sensitive frontier area rife with land conflicts, where a neighboring country (Argentina) had repeatedly requested the removal of people living in the park. Iguaçu was also one of the oldest protected areas – the second national park established in Brazil in 1939. In the 1970s and 1980s, the IBDF would resume its partnership with INCRA to relocate families from other protected areas such as the Serra da Canastra and Ubajara national parks and the Poço das Antas Biological Reserve.[99] And yet, the use of agrarian reform legislation, as seen in Iguaçu, never became the primary method through which the IBDF and its inheritor agencies attempted to rid national park lands of their inhabitants. In some cases, as in the Serra da Bocaina National Park between Rio de Janeiro and São Paulo, INCRA faced stiff political opposition from occupants with greater political clout and failed to remove them.[100] In other cases, using agrarian reform law was deemed politically unfeasible, and IBDF chose to purchase land at market values directly from claimants and dwellers.[101] There were also many parks that were home to indigenous peoples, which added further complication with different legislation and the involvement of other federal agencies (the case of the

---

[98] The Brazilian government would repeat the use of agrarian reforms tools to guarantee land for national park use in other areas of Brazil, particularly the Amazon, beginning in the mid 1970s. Maria Tereza Jorge Pádua (retired director of the IBDF's Department of Research and Nature Conservation), in discussion with the author, March 2020; Foresta, *Amazon Conservation*; Freitas, "Conservation Frontier."

[99] Gustavo Henrique Cepolini Ferreira, "A regularização fundiária no Parque Nacional da Serra da Canastra e a expropriação camponesa: da baioneta à ponta da caneta." (M.A. Thesis (Geography), São Paulo, University of Sao Paulo, 2013), 97–117; IBAMA, "Plano de manejo: Parque Nacional da Ubajara" (IBAMA, 2001), www.icmbio.gov.br/parnau bajara/planos-de-manejo; IBAMA, "Plano de manejo: Reserva Biológica de Poço das Antas" (IBAMA, 2001), www.icmbio.gov.br/parnaubajara/planos-de-manejo.

[100] IBAMA, "Plano de Manejo: Parque Nacional da Serra da Bocaina" (IBAMA, 2002), www.icmbio.gov.br/parnaserradabocaina/extras/62-plano-de-manejo-e-monitorias. html.

[101] Maria Tereza Jorge Pádua (retired director of the IBDF's Department of Research and Nature Conservation), in discussion with the author, March 2020.

indigenous peoples living inside the Iguaçu National Park is discussed in Chapter 6).[102]

In its essence, the removal and relocation of settlers from Iguaçu National Park was as much a matter of conservation policy as of national security imperatives. As seen in this chapter, the idea of promoting agrarian reform through frontier colonization guided much of the Brazilian land policy in the early 1970s. It not only addressed the question of developing Brazil's hinterland but also presented a solution for the pockets of land conflict scattered across the countryside. In western Paraná, the fear of a "subversive" revolt by peasants, tenants, and squatters colored the lens through which the military saw the problem at Iguaçu National Park. The desire to avoid rural conflict combined with the increase of federal powers over territory created the conditions for the removal of settlers from Iguaçu to occur.[103]

---

[102] Sérgio Brant Rocha, "Monte Pascoal National Park: Indigenous Inhabitants versus Conservation Units," in *National Parks without People? The South American Experience*, ed. Thora Amend and Stephan Amend (Quito: IUCN/Parques Nacionales y Conservación Ambiental, 1995); Dean, *With Broadax and Firebrand*, 335–36.

[103] Studying environmental policy from the 1970s on, Hochstetler and Keck argued that Brazil's "federalism" had a great impact on environmental policy. Throughout its history, Brazil had faced cycles of centralization and decentralization. The military regime was a phase of centralization, especially at its height in the early 1970s. Hochstetler and Keck, *Greening Brazil*, 14–16.

5

Surveillance and Evasion

The Border, 1940–1980

On April 14, 1968, park rangers at Iguazú National Park in Argentina had a fatal encounter with hunters while patrolling the park's back-country. The party of three included Enrique Miranda, who had worked at the park for fifteen years, and two rookies, Augustin Sosa and Bernabé Méndez. For two days they camped by the Santo Domingo River, near a salt lick that attracted animals and hunters, 200 meters away from the confluence with the Iguazu River. At 6:30 a.m., Méndez, who had left the camp to check the surrounding area, returned claiming to have heard voices by the river. Listening from the shores of the Iguazu, the agents heard a canoe, veiled by the morning fog, paddling away toward the Brazilian bank. They also heard bark-ing dogs in the forest behind them and turned back to find and kill the canines. It was a common practice among Brazilian hunters to let dogs loose in the forest to corral prey, and Argentine rangers would usually kill the animals if they had the chance. The rangers split up to cover more ground, as they believed it was safe to be alone in the bush – it would be a few hours before the hunters whose voices they had heard on the river returned from Brazil to collect the dogs. But they had misjudged the possibility that hunters were still in the area, and a few minutes after the rangers split up, Miranda and Sosa overheard Méndez arguing with an unknown person. They ran toward him and arrived in time to see a hunter pointing a rifle at Méndez. As both Miranda and Sosa stated in their later testimonies, they believed the hunter had been waiting for the rangers, and when Méndez ordered him to drop his weapon, he started shooting and fled the scene along with two other individuals who had been lurking nearby. Méndez was shot in the chest and died on the spot.[1]

Miranda, the leader of the surveillance excursion, was partially blamed for Méndez's death because he had not requested that deputy gendarmes accompany the surveillance expedition. Since March of that year, after a previous shooting incident with hunters, excursion leaders were required to ask the Argentine National Gendarmerie in Puerto Iguazú for deputies to accompany park rangers in the backcountry. This measure was one of several instituted by the park director of forests at the Argentine national park service, Roberto Ferreyra, to curb the activities of Brazilian hunters and loggers. Per Ferreyra's orders, gendarmes should accompany rangers in case of a confrontation with hunters. Argentine national park rangers carried firearms, but gendarmes had better weapons and experience patrolling the border. Nevertheless, the rangers preferred to travel light and believed additional personnel could complicate the logistics of backcountry excursions. On the morning of April 9, Miranda was overwhelmed by the last-minute arrangements for the expedition, including the need to find a truck and a driver to take the party to the edge of the park, as all of the park's vehicles were in use elsewhere. The expedition ended up leaving late and without backup. In retrospect, park administrators believed someone might have tipped hunters off about the absence of gendarmes, which would support the rangers' claim that the confrontation was an ambush. Despite that, Miranda and Ferreyra faced administrative sanctions for organizing an expedition without the proper backup. Violence was always a possible outcome for the rangers involved in these expeditions.[2]

This tragic encounter between park rangers and hunters provides a snapshot of the overlapping territories that constituted Iguazú National Park in Argentina and Iguaçu National Park in Brazil. Together, visitors, law enforcement officers, park administrators and personnel, hunters, heart-of-palm harvesters, and animals established a landscape of different and competing territories across the two border parks. As briefly discussed in the introduction, environmental law and park regulations classified

---

[1] Secretaría de Parques Nacionales to Dirección General de Parques Nacionales, "Sumario instruido c/ motivo homicidio de ex-agte. D. Bernabé Mendez," Expediente 4804, year 1968, APN, 11, 19–30. According to José Gorgues, Méndez was new and inexperienced, and instead of immediately looking for cover, he decided to stay out in the open, foolishly asking the hunter to surrender. José Gorgues (retired Iguazú National Park employee), in discussion with the author, August 2014.

[2] Secretaría de Parques Nacionales to Dirección General de Parques Nacionales, "Sumario instruido c/ motivo homicidio de ex-agte. D. Bernabé Méndez," 1–19.

most of the area of the two parks – over 95 percent of their combined
territory – into categories where outside visitors were banned. It was the
duty of national park administrators to enforce this ban through a series
of surveillance practices. This chapter focuses on how two groups, rangers
and wardens on the one hand, and hunters and heart-of-palm collectors
on the other, constructed the restricted areas of the two border national
parks as spaces of nature through a series of spatial practices. It shows
how backcountry surveillance, and the responses to it, shaped Iguazú and
Iguaçu into transboundary but nationalized spaces of forests and wildlife
surrounded by a changing agricultural landscape.[3]

Surveillance, as practiced in the two national parks, is one of the tools
employed in the territorial control of protected areas. It is among the
many practices that produce the space of a national park, along with
drawing boundaries on maps and signaling their existence on the ground
through signposts, fences, or roads. Surveillance, mapping, and fencing
are all aspects of what geographer Robert Sack terms *human territoriality*:
the control of people through the mediation of space.[4] In Iguazú and
Iguaçu, boundaries were used to divert specific groups of people from
penetrating park space and prevent them from engaging in certain behaviors. Environmental legislation and park regulations prohibited local
settlers from entering the park area and capturing or killing wildlife
while giving rangers a mandate to patrol the backcountry, arrest hunters,
and slaughter hunting dogs inside that space.

Inside the two parks, the discourse of park officials and environmental
legislation classified any illegal act of hunting as *furtivo*, a cognate to the
English "furtive," which in Iberian languages conveys the dyad of theft by
stealth. Those called "poachers" in English were referred in Spanish as
cazadores furtivos and, similarly, *caçadores furtivos* in Portuguese. In

---

[3] Tragic encounters like this were not exclusive to Argentina. In 1970, another expedition to
the southeastern corner of Iguaçu National Park in Brazil also resulted in a casualty, with
the murder of Brazilian national park warden Alvício Vargas by heart-of-palm "thieves."
Pedro Berg (retired Iguaçu National Park employee), in discussion with the author,
October 2013; Eugênio Cichovski to IBDF, "Circular 191, de 1° de agosto de 1968,"
October 15, 1968, Pasta Documentos Diversos, Parque Nacional do Iguaçu, Informações
Complementares, PNIB-A; Congresso Nacional do Brasil, "Projeto de lei de pensão para
viúva de Alvício de Vargas, morto em serviço no Parque Nacional do Iguaçu," in
Congresso Nacional: Anais do Senado, vol. II (Brasília: Congresso Nacional do Brasil,
1973), 135–36, 235–36; "Pensão à viúva de servidor no Parque do Iguaçu," Diário do
Paraná, August 12, 1970; Brazil, Law 5598, August 11, 1970; Adilson Simão (Iguaçu
National Park Director, 1974–86) in discussion with the author, October 2013.
[4] Sack, *Human Territoriality*.

parallel fashion, less mobile activities such as illegal logging or the harvesting of heart of palm were simply treated as theft of state property. In the case of hunting, evasion and its counterpart surveillance were embedded in the very term used in law to define the illegality of the activity. Hence, the spatial focus of this chapter. Hunters were considered *furtivos* if they were caught inside the boundaries of an area – the two parks – where such activities were banned. To avoid awkward translations such as "furtive hunter," I will use, throughout this chapter, the standard English terms "poaching" and "theft" to highlight instances when the activities of hunting animals and harvesting plants were deemed illegal by the discourse and actions of park authorities.[5]

As adjacent but independent parks, Iguazú and Iguaçu were not only defined by the border delimiting park from nonpark lands but were also divided by an international boundary, the Iguazu River, that separates Argentina from Brazil. Initially, the two governments established their parks as tools for the effective occupation of their respective border zones, and this concern persisted during the following decades. This geopolitical mandate explains why park administrators on both sides came to see transboundary incursions as an existential threat to the integrity of their parks. The concern with border crossings was particularly salient among Argentine park officials, who blamed the settlers living in the nearby Brazilian park for most of the unauthorized hunting and heart-of-palm logging occurring in Iguazú before the 1970s.

This chapter portrays conflicts over local, national, and transnational territories at the Triple Frontier area between the 1940s and the 1970s. Unlike previous chapters, which focused on diachronic narratives of change, here the approach is mostly synchronic, casting light on how spatial practices (i.e., the repetition of social acts mediated by space) create territories of protected nature in a borderland setting. It reconstructs a landscape rather than weaving a narrative. Change is not absent, however, as the period witnessed an evolution in the policy and meaning

---

[5] Scholars like Karl Jacob have demonstrated how new conservation laws "create new crimes." Behavior that before was considered customary – that is, hunting and logging – becomes lawless. However, the case of the two Iguazu parks complicates this picture, as the settlers who practiced hunting and logging inside the protected areas arrived after the parks were created. Furthermore, as Jacob recognizes, one should not romanticize local opposition to conservation law. In frontier areas such as the Triple Frontier in the 1950s and 1960s, newcomers' behavior toward the natural world could be quite destructive. Karl Jacoby, *Crimes against Nature: Squatters, Poachers, Thieves, and the Hidden History of American Conservation* (Berkeley: University of California Press, 2001), 2, 194.

of national parks, culminating in the eviction of settlers and extirpation of population centers from park territories. Also, during this period the national governments slowly strengthened their capacity to enforce their territorial mandate over the parks. This chapter focuses primarily on how park administrators, rangers, and wardens in both Brazil and Argentina employed surveillance tactics to curb poaching and illegal plant harvesting in the parks. It also shows how the local population engaging in such activities on both sides of the international border reacted, sometimes violently, to the enforcement of park law.

WILDLIFE POACHING AND HEART-OF-PALM THEFT
AT THE BEGINNING OF THE PARKS

In its first decade of existence, the Argentine Iguazú National Park lacked personnel and infrastructure to carry out its mandate to protect the park territory against poachers. The case of a squatter living on the eastern border of the park in 1940 illustrates the limited territorial powers of the Argentine national park administration in Iguazú. In September 1940, National Gendarmerie officers stationed in Puerto Aguirre (future Puerto Iguazú) heard news of a settler living on the eastern outskirts of the park, near the Yacuy River. The settler, Lorenzo Silveira, hunted park animals and used dynamite for large-scale fishing in park waters, selling game meat and dried fish in the Brazilian town of Foz do Iguaçu. Silveira lived forty-five kilometers away from the falls zone, in an area that was difficult to access, reachable only on horseback. At the time, the Argentine national park had no rangers or park outposts in the backcountry, but news of the use of explosives inside the park, in a national security border area, demanded a firm reaction from the authorities. Without a ranger corps at their disposal, park administrators improvised a surveillance excursion, probably one of the first of its kind, with three park assistants (*ayudantes*), a park hand (*peón*), and an outside gendarme. The settler, an Argentine national squatting a plot of land inside the park, was evicted and his shack destroyed.[6]

At the time, fishing was still allowed in park waters and the Argentine national park service even published brochures promoting angling for visitors to Iguazú. However, large-scale fishing, with the use of explosives by locals, was a different thing, and this led the national park agency to

---

[6] Parque Nacional Iguazú to Dirección de Parques Nacionales, Expediente 5520, year 1940, APN.

ban "fishing with dynamite" in park waters.[7] The situation also exposed the need for a ranger corps to project the national park administration's power to the territories under its jurisdiction. The idea of a ranger corps had already been proposed at a national level by conservationist Hugo Salomon, who was inspired by the game wardens he saw in the African colonial parks he visited between 1937 and 1939.[8] In Iguazú, park administrators transformed a few park employees – in general, local young men hired as park assistants or hands – into park rangers (*guardaparques*).[9] This first cohort of rangers received no systematic training, but they were required to know the terrain and possess backcountry skills such as swimming, shooting, machete wielding, and horse riding. The newly appointed rangers also had to wear a badge and a uniform, especially when patrolling the perimeter of the park, thus bringing the presence of the national park administration to the backcountry in a visual and bodily medium. To some, however, outdoor skills and khakis were not enough. Scientists in the national park agency voiced criticism of the new ranger program over the recruits' lack of training and inadequate knowledge of the local flora and fauna. They believed the new rangers were unprepared for their role as the embodiment of national park rules and legislation.[10]

Internal criticism did not impede the Argentine national park agency from pursuing its ranger plan, and with the initial group of *peones* donning the ranger uniform, administrators launched the first surveillance excursions to Iguazú's eastern backcountry, setting a pattern that continued in the years that followed. To patrol the park's strict preservation area, rangers in Puerto Iguazú would load a truck with a boat and gear in the early hours of the morning and take Highway 101 to the eastern edge of the park. From there, they would sail down the Yacuy Arroyo, a

---

[7] Dirección de Parques Nacionales, "Parque Nacional del Iguazú" (Buenos Aires: Dirección de Parques Nacionales, 1936, 1937, 1940), BNRA; Ministerio de Agricultura de La Nación, Dirección de Piscicultura y Pesca, *Recopilación de leyes, decretos, resoluciones y ordenanzas sobre pesca, caza marítima e industrialización* (Buenos Aires, Ministerio de Agricultura de La Nación, 1945), 37–44, BNRA; Dirección de Parques Nacionales, *Qué son los Parques Nacionales*, 14–15.

[8] Salomon, "Nociones generales," 33–36.

[9] This was the case of José Gorgues, a local young man hired as a park hand in 1937 at the age of 19. He was promoted to park ranger in 1940. José Gorgues (retired Iguazú National Park employee), in discussion with the author, August 2014.

[10] "Reglamento de guarda-parques," in Dirección de Parques Nacionales, *Decreto reglamentario de la ley 12103 y recopilacion de reglamentos vigentes* (Buenos Aires: Ministerio de Agricultura, 1940), 109–11, APN-B; Alberto F. Anziano, "Informe Comisión Técnica al Parque Nac. Iguazu, 1953" (Buenos Aires, 1953), Pliego 17, APN-B.

tributary of the Iguazu that crisscrossed the park's eastern boundary, until they reached the confluence of the two rivers. At this point, the party would continue downriver on the Iguazu, looking for signs of wildlife poaching and heart-of-palm extraction on the Argentine banks until they reached the falls area. Surveillance expeditions like these could last between three and seven days, depending on the level of the Yacuy (which in the dry season required portage at some points) and whether they made stops along the route.

By the end of the decade, surveillance excursions such as these were being launched once or twice a year, and rangers started reporting the first signs of "Brazilian" hunters trespassing in the Argentine park. In a 1948 expedition, for example, rangers found abandoned hunting camps on the banks of the Iguazu. They also discovered an empty shack amid a few cultivated plots near the park's eastern edge. Rangers failed to encounter any actual hunter or squatter, but they argued that the hunting camps and shack were unquestionably evidence of Brazilian invaders. To support their claim, they cited the presence of objects of Brazilian origin at different locations. In truth, objects from across the border were fairly weak evidence, as products from both countries were commonly sold throughout the borderland.[11]

A surveillance trail was built at the eastern limit of the Argentine park in 1947 both to serve as a physical demarcation of the park's boundary and to facilitate surveillance by land. However, rangers visited the area only once after that, and the forest soon encroached upon the trail. The construction of three ranger outposts in 1949, one of them in the backcountry where Highway 101 crossed the park's eastern perimeter, established a permanent base for surveilling the area. Now the park had a ranger permanently deployed in the area of strict preservation to curb poachers.[12]

The 1950s saw an increase in the frequency of expeditions. In 1958 alone five were launched, leading to the arrest of nine hunters, two of them Brazilian.[13] The presence of a ranger outpost at the eastern boundary

---

[11] Intendencia Iguazú to Administración General de Parques Nacionales y Turismo, Expediente 5268, year 1948, APN-B.

[12] Ibid.; Intendencia Iguazú to Dirección de Parques Nacionales, Expediente 1326, year 1943, APN; Intendencia Iguazú to Dirección de Parques Nacionales, Expediente 1326, year 1943, APN; Administración de Parques Nacionales y Turismo, "Memoria correspondiente al año 1949" (1950), 119, APN-B.

[13] "Memoria anual – División Bosques – 1958," in Dirección de Biblioteca Parques Nacionales to Dirección General de Parques Nacionales, "5/59 eleva memoria corresp. año 1958," Expediente 795, year 1959, 20–21, APN.

seemed to have curtailed transgressions or at least made them noticeable, but work conditions for park agents were far from ideal. Rangers stationed on Iguazú's outskirts remained isolated from the rest of the park, and the lack of radio equipment meant they had to rely on passing vehicles for communication. On February 2, 1959, ranger Enrique Miranda, deployed at the eastern outpost, had to ask a truck driver to inform park administrators of the recent arrest of two armed Paraguayan lumbermen who had entered the park to hunt birds.[14]

Once the Argentine national park service had been active in the region for several decades, locals had become aware of the prohibitions enforced by the agency, but most were ignorant of the actual lines that defined the space where those prohibitions were in force. Locals caught inside the park's strict preservation area confessed to knowing about the ban on hunting and possession of arms in park territory. However, many claimed to be ignorant of where the park actually began, especially those entering via the park's eastern section. A physical border did exist in the form of a line of boundary stones installed in 1948 by Emilio Dalponte, a land surveyor hired to demarcate the eastern limits of the park. Dalponte recognized that signaling the border physically on the landscape was a prerequisite for park administrators to lay claim to the park's territory. He had installed one boundary stone every thousand meters (for a total of about twenty-five boundary stones). In 1953, a new revision of the eastern limit moved the boundary line seventy-two meters east. Instead of moving all the stones to the new location, however, Dalponte had decided to install only six new stones in the vicinity of Highway 101, where a ranger outpost was located.[15]

Visual markers of territorial limits are essential in transforming large pieces of land into protected areas. Argentina's Iguazú National Park, like many other parks and reservations, was not only a *place*, a space that gained meaning through a series of social practices; it was also a *territory*, a bounded space demanding conscious effort – and the deployment of power over space – to maintain it. Deploying park rangers in the backcountry was one way of enforcing the park territory, but it also required other techniques, including making the boundary obvious to possible intruders. Assessed from this angle, a sparse line of boundary stones

---

[14] Intendencia Iguazu to Dirección General de Parques Nacionales, Expediente 544, year 1959, APN.

[15] Intendencia Iguazú to Administración General de Parques Nacionales, Expediente 1385, year 1962, 6, 20, APN.

hidden on the forest floor served as an ineffective method for communi-
cating the existence of an impassable limit. Nevertheless, the stones acted
as an ex post facto justification for arresting trespassers. It is clear that,
given the limited resources, the stones worked not as a deterrent to
possible intruders but as a material legitimation of park authorities'
actions against locals.[16] The uncertainty of the boundary even sometimes
allowed the expansion of the park's territorial powers beyond its borders.[17] This happened in 1962 when park rangers moved to shut down a
heart-of-palm harvesting operation that had felled 3,500 palm trees in an
area adjacent to the park. The operation, owned by former park settler
Nicolás Jewgeniuk, was located outside park boundaries, beyond its
eastern limits, but the lack of certainty about the park's eastern border
allowed rangers to assert authority over Jewgeniuk's activities.[18]

Things were different in Brazil. Before its thirtyfold expansion in 1944,
Iguaçu National Park lacked a police force to enforce the mandate of the
Brazilian Forest Service over its territory. State troopers in Foz do Iguaçu
and the local army battalion patrolled the park intermittently as part of
their border protection duties; police officers sometimes ended up enforcing environmental regulations. On a river border patrol in 1943, for
example, police officers stopped hunters in the park near Poço Preto, a
small port on the Brazilian side of the Iguazu and a popular angling spot.
Two of the three hunters were Brazilian, and the other an unidentified
Spanish-speaking foreigner. The police apprehended their firearms for
"hunting without a license in Brazilian territory," but their report failed
to mention the important fact that they were also acting inside the new
national park created in 1939. Indeed, Brazilian police officers initially
seemed oblivious to the park's existence at this point.[19]

After the expansion of Iguaçu in 1944, park administrators in Brazil
hired a group of watchmen from among the local population to guard the
new area. Between 1945 and 1947, the national park administration at
Iguaçu established six park outposts, two near the falls and four in the
newly expanded backcountry, where they deployed the new wardens and

---

[16] Nail, *Theory of the Border*, 47–63.   [17] Sack, *Human Territoriality*, 32–33.
[18] Intendencia Iguazú to Administración General de Parques Nacionales, Expediente 1385,
    year 1962, APN; "Nicolás Jewgeniuk," Settlement Cards, Iguazú National Park,
    Programa Pobladores y Comunidades, APN-P.
[19] Benedito de Almeida Prohmann a Glaucio Guiss, Delegado, "Relatório de diligencia
    efetuada na percorrida da fronteira Brasil-Argentina até a foz do Rio Santo Antonio,"
    March 23, 1943, DOPS/PR – Pastas Temáticas – Delegacia de Polícia de Foz do Iguaçu –
    Número: 0499b, Topografia: 55, Data: 1942–81, APP.

their families.[20] It was the most they could do in a time when the park was experiencing funding shortages.[21] Though the Brazilian Forest Service had the resources and structure to recruit and train rangers, their primary conservation goal in the 1940s was to protect trees, not wildlife. At the time, conservationists within the agency were fixated on protecting the remaining forests of western Paraná from the destruction caused by the advance of colonization and logging companies. One of their projects, never put into practice, was to create a federal ranger corps to protect forests throughout the short-lived Territory of Iguaçu (1943–46). Their only accomplishment, however, was to assign a volunteer forest deputy who alone was in charge of protecting an area of more than six million hectares, a territory the size of West Virginia.[22]

By the late 1950s, Iguaçu National Park in Brazil had nine uniformed but poorly equipped wardens to watch an area of over 160,000 hectares. Of these, five operated in the falls area and four in the backcountry, the area expanded in 1944, in outposts located at different points along the roads that delimited the northern perimeter of the park.[23] Wardens lacked the training and the means to enforce Iguaçu's environmental regulations.[24] Stationing a few wardens in the backcountry did work as a source of information about and deterrence against squatting and logging inside park lands, as well as to prevent fires. Ultimately, though, their capacity to curb undesired activities was quite limited, as they guarded a territory contested in the higher spheres of state and federal politics. As settlement on park land gained steam in the late 1950s, the area of the future São José and Santo Alberto villages became off-limits for park wardens on surveillance

---

[20] Eugênio Cichovski to IBDF, "Circular 191, de 1º de agosto de 1968," October 15, 1968, Pasta Documentos Diversos, Parque Nacional do Iguaçu, Informações Complementares, PNIB-A; Mário Câmara Canto, "Relatório que apresenta o administrador do Parque Nacional do Iguassú," September 25, 1946 (Foz do Iguaçu, 1946), PNIB-A.

[21] Mário Câmara Canto to Departamento de Parques Nacionais, "Sugestões referente às obras do P.N. do Iguaçu," May 29, 1947, PNIB-A.

[22] João Augusto Falcão, "A defesa florestal do Território do Iguaçu," July 22, 1944, in *O Serviço Florestal no biênio 1943–1944*, 133–35, MA.

[23] João Cleophas, *As atividades do Ministério da Agricultura em 1952* (Rio de Janeiro: Ministério da Agricultura, Serviço de Informação Agrícola, 1953), 312–13, MA.

[24] Unlike Argentina, Brazil never developed a professional corps of trained park rangers. Locally hired hands guarded the Brazilian parks. They were poorly paid, unprepared, and unequipped for the task of defending the parks. According to Maria Tereza Jorge Pádua, many ended up developing a sense of duty and "a passion for the natural environment," despite their lack of resources. Maria Tereza Jorge Pádua (retired director of the IBDF's Department of Research and Nature Conservation), in discussion with the author, March 2020.

trips. In his 1959 report, for example, Iguaçu National Park director Mário Pimentel de Camargo recognized that in the occupied area wardens no longer had the power to prevent logging or poaching.[25]

Other sectors of the park had different legal statuses, and also suffered the threat of land grabbing. One example is the northeastern section of the park, whose integrity as a protected area was threatened in 1957 by a land-grabbing operation launched by Moysés Lupion de Troia, the governor of Paraná. The presence of national park wardens in the area did little to prevent the Lupion administration from hiring a company to survey and parcel national park lands for future colonization. The government of the state of Paraná abandoned its plans of illegally parceling and selling the federal land only after a Paraná opposition politician, Federal Deputy Bronislau Ostoja Roguski, carried out a denunciation campaign in national newspapers.[26]

Owing to its sensitive nature as a borderland park, Iguaçu continued to be occasionally patrolled by troops from the First Border Battalion, stationed in Foz do Iguaçu. The Brazilian Army had its own agenda, however, and gave precedence to fighting the smuggling of products such as coffee rather than other activities such as hunting and logging. Park officials in Brazil also understood that they could not rely on this cooperation with military forces, as the army sometimes went long stretches without offering any help to park operatives.[27]

In their first decades, both Iguazú and Iguaçu employed a small contingent of ill-trained uniformed wardens and rangers to exert national park power over their respective territories. But the similarities end here. Whereas in Argentina the rangers' main goal was to curb wildlife poaching and heart-of-palm theft, in Brazil wardens acted as deterrence against attempts at logging and land grabbing, reflecting the greater push to colonize the frontier on the Brazilian side of the border. Clearly, wardens in Brazil were only partially effective, for much of the park lands' fate depended on other political and legal actors. The presence of a warden outpost, for example, did little to prevent settler occupation in São José and Santo Alberto.

Another critical distinction between the two parks relates to the spatial practices employed in surveillance. In Argentina, park authorities opted

[25] Mário Pimentel de Camargo, "Relatório anual 1959" (Foz do Iguaçu, 1959), 5, PNIB-A.
[26] "Moysés Lupion cobiça nova Gleba da União," *O Estado de São Paulo*, December 18, 1957; "Lupion não concretizará audacioso assalto à Gleba," *O Estado de São Paulo*, December 20, 1957.
[27] "Críticas às devastação das matas paranaenses," *Diário do Paraná*, July 15, 1959, 2.

for backcountry expeditions as a strategy to maintain the park's territorial integrity. The Argentine park was smaller, allowing rangers to rely on roads and waterways to cover its perimeter. Argentine rangers' mobility and occasional visits to the backcountry also allowed a higher degree of independence from the local population. After all, the areas surrounding Iguazú National Park in Argentina were still sparsely populated. In Brazil, on the other hand, wardens were deployed with their families in backcountry outposts adjacent to booming population centers. Backcountry wardens, unlike their Argentine counterparts, rarely organized routine surveillance expeditions because of a lack of vehicles. With no means of transportation and limited mobility, Brazilian wardens were forced to develop ties with neighboring communities. Integration eventually led to compromise. Therefore, to prevent hunting, a favorite activity among locals, was never a priority before the 1970s.

HUNTING ON THE TRIPLE FRONTIER

During the first half of the twentieth century, hunting was an important resource for the diets of the Guarani *obraje* workers in the borderland, including laborers in the logging operation that preceded Iguazú National Park in the 1920s. People living in the Triple Frontier area employed several hunting techniques using traps and bait, but the most common method involved ambushing animals from atop makeshift platforms set up in trees next to salt licks and water holes. Such tree stands were known in Portuguese as *jirau*, a Tupi word meaning "platform," and were used throughout Brazil by rural dwellers engaged in subsistence hunting in forested areas. Brazilian settlers introduced the method to Argentina, and in northern Misiones it came to be known as *sobrado*, a Portuguese term for a two-story house. Perched the entire night on a tree platform near a salt lick, hunters could wait for peccary, deer, and tapir without being seen or scented.[28]

Despite the risk of being mauled if they missed a shot, hunters also used tree stands to ambush jaguars, which required large-caliber guns. Dogs or traps, however, were far more common in jaguar hunting than *sobrados*. Canines were used particularly by sportsmen seeking the thrill of a chase, as

[28] Muello, *Misiones, las cataratas del Iguazú*, 73–76, 90, 106–8, 120; Germán de Laferrère, *Selva adentro* (Buenos Aires: Editorial Argentina "Arístides Quillet," 1945), 169–72; Sérgio Buarque de Holanda, *Caminhos e Fronteiras*, 4th ed., (São Paulo: Companhia das Letras, 2017), 73–74, 112–15.

jaguar hounds could spot a track, find the animal, and chase it up a tree. Once cornered by dogs, jaguars were shot by hunters from the ground. Commercial hunters in search of pelts preferred traps to using dogs, a less laborious method that required only setting jaguar traps in the right spots. They took advantage of the fact that jaguars, especially mothers with cubs, tended to stick to certain routes unless disturbed by humans, reusing the same paths from their dens to their preferred water holes. Despite the animals' stealth, well-seasoned hunters could find a jaguar track, sometimes through its association with tapir footprints. Upon finding a track, a hunter would hide a leghold trap underneath the foliage below a hanging piece of meat, which also helped to disguise the metallic scent of the trap.[29]

On the Brazilian side of the Iguazu, hunting was also ubiquitous, and game meat was part of the diet of the settlers arriving from the Brazilian state of Rio Grande do Sul in the 1950s.[30] The opening of the new BR-277 as a dirt road between 1950 and 1953 attracted many Italian- and German-Brazilian migrants from Rio Grande do Sul to the park environs. The newcomers relied not only on agriculture and livestock, particularly pigs and chickens, but also on hunting for their dietary needs. At the canteen opened by Edmundo Carlos Bierdorf in Medianeira in 1951, for example, game meat was a common menu item. Bierdorf was a southern pioneer who had moved to the area years earlier to work in the lumber industry. In Medianeira, adjacent to Iguaçu, he established a logging business, employing mostly Guarani and mestizo workers, many from Paraguay. He also opened a canteen to cater to both lumberjacks and the new families arriving from Rio Grande do Sul. The canteen's menu included not only pork and chicken, common items in the diet of the white newcomers, but also deer, agouti, and tapir meat, which were enjoyed by Guarani and Euro-Brazilians alike.[31]

---

[29] Germán Dras, "La caza del jaguar en los montes de Misiones," *Leoplán*, October 9, 1940, CIES; Intendencia Iguazú to Administración General de Parques Nacionales y Turismo, Expediente 5268, year 1948, APN-B.

[30] The Brazilian Army lieutenant Lima Figueiredo described the area of Iguaçu National Park as being "infested with jaguars" in the 1930s, before the creation of the park. In an expedition to the area he spotted tree stands (*jiraus*) installed by local hunters near the area's many "riverine clayish salt licks." While traveling through the area, Lima Figueiredo and his party killed one jaguar, and the animal's salt-cured flesh fed the group for the rest of their trip while the head was kept as a trophy. See Figueiredo, *Oéste paranaense*, 48–61; "Nas divisas do extremo norte," *O paiz*, March 9, 1929.

[31] Hildegarde Maria Rohde, Elza Lorenzzoni Biersdorf, and Associação dos Professores Aposentados de Medianeira, *Resgate da memória de Medianeira* (Medianeira, Paraná: CEFET-PR, 1996), 83–92, 188–208.

Besides supplying part of the newcomers' diet, hunting also served as a gendered form of social bonding for the white male settlers. It was common for men to go out into the forest on weekends to drink yerba mate and hunt. One of the most sought-after species was the peccary, which at that time lived in sounders of a hundred or more individuals, making hunting the swine a risky but fulfilling activity. Hunting was a lure to the region, as the abundance of game led southern farmers to move into the area.[32] Among these was Alfredo Brol, who arrived with his family at the Brazilian side of the border in 1936, at the age of eighteen. His father was a muleteer who had fallen in love with the region for its abundance of game. The Brols lived in a property straddling the border of the future Iguaçu National Park, where they raised pigs, which in turn attracted jaguars and cougars. As with other white settlers from southern Brazil, hunting occupied much of the free time of male members of the extended Brol family. Brol's son-in-law, Ermínio Mezzo, estimated that he had killed over three thousand deer in the area. He also captured snakes to sell to a tanner in Argentina. Like his father-in-law, Mezzo was from Rio Grande do Sul and had been drawn to the region for its abundance of game, settling in the area and marrying into the Brol family. The creation of the park in 1939 created another incentive for hunters: during the first years of Iguaçu, the Brols would sell jaguar hides to the wealthy tourists who flew in from Curitiba and São Paulo to see the falls.[33]

Hunting continued in the following decades among settlers on both sides of the border. Juan Hoppe, for example, easily found a jaguar trap to borrow in Puerto Iguazú in 1977 when he realized an animal was preying on his pigs and chickens within the Argentine national park. Jaguar traps (*trampas tigreras*) were sold in the local hardware store in Puerto Iguazú, as confirmed by Celso Schreiner, who lent the equipment to his friend Hoppe. Schreiner knew hunting was prohibited in the park and thought Hoppe, as an old settler (*poblador antiguo*), would know better than to use the trap inside the park. It was clear, however, that there was a clientele still eager to buy hunting gear in the area well into the 1970s, including jaguar traps.[34]

---

[32] Rohde et al., *Resgate da memória de Medianeira*, 83–92, 188–208; Marcos Sá Corrêa, *Meu vizinho, o Parque Nacional do Iguaçu* (Cascavel, Brazil: Tuicial, 2009), 82.

[33] In his 1993 interview, Mezzo flatly distanced himself from trophy hunters, arguing that he "never killed animals just for sport," and that he would hunt for his own "consumption or to sell their meat and hide." Interviews with Alfredo Brol and Ermínio Mezzo, *Gazeta do Iguaçu*, June 20, 1993, in "Foz 80, memória," BPEENR.

[34] Servicio Nacional de Parques Nacionales, Expediente 2960, year 1978, APN; Asesoría Jurídica to Administración de Parques Nacionales, "Memorandum 1147 – Informa sobre

Hunting also generated income for those involved in the sale of jaguar hides. The arrest of two hunters in the winter of 1975 at the Santo Domingo salt lick, in the Argentine park, sheds light on the modus operandi of commercial hunters. The Argentine Pedro Ramón Lambare and the Paraguayan Ramón Santiago Armoa were arrested on the night of July 11, 1975, while hunting animals for their pelts. At the time of their arrest, they had already caught and killed several monkeys, coatis, rabbits, peccaries, opossums, and birds. They captured the animals with nine leghold traps set around the salt lick. The two lived in Puerto Iguazú and allegedly hunted only in Paraguay, across the Paraná River, but the recent arrival of numerous Brazilian settlers in the area pushed them out of their hunting grounds. They knew about the hunting ban inside the Argentine national park but decided to try their luck there, since they knew it harbored plenty of animals. They were caught in the act by rangers after a few days of hunting, and in an attempt to make examples out of them – after all, they lived in Puerto Iguazú – the park administration applied a fine of 23,000 pesos. A heavy fine, to be sure, but it was less than the value of a single jaguar hide, 40,000 pesos.[35]

In his book on poaching and American conservation, historian Karl Jacoby has described the different ways the local population living near the Yellowstone National Park engaged in and justified poaching. According to Jacoby, there were those who hunted for personal consumption, which they recognized as an illegal act that was justified by their natural right to subsistence, and there were those who poached for commercial purposes, an objectionable predatory activity in the eyes of locals engaged in subsistence hunting. The distinction between the two types of poaching was not always clear, however, because "subsistence poachers"

el estado de trámite del expediente judicial Servicio Nacional de Parques Nacionales c/ Hoppe Juan s/ desalojo que tramita por ante el Juzgado Federal Posadas," Expediente 2674, year 1979, APN.

[35] Carpeta 159, July 11, 1975, "Sumario protec. fauna, flora, disp. 70 Ramón R. Lambare y Ramón Armoa," Caja Infracciones, Sumarios, Multas, PNIA. Jaguars were difficult to kill, but they attracted specialized hunters with special firearms and ammunition (*munición tigrera*). Commercial hunters seeking to profit from the selling of hides were not the only ones after the big cats. Neighboring Paraguay received a fair number of wealthy trophy hunters from Buenos Aires. Jaguar hunting there was legal, but the animal was becoming rarer. Weekend hunters would receive calls when *obraje* workers sighted a jaguar in the forest, and those with the means would quickly travel to eastern Paraguay to hunt the sighted animal. Servicio Nacional de Parques Nacionales, Expediente 0433, year 1978, APN. See also Carlos Rebella, *Caza mayor* (Buenos Aires: Albatros, 1974), 143–45; Víctor José Grignaschi, *Astas y colmillos: Relatos de caza* (Buenos Aires: Britania, 1983), 81, 90–92.

sold by-products of their hunts to the market, and commercial hunters also consumed game meat. In the Triple Frontier area, the line between the two activities was similarly blurry, as the same settlers who engaged in subsistence hunting also sometimes took the opportunity to profit from the sale of jaguar hides to tourists visiting the falls.[36]

LEGISLATION

The banning of hunting in and around the two national parks was a long process that evolved in parallel on either side of the border. Unlike Yellowstone, whose 1872 act provided against "the wanton destruction of fish and game ... and against their capture for the purposes of merchandise or profit," the first national park laws in Argentina and Brazil said little about managing the vertebrate animals found inside national park territories.[37] In the two countries, hunting and fishing in national parks came to be regulated either by internal park rules or by broader pieces of legislation that dealt with wildlife in the national context.

In Argentina, the influence of Hugo Salomon and the National Commission for South American Fauna led to the passage of hunting bans in the 1920s, even before the creation of Iguazú National Park. In that decade, the Argentine federal government prohibited the hunting of several birds and a few selected mammals in the federal territories of Formosa, Chaco, and Misiones. Notably absent from the list were big cats as well as reptiles and fish. New laws also established hunting seasons throughout Argentina. These hunting regulations were, however, mostly just for show, as they were silent regarding enforcement – it was up to local police forces to carry them out. The act of hunting itself was not penalized, only possessing by-products of hunting, which incurred fines but not incarceration.[38]

Argentina's 1934 National Park Act did not ban hunting and fishing in national parks but gave the national park agency discretion to regulate

---

[36] Jacoby, *Crimes against Nature*, 139, 146.

[37] United States, "An Act to Set Apart a Certain Tract of Land Lying Near the Head-Waters of the Yellowstone River as a Public Park," March 1, 1872, in Library of Congress, *A Century of Lawmaking for a New Nation: U.S. Congressional Documents and Debates, 1774–1875*, 32–33, http://memory.loc.gov/cgi-bin/ampage?collId=llsl&fileName=017/llsl017.db&recNum=73; Argentina, Law 12103, "Ley de Parques Nacionales," September 29, 1934; Brazil, Decree 1713, June 14, 1937; Brazil, Decree-Law 1035, January 10, 1939.

[38] Liebermann, "Breve ensayo," 227–44; Dennler de la Tour, "Protección y conservación," 34–35.

those activities inside the territories it controlled. It was up to the agency to ban hunting in the parks. In Iguazú National Park, hunting was prohibited in the park's early years owing, again, to the lobby of the National Commission for South American Fauna. Even so, park administrators began to enforce the hunting ban only after 1940, when a new resolution included fishing on the list of forbidden activities. Despite these changes, a total hunting ban was not incorporated into law until 1950, when the Argentine government prohibited hunting in all lands under federal jurisdiction, including national parks and federal territories (Misiones was a territory until 1953).[39]

In Brazil, a few months after gazetting Iguaçu National Park in 1939, the Vargas regime promulgated a new hunting law updating the previous 1934 hunting and fishing act.[40] The new law allowed the hunting of wildlife in Brazilian territory for all purposes, including commercial hunting, which was now to be licensed by the federal government. Animal products such as pelts, hides, and dead butterflies could be sold and even exported. Hunting was also permitted on most public lands, but prohibited in "parks and wildlife sanctuaries." Thus, the new law made Iguaçu National Park a hunting-free territory just months after its creation. Under the new law, hunting transgressions were considered misdemeanors, punishable by fines, confiscation, and brief incarceration – no more than sixty days – a penalty applied only to repeat offenders. This hunting law received minor revisions in 1943, retaining the concept of wildlife as an economic resource to be regulated and taxed.[41]

---

[39] Under Exequiel Bustillo, the Argentine National Park Agency turned a blind eye to hunting inside the park, and wild animal hides and dead butterflies were sold to tourists in a store near the falls. The park administration prohibited hunting and fishing only after conservationists lobbied against the practice in 1940. Dennler de la Tour, "Protección y conservación," 43–46; Argentina, Law 12103, "Ley de Parques Nacionales," September 29, 1934; Argentina, Decree 12054, "Atribuciones y deberes de la Administración General de Parques Nacionales y Turismo," April 30, 1946; Argentina, Law 13908, "Conservación de la fauna," July 19, 1950.

[40] The original 1934 Fishing and Hunting Act was the result of Minister of Agriculture Fernando Costa's experience as state secretary of agriculture to the state of São Paulo in 1927. In that role, Costa introduced new state regulations on fishing and hunting, including the need for licensing, to promote the rational management of fish and game resources in the state. "Caça e pesca" and "A natureza e sua exploração," *Boletim do Ministério da Agricultura* 27, no. 1–3 (1938): 113–15, 122–24, SU.

[41] Brazil, Decree-Law 1210, "Código de caça," April 2, 1939; Brazil, Decree-Law 1768, November 1939; Brazil, Decree-Law 5894, October 20, 1943; Instituto de Biologia e Pesquisas Tecnológicas, Estado do Paraná, Serviço de Proteção à Caça e Pesca, *Portaria n. 410 do Ministério da Agricultura* (Curitiba: Papelaria São José, 1946), APP.

Brazilian law banned hunting inside Iguaçu National Park from year one but allowed the practice outside the park until 1961. In that year, Brazilian president Jânio Quadros signed a decree establishing a five-year moratorium on hunting in dozens of municipalities in the states of Mato Grosso and Paraná, including Foz do Iguaçu, encompassing most of the area surrounding the national park.[42] Finally, in January 1967, when the country was under military rule, a new law passed by Congress prohibited the hunting of all animals native to Brazil. According to the law, all of the country's wildlife became the property of the federal government, and their "utilization, persecution, destruction, hunting, or capture" was prohibited. Exceptions would be made for "regional peculiarities" (e.g., subsistence hunting by peasant communities). Thus, trophy and commercial hunting, as well as the sale of hunting by-products, became punishable by law, a prohibition that is still in effect in present-day Brazil. Violators were punished with three months to a year in prison and a fine of ten times the official monthly minimum wage.[43] It is important to note, therefore, that whereas in Brazil hunters caught in the act could face time in jail, across the Iguazu River, in Argentina, the penalty was only a fine. Despite the many flaws in the enforcement of environmental laws in Brazil, this discrepancy may have influenced the decisions of Brazilian hunters to cross the border to poach in Argentina.[44]

The Brazilian legal ban on hunting did not translate into full enforcement. In a 1976 interview, Roberto Ribas Lange, who worked as an environmental inspector for the Secretary of Agriculture of the state of Paraná, explained that the lack of jurisprudence hindered the application of environmental legislation in Brazil. The Brazilian state never actually enforced any of the several iterations of the hunting legislation passed since the 1930s. Lange claimed that judges and prosecutors were unfamiliar with the hunting law and frequently dismissed poaching charges as "ridiculous." In three years as an environmental inspector, Lange failed to bring a single violator to court. Law enforcement officers also usually

[42] Brazil, Law 4771, "Novo código florestal," Art. 26, September 15, 1965; Brazil, Decree 50880, June 1961.

[43] Although hunting was prohibited in the Brazilian Iguaçu National Park, fishing was still allowed, and tourists could come to the park to angle. René Denizart Pockrandt, "Parque Nacional do Iguaçu," *Diário do Paraná*, September 26, 1965; Pockrandt, "Relatório das atividades e problemas do parque," 70; Brazil, Law 5197, January 3, 1967.

[44] This difference in the penalties faced by poachers on either side of the border was pointed out to me by Daniel de la Torre, former Iguazú National Park ranger and director of infrastructure works for the APN. Daniel de la Torre, in discussion with the author, August 2014.

dismissed hunting violations as minor offenses, unworthy of the attention of the Brazilian judicial system. IBDF officials had difficulty convincing members of the Brazilian police forces to do the bureaucratic work of pressing charges against poachers. When police officers cooperated, they usually proved unable to conduct a proper investigation and collect good evidence, leading to many dismissed cases. As a federal agency, the IBDF had its method of punishment – applying fines. But just as judges and police officers were disinclined to pursue legal charges against poachers, IBDF employees were unwilling to proceed with fine collection, as the cost of doing so usually exceeded the fines' monetary value. Lange calculated that in the ten years before 1976, IBDF had not made any effort to collect the fines it had issued. The only people who paid were the ones who chose to do so.[45]

POACHING AND SURVEILLANCE IN BRAZIL

Until the 1960s, police officers in Brazil were uninterested in enforcing environmental legislation, despite their legal obligation to do so. Iguaçu was a special case among the country's protected areas because officers had to enter the park to patrol sections of the border with Argentina, and there were times when the park provided justification for police to seize firearms in encounters with local hunters. But such events were uncommon, for law enforcement's goal was to patrol the border, not combat poaching.[46] Park directors in protected areas, for their part, had to deal with a lack of resources and trained personnel, which seriously undermined their ability to prevent activities such as poaching and illegal logging. With meager resources, park directors in Brazil's Iguaçu National Park were lenient with hunters and viewed backcountry wardens primarily as a physical deterrence against illegal land occupation inside

---

[45] Roberto Ribas Lange, interviewed in "Mesa redonda," *Referência em planejamento* 1, First Semester of 1976, 48; Instituto Brasileiro de Desenvolvimento Florestal, Delegacia Estadual do Paraná, "Relatório de exercício 1975," 203, PNIB-A.

[46] An example of one such case: while patrolling the border, police officers from Foz do Iguaçu seized the firearms of three men in Iguaçu National Park in 1943. The agents reported that the men did not have licenses to own the guns or hunt. Of course, they overlooked the fact that a hunting license would be needed only if the men were outside the park, as hunting was strictly prohibited inside Iguaçu. Glaucio Guiss, "Cópia do relatório de diligência efetuada na percorrida da fronteira Brasil-Argentina," March, 23, 1943, Secretaria de Estado de Segurança Pública, Divisão de Segurança e Informações, DOPS/PR – Pastas Temáticas – Delegacia de Polícia de Foz do Iguaçu – Número: 0499b, Topografia: 55, Data: 1942–1981.

park territory, which they understood as a more pressing issue. Mário Pimentel de Camargo, Iguaçu park director in 1962, confirmed this rationale by attesting that the presence of wardens in the extreme north-eastern fringe of the park made "surveillance against any kind of invasion of those lands ... complete." Camargo had little control over the wave of settlers arriving in the São José and Santo Alberto sections of the park, but he believed that the depopulated eastern sector was secured against squat-ting by the deployment of park wardens in the area.[47]

Once agricultural engineer René Denizart Pockrandt was appointed park director in February 1965, he overhauled the park's daily operations, includ-ing an attempt to improve the efficacy of surveillance and a focus on curbing wildlife poaching and heart-of-palm theft.[48] Two years into Pockrandt's tenure, wardens had managed to arrest a small number of "intruders, hunters, and heart-of-palm thieves," who were delivered to the local police and charged with environmental violations. Very few, however, were caught in the act and eventually most were released. Pockrandt believed that, despite personnel limitations, hunting in the park had decreased during his two years as the head of Iguaçu.[49] Violators were arrested, their hunting gear was confiscated, and they were transferred to local police stations. In his 1967 annual report, Pockrandt mentioned ongoing investigations against poachers and illegal loggers being carried out in most of the municipalities that bisected the park, a testimony to the broad territorial range the new park director achieved despite the limited resources at hand. The exceptions – the municipalities of Medianeira and São Miguel do Iguaçu – included the areas occupied by settlers, over which the park administration had no territorial control at the time.[50]

Determined to contain both settler encroachment and natural resource depletion, Pockrandt urgently demanded that his superiors in Brasília hire

---

[47] Mário Pimentel de Camargo, "Relatório anual de 1962," 5.
[48] A piece in *O Estado de São Paulo* in April 1965 describes the park as having been "abandoned for the last twenty years," with a shuttered park headquarters and museum, crumbling infrastructure, broken vehicles, pigs and chickens being raised by park employ-ees, clandestine river ports operated by smugglers, and so on. Pockrandt overhauled the park administration: he opened the park headquarters, renovated park buildings, requested that twenty officers from the state police be stationed in the park, and started pushing for a solution to the settlers living on park lands. "Parque nacional abandonado há vinte anos," *O Estado de São Paulo*, April 23, 1965.
[49] Pockrandt, "Relatório das atividades e problemas do parque," 4.
[50] Pockrandt reported the seizure of over forty firearms and cold weapons since he had been appointed to Iguaçu National Park. Pockrandt, "Relatório das atividades e problemas do parque," 70–71.

fifty "surveillance assistants." He was especially concerned with protecting the eastern section delimited by the Gonçalves Dias and Silva Jardim
Rivers. This area represented two-thirds of the park and harbored old-
growth forests and a grove of over 30,000 Paraná pine trees (*Araucaria
angustifolia*). Unlike Iguaçu's western sections, the eastern area had
avoided settler colonization, but in the 1960s it faced the threat of wildlife
poaching, heart-of-palm theft, and, on its borders, land grabbing spurred
on by politicians from neighboring municipalities. The park director also
requested jeeps, horses, motorboats, and better weapons. Skeptical that
all his demands for an overhaul in park surveillance would be met,
Pockrandt also suggested the installation of an army outpost in the park
as an alternative.[51]

As of 1967, the Brazilian park had a small surveillance team: eight
forest wardens (*guardas florestais*), who were civil servants, and four
surveillance assistants (*auxiliares de vigilância*), hired as contract employees (i.e., without tenure). Six park wardens and assistants worked in the
falls zone, controlling the park entrance, charging entrance fees, and doing
sporadic motorized patrols within a thirty-kilometer radius around the
falls. The other six were deployed in the backcountry, to places located
over 150 kilometers from park headquarters, in precarious housing and,
unlike their colleagues by the falls, without vehicles. They had to cover an
area of over 115,000 hectares (roughly 100,000 football fields) on foot
and fight trespassers with .32 and .38 caliber revolvers. Wardens were ill-
equipped to go after hunters in the backcountry, but they served as
informants about less mobile activities such as heart-of-palm theft and
illegal logging, as deterrence against land occupations, and as points of
contact between the local population and park administrators, who gen-
erally came from outside the region.[52]

The desire to reach out to locals might explain why Brazilian park
directors initially established warden outposts (*casas de guardas florestais*) in the backcountry at the edges of the park, alongside highways,
and close to adjacent towns. They created the first four outposts in the

[51] Pockrandt, "Relatório das atividades e problemas do parque," 5–8, 78–79; Eugênio
Cichovski to Secretário Geral do IBDF, January 29, 1968, Documentos Diversos 1966 a
1979, 2–5, PNIB-A.
[52] Pockrandt, "Relatório das atividades e problemas do parque," 3–4; Instituto Brasileiro de
Desenvolvimento Floresta, "Pessoal," c. 1969, PNIB-A; Eugênio Cichovski to Secretário
Geral do IBDF, January 29, 1968, 5; Eugênio Cichovski to IBDF, "Circular 191, de 1° de
Agosto de 1968," October 15, 1968, Pasta Documentos Diversos, Parque Nacional do
Iguaçu, Informações Complementares, PNIB-A.

1940s, by the old Foz do Iguaçu road that served as the park's northern border. It was only after Pockrandt's tenure that the park installed new warden outposts in other areas.[53] The all-male wardens lived in these outposts with their families, some of which had as many as ten members; the children attended school in neighboring communities. The wardens were poorly paid and supplemented their income by growing subsistence crops. Park directors had always allowed wardens to cultivate produce, but Pockrandt imposed some limits: no more than two hectares of crops and confined animals. The new director also aimed to overhaul the policy that viewed park outposts as a necessary link between Iguaçu National Park and surrounding communities. Pockrandt saw complicity with malfeasance as one of the main problems in the backcountry and wanted to isolate wardens from the pressure exerted by local politicians to overlook violations by rotating wardens among outposts each year.[54]

Another way Pockrandt addressed the need to improve surveillance was by reforming the behavior of park wardens. He made it his mission to eliminate alcoholism, lack of discipline, and the "culture of violence and vendetta" that was "part of the environment in which they had always lived." The director implemented a martial culture, with clean uniforms, identification, and strict control of behavior, cracking down on lenience toward illicit activities in the park.[55] But Iguaçu continued to suffer from a chronic lack of skilled personnel, as these changes did little to improve the reality that a small number of untrained wardens were responsible for protecting a huge territory.[56] Indeed, six ill-equipped and poorly paid wardens, scattered along the park fringes, could hardly hope to patrol

[53] Pockrandt, "Relatório das atividades e problemas do parque"; René Denizart Pockrandt to Diretor Geral do Departamento de Recursos Renováveis/IBDF, "Verificação 'in loco' de invasão," January 20, 1966, Pasta Documentos Diversos, Parque Nacional do Iguaçu, Informações Complementares, PNIB-A.

[54] Pockrandt, "Relatório das atividades e problemas do parque," 68. In his work on American national parks, Jacoby summarizes the dilemma of foresters who, often times, were hired in the communities they were supposed to patrol. Jacoby, *Crimes against Nature*, 38–39.

[55] In a few instances, park employees got involved in hunting. One such employee was Joraci dos Santos, a contract watchman at the park entrance, who was suspended for twenty-three days for helping hunters act inside the park in 1966. Eugênio Cichovski, Portaria 1, January 2, 1968, Iguaçu National Park, Pasta Documentos Diversos, 1968, PNIB-A; Pockrandt, "Relatório das atividades e problemas do parque," 3.

[56] As late as 1967, the park had no administrative employees. This is reflected by the scant paper trail produced by the park prior to the 1970s. The creation of the IBDF in 1967 changed this situation. Pockrandt, "Relatório das atividades e problemas do parque," 2.

Iguaçu's entire backcountry on foot. Several sections of the park's boundaries, some more than a hundred kilometers long, were practically defenseless against poachers.[57]

As a park adjacent to an international border during the Brazilian military dictatorship, Iguaçu's lack of control over its territory was sometimes a point of tension between park administrators and other state agencies. At the end of the 1960s, local law enforcement pushed park administrators to send a surveillance expedition to an isolated corner of the park. The park director at the time, Eugênio Cichovski, had identified an island on the Iguazu River (Ilha do Sol or Ilha do Pesqueiro) as a haven for poachers. The island, a narrow, twenty-hectare stretch of forest 1.5 kilometers long and 130 meters wide on the upper Iguazu, harbored three permanent Brazilian "squatters" (*posseiros*), one of whom claimed to have acquired the island from a previous dweller who had first arrived in the area in 1940. Cichovski initially believed the island to be outside of park territory, which meant he lacked the legal mandate to act. That all changed in September 1969, when the police department of Foz do Iguaçu demanded that the park take the necessary measures to deal with the "criminals and fugitives from Brazil and Argentina who infested the island," which they assumed was part of the national park.[58]

Cichovski acquiesced, and on September 29 a patrol consisting of two wardens and eight police officers disembarked on the island and arrested nine individuals. Of these, six were identified as hunters, bearing firearms and possessing hunting dogs. Several rifles and handguns were confiscated. The prisoners, demonstrating knowledge of the territorial uncertainties posed by the island, claimed their arrest was wrongful because the Brazilian national park had no jurisdiction over the area. They claimed that the island, like all unclaimed river islands, was a territory of the Brazilian Navy (Capitania dos Portos), and that one member of the group, Helmut Horst, from Medianeira, had the navy's permission to be there, a claim that was promptly denied by the local navy office. Although the 1944 legislation expanding the park was silent about the Brazilian

---

[57] Pockrandt, "Relatório das atividades e problemas do parque," 74.

[58] Eugênio Cichovski to IBDF director in Paraná, October 7, 1969, Documentos Diversos 1966 a 1979, PNIB-A, 1; Captain Wilson de Almeida Garret to Iguaçu National Park, September 15, 1969, Documentos Diversos 1966 a 1979, PNIB-A; Eugênio Cichovski to Capitania dos Portos, September 29, 1969, Documentos Diversos 1966 a 1979, PNIB-A; Mário Moutinho de Carvalho to Eugênio Cichovski, September 30, 1969, Documentos Diversos 1966 a 1979, PNIB-A.

river islands of the Iguazu, Cichovski came to view them as part of the park's territory.[59] Expeditions like this, which brought park wardens and police officers to the backcountry of Iguaçu National Park, were still relatively rare in Brazil. Into the late 1960s, the ability of Iguaçu's park administrators to survey and control the park's territory on a regular basis was still severely limited by lack of human and financial resources. Across the border, in Argentina, Iguazú National Park's administration had been organizing surveillance expeditions since the late 1940s, also in a sporadic manner. In the 1960s, however, as settlers began to establish themselves in the Brazilian park across the Iguazu River, park administrators in Argentina had an excuse to increase the number of expeditions and demand increased investment in surveillance infrastructure such as service roads. This transboundary dynamic supported the image constructed by Argentine park officials of a park threatened by incursions of hunters coming from Brazil.

TRANSBOUNDARY POACHING IN ARGENTINA

In his 1960 report on the state of the park, Juan Daciuk, of the Argentine national park agency's nature protection office, was one of the first to sound the alarm about Brazilian hunters crossing the border to hunt in Argentine territory. He noted that, given the limited, "almost nonexistent surveillance in the strict preservation zone," it would be very easy for Brazilian hunters, like the ones he had seen operating in Brazil on the other bank of the Iguazu, to cross the river and "repeat such slaughter" in Argentina.[60] As seen in Chapter 3, Daciuk later visited Iguaçu National Park in June 1962 to investigate the alleged incursions of Brazilian hunters across the border. Once there, he was informed by Mário Pimentel de Camargo, the director of Iguaçu, that the 9,000-hectare area currently inhabited by twenty-two families was, by law, part of the Brazilian national park, and that park directors had been requesting the government evict the settlers since the early 1950s.[61]

---

[59] Eugênio Cichovski to IBDF director in Paraná, October 7, 1969, Documentos Diversos 1966 a 1979, PNIB-A, 1–2. In 1981 the islands were definitively incorporated into the territory of Iguaçu National Park by new legislation redefining its limits; see Brazil, Decree 86676, December 1, 1981.

[60] Juan Daciuk to Dirección General de Parques Nacionales, "Eleva informe técnico ref. viaje de estudios al Parque Nacional Iguazú mes de enero ppdo.," Expediente 1746, year 1961, APN, 23.

[61] Juan Daciuk to Dirección General de Parques Nacionales, "Expone conveniencia de que se tramite un pedido a autoridades del Brasil, a fin de lograr desalojo de intrusos en un

The visit generated the first international cooperation between the administrations of the two parks. Argentine park officials did their part by requesting that the Ministry of Foreign Affairs in Buenos Aires intervene with the Brazilian government. They had the support of Brazilian park officials, who believed the international pressure would persuade Brasília to evict settlers from the Brazilian park. In the following months, a vertical chain rose from Argentine rangers complaining about Brazilian hunters trespassing in Iguazú to the ministry of foreign relations in Buenos Aires, bringing the fight against poaching to the highest echelons of the Argentine government. When two Argentine rangers, a longtime park employee José Gorgues and a rookie agent Bernardo Godoy, survived "an attack by dozens of Brazilian hunters" from across the river, the incident reverberated through several levels of state bureaucracy and become a minor border conflict between the two nations. By 1963, the Brazilian government had promised the Argentine foreign office it would solve the settler problem in Iguaçu – an issue that had to wait until the 1970s to be addressed. At the Argentine park, nevertheless, ranger Gorgues used the skirmish to demand boats, better firearms, and more agents.[62]

The Iguazu River provided hunters plentiful opportunities to evade national park surveillance. It acted both as a transportation corridor, connecting the two sides of the border, and as a fuzzy liminal zone, making it difficult for park agents to define the extent of their jurisdiction. The technical demarcation of the border between Argentina and Brazil, the river's thalweg, had been demarcated in 1910.[63] However, for park rangers, it was hard to know where the actual border lay while chasing poachers on a boat in the middle of the river. In its center lane, away from its banks, the Iguazu formed an enforcement limbo in practice. The impossibility of defining the border in the water emboldened poachers to attempt avoiding detention by sailing toward the opposite side of the river when spotted by park surveillance.

The binational setting of the two parks also made it difficult for rangers on the Argentine side to punish detained Brazilian hunters. Benjamin Cozzi, director of Iguazú National Park in the mid-1960s, made this point clear in his report on two Brazilian farmworkers arrested in

vasto sector del Par. Nac. País vecino a nuestro Parq. Nacional Iguazú," Expediente 2624, year 1962, APN-B, 1–9.
[62] Ibid., 10–23.
[63] Argentina and Brazil, "Artigos declaratórios da demarcação de fronteiras entre os Estados Unidos do Brasil e a República da Argentina," Rio de Janeiro, October 4, 1910, accessed at http://info.lncc.br/att1910.html.

Argentina. Despite catching the Brazilians in the act of poaching, rangers were forced to release them, as the only punishment meted out under Argentine hunting law was a fine. Even these modest financial penalties were ineffective in this case, for as soon as Brazilians were released, they would return to their home country, where the Argentine state had no jurisdiction to collect fines. The rangers' only option, Cozzi explained, was to seize foreign hunters' firearms and equipment, as other punitive measures would work only with Argentine nationals. The seizure of firearms, knives, and even boats became the standard punishment imposed on Brazilian hunters detained in Iguazú National Park in the 1960s. For example, when Brazilian citizens Benício Costa and Pedro Ferreira da Silva (who was only 16 at the time) were arrested in 1965 for bearing arms at the mouth of the Yacuy River, park officials questioned the two men, charged them a fine, and released them without their belongings, in this case a rifle, two machetes, and a boat. To people like Costa and Silva, farmworkers who entered Argentina in search of work on local estates, dispossession of the tools of their trades could pose a heavy burden.[64]

In 1968, the issue of Brazilian hunters operating in Iguazú forced Argentine park officials to demand once again that their diplomatic corps intervene. In April, park administrators in Argentina crossed the river to meet with René Denizart Pockrandt in Iguaçu, who promised to crack down on wildlife poachers and heart-of-palm harvesters based in Brazil. Pockrandt assured the Argentines that Brazilian authorities had taken measures to reclaim the occupied zones for the Brazilian park. In Argentina, the national park service once again asked the minister of foreign relations to step in. Because of the complex border entanglements connecting the two parks, the Argentines demanded that their own diplomats in Buenos Aires issue a request to Brazil to evict the Brazilian settlers who were living in the occupied area of the Brazilian park.[65] It is not clear whether the Ministry of Foreign Relations did anything, but by July 1968 the director of the Argentine National Gendarmerie, Jorge Esteban Cáceres Monié, reported that Brazilian authorities had burned all the shacks used by hunters on the Brazilian bank of the Iguazu River.[66]

[64] Dirección de Parques Nacionales, Expediente 0307, year 1964, APN, 1–11; Intendencia del Parque Nacional del Iguazú to Administración General de Parques Nacionales, Carátula de Expediente de Infracción 618, year 1965.
[65] Intendencia Iguazú to Dirección General de Parques Nacionales, Expediente 1812, year 1968, APN, 3.
[66] Ibid., 14.

The incursions of Brazilian hunters into Argentina also shaped debates on Iguazú National Park's infrastructure. Argentine park officials quarreled over competing ideas of modernity, the porosity of international borders, and the relationship between nature protection and national security. Disputes revolved around the construction of service roads designed to facilitate surveillance and curb poaching. Whereas proponents of the service roads saw them as an indispensable tool in the fight against hunting and heart-of-palm theft, others saw them as disruptive to the very wildlife they were designed to protect. The idea of constructing a service dirt road along the left bank of the Iguazu River was first proposed in 1958. The road would connect the falls area to the eastern limits of the park, facilitating the movement of rangers and other law enforcement officers on the northern edge of Iguazú National Park, where park boundaries formed the international border with Brazil.[67]

Juan Daciuk was one of the first critics of the construction of this road. In his 1961 report on the state of the park, he detailed the road's possible negative consequences to wildlife. He feared that a road might have a negative impact on the natural riverine slopes that formed the habitat for many species, including tapirs. He was also concerned about the effects on wildlife of noise produced by jeeps and other off-road vehicles. Daciuk believed the cost of maintaining a road in the middle of the forest would prove unsustainable.[68] As the critics of the planned road saw it, the Iguazu River was unquestionably the best option for surveillance. They agreed with seasoned rangers such as Julio Silveira, whose experience traveling the upper Iguazu convinced Daciuk of the advantages of the fluvial option. Daciuk suggested that instead of building a service road, park administrators should transform the ad hoc surveillance expeditions to the backcountry into a permanent feature of park policy.[69]

---

[67] Juan Daciuk to Dirección General de Parques Nacionales, "Eleva informe técnico ref. viaje de estudios al Parque Nacional Iguazú mes de enero ppdo.," Expediente 1746, year 1961, APN, 52.

[68] It could take only six months for a cleared walking trail to disappear amid the forest. That was the fate of the north–south trail that marked the eastern boundary of the park. Opened in July 1961, the trail was already overgrown by January 1962. Intendencia Iguazú to Administración General de Parques Nacionales, Expediente 1385, year 1962, APN.

[69] Juan Daciuk to Dirección General de Parques Nacionales, "Eleva informe técnico ref. viaje de estudios al Parque Nacional Iguazú mes de enero ppdo.," Expediente 1746, year 1961, APN, 24, 48; Juan Daciuk to Dirección General de Parques Nacionales, "... III viaje de interiorización al Parque Nac. do Iguassu, de la Rep. de Brasil ..." Expediente 2372, Year 1962, APN-B, 49.

Daciuk's criticism of the riverine road project was ignored, but not completely. In a glaring example of selective reception of information, Julio Peña, director of parks and reservations, used Daciuk's dire picture of invading gangs of Brazilian hunters as proof that the road was necessary. Peña adopted Daciuk's plan of building outposts along the shore of the Iguazu but disregarded the idea of using them solely as ports for river surveillance. For Peña, connecting the bases via dirt road would be more efficient. As part of an institution that still had a significant investment in building urban infrastructure in Puerto Iguazú and urban centers in other national parks, Peña shared a view that favored infrastructure over environmental concerns. This bias was part of the early ethos of the Argentine national park agency.[70]

Different interpretations on the need for a service road also pitted the conservationists within the Argentine national park agency against rangers and park personnel, the people who would actually use the road. In 1964, the director of museums, Alberto Anziano, demanded that the proposed road's width be narrowed to minimize impact on local fauna. Anziano argued that the errors of past administrations, including creating settlements inside the park and allowing another road (Highway 101, which cut across the park from east to west) to be built, had harmed the park's wildlife. He therefore requested that the dirt road be redesigned into a walking trail.[71] However, rangers and park director Benjamin Cozzi in Iguazú strongly opposed Anziano's plans, arguing that a walking trail would never solve the problem of mobility and surveillance. Taking matters in his own hands, Cozzi traveled the northern boundaries of the Argentine park to counter Anziano's depiction of a threatened animal population. Wildlife, according to him, was thriving and there was no need for the radical limitations on development proposed by Anziano.[72]

---

[70] Juan Daciuk to Dirección General de Parques Nacionales, "Eleva informe técnico ref. viaje de estudios al Parque Nacional Iguazú mes de enero ppdo.," Expediente 1746, year 1961, APN, 52.

[71] "Informe comisión cumplida por Anziano, Alberto al Parque Nacional Iguazú (sobre la conservación de las especies botanicas)," excerpt from Expediente 4779, year 1964, Carpeta 22, APN-B, 2–3.

[72] Ibid., 2–3, 24. Officials in Buenos Aires also contested the need for a surveillance road in an area in which the Iguazu River was the primary mode of travel. Park officials, for their part, called the notion of relying on boats alone for surveillance "childish." They argued that the river was not always navigable; that hunters could hide in the middle of the forest from rangers sailing down the river; and that agents on boats, without forest cover, were easy targets for hunters shooting from either bank. Intendencia Iguazú to Servicio Nacional de Parques Nacionales, Expediente 2098, year 1972, APN, 4–24.

In 1964, park officials in Iguazú sent Buenos Aires a budget proposal for constructing a fifty-seven-kilometer-long, three-meter-wide, leveled dirt road (called a "circumventing trail") connecting the upper falls to the park's eastern limit, with a planned thirty-three wooden bridges to allow the passage of off-road vehicles.[73] Construction of the service road faced several delays, budget cuts, and changes of heart by park and national park agency administrators. The work started only in 1968, and by 1969 twenty of the projected fifty-seven kilometers had been completed. In October of that year, rangers found evidence of "Brazilian" heart-of-palm harvesters operating in the park: a large cut of 1,500 palm trees in the middle of the forest, near the riverbank. At around this time, the workers employed to build the road also started complaining of harassment by Brazilians crossing the river to hunt in Argentina.[74] Officers in Buenos Aires saw the palm tree cutting as an alarming sign and proposed a change of plans – completing the rest of the road as a walking trail. They believed continuing the proposed dirt road as a trail would be cheaper and faster and argued that surveillance along the river could be done perfectly well on foot and horseback instead of by jeep.[75]

Officials in the Argentine park were not happy with this change of plans. The dirt road was the brainchild of Ramón Víctor Pablo Elías, who had proposed it in 1958, when he was the director of Iguazú. In the late 1960s, he was back as park director and pressed for the road to be completed. He ridiculed the new proposal from Buenos Aires and the idea of using riding animals for surveillance. He argued that horses would have a difficult time acclimatizing to the area, that jaguars could scare the horses and cause accidents, and, more important, that giving up on building a road meant moving away from modern methods of transportation. Elías contended that "it was not possible that in the era of the jet, one would consider employing mules [for patrolling the area]."[76]

The park director had the support of Anziano, the director of museums, who had changed his mind and was convinced that finishing the project as a dirt road was a necessary compromise to curb poaching. Anziano reminded

---

[73] Intendencia Iguazú to Dirección General de Parques Nacionales, Expediente 5880, year 1964, APN.

[74] Intendencia Iguazú to Dirección General de Parques Nacionales, Expediente 3653, year 1969, APN, 1–4.

[75] Milan Jorge Dimitri to Dirección General de Parques Nacionales, "S/N.° Elev. inf. ref. al P. Nac. Iguazú c/ motivo reciente viaje de estudio e inspección técnica," Expediente 1384, year 1969, APN, 1.

[76] Intendencia Iguazú to Dirección General de Parques Nacionales, Expediente 4055, year 1969, annexed to Expediente 3653, year 1969, APN.

the director of the Argentine national park service that Iguazú "had been suffering grave attacks, year after year, since 1943," from Brazilian hunters. Now, he pointed out in his report, a completed dirt road would be the only effective instrument to curb such "infiltrations." After a flight over the Iguazu River, he described its Brazilian bank as being occupied by kilometers of houses and shacks, all with their own "little docks and motorboats," from which the "poachers invading [the Argentine] park" originated. In his opinion, a dirt road that allowed rangers to circulate quickly along the banks was the best option for fighting transboundary poaching.[77]

The Argentine national park agency never finished the road as initially planned, completing only twenty-two of the envisioned fifty-seven kilometers. In 1974, the agency installed a ranger outpost at the end of the road, across the Apepu River. By then, the great majority of settlers in Brazil had already left the park, and the transboundary threat they represented was mostly gone. The dispute over building the road exposes the overlap of three types of spaces that contributed to the creation of the park as a nature protection area. The first, the space of surveillance, was legitimized by the need to protect a "natural" and "national" area from the incursions of foreign nationals. Rangers, the primary agents behind the construction of such territory, relied on periodic surveillance expeditions to perform their duties and required the construction of "modern," automobile-based transportation infrastructure. Spaces of poaching, on the other hand, stemmed from the spatial practices of Brazilian settlers and other hunters, who used topographical and political boundaries to subvert the rules set by national park proponents and managers. By using the river to enter and hunt in another country, Brazilians managed to dodge hunting prohibitions by negotiating the territorial limitations of Argentine environmental enforcement. Finally, spaces of animality were established in the overlap between the spaces constructed by humans, particularly those where territoriality was employed, and the territories established by nonhuman animals. Human actors used spaces of animality to produce arguments in favor of or against the road based on the potential conflicts a human–animal spatial overlap could generate.

TRANSBOUNDARY HEART-OF-PALM THEFT IN ARGENTINA

Vertebrate animals were not the only living things that humans sparred over inside the parks. Another primary source of conflict between rangers

---

[77] Alberto Anziano to Dirección General de Parques Nacionales, Expediente 4479, year 1969, annexed to Expediente 3653, year 1969, APN.

and locals was the harvesting of heart of palm from the territories of the two national parks. In the Iguazu borderlands, heart of palm was extracted from a native species of palm tree, the juçara (*Euterpe edulis*). The tree was common to southern and southeastern Brazil, northeastern Argentina, and eastern Paraguay, but by the 1970s it had become rare outside the two national parks. Like other palm trees, the juçara has a smooth trunk with a diameter of about twenty centimeters. Adult specimens can reach twenty meters tall. The tree has large pinnate leaves that can reach the length of three meters, with dozens of long leaf blades. Under its top leaf area, the tree has fruit stipes where the juçara berry grows. The juçara fruit is an edible black berry similar to the açaí berry, which is the fruit of another heart-of-palm-producing tree found in the Amazon rainforest, *Euterpe oleracea*. Harvesters were not interested in berries, however. Right above the berry stipes is the part that attracted them: a one-meter-long, bright-green meristem connecting the trunk to the leaves at the top. There, within the softer outer layer, lies the *palmito* or heart of palm, the inner core of the section preceding the leaves. The plant reproduces easily, but unlike other heart-of-palm species, *edulis* takes years to reach the stage of heart-of-palm production. To harvest it, palmiteiros cut down the entire tree to extract the meristem, which usually corresponds to just five percent of the length of the trunk. Heart-of-palm harvesting, therefore, is a misnomer, because its effects more closely resemble those of logging.[78]

In Iguazú, the juçara palm tree occurred in clusters, which facilitated harvesters' efforts. On a site in the eastern section of the park, for instance, Franco A. Devoto and Maximo Rothkugel found five hundred specimens of *edulis* in their 1926 survey, which comprised 58 percent of all the trees recorded in that hectare.[79] These clusters of palm trees would induce a spatial behavior analogous to the one created by the concentration of animals around salt licks – hunters, harvesters, and rangers met at specific nodes of hunting and harvesting

---

[78] Milan Jorge Dimitri et al., "La flora arbórea del Parque Nacional Iguazu," *Anales de Parques Nacionales* 12 (1974): 23, 56; Melina Oliveira Melito et al., "Demographic Structure of a Threatened Palm (*Euterpe edulis* Mart.) in a Fragmented Landscape of Atlantic Forest in Northeastern Brazil," *Acta Botanica Brasilica* 28, no. 2 (June 2014): 249–58; Dalva M. Silva Matos, et al., "Understanding the Threats to Biological Diversity in Southeastern Brazil," *Biodiversity and Conservation* 11, no. 10 (2002): 1747–58; Mauro Galetti et al., "Palm Heart Harvesting in the Brazilian Atlantic Forest: Changes in Industry Structure and the Illegal Trade," *Journal of Applied Ecology* 35, no. 2 (1998): 294–301.

[79] Devoto and Rothkugel, "Informe sobre los bosques," 210 and annexed table.

activity.[80] However, knowledge of the location of palm tree groves failed, for a series of reasons, to translate into prevention of heart-of-palm theft. First, the Argentine park simply lacked the people and resources to cover the entire park territory, including the known clusters of *edulis*, with periodic surveillance expeditions. Moreover, many groves of juçara were located deep in the forest, far from the routes taken by park rangers. Heart-of-palm harvesters also invested in sophisticated operations that involved many individuals, including lookouts and armed henchmen. Finally, the transnational nature of heart-of-palm theft – as with wildlife poaching, harvesters would cross the river from Brazil to cut heart-of-palm in Argentina – created severe limitations to the territorial power of Argentine officials.

All these issues were present in the case of a large heart-of-palm harvest discovered by park rangers in March 1967. Rangers were informed by Argentine settlers about the presence of Brazilian harvesters in the park, near the Apepu River. Suspecting a large heart-of-palm operation, Director Cozzi requested the backup of heavily armed gendarmes for the raid. Heart-of-palm theft was, indeed, different from the hunting performed by local farmers for reasons of leisure or subsistence. In the 1967 incident, for example, harvesters had established a complex structure involving several people, including lookouts, who fired their weapons when they spotted patrols. Harvesters had also hidden their trail from the riverbank, opening paths sixty meters inland to avoid being spotted by rangers in boats. The tip reporting the heart-of-palm operation gave the approximate location of the site, but rangers and gendarmerie officers still had to scour a few kilometers of the riverbank before finding the trailhead that led to the decimated palm tree grove.[81]

One of the shortcomings of the surveillance system in place in Iguazú was its focus on patrolling well-traveled paths. As forest ranger Roberto A. Ferreira revealed to his superiors in Buenos Aires, rangers usually stuck to known trails and navigable watercourses, never penetrating deep inland, as these were areas of "virgin forest" void of trails. Hunters and harvesters used the same pathways but went further into the forest by opening their own trails. Rangers counted on spotting trailheads to find new heart-of-palm cuts, which could be difficult if hunters and harvesters consciously

---

[80] Juan Carlos Montiel to Administración General de Parques Nacionales y Turismo, Expediente 9900, year 1948, APN, 8, 12–13.
[81] Intendencia Iguazú to Dirección General de Parques Nacionales, Expediente 1717, year 1967, APN, 1–29.

concealed their tracks. There were other problems. Surveillance tours were costly and tiresome – agents had to prepare to spend days sailing, hiking, and camping in the forest. An expedition would take at least five days, with stops in different locations for surveillance by foot. By the mid-1960s, rangers carried out four to five backcountry excursions per year, but in 1967, because of the large-scale heart-of-palm operation found in Apepu, they had to return to the area a few additional times to ensure the harvesters had not reappeared.[82]

In Apepu in 1967, rangers found a recent cut of over 17,000 palm trees. The site was deserted by the time they arrived. Park authorities estimated that it had taken ten to fifteen days of work and several people to complete the cutting. Harvesters had been not only careful to hide the trailhead but also were cautious to start the cutting right after the last surveillance expedition had passed through the area, as they knew it would be at least a month before rangers returned. The unprecedented scale of this operation led park authorities to launch a thorough investigation of the matter, and after a few months rangers arrested Juan Mendez, a Brazilian national who was caught armed inside the Argentine park, near Apepu.[83] Mendez was initially uncooperative, claiming not to understand Spanish, but eventually park authorities managed to extract information from him. Mendez was an employee of Roberto Esquivel, an Argentine national who had been accused of murder and fled to Brazil. Unsurprisingly to park officials, both Esquivel and Mendez lived across the river, inside the Brazilian park, right across from where the palm trees had been cut in Argentina.[84]

The fact that the accused lived in Brazil exposes government agents' limited power in cases of transboundary wildlife poaching and heart-of-palm theft. Through the national gendarmerie and the Argentine consul in Foz do Iguaçu, Argentine park officials demanded a response from Brazilian park authorities. The response came from the Brazilian Army instead, as the Brazilian park lacked de facto control over the settled area across the river. Colonel Jayme de Paiva Bello, then commander of the First Border Battalion in Foz do Iguaçu, promised to probe into the clandestine heart-of-palm canneries in Brazil that marketed illegally harvested heart-of-palm from Argentina.[85] Unlike the hunting cases, the

[82] Ibid., 4–5, 32–47.
[83] Intendencia del Parque Nacional del Iguazú to Dirección General de Parques Nacionales, Carátula de Expediente de Infracción 3118, year 1967, APN, 1-2.
[84] Ibid., 3-7.
[85] Intendencia Iguazú to Dirección General de Parques Nacionales, Expediente 1717, year 1967, APN, 4.

extraction of heart of palm was treated as a penal offense by Argentine park officials, who considered it theft of park property. However, authorities had little chance to arrest Esquivel, despite his Argentine nationality, because he lived in Brazil. Though he was also wanted for murder in his home country, he was a low-profile criminal, rendering extradition unlikely. Nevertheless, this case of a large heart-of-palm cut that had taken place under Argentine park rangers' noses added to the pressure to finally build the long-planned riverine road.[86]

The following year, the director of forests, Roberto Ferreyra, implemented a few measures to improve surveillance in the backcountry, including increasing the frequency of expeditions and always sending gendarmes to accompany them. Ferreyra also tested overlapping expeditions. Violators from Brazil, he argued, waited for a patrol to pass before entering the park. Hence, starting in March 1968 new expeditions were launched while the previous ones were still only midway along the upper Iguazú. Rangers also started leaving Puerto Iguazú at dawn to avoid being spotted by lookouts. Ferreyra believed hunters in the backcountry were being warned via radio by people in town who spotted the patrols leaving for the backcountry. Harboring an urban settlement inside a national park threatened the element of surprise in national park surveillance operations.[87]

These measures were temporary, as they were devised to last until the surveillance trail was completed. Even so, they strained park and gendarmerie resources to their limits. In March, an expedition organized by ranger Delfin Gorgues (José's Brother) had failed to include deputy gendarmes. According to Gorgues, his request for agents had been denied by the National Gendarmerie, as the park already had an expedition in the backcountry with two deputies. The April expedition also failed to include gendarme backup, which resulted in the tragic death of ranger Bernabé Méndez. Rangers were overburdened by preparations, which including purchasing supplies, fuel, and ammunition as well as procuring transportation to haul agents, gear, and boats to the backcountry. Requesting gendarme backup was at the bottom of their list of priorities.[88]

In subsequent years, Argentine rangers continued to find new cuts of palm trees in the park's backcountry. In 1969, they found a cut of 1,500

---

[86] Ibid., 4, 47.
[87] Secretaría de Parques Nacionales to Dirección General de Parques Nacionales, "Sumario instruido c/ motivo homicidio de ex-agte. D. Bernabé Méndez," 8–13.
[88] Ibid., 1–7, 14–19.

trees.[89] In 1970, two other cuts were found in different areas, totaling over 3,000 specimens.[90] In 1971, two new large heart-of-palm operations were discovered, one of them just three kilometers from a new permanent ranger camp set up on the banks of the Iguazu River, with over 2,800 palm trees cut.[91] In January 1972, rangers discovered still another palm tree cut of 1,300 specimens. In the years since 1967, rangers had failed to make arrests and establish a clear connection between heart-of-palm harvesting and settlers living in Brazil. This time, however, individuals on a boat moored on the Brazilian side of the Iguazu River watched the rangers while they inspected the clearing. A few days later, in Iguaçu, the Brazilian Federal Police arrested two settlers with a truck loaded with palm tree logs. The two men, Antônio Nobre de Assunção and Auri Uhlmann, confessed to having extracted the palm trees from the Argentine park with the intention of selling the palmito to Brazilian canneries. Across the river, Argentine park authorities believed the two Brazilians to be responsible for the palm tree cut in their park in January. Assunção, known as "Polaco Preto" (Black Polack), was a notorious heart-of-palm harvester in Brazil.[92]

All evidence pointed to the Brazilians as the culprits of the recently discovered heart-of-palm clearing. However, the two Brazilians might also be lying about the origin of the palm tree logs. One of the two men, Uhlmann, was a settler living in the Brazilian park during the removal process. He had no land deed and was not eligible for compensation, but he stayed in the park until 1978, trying to push INCRA for land indemnity. By 1972, with the process of settler removal under way, being caught with heart of palm extracted from the Brazilian park could jeopardize one's prospect of receiving compensation. If Uhlmann had cut heart of palm in Brazil, it would make sense to lie about the origin of the palmito, as the penalty for contraband would incur only the apprehension of the palm logs. In this complicated transboundary context, with shifting spatial configurations, it was difficult to obtain concrete evidence of

[89] Intendencia Iguazú to Dirección General de Parques Nacionales, Expediente 3653, year 1969, APN.
[90] Intendencia Iguazú to Dirección General de Parques Nacionales, Expediente 1691, year 1970, APN.
[91] Escuadrón Eldorado to Servicio Nacional de Parques Nacionales, Expediente 2078, year 1971, APN; Intendencia Iguazú to Servicio Nacional de Parques Nacionales, Expediente 0838, year 1972, APN.
[92] Jayme de Paiva Bello, "Parque Nacional do Iguaçu, relatório de 1972," 1972, PNIB-A, 8; Pedro Berg (retired Iguaçu National Park employee), in discussion with the author, October 2013.

Brazilians' involvement in wildlife poaching and natural resources theft in the Argentine park. Nevertheless, Argentine authorities issued an arrest warrant for Assunção and Uhlmann and asked Brazilian authorities that the two be extradited, which never occurred.[93]

Rangers and park administrators in Argentina insisted that most hunters and harvesters were Brazilians who lived in the settlements located inside Iguaçu National Park. In an interview, former Iguazú National Park ranger José Gorgues also made it clear that park agents and deputy gendarmes in the 1960s and 1970s believed all heart-of-palm harvesters were from Brazil. Gorgues also indicated that rangers in the Argentine park feared the Brazilians, who were more numerous and had better boats and heavier guns.[94]

HEART-OF-PALM OPERATIONS AND THE LACK OF TERRITORIAL CONTROL IN BRAZIL

Across the border, heart-of-palm theft was an even bigger problem for Brazilian park wardens, as it reached a larger scale and threatened government control over park territory. Unlike Argentina, the heart-of-palm problem in Brazil did not entail transnational issues, as all harvesters operating inside the park originated in Brazil. However, it made explicit the limitations of the national park's power over its territory and its lack of jurisdiction in the area where most transgressors were based – outside park boundaries. Park authorities' need to project their power outside park borders came to the fore in 1967, when the director of Brazil's Iguaçu National Park, René Denizart Pockrandt, called for the creation of a police station in the park to monitor environmental crimes in the border zone. The new Forest Act passed by Congress in 1965 had expanded the power of park authorities to detain, investigate, and criminally charge all environmental offenders caught *inside* protected areas.[95] It was not enough. Pockrandt's primary goal was to fight heart-of-palm theft, and to do so, he argued, it was also necessary to give the park agents the power to enforce conservation laws *outside* the park.

---

[93] Ministerio de Economia to Ministerio de Justicia, Expediente 1802, year 1975, 27–28; Intendencia Iguazú to Servicio Nacional de Parques Nacionales, Expediente 0838, year 1972, APN, 1–6, 23, 36–56.

[94] José Gorgues (retired Iguazú National Park employee), in discussion with the author, August 2014.

[95] Brazil, Law 4771, "Novo código florestal," Art. 33, September 15, 1965.

The park director wanted to shut down the numerous heart-of-palm canneries operating in neighboring Brazilian towns. There were five of them, in Medianeira, Matelândia, Céu Azul, Capitão Leônidas Marques, and Capanema, all supplied by palm trees cut inside the parks in Brazil and Argentina. Local businessmen hired gangs of daily laborers, usually landless farmers, to enter the park and cut the trees. Contractors provided laborers with boats and oxcarts to transport palm logs from deep inside the park to points where trucks waited to haul the logs to the canneries. They paid taxes on their palmito sales as if it had been cut outside the park, in one of those municipalities. Heart of palm was canned in glass jars and sold as a delicacy in the urban markets of Rio de Janeiro, São Paulo, and Curitiba. Pockrandt wanted extended territorial powers to sever the heart-of-palm commodity chain's middle links: the canneries.[96]

However, granting park agents extensive territorial powers on paper would not improve their meager capacity to exert park power in the real world. Territorial control was a function of people, resources, and training. Park wardens in Brazil were not equipped to face off with large heart-of-palm operations or raid canneries in neighboring towns. Thus, like their Argentine counterparts, Brazilian park officials started requesting backup from the police (and later the army) during raids. It was a necessary measure, as every time a patrol of park wardens and state police officers came across a palm tree operation inside the park, they met with armed resistance from harvesters. A survey of local canneries and the traffic of trucks loaded with palm logs produced by the park administration estimated that over 50,000 palm trees were illegally extracted every month in the Brazilian park in the late 1960s. The number might be hyperbolic, but even if the real figure were one-tenth of this estimate, 5,000 *per month* would still make the 3,000 or 4,000 palm trees cut *per year* in the Argentine park pale in comparison.[97]

In July 1967, Pockrandt asked Colonel Arídio Martins de Magalhães, commander of the First Border Battalion stationed in Foz do Iguaçu, to help curb heart-of-palm theft and regain control of the park's territory. Using rhetoric similar to that used in Argentina – that harvesters were stealing federal property (palm trees) from federal public lands – Pockrandt persuaded Magalhães to send a patrol of ten soldiers and a sergeant to investigate heart-of-palm extraction near

---

[96] Pockrandt, "Relatório das atividades e problemas do parque," 69; Eugênio Cichovski to Secretário Geral do IBDF, January 29, 1968, 3.

[97] Pockrandt, "Relatório das atividades e problemas do parque," 73–74.

Leônidas Marques, on the park's eastern border. The goal was to intimidate harvesters into stopping their activities. To the military's surprise, the patrol met fierce resistance from heavily armed henchmen. A shootout ensued, and the heart-of-palm harvesters scattered into the forest. The military reported the presence of more than five hundred workers in the area, a far cry from the thirty or so individuals they expected to find. A few days later, Magalhães sent an entire platoon to the area to "inform locals [of the prohibition against heart-of-palm harvesting in the area], arrest those caught in the act, confiscate firearms, and make the local police chief in Leônidas Marques take action to curb such illegal activities."[98]

Magalhães saw the army's involvement as a temporary solution for the problem of heart-of-palm theft in the Brazilian park. He argued that his border battalion lacked the manpower and resources to go after harvesters, and doing the work of park wardens was a distraction from the military's primary mission of patrolling the international border with Argentina and Paraguay. The IBDF, he suggested, should establish its own surveillance structure, preferably by hiring at least fifty rangers to cover the entire park. Nonetheless, park directors in Iguaçu continued to request help from the army. In 1968, for example, such a request was made after an employee working for a federal land agency was shot by harvesters in the park's backcountry.[99] Since the military dictatorship was in power at the time, calling for the army to intervene served to intimidate those involved in the heart-of-palm industry. Five days later, nine heart-of-palm workers voluntarily surrendered to the authorities.[100]

The army was not always on call, and park wardens on their own had little power to enforce the federal mandate over park space. There were times, for example, when local hunters would complain to the local police about park wardens seizing their weapons, and police officers would force the wardens to return the firearms to their owners, as Aparecido Ramalho Teixeira complained in November 1968. Teixeira was 26 then, a young surveillance assistant who had worked in the park for the last eight years and been recently transferred to a new outpost in Leônidas Marques created in 1968. Having attempted to do things by the book, Teixeira

---

[98] Ibid., 75.   [99] Eugênio Cichovski to Secretário Geral do IBDF, January 29, 1968, 6.
[100] Oswaldo Euclides Aranha to Iguaçu National Park director Francisco Beltrão, January 11, 1968, and Wilson Dalago, "Termo de apresentacão," 1968, Documentos Diversos 1966 a 1979, PNIB-A.

was then humiliated by police officers from adjacent towns, who forced him to return confiscated firearms to hunters from Capanema.[101]

In the region's dispossessed peasants and settlers threatened by land speculators and colonization companies, heart-of-palm harvesters found an easily tapped labor pool. Like many areas in western Paraná, the municipality of Leônidas Marques, at the eastern border of Iguaçu National Park and a hotspot of illegal heart-of-palm extraction, was plagued with land conflict. The new military regime had still a limited reach in the region, and officials from federal land agencies continuously received death threats from land grabbers (*grileiros*). In 1967, squatters (*posseiros*) took up arms and marched to the town of Leônidas Marques to pressure the federal government to issue land titles. The state government sent more than 100 police officers to the region, and an agreement between squatter leaders and federal officials averted the confrontation. It was in this environment of violent land conflicts, limited federal power, a dispossessed population of squatters who were armed and justifiably confrontational, and an army of henchmen working for local businessmen managing shady colonization companies and logging operations that park administrators had to work to curb commercial heart-of-palm harvesting inside park territory.[102] Violence was a common feature of life at the border, and Pockrandt, a city man whose family remained in Curitiba during his tenure as park director, lived in fear of being attacked in his park residence by hunters or heart-of-palm harvesters. He had two men stand guard at his house at night and on outings made sure to always be accompanied by at least one armed employee. Pedro Berg, who worked as a guard for Pockrandt in the late 1960s, explained that "most [park] directors had night watchmen, especially this one, as he was very afraid [of being attacked]."[103]

The assignment of fifty state troopers to Iguaçu National Park in 1970 tipped the balance against the clandestine heart-of-palm industry. Officers were hired primarily to deal with the removal of settlers from the Brazilian

---

[101] Aparecido Ramalho Teixeira to Iguaçu National Park director, Parque Nacional do Iguaçu, November 5, 1968, Pasta Documentos Diversos, 1968, PNIB-A; Eugênio Cichovski to Secretário Geral do IBDF, January 29, 1968, 3.

[102] Secretaria de Estado de Segurança Pública, Divisão de Segurança e Informações, DOPS/PR – Pastas Temáticas – Questões de Terras Gleba Andrada – Número: 1655, Topografia: 199, Data: 1966, APP; State of Paraná, Companhia de Desenvolvimento do Paraná, "O Paraná e a economia madeireira" (Paraná: 1964), 5.4–5.14, IPARDES.

[103] Pedro Berg (retired Iguaçu National Park employee), in discussion with the author, October 2013.

park, but they were also employed in enforcing the park's conservation mandate. As police officers, they could shut down illegal canneries and stop heart-of-palm trucks outside park territory.[104] In the period of just one month, April 1970, state troopers stationed at the park shut down eleven clandestine heart-of-palm canneries in the border region. The canneries had been established by employees of the Brazilian Postal Service from Rio de Janeiro who, taking a leave of absence from their work, moved to the region to exploit heart of palm. They planned to stay in the border zone for two years, during which time they would hire local businessmen to go into Iguaçu National Park for palm trees. The men saw the park as an unguarded source of heart-of-palm harvesting and an opportunity for easy profits. They planned to export the product to consumer markets in Europe, particularly France, where the vegetable had become popular as an exotic delicacy.[105]

The presence of state troopers did not eliminate environmental violations in the Brazilian park overnight, and in the years to come park administrators continued to complain about police officers' corruption and insubordination. Still, the arrival of the police brought a substantial improvement to the federal government's ability to control the park territory, and park administrators no longer had to persuade local army commanders to intervene against heart-of-palm harvesters. But its dependence on police officers, supplied by the government of the state of Paraná, sheds light on the limitations of the IBDF, a federal agency, to wield power over a territory owned and controlled by the federal

[104] Ministério da Agricultura, Divisão de Segurança e Informações, "Pedido de busca n° 05/ PSI/DSI/MA/75 Desenvolvimento do setor primário – Colonização OCOI – 5.1," February 28, 1975, Pasta 2.6, Fundo Parque Nacional do Iguaçu, ICMBio; Eugênio Cichovski to Secretário Geral do IBDF, 299/68, October 15, 1968, Pasta Parque Nacional do Iguaçu – Informações Complementares, PNIB-A; Instituto Brasileiro de Desenvolvimento Florestal, "Termo de acordo," May 7, 1970, Pasta Termo de Acordo de Contrato IBDF com a Secretaria de Agricultura do Estado do Paraná, PNIB-A; "Colonos no parque," *Diário do Paraná*, July 3, 1971.

[105] "Parque do Iguaçu era abastecedor de palmitos," *Diário do Paraná*, April 4, 1970; "O governo fecha fábricas de palmito," *Diário do Paraná*, May 9, 1970; "Polícia Florestal evita desmatamento," *Diário do Paraná*, December 3, 1970. A couple of days later that same month, April 1970, park wardens stopped a truck with 3,000 palm logs. Gunfire broke out between wardens and harvesters, and the skirmish ended with several injured and one dead, harvester Florentino Mendes. After the shooting, the cannery that had been supposed to receive the load was fined and closed, but it managed to resume its activities after paying the fine. In 1972 the same cannery was once again shut down by the IBDF and the state police. "Fechada fábrica que tirava palmito do parque," *Diário do Paraná*, April 12, 1972; Pedro Berg (retired Iguaçu National Park employee), in discussion with the author, October 2013.

government. It was a continuation of the decades-long, usually conflictive but occasionally cooperative relationship between the state and federal governments at Iguaçu National Park.

SPATIAL PATTERNS OF TRANSBOUNDARY PARK VIOLATIONS

Throughout the 1960s, Argentine park officials continued to blame the settlers living in Brazil's Iguaçu National Park for most of the poaching and heart-of-palm theft recorded in Argentina's Iguazú. In their field reports, rangers claimed that Brazilian settlers across the river took advantage of their location, using the river to move across the border to penetrate the Argentine park and engage in violation free of penalties. Yet Argentine surveillance work and detentions produced little direct evidence to support the claim that most of the offenders were Brazilian. In a sample of seventy-four people (all of them males) accused of environmental violations in the Argentine park over four decades, only eight individuals, about 10 percent of the total, lived in Brazil.

A nationalist bias likely underpins Argentine park officials' claims blaming Brazilians for poaching and heart-of-palm theft. Rangers and administrators in Iguazú, influenced by a view of the border as a porous threshold allowing the penetration of dangerous alien elements, may have overstated the role of Brazilian settlers in the environmental violations recorded in the Argentine park. It is useful, therefore, to assess the validity of their claims by looking at a different type of evidence – the correlation between where violations took place and the location of settlers in the Brazilian park. Examining the changing spatial patterns of hunting can help place the wrongdoers' origin.[106] If the Argentine park rangers were correct, geolocating cases of environmental violations would reveal a cluster of cases next to where Brazilian settlers lived across the Iguazu River and the dispersal of this cluster after they were evicted in the early 1970s.

The following analysis uses seventy-six cases of poaching recorded by park rangers between 1960 and 1980 in Iguazú National Park in Argentina. The incidents were recorded in documents found in the Argentine national park agency's archive, in Buenos Aires and at the Iguazú National Park archive in

---

[106] I focused solely on hunting violations for they comprised the majority of cases collected in the archives.

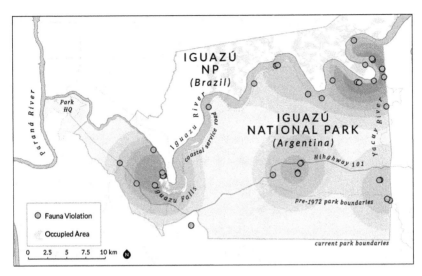

MAP 5.1 Fauna violations at Iguazú National Park (AR), 1960–74

Misiones.[107] Hunting was part of the culture of many families in the border-land region, so it is likely that the removal of settlers from Iguaçu, Brazil, affected the practice in Iguazú, Argentina. Testing the role of these communities in the spatial patterns of wildlife poaching required dividing the data set into two periods, 1960–74 (thirty-five poaching events) and 1974–80 (forty-one poaching events). Evictions in Brazil started slowly in 1970, but gained steam two years later; by 1975, 80 percent of settlers had been removed. Maps 5.1 and 5.2 reflect this periodization. They use a geographical information system (GIS) statistical tool, Kernel Density, to show clustering and dispersion in the spatial distribution of points for the two selected periods.

The two maps reveal an evident change in the spatial distribution of events across the Argentine park. In the 1960–74 period, a cluster of poaching cases took place in the northeastern corner of the park, where the settlers in the Brazilian park lived right across the river until the early 1970s. In the 1975–80 period, on the other hand, a southward shift in the location of poaching events occurs, despite no changes in backcountry

---

[107] These documents identify a series of poaching events, including detailed metadata such as time, date, type of violation, number of rangers and transgressors involved, place of origin of transgressors (when this information was available), and, of course, location. To geolocate these environmental violations, each event was assigned to a point within a region that, although not precise, was limited enough to allow for a minimum degree of spatial certitude.

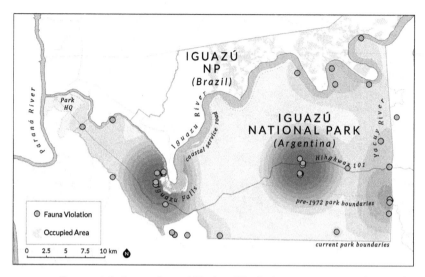

MAP 5.2 Fauna violations at Iguazú National Park (AR), 1975–80. Both maps by
Frederico Freitas

surveillance expeditions. In the first fifteen years, there are at least sixteen
recorded poaching events in the northeastern section of the park, across
from the Brazilian settlements. In the following six years, there are only five
poaching cases recorded in the same area. Events concentrated around the
falls area (nine events) and the Santo Domingo salt lick (nine events). This
change confirms contemporary impressions by Argentine rangers and park
administrators that the presence of settlers across the river in Brazil was,
indeed, a significant source of poaching in the Argentine park.[108]

***

To create Iguazú and Iguaçu as spaces of protected nature, national park
agents had to remove dwellers living inside the park and prevent undesirable
activities such as hunting and heart-of-palm harvesting within park boundaries. The result was similar – ridding the parks of unacceptable human

---

[108] This assessment is based on data that is incomplete at best, due to the fragmentary nature
of the reporting and archiving processes. Studies carried out in the United States, for
example, demonstrate that hunters are rarely caught inside national park areas, with
authorities registering only about 2 or 3 percent of all cases of poaching (see Jacoby,
Crimes against Nature, 115). Therefore, any patterns of poaching deriving from the
plotting of a few cases on a map should be read as an indication of possible trends, not as
statistically sound analysis.

practices. However, settler removal and curbing of poaching and plant theft contained more differences than similarities. First, they had distinct chronologies. Settlements inside the parks, particularly in the case of Argentina, were not always seen as a problem – quite the opposite – a view that changed as ideas about conservation evolved. Hunting and heart-of-palm harvesting, on the other hand, were prohibited since the inception of the parks. Settlement and poaching were also different in terms of the spatial practices they entailed – inhabiting inside a boundary in contrast to incursions from outside. Moreover, they diverged in the type of space they created, as hunting and heart-of-palm harvest, however large their scale, never caused a radical land cover transformation in the manner of permanent settlements. Finally, there were also distinctions in how park authorities opposed them. As seen in Chapters 3 and 4, removing settlers from the Iguazu parks entailed massive state investment, reallocation of resources, legislation changes, eviction and relocation of people, court battles, and destruction of property. Fighting poaching and heart-of-palm theft mostly required surveillance and enforcement of land and riverine borders.

In the end, a pivotal difference lay in the lasting challenge hunting and heart-of-palm harvesting imposed on the national park order. The settler issue was solved in the 1970s, but the two parks continued to fight in the following decades against wildlife hunting and heart-of-palm harvesting. In Argentina, population growth in Puerto Iguazú and Caburei, at the eastern boundaries of the park, brought new pressures and a shift in the spatial patterns of poaching in Iguazú National Park. Hunters now came mostly from Argentina but, like their Brazilian counterparts from the 1960s, many of them entered the park for sport or subsistence hunting. Along the new southern boundaries of the park, the presence of neighboring forest plantations generated new conflicts, as logging company employees would use their free time to enter park areas to hunt.[109] In Brazil, the presence of fifty

---

[109] Intendencia Iguazu to Serviço Nacional de Parques Nacionales, Expediente 1992, year 1972, APN; Carpeta 2, "Infracción caza," May 15, 1972, Caja Infracciones, Sumarios, Multas, PNIA; Luis Guilhermo Placci, "Relevamiento del área afectada por el corte de palmitos (*Euterpe edulis*) en el Parque Nacional Iguazú, Misiones, informe sobre el daño ecológico," December 1991, DRNEA; D. Fiorentiny and G. A. de la Fuente, "Comisión a fines de coordinar las tareas de reconocimiento ambiental, planificación y proyectar la infraestructura necesaria para vigilancia," Expediente 2326, year 1972, 1–2, 16–28, APN-B; Teodoro Portillo to Iguazú National Park Director, November 16, 1977, Carpeta "Varios," PNIA; Daniel de la Torre to R. Foerster, March 1978, Carpeta "Varios," PNIA; Daniel de la Torre to R. Foerster, September 1, 1978, and Reinhard Foerster to Iguazú National Park Director, September 4 and September 27, 1978, both in Carpeta "Actas Infracción 18/11/1974–29/09/1978," PNIA.

state police officers improved the national park administration's ability to curb violations inside and outside park boundaries. In the 1970s alone, the police arrested several hunters acting in the park; confiscated thousands of dead and live animals (the illegal trade of tortoises and birds was gaining traction); and shut down a clandestine slaughterhouse in a nearby town that sold bush meat taken from the park to local steakhouses. Groups of heart-of-palm harvesters continued to act in the Brazilian park, but the police presence made their lives more difficult. On behalf of the IBDF, state troopers stationed in Iguaçu shut down canneries and apprehended trucks loaded with palm logs. The alliance between the federal environmental agency and the police department of the state of Paraná allowed the park to extend its spatial power beyond its borders.[110]

Thus, surveillance continued. In the decades after the two parks' creation, biodiversity conservation became the paradigm for protected areas in South America, and Iguazú and Iguaçu National Parks arrived at the twenty-first century as islands of subtropical rainforest surrounded by a sea of crop and grazing fields and pulp monoculture. As spaces of nature, these parks demanded surveillance work, laborious and tiresome. It was through, among other things, the enforcement agents' toil, deployment to isolated backcountry areas, and excursions throughout the territories that parks like Iguazú and Iguaçu emerged in their current form. This chapter has attempted to understand the spatial practices that built national parks as spaces of nature in a period when the focus of park officials in the two countries shifted from border colonization and tourism development to species, and later biodiversity conservation.

---

[110] This relationship was not always peaceful, because park administrators considered the state troopers acting in the park to be unprepared, unfocused, soft on poaching, and easily corrupted. Adilson Simão, "Relatório anual 1978," January 15, 1979, Relatórios Anuais do Parque Nacional do Iguaçu, 1972–1985, Fundo Parque Nacional do Iguaçu, ICMBio; Angela Tresinari Bernardes Quintão, Informação No. 150/80/DN, July 4, 1980, Documentos Diversos, Fundo Parque Nacional do Iguaçu, ICMBio; "Relatório no. 003/ 80 – ASI/IBDF," February 1980, Documentos Diversos, Fundo Parque Nacional do Iguaçu, ICMBio; Adilson Simão (Iguaçu National Park director, 1974–86) in discussion with the author, October 16, 2013. See also "Os inquilinos do Parque estão saindo," *Referência em planejamento* 1, First Semester of 1976; "Fabrica artesanal de caça," *O Estado de São Paulo*, January 29, 1977; "Fauna de Iguaçu constitui cardápio de restaurantes," February 2, 1977; Jayme de Paiva Bello, "Parque Nacional do Iguaçu – Anexo C ao relatório anual de 1974," January 13, 1975, Relatórios Anuais do Parque Nacional do Iguaçu, 1972–1985, Fundo Parque Nacional do Iguaçu, ICMBio; Instituto Brasileiro de Desenvolvimento Florestal, Delegacia Estadual do Paraná, "Relatório de exercício 1975," 154–55, 202, PNIB-A.

6

The View from Above

The Borderland, 1940–2014

In a 1996 interview, Brazilian environmentalist Paulo Nogueira Neto recalled the experience that led to his conversion to conservationism. It happened between 1938 and 1940, while his father was living in exile in Argentina during the Estado Novo, the dictatorial period imposed on Brazil by Getúlio Vargas. Still in his late teens, Nogueira Neto stayed behind in São Paulo, but as a member of a wealthy *Paulista* dynasty, he was able to fly with his family to Buenos Aires regularly to visit his father. Since 1935, Foz do Iguaçu had been connected to the rest of the country via an airstrip built by the army, which was later upgraded into a small airport with funds from Iguaçu National Park. By the late 1930s, Panair do Brasil, a Pan Am subsidiary, was operating a Rio de Janeiro–Asunción–Buenos Aires route with a layover at the border town. The periodic airplane trips to the Argentine capital allowed Nogueira Neto to experience something unique in the 1930s – the opportunity to look down upon the vast expanses of forests that covered the Triple Frontier area. As he recalled six decades later:

When we left Curitiba there were some farms, but minutes later there was nothing more: no roads, no houses, only forest, forest, all the way to Foz do Iguaçu, which was a military garrison, a border post, and a landing strip. After Foz do Iguaçu it was forest again all the way to Asunción in Paraguay. I saw this. I saw this forest disappear. What is left? A protected area, that is Iguaçu National Park, created before the occupation of the region. This happened in 1938, 1940, and it made a lasting impression on me, as the only thing left is the park.[1]

---

[1] Urban, *Saudade do matão*, 157. On the building of the airstrip, see Mário Câmara Canto, "Relatório que apresenta o administrador do Parque Nacional do Iguassú,

239

A traveler in 1980 flying from Curitiba into the new international airport in Foz do Iguaçu would have seen a different landscape from her window. Instead of the continuous carpet of forests that amazed Nogueira Neto, she would have seen a patchwork of narrow, irregularly shaped crop fields separated by winding backcountry roads and isolated slivers of riverine vegetation. She would also have noticed the grayish polygons of the many cities and towns that did not exist in 1940. As her airplane approached Foz do Iguaçu, she would have been surprised to encounter the massive dark green expanse of Iguaçu National Park. If her gaze had wandered to her left, she would have spotted a similar area of forests south of the Iguazu River, in Iguazú National Park in Argentina. As Paulo Nogueira Neto points out, the two national parks were created before the large-scale colonization of this border area. Trees remained standing inside the two parks, but the construction of new roads, clearing of forests for farms, and formation of new towns radically transformed the landscape outside them.

Like our airplane travelers, historical and hypothetical alike, this chapter looks at Iguaçu and Iguazú National Parks from above to understand the changes in their landscapes from their creations to the present. A wealth of historical aerial imagery and satellite data produced on this border area between the 1950s and the 2010s makes this change in perspective possible. Up until the 1970s, analogue, film-based cameras and sensors mounted on airplanes and first-generation satellites photographed many different regions of the globe. Environmental scientists, geographers, and archaeologists have used these images in their study of past landscapes, but up until recently, historians, even those conversant in the use of geographic information systems (GIS), have neglected these sources. This chapter helps correct this oversight, analyzing and interpreting a series of historical images produced from airplanes and satellites to understand the evolution of specific human and natural features across time.[2]

referente ao 1° semestre do corrente ano" (Foz do Iguaçu, 1944), PNIB-A; and João Gomes Ribeiro Filho, *Relatório apresentado ao presidente da República dos Estados Unidos do Brasil pelo general de divisão João Gomes Ribeiro Filho, Ministro de Estado da Guerra, em maio de 1936* (Rio de Janeiro: Imprensa do Estado Maior do Exército, 1936), 20, 67–69. On the 1930s airplane routes to Foz do Iguaçu, see Sasaki, *Pouso forçado*.

[2] Here, I follow the lead of David Biggs, who first proposed using historical satellite imagery to answer historical questions about space, environment, and society. David Biggs, "Frame

This study employs four sets of aerial and satellite imagery to assess the radical changes in the landscape of this border area. The most important sets are formed by high-resolution aerial images produced by the government of Paraná in 1953 and 1980. They provide snap-shots of the landscape of Iguaçu National Park and the surrounding area immediately before the arrival of settlers and after their removal from the park. They show the radical transformation happening at the borderland in this period. The study also uses satellite imagery produced by the US government in 1967. It captures the state of the national parks at the height of the arrival of settlers in western Paraná. High-resolution satellite imagery produced between 2009 and 2014 provides a view of the evolution of the borderland landscape in the twenty-first century.

SIXTY YEARS OF LAND USE AT THE BORDER

The following maps (Maps 6.1–6.4) show the evolution of the land cover in Iguaçu National Park and the surrounding area based on visual inter-pretation of the aerial and satellite images.[3] Map 6.1 shows most of the area inside and outside the Brazilian park covered by forests (black) in 1953. Iguaçu National Park itself presented very few stretches of cleared forest (light gray). Forest covered the majority of the area outside the Brazilian park, including the section in the Argentine territory east to Iguazú National Park. Some patches of cleared land had already started to open up in Brazil, outside the northern boundaries of Iguaçu, particu-larly along the axis of the new Highway BR-277, completed that same year (for the road's route, see Map 6.5). The highway was a magnet attracting thousands of internal Brazilian migrants to western Paraná. The early effects of this migration are visible in the northeastern corner

DS1050-1006DF129: March 20, 1969," *Environmental History* 19, no. 2 (2014): 271–80; David Biggs, "New Spaces for Stories: Technical and Conceptual Challenges to Using Spatial Imagery in Environmental History," Environmental History Field Notes (blog), 2014, http://environmentalhistory.net/field-notes/2014-biggs/.
[3] I divided land cover into five basic classes: forest, cropland/recently cleared, urban, natural field, and water. No fine-grained distinction was made between old- and second-growth forests, and the visual assessment of the images did not identify pulpwood and timber plantations in the area surrounding Iguaçu National Park. Likewise, no distinction was made between different types of croplands, or between cropland and pasture – the latter being an unnecessary distinction, for extensive cattle ranching is rare in this area.

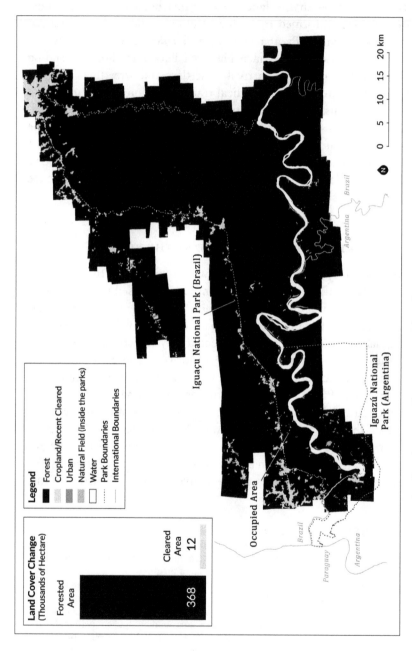

MAP 6.1 Land cover at Iguaçu National Park, 1953. Map by Frederico Freitas

Legend

- Forest
- Cropland/Recent Cleared
- Urban
- Natural Field (inside the parks)
- Water
- Park Boundaries
- International Boundaries

Land Cover Change
(Thousands of Hectare)

Forested Area
368

Cleared Area
12

Iguaçu National Park (Brazil)

Iguazú National Park (Argentina)

Occupied Area

Brazil
Argentina

Paraguay
Argentina

N

0   5   10   15   20 km

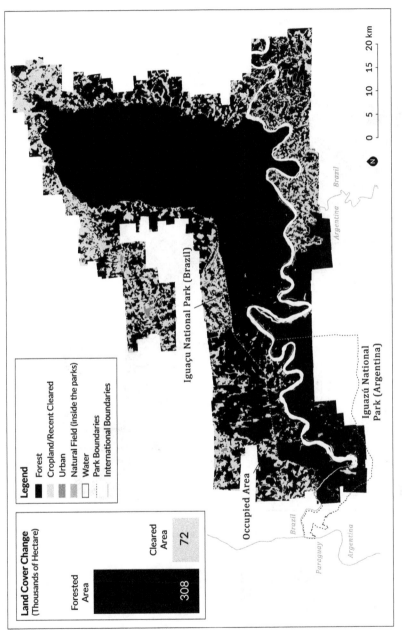

Legend

- ■ Forest
- ▨ Cropland/Recent Cleared
- ▦ Urban
- □ Natural Field (inside the parks)
- Water
- ┈┈ Park Boundaries
- ─── International Boundaries

Land Cover Change
(Thousands of Hectare)

Forested Area — 308

Cleared Area — 72

Iguaçu National Park (Brazil)

Iguazú National Park (Argentina)

Occupied Area

0   5   10   15   20 km

Brazil
Argentina
Paraguay

MAP 6.2   Land cover at Iguaçu National Park, 1967. Map by Frederico Freitas

243

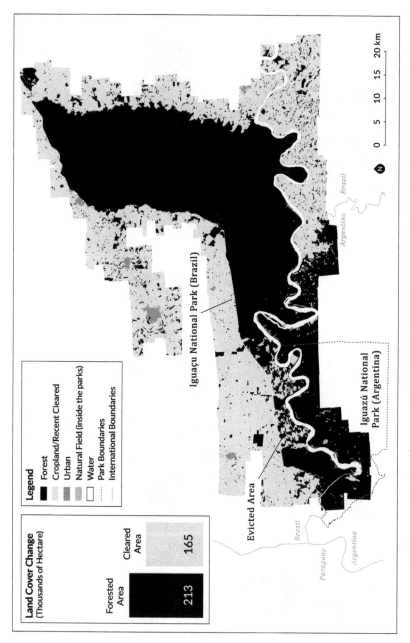

Land Cover Change
(Thousands of Hectare)

Forested Area	Cleared Area
213	165

Legend

- Forest
- Cropland/Recent Cleared
- Urban
- Natural Field (inside the parks)
- Water
- Park Boundaries
- International Boundaries

Iguaçu National Park (Brazil)

Iguazú National Park (Argentina)

Evicted Area

Paraguay

Brazil

Argentina

Argentina

Brazil

N

0   5   10   15   20 km

MAP 6.3 Land cover at Iguaçu National Park, 1980. Map by Frederico Freitas

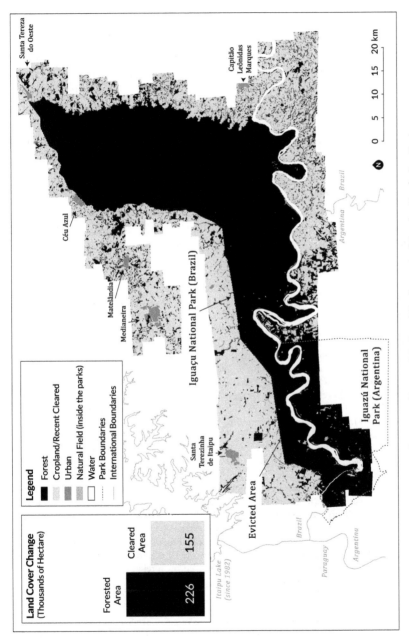

Land Cover Change
(Thousands of Hectare)

Forested Area
226

Cleared Area
155

Legend

- Forest
- Cropland/Recent Cleared
- Urban
- Natural Field (inside the parks)
- Water
- Park Boundaries
- International Boundaries

Santa Tereza do Oeste

Céu Azul

Matelândia

Medianeira

Iguaçu National Park (Brazil)

Santa Terezinha de Itaipu

Itaipu Lake (since 1982)

Paraguay

Argentina

Brazil

Evicted Area

Iguazú National Park (Argentina)

Argentina

Brazil

Capitão Leônidas Marques

0 5 10 15 20 km

MAP 6.4 Land cover at Iguaçu National Park, 2014. Map by Frederico Freitas

245

of the Brazilian park, where the town of Santa Tereza do Oeste was forming.[4]

The situation changed significantly in 1967 (Map 6.2). Outside the park on the Brazilian side of the border, the forest was being cleared to make way for small farms, and 35 percent of the 1953 forest cover was already gone. Inside the park, settlers had already started to arrive in the narrow southwestern strip of parklands clinging to the meanders of the Iguazu River. They founded the villages of Santo Alberto and São José and opened roads and farms. They cleared about 1,545 hectares of forest in this section of the park between 1953 and 1967, 31 percent of the total area that had been cleared by the time of the eviction in the 1970s. In Argentina, across the international boundary, the lands both inside and outside Iguazú National Park show only minor signs of disturbance. Colonization happened on a different timeline south of the border.[5]

Based on aerial images taken in 1980, at the tail end of the eviction of settlers from the Brazilian park, Map 6.3 reveals the marks of a colonization process at its apex. Most of the area in Brazil outside Iguaçu National

---

[4] The 1953 map is based on aerial images produced by the Department of Geography, Land, and Colonization (Departamento de Geografia, Terras e Colonização, DGTC) for the state of Paraná between 1952 and 1953. Paraná celebrated 100 years in 1953 and launched a campaign to survey its territory. The administration of Governor Moisés Lupion intended to produce data to bolster its efforts to lay claim to Paraná's disputed public land and, ultimately, colonize its western borderlands. Departamento de Geografia, Terras e Colonização, Set of Orthorectified Aerial Photographs of the State of Paraná, 1:25,000 (State of Paraná, Brazil), 1953 (235 images), ITCG. See also Departamento de Geografia, Terras e Colonização do Estado do Paraná, "Relatório das atividades geográficas desenvolvidas no Estado do Paraná, apresentado à XIII Sessão Ordinária da Assembleia geral do CNG," 1953, Comissão Especial da Faixa de Fronteiras, Conselho de Segurança Nacional – Presidência da CEFF, Lata 152, Pasta: Governos Estaduais Paraná: 1950–56, AN-RJ; Reinhard Maack, *Geografia física do Estado do Paraná* (Curitiba: Universidade Federal do Paraná, 1968), 68; Ely Bergo de Carvalho, "O estado jardineiro e a gestão das florestas: Uma história do Departamento de Geografia, Terras e Colonização na gestão do sertão paranaense (1934–1964)," in *História ambiental no sul do Brasil: apropriações do mundo natural*, ed. Jó Klanovicz, Gilmar Arruda, and Ely Bergo de Carvalho (São Paulo: Alameda Editorial, 2012); Tourinho, *Toiro passante*, 548; Gregory, *Os eurobrasileiros*, 18.

[5] The 1967 map is based on CORONA satellite images produced in 1967. CORONA was a secret satellite reconnaissance program run between 1958 and 1972 by the US Central Intelligence Agency and the US Air Force that spied on foreign countries from the safe distance of low orbit. Declassified images DS1044-2124DF027, DS1044-2124DF028, and DS1044-2124DF029, November 10, 1967, Sioux Falls, South Dakota: US Geological Survey (USGS) Earth Resources Observation and Science (EROS) Center. See also John Cloud, "Hidden in Plain Sight: The CORONA Reconnaissance Satellite Programme and Clandestine Cold War Science," *Annals of Science* 58, no. 2 (2001): 203–9; John Cloud, "Imaging the World in a Barrel: CORONA and the Clandestine Convergence of the Earth Sciences," *Social Studies of Science* 31, no. 2 (2001): 231–51.

Park had already been converted to cropland, and forests covered only 16,972 hectares in small clumps scattered among farms. Compared to the 167,317 hectares of forest in 1953, this number represents a reduction in forest cover of 89 percent. Inside Iguaçu National Park, the area occupied by settlers between the late 1950s and early 1970s appears as patches of light gray amid a sea of black. The footprint of their farms is evident in the images, as the forest had not had yet time to encroach on the recently emptied lots. The area of vacant farms comprised about 4,894 hectares in 1980, more than the 4,164 hectares described in the 1971 survey – an indication that forest continued to be cut even after the start of the eviction process (see Table 4.1 in Chapter 4). In the entire area covered by the selected aerial images, between 1953 and 1980, forest cover shrank from about 368,000 hectares to 213,000 hectares. Most of this conversion from forest to cropland and urban areas occurred in Brazil, outside Iguaçu National Park, with a smaller share happening inside the Brazilian park and in Argentina. This study does not distinguish the quality of the intact forest, but it does show the effectiveness of these national parks for impeding landscape transformation.[6]

The enforcement of Iguaçu National Park's territorial mandate as a protected area also served to "create nature," in the form of regrown forests in the 4,894-hectare area cleared by settlers in the 1960s and 1970s. In the 2014 map (Map 6.4), the section of the Brazilian park previously used for farming had now been overtaken by secondary forest as the result of the eviction of settlers in the 1970s. On the one hand, this was mainly the result of the natural encroachment of the forest, as the national park administration never took direct measures to reforest the area. On the other hand, the regrowth of the forest in this previously occupied section of the park – as well as the continued presence of old-growth forest in the other areas – was the result of a series of spatial policies and practices that aimed to create Iguaçu as a space of nature devoid of humans. The 2014 map also shows other important changes. One is the consolidation of urban areas along the axis of Highway BR-277, where towns such as Medianeira and Matelândia bloomed. Another change is the advance of the colonization frontier in Argentina, along the eastern limits of Iguazú National Park. I will discuss these two changes in

---

[6] The 1980 map is based on another statewide aerial survey carried out by the government of Paraná. Fundação Instituto de Terras e Cartografia, Set of Orthorectified Aerial Photographs of the State of Paraná, 1:25,000 (State of Paraná, Brazil), 1980 (334 images), ITCG.

further detail in the following sections. Finally, the period between 1980 and 2014 witnessed the growth of forested areas in Brazil, outside Iguaçu National Park. The area of forests outside the park grew almost 100 percent, from 16,972 to 30,436 hectares. Reforestation was fragmented, as the map shows, with slivers of black amid the light gray of croplands.[7] This timid regrowth in forested areas outside the park was most likely the result of improvements in the enforcement of environmental legislation in Brazil in the 2000s.[8]

The analysis of sets of historical satellite and aerial images offers an expansive view of critical moments of this borderland, shedding light on the impact of the national parks on this landscape at a regional scale. However, a view from above can also open a window into smaller-scale stories about the evolution of specific processes happening in particular places inside the parks, on their borders, and outside their territories. The following sections focus on these smaller narratives of spatial change, showing disputes involving different human agents over land, natural resources, and dwelling rights that were ultimately mediated by their interaction with the space of the borderland.

LOGGING THE FOREST

Part of the original territory of the Atlantic forest biome, the Triple Frontier area was still covered by forests in the 1950s. As a biome, the Atlantic forest comprised a mosaic of smaller and distinct forest formations, and this chapter focuses on the two subset forest types found at the borderland – Upper Paraná

---

[7] The 2014 map is based on high-resolution satellite imagery produced between 2009 and 2014 made available by ESRI's ArcGIS world imagery base map. For the area of the park, ArcGIS composes a mosaic with images from Digital Globe (miscellaneous satellite imagery, 1m resolution, 2009–13); GeoEye (Ikonos satellite, 1m resolution, panchromatic, 2000–11); and CNES/Airbus DS (SPOT 5 satellite, 2.5m resolution, panchromatic, 2004–12). See Esri, "World Imagery Contributors," March 17, 2016, accessed April 20, 2016, http://esriurl.com/WorldImageryContributors.

[8] Since 1965, a mostly unenforced piece of Brazilian legislation required that rural land-owners keep 20 percent of rural properties covered by forests. In the 2000s, changes in policy, technology, and enforcement led property owners in some areas of Brazil to reforest their holdings. Brazil, Decree 23793, "Código florestal," January 23, 1934; Brazil, Law 4771, "Novo código florestal," September 15, 1965; Brazil, Law 12651, "Novo código florestal," May 25, 2012. With the passage of a significant revision of the Brazilian Forest Code, the Brazilian Forest Service started surveying the status of forest reserves in all the rural estates in the country. This survey is still being carried out, but the up-to-date data can be accessed online at "SICAR – Sistema Nacional de Cadastro Ambiental Rural," 2019, accessed at www.car.gov.br/publico/imoveis/index.

Atlantic forests and Araucaria moist forests.[9] The wide valleys of the Paraná, the Iguazu, and the Uruguay were dominated by Upper Paraná Atlantic forests, a highly diverse, dense subtropical forest. This type of forest contains a high canopy of about twenty-five meters that intersects with several other lower strata constituted by shade-tolerant and stunted trees. No single tree dominates this forest, but one of its iconic species is the juçara palm tree (*Euterpe edulis*), whose heart of palm provided sustenance for indigenous people and the different waves of settlers into the region. The juçara palm is usually associated with the peroba rosa (*Aspidosperma polyneuron*), a hardwood used in construction and furniture making in Brazil. Other valued timber trees present in Upper Paraná Atlantic forests are cabreúva (*Myrocarpus frondosus*), ipê (*Tabebuia* ssp.), louro-pardo (*Cordia trichotoma*), and, especially, Argentine cedar (*Cedrela fissilis*). According to a 1960s Argentine scientist, the vegetation in this forest was "luxurious, entangled, with dense underbrush replete with bushes, giant ferns, thick weeds, and vines. A machete and ax are necessary to open the way."[10] However much Argentine informants from the country's temperate and treeless regions liked to employ tropes of a Misiones covered by impenetrable jungle, these are not tropical rainforests in the same sense as the Amazon rainforest or the forests of coastal Brazil. Upper Paraná

---

[9] Scholars have called Upper Paraná Atlantic forests and Araucaria moist forests many different names since the nineteenth century. Most of these denominations are based on a provincial understanding of the place they occupy in a given country's vegetation mosaic. In the case of Upper Paraná Atlantic forests, Argentine authors, as discussed in the introduction, employ the term *selva missioneira* (Misiones jungle), which implies it is limited to Argentina. Brazilian authors, on the other hand, use a seemingly technically precise term, *floresta estacional semidecidual* (seasonal semideciduous forest), which betrays a parochial understand of vegetation formations, for it classifies Upper Paraná Atlantic forests solely in relation to other environments found within Brazil. Whereas in Brazil this might be the only forest environment with these specific characteristics, in other countries one can find other forests that are seasonal and semideciduous but have distinct species, ecologies, and landscapes. These forest formations, which are part of the larger Atlantic forest biome, straddle international boundaries. To avoid applying country-centered names to transnational environments, I have chosen to employ the nomenclature of terrestrial ecoregions as used by conservation organizations such as the World Wildlife Fund and the Nature Conservancy since the early 2000s. World Wildlife Fund, "Terrestrial Ecoregions of the World | Publications | WWF," World Wildlife Fund, August 1, 2012, www.worldwildlife.org/publications/terrestrial-ecoregions-of-the-worl d; Jonathan M. Hoekstra and Jennifer L. Molnar, *The Atlas of Global Conservation: Changes, Challenges and Opportunities to Make a Difference* (Berkeley: University of California Press, 2010); Olson and Dinerstein, "The Global 200"; Olson et al., "Terrestrial Ecoregions of the World."
[10] Domingo Cozzo, *La Argentina forestal* (Buenos Aires: Editorial Universitaria de Buenos Aires, 1967), 45–49.

Atlantic forests receive a good annual amount of rain, between 1,500 and 2,000 mm, but precipitation is concentrated in the warmer months. During its colder and drier short winter, rainfall decreases to a third of the amount registered in wetter months, and between 20 and 50 percent of the trees shed their leaves. The southern reaches of the forest commonly experience a few nights of frost every year, which prevented the introduction of coffee cultivation to the Triple Frontier area.[11]

In areas of higher altitude, away from the main rivers, a distinct type of forest was found, Araucaria moist forests. This environment was dominated by the species that single-handedly defined the logging industry in Brazil in the twentieth century, the Paraná pine (*Araucaria angustifolia*), also known as *kuri'y* by Guarani-speaking locals. The tree is a conifer, one of the two species of the *Araucaria* genus in South America, and one of the few species of conifers native to Brazil. It grows in straight trunks with branches concentrated at the crown of the tree, turned upward like a candelabra. In the late 1800s, it was possible to find individuals reaching forty meters in height, but excessive logging has decimated older specimens, and the tallest individuals reach only about twenty meters today. In the twentieth century, the tree was logged almost to extinction for timber, pulpwood, and firewood. Over 97 percent of the original area of the Araucaria moist forests was logged, and only a few sustainable groves of Paraná pine survive to this day. In the 1950s, Araucaria moist forests could be found at elevations above 500 meters, which are common in a wide central band across the three southern states in Brazil – Paraná, Santa Catarina, and Rio Grande do Sul. The forest type was also present in a small area of highlands in eastern Misiones in Argentina. The forest is highly diverse, but its upper canopy is dominated by Paraná pine, which can constitute more than 40 percent of all individual trees. It shares many

---

[11] Reinhard Maack, *Mapa fitogeográfico do Estado do Paraná* (Curitiba: Instituto de Biologia e Pesquisas Tecnológicas, Instituto Nacional do Pinho, 1950), SU; Reinhard Maack, *Geografia física*, 130, 163, 198–200, 218–23; Lucas A. Tortorelli, *Maderas y bosques argentinos* (Buenos Aires: Editorial Acme, 1956), 19–37; Instituto Brasileiro de Geografia e Estatística, *Mapa de vegetação do Brasil*, 1:5,000,000 (Brasília: Ministério do Planejamento, Orçamento e Gestão, 2004), https://mapas.ibge.gov.br/tematicos/vegetacao.html; Alejandro R. Giraudo et al., "Status da biodiversidade da Mata Atlântica de interior da Argentina," in *Mata Atlântica: Biodiversidade, ameaças e perspectivas*, ed. Carlos Galindo-Leal and Ibsen de Gusmão Câmara (Belo Horizonte: Fundação SOS Mata Atlântica and Conservação Internacional, 2005), 162–63; Eunice Sueli Nodari, "Crossing Borders: Immigration and Transformation of Landscapes in Misiones Province, Argentina, and Southern Brazil," in *Big Water: The Making of the Borderlands between Brazil, Argentina, and Paraguay*, ed. Jacob Blanc and Frederico Freitas (Tucson, AZ: University of Arizona Press, 2018).

plant and animal species with Upper Paraná Atlantic forests, but it also presents a high incidence of species that are less common or absent in those lower altitudes, among them conifers such as the Paraná pine and the pinheirinho bravo (*Podocarpus lambertii*). Araucaria moist forests also present a high incidence of yerba mate (*Ilex paraguariensis*), which, together with the abundance of conifers, made the environment one of the main economic engines in the state of Paraná before the conversion of the state's economy to agriculture. Unlike Upper Paraná Atlantic forests, the Araucaria moist forests receive rainfall the entire year, with no significant reduction in the winter. They also have a colder climate, with some higher areas recording light snow a few times per decade.[12]

The two parks are established in the lowlands alongside the Iguazu River, in areas of Upper Paraná Atlantic forests, but a northeastern corner of the Brazilian park, where the landscape rises to altitudes of 750 meters, contains groves of the coveted Paraná pine. In this section of Iguaçu National Park, the Upper Paraná Atlantic forests transition into Araucaria moist forests, with specimens of juçara palm tree, typical of the former, interspersed with Paraná pine and yerba mate, which characterize the latter. About 10 percent of the Brazilian park encompasses areas of Araucaria moist forest, but the present size of the actual groves of Paraná pine is limited to only a few hundred hectares that harbor relatively young individuals. A 2018 dendrochronological survey calculates the park's average Paraná pine age to be forty-seven years old at the edges of the park and seventy-one years old at the center – a young population indeed, for the species can reach four hundred years. The young age and low density of specimens of Paraná pine in this section of Iguaçu are a testimony to the preceding decades of logging, which continued in this area until the 1960s, as demonstrated by the clearings in this section of the park, along its northernmost boundary, in Maps 6.1 and 6.2.[13]

---

[12] Maack, *Geografia física*, 193–94; John Robert McNeill, "Deforestation in the Araucaria Zone of Southern Brazil, 1900–1983," in *World Deforestation in the Twentieth Century*, ed. John F. Richards and Richard P. Tucker (Durham: Duke University Press, 1988); Maria Fabiana Rau, "Land Use Change and Natural Araucaria Forest Degradation: Northeastern Misiones – Argentina" (PhD diss., University of Freiburg, 2005), 2–10; Instituto Brasileiro de Geografia e Estatística, *Mapa de vegetação*; Giraudo et al., "Status da biodiversidade," 162–63; Nodari, "Crossing Borders"; Mark Robinson et al., "Uncoupling Human and Climate Drivers of Late Holocene Vegetation Change in Southern Brazil," *Scientific Reports* 8, no. 1 (2018): 7800.

[13] Carlos Alberto Teixeira Coelho Júnior, *Pelas selvas e rios do Paraná* (Curitiba: Guaíra, 1946), 115; Wanderbilt Duarte de Barros, *Parques nacionais do Brasil*, Série documentária 1 (Rio de Janeiro: Serviço de Informação Agrícola do Ministério da

Other areas of Iguaçu National Park, close to the banks of the Iguazu River, were also subject to selective logging carried out by *obrajes* before the creation of the park, but the record here is sparse. There was at least one *obraje*, granted by the state government to one Ramon Lopes, a Uruguayan citizen, operating inside the Brazilian park. Lopes cut mainly Argentine cedar, leaving other valuable timber trees standing, although contemporary witnesses attest to a considerable degree of forest destruction caused by loggers' opening of clearings and trails for the cutting and transportation of logs. Nevertheless, the effects of this logging operation on the landscape of the future park were limited by its distance from the Paraná River, the main waterway connecting this borderland region to the largest market for timber, Buenos Aires.[14] The situation was different in the area of the future Argentine Iguazú National Park, where federal employees extensively documented the ongoing operation of an *obraje* inside the park while surveying the land for nationalization (see Chapter 1). Similar to the *obraje* in Brazil, loggers operating on the Ayarragaray estate cut mostly Argentine cedar, despite the myriad of valuable timber species available in this stretch of subtropical forest.[15]

Why Argentine cedar? Because of its light density – for a log to float, it needs to have a density lower than water's, that is, 997 kg/m³. With a wood density of 530 kg/m³, the Argentine cedar, which is not a real coniferous cedar but a flowering tree from the mahogany family, was even lighter than the Paraná pine (density: 550 kg/m³), a true softwood. The cedar was also considerably lighter than other popular hardwoods such as cabreúva (910 kg/m³), ipê (1,010 kg/m³), and louro-pardo

Agricultura, 1952), 62; Centro de Pesquisas Florestais da Universidade do Paraná and Instituto Brasileiro do Desenvolvimento Florestal, *Inventário de reconhecimento do Parque Nacional do Iguaçu* (Curitiba, Brazil: IBDF/CPF-UFP, 1968), 9–25; Harold Edgard Strang and Henrique Pimenta Veloso, "Alguns aspectos fisionômicos da vegetação no Brasil," *Memórias do Instituto Oswaldo Cruz* 68, no. 1 (1970): 9–76; Instituto Paranaense de Desenvolvimento Econômico e Social and Fundação Édison Vieira, "Estudos para a formulação de políticas de desenvolvimento do Setor Florestal," vol. III (Curitiba: CODESUL, IPARDES, 1982), IPARDES; Marcela Strucker Kropf and Alci Albiero Júnior, "Araucárias do Parque Nacional do Iguaçu: Implicações para sua conservação," in *Fronteiras fluidas: Floresta com araucárias na América meridional*, ed. Eunice Sueli Nodari, Miguel Mundstock Xavier de Carvalho, and Paulo Zarth (São Leopoldo, Brazil: Editora Oikos, 2018).

[14] The *obraje* was located at the mouth of the Represa River, a tributary of the Iguazu that bisects Iguaçu National Park north to south. Figueiredo, *Oéste paranaense*, 74–77.

[15] Cozzo, *La Argentina forestal*, 45–49.

(780 kg/m³).[16] Before a reliable land connection between this borderland and consumer markets was built, timber rafting on the Paraná was the only way to transport logs to buyers in Buenos Aires. In areas of Upper Paraná Atlantic forest, devoid of Paraná pine, the floatable Argentine cedar made the development of a timber industry possible. Logs were transported by mule or oxcarts to the dozens of small *obraje* ports on the banks of the Paraná, where they were tied together for river transportation. Rafts made of 200 logs of Argentine cedar were floatable enough to allow for the transport of a smaller amount of denser timber from other types of trees with them, but most logs produced in areas such as the Arrayagaray estate were cedar. The selective cutting of cedar along with a few other species (cabreúva, ipê, and louro-pardo) did not eradicate these trees from Iguazú, for they tended to occur in isolation in the middle of the forest and were often missed by the Guarani scouts who surveyed the territory of the *obrajes* searching for prime hardwood specimens. Also, loggers avoided cutting young trees and would wait a few years before revisiting previously logged areas. Some sections in the territory of the future Argentine park, for example, were logged three different times in the four decades that preceded its nationalization in 1928. As seen in Chapters 1 and 2, the *obrajes* that operated on the banks of the Paraná in Brazil and Argentina, including in the future area of the national parks, also gathered yerba mate, which caused even less impact on the landscape. Overall, the *obraje* era, which extended into the 1930s, had a moderate impact on the forest, for their logging and mate gathering mostly affected select species of trees.[17]

INDIGENOUS LABOR

As seen in previous chapters, the early twentieth-century *obrajes* employed primarily workers of Guarani descent, usually in slavery-like conditions of

[16] "Informações sobre madeira," Instituto de Pesquisas Tecnológicas, accessed at www.ipt.br/consultas_online/informacoes_sobre_madeira/busca. Since colonial times, the absence of floatable timbers had imposed hurdles for the development of the logging industry in areas of Atlantic forest. In tropical and subtropical South America, most high-quality woods were extremely dense. Miller, *Fruitless Trees*, 132–34.

[17] Devoto and Rothkugel, "Informe sobre los bosques"; Muello, *Misiones*, 28–48; Maria Buchinger and Rodolfo Falcone, "Nota preliminar sobre las especies argentinas del género *Cedrela* L." *Darwiniana* 10, no. 3 (1953): 461–64; Tortorelli, *Maderas y bosques*, 30, 483–92; Giraudo et al., "Status da biodiversidade," 165; M. Barstow, "*Cedrela fissilis*," *The IUCN Red List of Threatened Species*, 2018, accessed October 11, 2019, https://dx.doi.org/10.2305/IUCN.UK.2018-1.RLTS.T33928A68080477.en.

debt bondage. A sizable contingent of these laborers were Mbya or
Ñandeva, the two Guarani populations living at the borderland. Others
had Guarani ancestors and spoke Paraguayan Guarani – still widely used by
mestizos in Paraguay today – but did not see themselves as Indians.
Contemporary Brazilian sources commonly depicted these varied ethnic
groups as "Paraguayans" even though, legally speaking, many were
Brazilian citizens, having been born on the Brazilian side of the border.
They were also called *índios* or *bugres* (the latter a slur for indigenous
peoples), despite some not identifying themselves as such.[18] Ñandeva
groups inhabited the banks of the Paraná and were some of the first to be
employed by *obrajes* in the late nineteenth century. Eventually Mbya
groups coming from the Itakyry region in Paraguay moved to the
Brazilian side of the border between the 1920s and 1950s, crossing into
areas inhabited by the Ñandeva. Their journey was part of a multigener-
ational quest for the mythical "land without evil," a place free of pain and
suffering that occupies a central place in the cosmogony of the Guarani.
Mbya groups entered western Paraná and Misiones in the first half of the
twentieth century on their way to the land without evil, which they believed
could be found somewhere in eastern South America. The Mbya joined the
Ñandeva and other nonindigenous laborers working in the local *obrajes* on
the banks of the Paraná River, but many eventually moved on in their
decades-long eastward migration before finally settling on the coast of
São Paulo years later.[19]

[18] José Maria de Brito, "Descoberta de Foz do Iguaçu e fundação da Colônia Militar,"
Boletim do Instituto Histórico, Geográfico e Etnográfico Paranaense 32 (January 1977):
45–72; José Francisco Thomaz do Nascimento, "Viagem feita por José Francisco Thomaz
do Nascimento pelos desconhecidos sertões de Guarapuava, Província do Paraná, e
relações que teve com os índios coroados, mais bravios daqueles lugares," *Revista
Trimensal do IHGB* 49 (1886): 267–81; Nestor Borba and André Pinto Rebouças,
Excursão ao salto do Guayra: O Parque Nacional (Rio de Janeiro: Casa Mont'Alverne,
1897), 8–9, 21, 30–32; Wachowicz, *Obrageros, mensus e colonos*, 46–50; Gregory, *Os
eurobrasileiros*, 159–61; Sarah Iurkiv Gomes Tibes Ribeiro, "A construção de um discurso historiográfico relativo aos guarani: Ensaio de teoria e metodologia," *Tempos
históricos* 5–6 (2003–04): 161–83; Evaldo Mendes da Silva, "Folhas ao vento: A micromobilidade de grupos Mbya e Nhandéva (Guarani) na Tríplice Fronteira" (PhD diss.,
Federal University of Rio de Janeiro, 2007), 61–66.
[19] Egon Schaden, *Aspectos fundamentais da cultura guarani*, 2nd ed. (São Paulo: Difusão
Européia do Livro, 1962), 9–18, 20–22, 46–47, 161–74; Penny Seymoure, "The Fight for
Mbya Lands: Indigenous Rights and Collective Rights," in *Tourism in Northeastern
Argentina: The Intersection of Human and Indigenous Rights with the Environment*,
ed. Penny Seymoure and Jeffrey L. Roberg (Lanham, MD: Lexington Books, 2012), 22–
37; Rubia Carla Formighieri Giordani, "Os guarani no Oeste Paranaense e a (re)
constituição de territórios originários," *Guaju – Revista brasileira de desenvolvimento*

In the 1930s, the Brazilian industry of wild yerba mate was in decline and the Argentine-controlled *obraje* companies, which now faced the opposition of a nationalist federal government in Brazil and the competition of mate plantations at home, left western Paraná. Brazilian entrepreneurs, mostly from Rio Grande do Sul, formed joint-stock colonization companies to purchase these lands from previous owners or the state government, at times in dubious transactions. The new proprietors exploited timber, demand for which grew in the 1940s and 1950s in tandem with the increasing urbanization of Brazil and reconstruction efforts in Europe, and sold parcels to settlers from other areas of Brazil.[20] Initially, these logging and colonization companies employed the same *obraje* workers of Guarani descent, including Mbya and Ñandeva, to build roads, demarcate lots, extract timber, and clear the first patches of forest for colonization projects. In areas of Upper Paraná Atlantic forests, the type of clearing now performed by Guarani workers was a departure from previous logging patterns, changing from selective cutting of Argentine cedar to clear-cutting and converting patches of forest into farms and villages.[21]

As the population of white Brazilian settlers gradually increased, the need for Guarani labor decreased. At the same time, the pressure of new settlers coming mostly from the Brazilian state of Rio Grande do Sul pushed the Guarani to the fringes of the borderland. Some clustered in communities by the banks of the Paraná, others proceeded with their eastward migration toward the coast or moved to Misiones in Argentina or to eastern Paraguay, where the demographic pressure was less intense.[22] Local authorities

---

territorial sustentável 1, no. 1 (2015): 146, 150; Gustavo Kenner Alcântara et al., *Avá-Guarani: A construção de Itaipu e os direitos territoriais* (Brasília: Escola Superior do Ministério Público da União, 2019), 2 1; Ministério Publico Federal, "Ação civil originária n° 238/2019-SDHDC/GABPGR, Sistema único n° 280475/2019," 2019.

[20] Temístocles Linhares, *Paraná vivo: Sua vida, sua gente, sua cultura* (Rio de Janeiro: José Olympio, 1985), 62–66; Freitag, *Fronteiras perigosas*, 82–83.

[21] Argentine cedar continued to be the most prized hardwood in areas of Upper Paraná Atlantic forest. In the Brazilian town of Toledo, for example, where large mechanized mills were already operating by the mid-1950s, 80 percent of all the hardwood produced was Argentine cedar. Kalervo Oberg and Thomas Jabine, *Toledo, a Municipio on the Western Frontier of the State of Paraná* (Rio de Janeiro: United States Operations Mission to Brazil, 1957), 25–26.

[22] Settler Leonardo Wychoski recalls a community of fifty-two Guarani living north of the border of Iguaçu National Park moving to Paraguay after they were forced to sell their land to a colonization company. "Jagunços, feiticeiros e índios: Entrevista com Wychoski," *Nosso tempo*, March 10, 1983. See also Sarah Iurkiv Gomes Tibes Ribeiro, "Fronteira e espacialidade: O caso dos guarani no oeste do Paraná," *Varia Scientia* 6, no. 12 (2006): 175–77; Silva, "Folhas ao vento," 61–66; Giordani, "Os guarani," 152–53.

forcibly took some Guarani families living close to the new settlements to an indigenous reservation created in the central area of the state of Paraná, the Rio das Cobras outpost, which had initially been devised to receive members of the Kaingang people, an indigenous group of the Gê-linguistic trunk.[23] Despite being pushed to the fringes of the newly settled areas, the Guarani who remained on the Brazilian side of the borderland did not isolate themselves from the settler society. They continued to engage in a number of work-related activities with the arriving settlers, building roads and bridges, clearing land, and working as farm laborers in the new white settlements. By and large, indigenous labor was crucial in the development and settlement of the region.[24]

HIGHWAYS AND COLONIZATION COMPANIES

The BR-277, the primary settler entryway to western Paraná in the late 1950s, was also built in part with indigenous labor. Contractors initially tapped into the Guarani population's experience as loggers to clear the forest along the highway's planned route.[25] The Vargas administration started to plan this highway in 1941 in the context of the March to the West, when a commission created to expand the road network in southern Brazil decided that Foz do Iguaçu needed a new, more reliable land connection to the Atlantic. In the section of the BR-277 close to Iguaçu National Park, army engineers chose to avoid the path of the old dirt road built by the state of Paraná in 1920 and create a new route. The 1940s project provided for a new two-lane, macadamized highway running on dry land between the Iguaçu and the Paraná, thus avoiding the many creeks and springs that made the 1920s road impassable for most of the year (see Map 6.5). The federal government opened the BR-277 as a dirt road in 1951, promising to add macadam in the years to come. Progress was slow, and as late as 1958, there were still large sections to be macadamized. Transportation during heavy rains still posed a challenge in the

---

[23] Maria Lucia Brant Carvalho, "Das terras dos índios a índios sem terras, o Estado e os guarani do Oco'y: Violência, silêncio e luta" (PhD diss., University of São Paulo, 2013), 348.

[24] José Augusto Colodel, *Matelândia: História e contexto* (Cascavel, Brazil: Assoeste, 1992), 218, 243–45; Gregory, *Os eurobrasileiros*, 99, 132–34; Silva, "Folhas ao vento," 61–66; Alcântara et al., *Avá-guarani*, 39–41.

[25] Ian Packer and Centro de Trabalho Indigenista, "Violações dos direitos humanos e territoriais dos guarani no Oeste do Paraná (1946–1988): Subsídios para a Comissão Nacional da Verdade" (Brasília: Centro de Trabalho Indigenista, Comissão Nacional da Verdade, 2014), 19–20, 25–26.

1950s, but the BR-277 would never completely shut down as had happened with the old road, where flash floods regularly washed away bridges. As early as 1951, a weekly bus route started connecting Ponta Grossa, 500 kilometers to the east, to Foz do Iguaçu via the BR-277, eventually bringing the first prospective settlers to the region. With the new highway, travel time from Curitiba to Foz do Iguaçu was slashed from two weeks to two days.[26] The BR-277 was entirely asphalted in 1969 after a series of international treaties, and the construction of a bridge on the Paraná, amplified its geopolitical importance to Brazil, giving the country control over the first land connection between landlocked Paraguay and the Atlantic.[27]

The federal government built the BR-277 for geopolitical reasons, first to connect the borderland to the west to its Atlantic core to the east and then to bring Paraguay into its orbit. The government of Paraná took the opportunity of the construction of the federal highway to ramp up its plans to colonize the borderland and began installing a network of side roads in the 1950s. One of them, the PR-495, cut through the heart of Iguaçu National Park, connecting the town of Capanema, south of the Iguazu River, to Medianeira on the BR-277 (see Map 6.5). This side road, later known as the *Estrada do Colono* (Settler's Highway), was finished in 1954 with the help of local colonization companies, who lent the state government machinery to expedite the clearing of the forest. For the next two decades, the PR-495 would

[26] The highway was first named BR-35, then BR-37, and finally BR-277. Brasil, Decree-Law 3196, April 14, 1941; Americo R. Netto, "A Marcha para Oeste em automóvel: Ciclos evolutivos da rodovia para a Foz do Iguaçu, III conclusão," *Rodovia* 42, July 1943, DER-PR; Coelho Júnior, *Pelas selvas e rios*, 137–38, 177; Instituto Brasileiro de Geografia e Estatística, *Sinopse estatística do município de Foz do Iguaçu* (Curitiba: Departamento Estadual de Estatística do Estado do Paraná, 1950), 28–31, APP; "Instantâneos de Fóz do Iguáçu," *A notícia*, November 30, 1952; "Ligação vital," *A notícia*, March 10, 1954; Araken Távora, Cid Destefani, and Hermes Astor, "BR-277: A grande estrada," *Panorama*, 1967–68, DER-PR; "Da estrada estratégica à BR-277," in *Memória de Foz do Iguaçu* 2 (1982), 23, BPEENR; Rohde et al., *Resgate da memória de Medianeira*, 53, 65–70; Joel Wolfe, *Autos and Progress: The Brazilian Search for Modernity* (Oxford: Oxford University Press, 2010), 96.

[27] "Foz do Iguaçu faz história: Quarto encontro dos presidentes do Paraguai e do Brasil," *A notícia*, November 30, 1958, BPEENR; Távora et al., "BR-277"; "Costa inaugura a BR-277 e exalta a cooperação entre Brasil e Paraguai," *Folha de São Paulo*, March 28, 1969; "Da estrada estratégica à BR-277," 21, BPEENR; Foweraker, "Political Conflict on the Frontier," 41, 84–85; Bridget María Chesterton, "From *Porteño* to *Pontero*: The Shifting of Paraguayan Geography and Identity in Asunción in the Early Years of the Stroessner Regime," in *Big Water: The Making of the Borderlands between Brazil, Argentina, and Paraguay*, ed. Jacob Blanc and Frederico Freitas (Tucson: University of Arizona Press, 2018), 249–50.

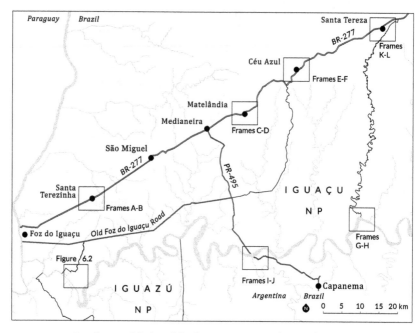

MAP 6.5 Iguaçu National Park, c. 1980. Map by Frederico Freitas

become the gateway for settlers traveling north to western Paraná from Rio Grande do Sul. In just one month in 1969, 2,190 families of settlers took their trucks loaded with their belongings onto the barges across the Iguazu connecting Capanema to the road inside Iguaçu National Park. The road's existence, however, represented a challenge to park administrators, as Paraná's Division of Highways (Departamento de Estradas de Rodagem do Paraná, DER/PR) had built it through park territory without the authorization of the Forest Service, which administered the protected area. Brazilian federal agencies evicted settlers and regained control of the park's public land in the 1970s, but the Estrada do Colono remained in operation, a reminder of the challenges the state government had mounted in the 1950s against federal domain in Iguaçu. In the 1980s, park administrators began lobbying for the road to be closed, provoking the ire of neighboring settler communities, who wanted to keep open a road that was the only direct connection between farmers living north and south of the park.[28]

---

[28] This road, first named R-25, was temporarily incorporated to the highway BR-163 in the 1970s, which connects southern Brazil to Amazonia. It was later closed by federal

The two new highways linked this corner of western Paraná to the rest of the state and southern Brazil. They served as reliable arteries for the circulation of buses and trucks, the primary modes of motorized transportation in the Brazilian countryside in the 1950s, inaugurating a land connection to a border zone that had historically been dependent on its fluvial linkage to Argentina.[29] With the roads functional, realtors working with the colonization companies could bring settlers from Rio Grande do Sul to see available land before they decided to purchase.[30] Between 1945 and 1954, the state government re-demarcated the land around Iguaçu National Park, dividing the territory into large estates. Private colonization companies and individual realtors acquired the newly retitled land and divided it into small lots for sale. Similar to much of the land in Paraná, different parties had already laid claim to the land in the area of Iguaçu National Park, but the new colonization companies had connections in the government of Paraná, which lubricated the process of making their land purchases official at the state level. There were already people living on some estates – Guarani communities, non-Guarani squatters of mixed-race descent (known as *caboclos*), white settlers from previous colonization initiatives. Those who ended up entangled in the resale of their lands were forced to leave by the companies' henchmen, a pattern repeated in many areas of Paraná in this period. After taking control of the land, the new companies followed in the footsteps of the old *obrajes* and, in the first years, logged their land and exported timber downriver to Argentina. They reinvested the profit from timber in building the infrastructure necessary to establish settlers, which included clearing lots, opening roads, and founding schools and churches.[31]

---

prosecutors in 1986 for its impact on the park environment. Eleven years later, in 1997, politicians and farmers from neighboring towns occupied the remnants of the road inside park territory, forcing its reopening. It remained in partial operation until it was closed again by the Brazilian Federal Policy and the Brazilian Army in 2001. Paraná, "A concretização do plano de obras do governador Moysés Lupion, 1947–1950" (1951), 368, APP; "Situação das estradas do sudoeste do estado," *Divulgação e propaganda rodoviária* 15, 1968, DER-PR; Os gaúchos pioneiros," *Veja*, April 23, 1969, 18; Rohde et al., *Resgate da memória de Medianeira*, 55; 260–1; Cynthia Roncaglio, *Das estradas às rodovias: Meio século de rodoviarismo no Paraná* (Curitiba: DER-PR, 1996), 35; Processo n° 00.00.86736-5 – Ação Civil Pública/Ministério Público Federal vs. IBDF e Municípios Lindeiros ao PNI – Assunto: Fechamento da Estrada do Colono – Pastas 1–13 (1986–2001), JFP-C.

[29] Os gaúchos pioneiros," 18; Wolfe, *Autos and Progress*, 81.

[30] Colodel, *Matelândia*, 207–13, 226–27; Gregory, *Os eurobrasileiros*, 167–69.

[31] Paraná, "Relatório apresentado a S. Excia. o Snr. Dr. Getúlio Vargas M. D. Presidente da República pelo Snr. Manoel Ribas Interventor Federal no Estado do Paraná, exercício de

TABLE 6.1 *Colonization projects along the BR-277*

Municipality	Colonization company	Beginning of colonization	Year the location became a municipality	Population (2019 estimate)
Santa Terezinha de Itaipu	Colonizadora Criciúma	1952	1982	23,465
São Miguel do Iguaçu	Colonizadora Gaúcha	1948	1961	27,452
Medianeira	Colonizadora Bento Gonçalves	1949	1960	46,198
Matelândia	Colonizadora Matelândia	1950	1960	17,943
Céu Azul	Colonizadora Criciúma	1952	1968	11,765

Source: IBGE, Cidades@, cidades.ibge.gov.br

In the area immediately north of Iguaçu National Park, five different colonization projects started between the late 1940s and early 1950s, giving rise to the towns of Céu Azul, Matelândia, Medianeira, São Miguel do Iguaçu, and Santa Terezinha de Itaipu (see Table 6.1) along the BR-277's route. A different colonization company was behind each project, but they were, for the most part, controlled by the same small cadre of majority shareholders operating from Curitiba. The companies also had a myriad of smaller shareholders, mostly from Rio Grande do Sul, in some cases all from the same town. For Matelândia, for example, 55 percent of its ninety-two shareholders originated in the same town, Farroupilha in Rio Grande do Sul.[32]

1932 a 1939" (1940), 23, APP; Paraná, "A concretização do plano de obras do Governador Moysés Lupion, 1947–1950" (1951), 315, 338, 364, 370, APP; Oberg and Jabine, *Toledo*, 19–23, 33, 123–26, 145–46; Westphalen, Machado, and Balhana, "Nota prévia," 6–7, 15; Keith Derald Muller, *Pioneer Settlement in South Brazil: The Case of Toledo, Paraná* (The Hague: Martinus Nijhoff, 1974); José Augusto Colodel, *Obrages e companhias colonizadoras: Santa Helena na história do Oeste Paranaense até 1960* (Santa Helena, Brazil: Prefeitura Municipal, 1988), 191–238; Interview with Etelvino Salvatti, *Gazeta do Iguaçu*, April 14, 1994, in "Foz 80, Memória," BPEENR; "Jagunços, feiticeiros e índios"; Freitag, *Fronteiras perigosas*, 29–30.

[32] Departamento de Terras e Colonização, Paraná, "Mapa do município de Foz do Iguaçu," 1941, Comissão Especial da Faixa de Fronteiras, Conselho de Segurança Nacional, Lata

This section of western Paraná had been exploited for timber and yerba mate by the *obrajes* since the late nineteenth century, but from a bird's-eye perspective, the impact of human labor on the landscape in the 1950s was limited. Some tree species had been extensively cut in some areas – particularly Argentine cedar – but the logging was selective and loggers left much of the forest standing. More comprehensive clearings were limited to a small network of trails and the circumscribed space surrounding the *obraje* ports on the banks of the Paraná. The borderland, viewed from an airplane window, was still a carpet of forests. But the opening of new land routes into the region coupled with the arrival of colonization companies radically transformed the landscape. The change is evident in the images in Figure 6.1, which show the evolution of three different colonization projects established alongside the BR-277 between 1953 and 1980. The images are formed by a mosaic of historical aerial photographs georeferenced in GIS (to locate the frames in the area surrounding Iguaçu National Park, see Map 6.5). Frame A shows the project closest to Foz do Iguaçu, Santa Terezinha de Itaipu, in 1953 as a small cluster of cleared rectangular shapes alongside the recently opened BR-277. A carpet of trees covers everything else. The colonization company had already traced the future town's main thoroughfare perpendicular to the BR-277 but had yet to clear most of its urban lots. The 1980 images in Frame B show a small town laid out in the Cartesian grid commonly found in the urban plans of western Paraná colonization companies. Newspaper ads, such as a 1955 one describing Santa Terezinha's "high-quality lands, magnificent roads, in lots duly mapped and demarcated," played a crucial role attracting settlers to this Paraná frontier. Ads also emphasized the infrastructure available to settlers for the exploitation of timber with "warehouses, sawmills, transportation, etc." and the proximity to a major river port in Foz do Iguaçu.[33]

Frames C and D show another colonization project, the future town of Matelândia, whose urban footprint was already mostly cleared in 1953.

152/1940–48, AN-RJ; "Santa Terezinha, ontem, hoje," *Nosso tempo*, March 10, 1983; Rohde et al., *Resgate da memória de Medianeira*, 37–38, 58; Colodel, *Matelândia*, 172–201; Antonio Marcos Myskiw, "Colonos, posseiros e grileiros," 100–12.

[33] *A notícia*, April 15, 1955, p. 4, BPEENR. In Rio Grande do Sul, the main source of knowledge about real-estate opportunities outside the state was ads posted in local newspapers by different colonization companies. The companies targeted specific ethnic communities, publishing advertisements in Italian or German. The ads praised the fertility of the lands, the favorable conditions of payment, the good location, the new transportation options, and so on. See Eunice Sueli Nodari, *Etnicidades renegociadas: Práticas socioculturais no oeste de Santa Catarina* (Florianópolis: Editora da UFSC, 2009), 42–43.

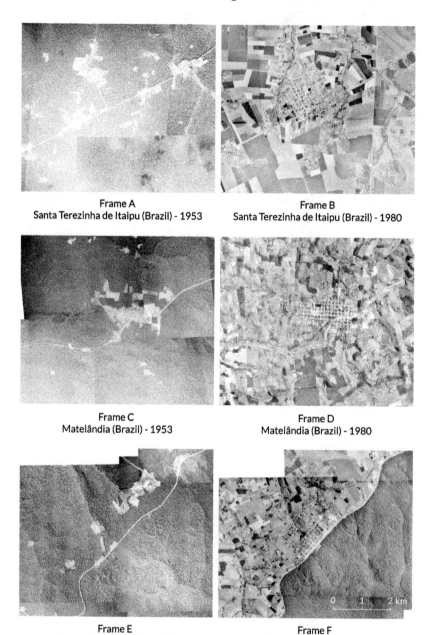

Frame A
Santa Terezinha de Itaipu (Brazil) - 1953

Frame B
Santa Terezinha de Itaipu (Brazil) - 1980

Frame C
Matelândia (Brazil) - 1953

Frame D
Matelândia (Brazil) - 1980

Frame E
Céu Azul, Brazi (Brazil) - 1953

Frame F
Céu Azul (Brazil) - 1980

FIGURE 6.1 Colonization projects and towns in western Paraná. Source (images):
ITCG

Colonization companies sold three types of land: urban lots of about 0.1 hectares, semiurban lots of about 2.5 hectares, and rural lots of about 25 hectares. The contrast between the two Matelândia frames demonstrates that, in their first years, companies concentrated their efforts on establishing an urban core by clearing the forest around their local offices and demarcating lots and blocks for future towns. Settlers purchasing rural parcels would be responsible for cutting their own trees (which were still mostly intact in 1953), hiring loggers if need be but borrowing or renting machinery from the company. Bottom frames E and F show the newest colonization project in the region, Céu Azul, which was established in 1952 and whose first families of southern settlers arrived in 1953, the year the image was captured. Frame E reveals a very incipient clearing where the project's urban core would later develop, as well as other areas outside the future town that had already been extensively logged. Similar to the other panels, frames E and F are bisected diagonally by a white line, the BR-277, which bounds the territory of Iguaçu National Park at the bottom right half of the frame. The 1953 frame reveals the existence of areas of recovering forest inside the park (in the upper right of frame F), demonstrating that some clearing – whether caused by humans, wildfire, or a mixture of both – had occurred inside park boundaries a few years before. By the time the photograph was taken, the forest in Iguaçu was already recovering, but conversion into nonforest land continued in the adjacent area outside the park. In contrast, the 1980 image shows the formation of a stark boundary between park and nonpark lands, with the area inside Iguaçu mostly covered by forests and the area outside the park completely taken over by farms. This sharp division between protected and nonprotected landscapes reveals a pattern reproduced in hundreds of other aerial images from the 1980 data set and made explicit in the land cover maps, which were based on these images (Maps 6.1–6.4). It offers evidence of the concrete role played by Iguaçu National Park in maintaining the last remaining stretch of Upper Paraná Atlantic forests intact amid rapid landscape changes outside its boundaries.

A CONTINUOUS NORTHWARD MIGRATION

The settlers arriving in this corner of western Paraná in the 1950s and 1960s were mostly German- and Italian-Brazilians from the country's southernmost state, Rio Grande do Sul. A 1961 survey calculates that 54 and 37 percent of settlers in western Paraná were of Italian and German descent, respectively. Another survey estimates that 68 percent of the settlers in the area in the late 1950s were from Rio Grande do Sul, and 16 percent arrived from Santa Catarina, another southern Brazilian state with a heavy presence of Germans and Italians.[34] European immigrants from what would later become Germany and Italy had begun settling in the high valleys and plateaus of Rio Grande do Sul in 1824. Similar to Paraná, this was an area of Upper Paraná Atlantic forests and Araucaria moist forests. Immigration from Europe continued to this area until the late nineteenth century, but after few generations, fragmentation and the small size of the estates – on average lots of 25 hectares, and many located in rugged terrain – pushed the descendants of the German and Italian settlers to new frontier areas. In the first decades of the twentieth century, they started migrating to northwestern Rio Grande do Sul, from there to western Santa Catarina, then crossed the Uruguay River toward south central Misiones in Argentina, and by the 1950s, arrived in southwestern and western Paraná. New generations continued to migrate northwestward in the 1970s, crossing the Paraná toward eastern Paraguay or penetrating the states of Mato Grosso, Rondônia, and Pará in Brazilian Amazonia. The first families of settlers to arrive in western Paraná encountered a subtropical rainforest similar to the one their German and Italian forebears had first cleared in Rio Grande do Sul in the nineteenth century, but with a flatter and gentler terrain, which facilitated the type of mechanized agriculture they later started practicing in the 1970s.[35]

---

[34] Oberg and Jabine, *Toledo*, 36; Lotário Brecht, "Relatório do plano de colonização empregado pela Pinho e Terras Ltda.," (Toledo: Pinho e Terras, 1961), as cited by Freitag, "Extremo-Oeste Paranaense," 181.

[35] Reinhard Maack and Alexander Marchant, *German, English, French, Italian, and Portuguese Literature on German Immigration and Colonization in Southern Brazil* (Cambridge: Harvard University Press, 1939), 419–22; Leo Waibel, *Capítulos de geografia tropical e do Brasil* (Rio de Janeiro: Instituto Brasileiro de Geografia e Estatística, 1958), 211–17, 225–28, 239–42; Westphalen, Machado, and Balhana, "Nota prévia," 5–7, xlv–xlvi; Robert C. Eidt, *Pioneer Settlement in Northeast Argentina* (Madison: University of Wisconsin Press, 1971), 7–10, 50–78; Foweraker, "Political Conflict on the Frontier," 30–39; Velho, *Capitalismo autoritário e campesinato*, 219; Pedro Calil Padis, *Formação de uma economia periférica: O caso do Paraná* (São Paulo: HUCITEC, 1981), 161; José Augusto Colodel, *Matelândia*, 213; Gregory, *Os eurobrasileiros*, 17, 28; Marcia Anita Sprandel, "'Aqui não é como a casa da gente...': Comparando agricultores brasileiros na Argentina e no Paraguai," in *Argentinos e brasileiros: Encontros, imagens e estereótipos*, ed. Alejandro Frigerio and Gustavo Lins Ribeiro (Petrópolis: Vozes, 2002), 188–201; Correa and Bublitz, *Terra de promissão*, 52–55, 70–82, 110–12; Nodari, *Etnicidades renegociadas*, 42; Juliana Bublitz, *Forasteiros na floresta subtropical: Uma história ambiental da colonização européia no Rio Grande do Sul* (PhD diss., Federal University of Rio de Janeiro, 2010), 13–15; Blanc, *Before the Flood*, 69, 174–79.

Table 6.2 shows population growth in three different areas of the Argentine–Brazilian borderland. For Brazil, the table shows population growth in the region of western Paraná, the group of forty-four municipalities around Iguaçu National Park, north of the Iguazu River, and southwestern Paraná, made up of thirty-two municipalities south of the Iguazu. The two regions are part of the Brazilian state of Paraná, and in the early 1900s they included only two municipalities, Foz do Iguaçu (western Paraná) and Clevelândia (southwestern Paraná), which were later split into smaller municipalities as migration and natural population growth created the conditions for new political subdivisions. In Argentina, the table shows the population of the entire province of Misiones, where Iguazu National Park was created. Misiones is geographically comparable in size to the combination of western and southwestern Paraná – the Argentine province is 29,801 km² in area, whereas the two regions within the state of Paraná are 24,015 km². The numbers show that in around 1950, Misiones already had over three times the population of the two border regions in Paraná combined. The colonization of Misiones had started earlier, in the southern and central areas of the state, with an influx of settlers from Brazil's Rio Grande do Sul and from Europe. Across the border in Brazil, the period between 1950 and 1970 saw the population in the region explode, growing fifteen times from a mere 70,398 to 1,081,108 people. This growth was the result of a wave of migration from other areas of Brazil, especially the two southern states, Rio Grande do Sul and Santa Catarina. As thousands of people, mostly farmers, settled in the area, the borderland was transformed into one of Brazil's breadbaskets. By 1980, population growth lost steam following a crisis in agricultural production and the emigration of farmers to other frontiers in Paraguay and Amazonia. This trend is clearly evident in southwestern Paraná, which lost population between 1980 and 1991, but in western Paraná population decline was offset by the building of the Itaipu Dam on the Paraná River, which attracted thousands of newcomers from other areas of Brazil.[36]

---

[36] Instituto Paranaense de Desenvolvimento Econômico e Social, *O Paraná: Economia e sociedade* (Curitiba: IPARDES, 1981); Cyrus B. Dawsey, "Push Factors and Pre-1970 Migration to Southwest Paraná, Brazil," *Revista geográfica* 98 (1983): 55; Wachowicz, *Paraná, sudoeste*; Hermógenes Lazier, *Análise histórica da posse de terra no sudoeste paranaense* (Curitiba: Biblioteca Pública do Paraná, Secretaria de Estado da Cultura e do Esporte, 1986); Maria Cristina Colnaghi, "O processo político de colonização do Sudoeste," in *Cenários de economia e política-Paraná*, ed. Francisco Moraes Paz (Curitiba: Editora Prephacio, 1991), 7–10; Urbano Theobaldo Mertz, "Um estudo das transformações sociais e econômicas de uma sociedade de colonos na região Oeste do Estado do Paraná" (MS thesis, Federal Rural University of Rio de Janeiro, 2000), 53–54, UFRRJ. On the colonization of Misiones, see Eidt, *Pioneer Settlement in Northeast Argentina*.

TABLE 6.2 *Population growth in western and southwestern Paraná (BR) and Misiones (AR)*

Brazil	1940	1950	1960	1970	1980	1991	2000	2010
Western Paraná	7,645	16,421	114,255	698,057	889,985	953,962	1,084,479	1,168,967
Southwestern Paraná	17,240	53,977	185,131	383,051	445,150	417,252	418,075	444,833
Total	24,885	70,398	299,386	1,081,108	1,335,135	1,371,214	1,502,554	1,613,800

Argentina	1947	1960	1970	1980	1991	2001	2010
Misiones	246,396	361,440	443,020	588,977	788,915	963,869	1,101,593

Source: IBGE (Brazil), INDEC (Argentina)

TABLE 6.3 *Area (km²) covered by native forests in the state of Paraná, Brazil, 1930–79*

	Araucaria moist forests	Other forest (including Upper Paraná Atlantic forests)	Total	Percentage of State of Paraná (%)
Primitive area	73,780	94,044	167,824	84.2
1930	39,580	89,444	129,024	64.7
1937	34,554	83,468	118,022	59.2
1950	25,224	54,610	79,834	40.1
1960	20,432	35,204	55,136	27.7
1973	4,340	12,796	17,136	8.6
1979	n/a	n/a	10,312	5.2

Source: Maack, *Geografia física do Estado do Paraná* (Curitiba: Universidade Federal do Paraná, 1968), 196; Instituto Paranaense de Desenvolvimento Econômico e Social and Fundação Édison Vieira, "Estudos para a formulação de políticas de desenvolvimento do Setor Florestal (Curitiba: CODESUL, IPARDES, 1982), 1:4, IPARDES

By the time the Itaipu reservoir was filled in 1982, the landscape of the borderland had already completed its transition from forest to farmland, the end of a process that had also affected other parts of Paraná. In the State of Paraná as a whole, the four decades between 1930 and 1979 saw native forest cover plunge from 64 percent to a mere 5 percent of the territory (see Table 6.3). Over these forty years, about 120,000 km² of native forests – an area equivalent to Pennsylvania – were transformed into farms, pastureland, and urban areas. An even more significant transformation occurred between 1963 and 1973, when an annual average of 3,700 km² of forests were cut or burned in the state. Logging continued to be Paraná's primary industry until it was outmatched by agriculture in the 1970s. Loggers exploited the vast groves of Paraná pine that covered most of the state's central highlands – the only significant native source of softwood in Brazil. Between 1947 and 1964, softwood, mostly native Paraná pine, made up an estimated 85 percent of all the timber officially produced in the state. With the opening of highways connecting the center and western sections of the state to the Atlantic coast, trees could be brought from Paraná to fuel Brazil's economic growth in the form of pulpwood, firewood, and timber. After the 1940s, foreign markets lost importance, and only about 10 percent of all the timber produced in the state of Paraná – soft and hardwood – was exported. Western Paraná, owing to its historical and hydrological connections to the River Plate basin since the *obraje* era, retained a considerable share of the dwindling export market, and 40 percent of exported timber in the state (but only 4 percent of all the timber produced) left the country through Foz do Iguaçu downriver to Argentina.[37]

Loggers prized Paraná pine, which in western Paraná grew in the highlands east of Iguaçu National Park, around the town of Cascavel. In this area, one settler, Etelvino Salvatti from Rio Grande do Sul, used to hire 80 workers to cut 1,200 logs of Paraná pine per week in the 1960s, which his company exported downriver from Foz do Iguaçu to Argentina.[38] Not everybody had the opportunity to exploit Paraná pine, however, as much of the region was covered by Upper Paraná Atlantic forests, which lacked the coveted softwood. Valued hardwood such as Argentine cedar was found in these areas, but not in great quantities. By the time settlers arrived in the region, much had been already cleared by *obrajes* and colonization companies.[39] Other tree species encountered by newcomers had little commercial value, and the settlers used fire, the least labor-intensive method at their disposal, to clear their land for agriculture. Some in the government saw the burning of the forest as a waste of resources. By the 1960s, policymakers had begun seriously considering the possibility that Paraná might run out of forests, which could bring about the collapse of the timber and pulp industries in the state, so they requested studies to assess the status of the state's forest reserves. One of the first of such studies, the 1966 survey led by Dutch FAO forestry engineer F. J. van Dillewijn, calculated the waste of valuable hardwood consumed by settler-caused fires. The study tagged the amount of timber burned by settlers in areas of Upper Paraná Atlantic forest with the current price of firewood (the cheapest

---

[37] "As exportações nacionais de madeira em face das alterações cambiais," c. 1950, Fundo Jesus Soares Pereira – Pasta Instituto Nacional do Pinho, CPDOC; Companhia de Desenvolvimento do Paraná, "O Paraná e a economia madeireira," 1964, IPARDES; "Florestas, neste ritmo daqui à dez anos nada restara da mata primitiva," *Referência em Planejamento* 2 (1976): 2–5; Aida Mansani Lavalle, *A madeira na economia paranaense* (Curitiba, Brazil: Grafipar, 1981), 18–19, 108; Instituto Paranaense de Desenvolvimento Econômico e Social and Fundação Édison Vieira, "Estudos para a formulação de políticas de desenvolvimento do Setor Florestal (Curitiba: CODESUL, IPARDES, 1982), 1:7, IPARDES.

[38] "Etelvino Salvatti: Um homem que acreditou no futuro da cidade," *Memória de Foz do Iguaçu* 2 (1982): 43, BPEENR; Interview with Etelvino Salvatti, *Gazeta do Iguaçu*, April 14, 1994, in "Foz 80, Memória," BPEENR.

[39] *Sinopse estatística do município de Foz do Iguaçu*, 34, APP.

type of wood) and concluded that Paraná was wasting 25 billion cruzeiros per year in burned forests and was poised to lose another 650 billion (or 2 billion US dollars in 2020 values) if it put its remaining forests to the torch.[40]

GUARANI DISPLACEMENT

As hundreds of thousands of incoming white settlers converted a vast expanse of forests into a mosaic of farms, they put enormous pressure on the Guarani communities still living at the borderland. The arrival of colonization companies and settlers in western Paraná steadily pushed the Guarani away from prime agricultural land at the border. The government, at both the federal and state levels, also contributed to this process by taking an assertive role in transforming the territory. Government agencies built highways and privatized public land – disputes between federal and state governments notwithstanding – which created an agriculturally productive territory for incoming Brazilian farmers of European descent. Adding to the pressure on the Guarani, a large portion of the Brazilian border area was closed off to human occupation by a protected area.

How did the establishment of Iguaçu National Park contribute to the displacement of the Guarani in the Brazilian borderland? Here, the written record is almost nonexistent. During my archival research, I could not find any evidence of indigenous communities living in the area of the park at the time of its creation. Archeological research conducted in the park has also failed to demonstrate evidence of early twentieth-century

[40] Reinhard Maack, "As consequências da devastação das matas no Estado do Paraná," *Arquivos de biologia e tecnologia, Curitiba* 8 (1953): 437–57; Comissão de Estudos dos Recursos Naturais Renováveis do Estado do Paraná and Companhia de Desenvolvimento do Paraná, "Inventário do pinheiro do Paraná," Curitiba, November 1966, IPARDES; Comissão de Estudos dos Recursos Naturais Renováveis do Estado do Paraná and Companhia de Desenvolvimento do Paraná, "Inventário do pinheiro no Paraná," (Curitiba: CODEPAR, 1974), 77–84; Universidade Federal do Paraná, Centro de Pesquisas Florestais, "Estudo das alternativas técnicas, econômicas e sociais do setor florestal do Paraná, sub-programa 'matéria-prima'" (Curitiba: Superintendência do Desenvolvimento da Região Sul and Instituto Brasileiro de Desenvolvimento Florestal, 1974); Secretaria de Estado da Indústria e do Comércio, Coordenadoria de Desenvolvimento Industrial, "Estudo sobre a adequação floresta-indústria no Estado do Paraná: Conclusões e proposições," Curitiba, March 1982, IPARDES; Banco do Brazil, "Conversor de moedas," www.bcb.go v.br/conversao; Banco do Brazil, "Calculadora do cidadão: Correção de valores IGP-DI (FGV) a partir de 02/1944," www3.bcb.gov.br/CALCIDADAO/publico/exibirFormCorrec aoValores.do?method=exibirFormCorrecaoValores.

Guarani dwelling inside Iguaçu. Indigenous artifacts found within park territory are from the colonial and precolonial eras.[41]

Evidence of Guarani presence in Iguaçu National Park can be found, however, in interviews with Guarani elders conducted by Brazilian anthropologists. It can also be inferred from the aerial photographs taken in 1953. In an interview, a Ñandeva elder woman, Narcisa Tacua Catu de Almeida, recalls living a decade during her teenage years in the Aldeia Guarani, an indigenous community in an area close to Iguazu Falls. According to Almeida, the Guarani living in the area were expelled by force in 1943, when many "were killed and their bodies thrown in the falls."[42] Another Guarani elder, Damásio Martines, refers to the same Aldeia Guarani close to the falls, explaining that it was the largest Guarani community in the area. The Ñandeva considered Iguazu Falls to be a place of religious significance, hence the importance of this community. Diverging from Almeida, however, Martines's version claims that the massacre that dispersed the community took place before the park's creation in 1939. He explains that those who perpetrated the massacre were not "police officers" but "Spaniards."[43]

Almeida claims the Aldeia Guarani was located where the international hotel broke ground in 1941. However, historical sources suggest that the area had been occupied by whites since at least 1915, with no indication of indigenous presence. It is possible that an *aldeia* was located nearby and park administrators hired the Guarani living there to clear the terrain for the construction of the hotel and other park infrastructure. Maybe park administrators started considering the Guarani a nuisance to visitors and pushed them away, first to another area inside Iguaçu, and then out of the park. Almeida also cites another Guarani community inside the park, the Aldeia São João Velho, located close to a namesake river. She claims to have moved there in 1943, after being displaced from the community by the falls, and to have lived there until

---

[41] Igor Chmyz and Rucirene Miguel, *Relatório técnico sobre a arqueologia e a etno-história da área do Parque Nacional do Iguaçu* (Curitiba: Centro de Pesquisas Arqueológicas/UFPR, 1999).

[42] Carvalho, "Das terras dos índios," 328–31.

[43] On the Brazilian side of the border, "Spaniard" is usually used to refer to anyone from Paraguay or Argentina. See Ian Packer and Centro de Trabalho Indigenista, "Violações dos direitos humanos e territoriais dos guarani no Oeste do Paraná (1946–1988): Subsídios para a Comissão Nacional da Verdade," Anexo 1, "Depoimentos Ava Guarani" (Centro de Trabalho Indigenista, Comissão Nacional da Verdade, 2014), 22, 27.

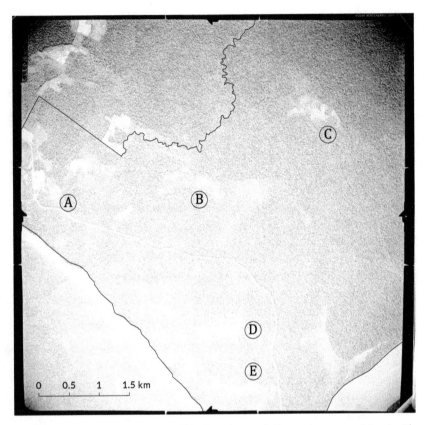

FIGURE 6.2 Frame 13349, possible locations of Guarani communities inside Iguaçu NP, Brazil, 1953. Source: ITCG

1962. Almeida argues the Guarani were permanently expelled from the Iguaçu National Park in that year.[44]

Almeida and Martines do not give precise locations for the two aldeias, but a visual analysis of one of the hundreds of aerial images taken in 1953 can help identify possible areas of previous Guarani occupation. Figure 6.2 presents an image covering the area of the peninsula formed by the curve of the Iguazu River. The area encompasses most of Iguaçu National Park before its 1944 expansion. The falls, not shown in the figure, are located just outside the bottom of the image. At the bottom left corner, across the river, Argentina is visible.

---

[44] Carvalho, "Das terras dos índios," 328–31.

The Guarani witnesses placed the second aldeia, São João Velho, close to the São João River, near a power plant built by the park in the 1940s. Analysis of the 1953 image reveals three possible areas – marked A, B, and C – where the community could have been located. Area A is the closest to the power plant and river, and a likely candidate for the Guarani community's location, as it is an area with clear signs of dwelling and agricultural use. If this is the site of the Aldeia São João Velho, it reveals that the Guarani were living quite near park personnel and would support my hypothesis that the park, similar to the neighboring colonization companies, initially employed poorly paid Guarani workers for menial tasks such as cutting trees.[45] Letters B and C also mark cleared areas in 1953. These, too, could be places where the Guarani were dwelling, as they are both located close to the São João River and adjacent to the Poço Preto trail – today used for limited tourist hiking.

Letters D and E show areas that had been previously cleared but long since abandoned and overgrown by the forest in 1953. They might indicate possible locations for the first Guarani aldeia, whose inhabitants were dispersed at some point in the 1930s or 1940s. All of this is speculative, as no written primary sources were found corroborating the existence of these aldeias inside the Brazilian park. Still, an archaeological investigation could easily confirm the existence of recent remains of Guarani occupations at the sites identified here.

After being forced out of Iguaçu National Park in the early 1960s, Narcisa de Almeida moved to another community, the Aldeia Colônia Guarani, located on the outskirts of Foz do Iguaçu. The Ñandeva had lived in this location since the 1910s, but in the 1960s, land speculators started selling deeds for lots occupied by the Guarani community. In the 1970s, INCRA officials started demarcating the settler-claimed lots in a bid to regularize them. Though they recognized that the area had been

---

[45] Area A could also be where the skilled workers brought in from other areas of Brazil to build roads, the hotel, and the power plant lived. Park administrators continually complained about the lack of skilled workers in the region, which led them to bring bricklayers, carpenters, and other tradespeople from outside. They also claimed they could not hire local workers as park employees because they were mostly "foreign" (i.e., Guarani and Spanish-speaking Paraguayans). It is unlikely, however, that park administrators relied on costly outside labor for tasks such as clearing the forest, as the region already had workers, many of Guarani descent, who specialized in this activity. Mário Câmara Canto, "Relatório que apresenta o administrador do Parque Nacional do Iguassú, referente ao período de abril, maio e junho de 1942" (Foz do Iguaçu, 1942), PNIB-A; Mário Câmara Canto, "Sugestões referentes às obras do P. N. do Iguaçu," May 29, 1947, Pasta Relatórios de Atividades 1947, PNIB-A.

inhabited by the Guarani, they chose to make indigenous displacement official by finding another area to which to relocate the indigenous community. In the view of INCRA officials working on the Colônia Guarani case, Iguaçu National Park was the obvious choice, as it was an area of largely untouched nature that had no indigenous inhabitants and was owned by the federal government. Such a choice shows a remarkable lack of communication among INCRA bureaucrats, as the same agency removing white settlers from Iguaçu was proposing relocating Guarani in the park.[46] Unsurprisingly, IBDF officials never seriously considered the possibility of settling the Guarani in the park in a time when it was being emptied of white settlers. The park director, Jayme de Paiva Bello, disingenuously dismissed any Guarani connection to the park by claiming that the "original" inhabitants of the area, the Kaingang, were not related to the Guarani. According to Bello, indigenous people "had long since disappeared from the park area" at the time of its creation in 1939.[47]

BOUNDARIES OF NATURE

By 1980, the transformation of forests into farmland outside Iguaçu National Park was almost complete – a change easily identifiable by comparing the 1953 and 1980 aerial images produced by the state government. Figure 6.3 shows three pairs of panels with a mosaic of aerial images of different sections of Iguaçu National Park during the two periods. Frame G shows the southeastern corner of the park in 1953, entirely covered by vegetation. The monotonous "gray" expanse of Upper Paraná Atlantic forests is interrupted only by the wide upper Iguazu River, which at this point divides western Paraná from southwestern Paraná, and

---

[46] Nelson Silva to FUNAI, "Ofício n° 045/76-Gab/4ª DR," February 2, 1976; "Ofício n° 045/76-Gab/4ª DR," May 23, 1976; Ismarth de Araújo Oliveira to Lourenço José Tavares Vieira da Silva, June 1976. All memos can be found in Ian Packer and Centro de Trabalho Indigenista, "Violações dos direitos humanos e territoriais dos guarani no Oeste do Paraná (1946–1988): Subsídios para a Comissão Nacional da Verdade" (Centro de Trabalho Indigenista, Comissão Nacional da Verdade, 2014), Anexo 7a, Anexo 7c, and Anexo 7d.

[47] Ironically, a previous director of Iguaçu, René Denizart Pockrandt, had suggested in 1967 settling indigenous people in the Brazilian park to improve its "touristic appeal." The Guarani eventually ended up occupying sections of the Iguaçu National Park in 2005 and 2013 as a way to pressure the Brazilian federal government to set aside more land for their communities. Pockrandt, "Relatório das atividades e problemas do parque," 81; Bello, "Parque Nacional do Iguaçu: Informação sobre o Parna." See also Freitas, "The Guarani and the Iguaçu National Park."

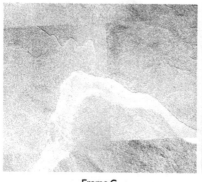

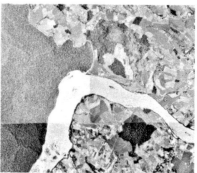

Frame G
Iguaçu Park SE Border (Brazil) - 1953

Frame H
Iguaçu Park SE Border (Brazil) - 1980

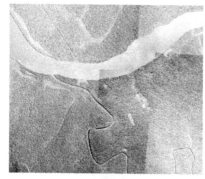

Frame I
Iguaçu Park South Border (BR and AR) - 1953

Frame J
Iguaçu Park South Border (BR and AR) - 1980

Frame K
Iguaçu Park NE Border (Brazil) - 1953

Frame L
Iguaçu Park NE Border (Brazil) - 1980

FIGURE 6.3 Iguaçu National Park borders. Source (images): ITCG

the narrow, winding line of the Gonçalves Dias River, which serves as the eastern boundary of the park.

The same area in 1980, shown in Frame H of Figure 6.3, reveals a landscape that has been radically modified in the areas outside the park. Where there was once dense forest, crop fields can be found. A few patches of forest persist outside the park boundaries in 1980, but these will be greatly reduced in the decades to come. In 1953, it would have been impossible for an observer without previous knowledge of the region's geography to identify the park's boundaries just by looking at this aerial overview. This situation had changed by 1980, with the carpet of forest on the left half of Frame H clearly distinguishing protected lands from the farms and crop fields dominant in the rest of the image.

The next pair of images in Figure 6.3, Frames I and J, show a section at the southern edge of Iguaçu National Park. In Frame I, a mosaic of 1953 aerial images, the main river forming a gentle "U" is again the Iguazu. On its northern banks is the territory of the Brazilian Iguaçu National Park. South of the river, Brazil is on the right and Argentina on the left. The San Antonio River, a small tributary of the Iguazu, demarcates the international border between the two countries. Similar to the previous pair of images, in these the landscape inside and outside Iguaçu National Park is uniform in 1953. Forests still cover the entire area. Inside the park, on the northern banks of the Iguazu River, an observer might notice the PR-495, the Estrada do Colono, still under construction. The highway was almost finished in the section inside Iguaçu National Park, but it had not yet reached the river.

In the 1980 mosaic, Frame J, the highway inside the park is completed, and it connects by ferry to another highway on the lower bank of the Iguazu River. In this area of Brazil, in the right bottom corner of Frame J, settlers have completed their transformation of the dense subtropical forest into farms. The advancement of settlements was considerably slower in Argentina (bottom right). A highway had recently connected the region to the rest of the province of Misiones, and the first settlements started to spring up, reproducing the pattern of landscape transformation that had occurred two decades earlier in Brazil. This corner of Misiones, sandwiched between Brazil to east and north and the Argentine Iguazú National Park to the west (not pictured here), was spared by the first colonization waves that transformed the rest of the province. Concerned that settlers from Brazil might start to colonize the area, the provincial government of Misiones launched its own colonization project in the mid-1970s. Their goal was to occupy their side of the border with "real settlers" (i.e., non-Brazilian ones) who spoke Argentina's "language" and venerated the country's "national symbols." Here, we see the same ideas that had guided the creation of Puerto Iguazú by the Argentine national park service four decades earlier making a comeback in the provincial plans of Misiones in the 1970s. In the bottom right corner of Frame J, the first results of this new policy are visible: the first cleared lots amid the forest.[48]

The third pair of aerial mosaics, Frames K and L, offer an example of how the enforcement of park boundaries served to reconstitute the forest inside these protected areas. The two frames show the northeastern corner of Iguaçu National Park, where its eastern boundary line, defined by the Gonçalves Dias River, meets its northern boundary, the BR-277. Frame K shows the area in 1953; the white line slicing the image from northeast to southwest is the BR-277. The black line, which I added to the images, marks the riverbed of the Gonçalves Dias that separates park from non-park lands. In contrast with the other 1953 images, Frame K reveals extensive clearings not only outside Iguaçu but also inside the triangle that marks this corner of park territory. Unlike the rest of the park, this area had extensive stands of coveted Paraná pine. The opening of the BR-277 triggered the rapid clearing of this area, with loggers ignoring park boundaries.

Similar to the villages of São José and Santo Antonio inside Iguaçu National Park (see Chapter 4) this was also an area where past state administrations had engaged in land grabbing.[49] The issue of fraudulent deeds by the state government allowed realtors to sell lots to settlers in this corner of the park, and by 1980 a small town, Santa Tereza do Oeste, had sprung up alongside the BR-277 in an area that was still nominally part of Iguaçu National Park. Because the area was in a far corner of the park, it was easy for officials at the IBDF to accept the partition of the area and the retracing of park boundaries, which

---

[48] Gobierno de la Provincia de Misiones, "Plano básico nº 1R (Plano de colonizacion 'Andresito') Contribuyente al Plan de Gobierno 1978 del Gobierno de la Provincia de Misiones," June 1978, Caja AH0011, Documento 34, AHC, 1–17; Oscar A. Álvarez to Major Emilio Sturns, RVPE/MRO 3953, August 7, 1978, Caixa 3.A 1/1, "Notas despachadas 1/07/1976 a 29/03/1979," PNIA.

[49] Departamento de Terras e Colonização, "Planta do terreno Colônia de São José da Foz do Iguaçu," December 21, 1937; Departamento de Terras e Colonização, "Imóvel São José," 1941, Dossiê PIC-OCOÍ, 1974–78, INCRA-Curitiba; "Moisés Lupion cobiça nova gleba da União," *O Estado de São Paulo*, December 18, 1957; "Lupion não concretizará audacioso assalto à gleba," *O Estado de São Paulo*, December 20, 1957; Mário Pimentel de Camargo, "Relatório anual 1959" (Foz do Iguaçu, 1959), 5, PNIB-A.

occurred in 1981.[50] Park officials initially tried to demand that the Estrada do Colono, which they claimed had been illegally built by the state government in the 1950s, be closed in exchange for the loss of the park territory.[51] Given that they had spent most of their political cachet in the recent eviction of settlers from the central area of the park, however, they had to accept the redrawing of the northwestern corner of the park without any compensation.[52] In the end, Iguaçu National Park lost only 1,178 hectares, or 0.7 percent of the park's 163,911 hectares at the time.

Frame L shows the northeastern corner of the park in 1980. I added the new park boundaries (in black), which were defined by presidential decree only in 1981.[53] The image illustrates the effectiveness of certain spatial practices in creating the park as a space of nature. In the 1960s, as Santa Tereza do Oeste grew into a town inside park territory, Iguaçu's directors installed a warden in this corner of the park, defining a tributary of the Gonçalves Dias River (marked in Frame L in black) as the new de facto boundary of the park. At this new border they also built a 30-meter metal observation tower to serve as visual marker signaling territorial control on

[50] "Ofício PARNA/FI-068/74," January 28, 1974, Pasta Documentos Diversos, 1974, PNIB-A; Antonio Silva Araujo, "Memorial descritivo das linhas que definem o perímetro da área do Parque Nacional do Iguaçu, situado na parte sudoeste do Estado do Paraná, nos municípios de Foz do Iguaçu, São Miguel do Iguaçu, Medianeira, Matelândia e Céu Azul," June 6, 1974, Pasta Documentos Diversos [1942] 1968 a 1981, Fundo Parque Nacional do Iguaçu, ICMBio; José Jusi, "Situação fundiária do Parna Iguaçu, n° 3102/77-DE PR," November 7, 1977, Pasta 2.6 – Documentos Diversos 1968 a 1986, Fundo Parque Nacional do Iguaçu, ICMBio.

[51] Instituto Brasileiro de Desenvolvimento Florestal, "Parque Nacional do Iguaçu: Histórico," 1975, Pasta Documentos Diversos, 1975, PNIB-A.

[52] The failed negotiation between the IBDF, INCRA, and the government of the state of Paraná to close the Estrada do Colono as compensation for the loss of territory in Santa Tereza do Oeste was recorded in the following documents: David de Oliveira Assoreira, "Informação n° 220/77/DN," November 24, 1977; Osiris Stenghel Guimarães to Alysson Paulinelli, November 21, 1977; "Of. 662/77-P /3977/77," December 23, 1977; Celso Soares de Castro to Alysson Paulinelli, December 23, 1977; Paulo Azevedo Beirutti to Oisiris Setenghel Guimarães, March 15, 1978; Oisiris Setenghel Guimarães to Paulo Azevedo Beirutti, April 10, 1978; "Relatório n° 003/80 – ASI/IBDF," 1980; Angela Tresinari Bernardes Quintão, "Informação n° 150/80/DN," July 4, 1980; Alfredo Gulin to Alipio Ayres de Carvalho, November 25, 1977; and Alfredo Gulin to Paulo Azevedo Berutti, April 17, 1978; all in Pasta Documentos Diversos [1942] 1968 a 1981, Fundo Parque Nacional do Iguaçu, ICMBio.

[53] Maria Tereza Jorge Pádua, "Of. N° 046/81-DN, Proposta de novos limites de Parque Nacional (minutas)," February 12, 1981, Pasta Documentos Diversos [1942] 1968 a 1981, Fundo Parque Nacional do Iguaçu, ICMBio; Brazil, Decree 86676, December 1, 1981.

that side of the tributary, and installed a fence creating a barrier between the BR-277 and the park between Santa Tereza do Oeste and Céu Azul.[54] All these measures served to halt the advance of settlers inside the park, whose forest by 1980 had recovered from the clearing that took place in the 1950s (as clearly shown in Frame L). These measures also meant accepting the existence of Santa Tereza do Oeste, defining a new de facto boundary between the town and the park that would later be cemented into law in 1981.

All in all, between 1953 and 2014, 154,919 hectares of forest inside Iguaçu National Park remained untouched, 95 percent of the present-day area of the Brazilian park. Deforestation and reforestation, both in the area occupied by settlers until the 1970s and in other areas that experienced wildfires or logging at the edges of the park, took place on less than 5 percent of the park territory. These figures offer a stark contrast to the pace of landscape transformation happening in Brazil outside Iguaçu, where, between 1953 and 1967, some 51,452 hectares of forests were cleared, with another 78,068 hectares cut between 1967 and 1980. Change also happened in the other direction outside the park, with the reforestation of 11,264 hectares of land. However, reforestation outside the protected area was minimal when compared to the scale of forest converted into farms and towns. In the end, the borders that define Iguaçu National Park actively prevented most of these changes from happening inside the park. Yet boundaries also produced the park as a space of subtropical forests maintained by human practices. It was the establishment and enforcement of a territory purportedly devoid of dwellers, of a space where temporary human presence was justified solely by the need to guard fauna and flora from the forces transforming the landscape outside it, which created the park as a territory of nature.

---

[54] Pockrandt, "Relatório das atividades e problemas do parque," 3–4; Jayme de Paiva Bello, "Quadro informativo Parque Nacional do Iguaçu – Data 08/Abr/1975," Documentos Diversos, PNIB-A; Instituto Brasileiro de Desenvolvimento Florestal, "Plano de ação – 1975" (Brasília: Ministério da Agricultura, 1975), PNIB-B; IBDF, "Parque Nacional do Iguaçu: Locação da vigilância e fiscalização no perímetro do parque," c.1977, Documentos Diversos, PNIB-A.

Epilogue: The Resilience of Boundaries

Iguazú and Iguaçu National Parks, 2020

In 1984, Iguazú National Park was listed as a UNESCO World Heritage Site a few months after Argentine authorities submitted its candidacy. The recognition, a point of pride for the newly elected democratic government of Raúl Alfonsin, was announced at UNESCO's Eighth World Heritage Convention in Buenos Aires in November of that year. Iguazú's designation as a World Heritage Site led Brazilian authorities across the border to rapidly cobble together a nomination for their own park, Iguaçu, a month later. It was the latest episode in the old catch-up game the two parks had been playing against each other for decades. It is clear that Brazilian authorities crafted Iguaçu's candidacy in response to the newly gained international status of their Argentine competitor. If Argentina now harbored a World Heritage Site on its side of Iguazu Falls, it was appropriate that Brazil received its own designation, for the Brazilian park included its share of the falls as well as expanses of endangered Atlantic forest.

However, such intricacies of transboundary competition were lost on UNESCO. As the officials assessing Iguaçu's candidacy saw it, the Brazilian park should be incorporated into the list *together with* the Argentine park, as one single "transfrontier World Heritage Site" under the name of "Iguazu, Iguaçu National Park of Argentina and Brazil." They envisioned a joint designation fostering cooperation and shared management between the two parks. Not surprisingly, the proposal was firmly rejected by Brazilian authorities, who insisted on submitting Iguaçu's candidacy "without any link to the concept of transfrontier heritage site." Brazilians conceived of Iguaçu National Park as an independent site, contending that the natural features and resources found inside it were unique to Brazil. UNESCO's evaluation, set out by IUCN officials, argued otherwise, considering the falls and the forest to be a transboundary site shared with Argentina. Poignantly, Brazilian officials also rejected UNESCO's proposal for the adoption of shared conservation norms and comanagement between the two parks. UNESCO eventually caved in and accepted Iguaçu as a separate World Heritage Site in 1986. In the following years, however, IUCN officials consulting for the UN agency continued to insist on the absurdity of having two separate entries for parks they considered part of a single transboundary complex of forests and waterfalls.[1]

The Brazilian authorities' insistence on having their own World Heritage Site at the borderland, independent of the Argentine one, reveals that ideas about national sovereignty and transboundary antagonism still shaped how government officials conceived of the two parks in the 1980s. Iguazú and Iguaçu had their backs turned to each other by design, existing since their inception as independent entities, albeit connected by the shared falls and international border between them. Up until the 1950s, there was little practical contact between Argentine and Brazilian park administrators. The 1960s witnessed the first exchanges between the two national parks, triggered by settlement inside the parks, transboundary poaching, and heart-of-palm theft. But local transboundary collaboration was still minimal, and in high-profile cases (e.g., the issue of Brazilian settlers from Iguaçu trespassing in Iguazú) park officials would ultimately pass problems up the chain of command for mediation by the Argentine and Brazilian chancelleries. None of this is surprising, as both Iguazú and Iguaçu were first established for geopolitical reasons – to incorporate a border region seen as too open to transboundary influences. Comanaging Iguazú and Iguaçu, as suggested by the IUCN officials assessing the case for UNESCO, was anathema to the parks' decades-long mission of exerting federal territorial sovereignty at the border. In this way, one can understand the stubborn pettiness of Brazilian

[1] IUCN, "Advisory Body Evaluation – Nomination to the World Heritage List No. 303 – Iguazú National Park" (UNESCO, December 31, 1983); UNESCO, "World Heritage Committee, Eighth Ordinary Session" (UNESCO, November 2, 1984); IUCN, "Advisory Body Evaluation – Nomination to the World Heritage List No. 355 – Iguaçu National Park" (UNESCO, December 27, 1984); UNESCO, "World Heritage Committee, Ninth Ordinary Session, SC-85/CONF.008/4" (UNESCO, October 24, 1985); UNESCO, "World Heritage Committee, Tenth Session, SC-86/Conf.003/3" (UNESCO, October 20, 1986); UNESCO, "World Heritage Committee, Thirteenth Session, SC-89/Conf.003/12" (UNESCO, September 1989); UNESCO documents can be found at http://whc.unesco.org /en/list/303/documents/; http://whc.unesco.org/en/list/355/documents/. Secretaria DN, "Proposta de inscrição do Parque Nacional de Iguaçu [*sic*] na lista do Patrimônio Mundial da UNESCO – Ata da reunião realizada no Palácio Itamaraty em 9 de junho de 1986," June 10, 1986, Pasta 2.6 – Documentos Diversos, 1968 a 1986, Fundo Parque Nacional do Iguaçu, ICMBio.

officials in refusing to share a designation as a World Heritage Site with Argentina.

In the years that followed, a series of changes in the two countries and particularly in the borderland made such geopolitical concerns increasingly outdated. Argentina and Brazil returned to democracy in the 1980s, and the newly elected governments willingly shed their military dictatorships' hypertrophied concerns about border security from their revised foreign policies. Furthermore, Argentina and Brazil, along with Paraguay and Uruguay, established the Mercosur trade bloc in the 1990s, which deeply integrated the economies of the four countries. Brazil became Argentina's leading trading partner in 1993, a position it has maintained since then.[2] At a local level, in 1982, Brazil and Paraguay finished Itaipu – at the time, the largest hydroelectric dam in the world – which radically transformed the Triple Frontier. The construction of the dam attracted hundreds of thousands of people into the area, mainly to cities such as Foz do Iguaçu and Ciudad del Este (Paraguay), and the border evolved from a backwater into a transnational center of commerce, energy, and tourism. The UNESCO World Heritage Site labels did contribute to transforming Iguazú and Iguaçu into significant destinations for tourists from Latin America, Europe, and the United States. Local travel agencies and tourism operators started selling Iguazu Falls as a landscape to be viewed from both sides of the border, and as a result an increasing number of visitors started crossing the border and visiting the two parks as part of a single experience.

Yet collaboration between the two parks continued to be difficult despite greater transnational policy alignment and increased transboundary flows of goods, people, and capital through the Triple Frontier borderland. In 1993, for example, the park directors at Iguaçu and Iguazú launched, with the support of the governors of the state of Paraná and the province of Misiones, the first joint operation against poaching and heart-of-palm theft across the two parks. The operation put together a backcountry patrol composed of Argentine park rangers and Brazilian state troopers and was covered by a local TV station from Foz do Iguaçu. Officials at the two parks believed that, with the Mercosur common market in effect, joint operations such as these would be well received by policymakers and bureaucrats in Brasília and Buenos Aires. They could not have been more wrong. In Argentina, the initiative was poorly

---

[2] Observatory of Economic Complexity, "Where Does Argentina Export To?," accessed January 2020, https://oec.world/en/visualize/tree_map/sitc/export/arg/show/all/2017/

received in the higher echelons of the Argentine National Park Agency, whose directors argued that Jorge Cieslik, the head of Iguazú National Park, did not have the authority to "celebrate international cooperation agreements" with Brazil. Cieslik was formally reprimanded and suspended for five days for undermining the tacit understanding that the parks existed to maintain the boundaries between the two countries, thus barring cooperation with the other side.[3]

Transboundary park collaboration increased nevertheless, especially in comparison to the preceding years of mutual disinterest.[4] In 1996, for example, a conference brought together officials from both parks to discuss transboundary conservation efforts in the Triple Frontier area. In the following year, government scientists working at the two parks started meeting to share technical information across the border.[5] Brazilian scientists monitoring large carnivores, for example, concluded they had to work with their counterparts in Argentina, since animals such as jaguars were great swimmers that refused to observe international and natural boundaries such as the Iguazu River.[6] Today, in the opinion of officials working at the two parks, collaboration occurs mostly at a "technical level" between scientists and rangers on an informal "one-on-one" basis. At an institutional level, on the other hand, there is an understanding that park directors and national park agencies have taken few concrete steps to work with the other side, despite continuous pressure by UNESCO representatives for more integration between the two parks. In the words of a veteran Argentine park ranger, "every five years UNESCO representatives visit the parks and conclude they have not advanced collaboration."[7]

---

[3] CUDAP: EXP-PNA:0001418/2012, Número original: 982/1993, Year 1993, APN.

[4] Marcela Strucker Kropf and Ana Alice Eleutério, "Histórico e perspectivas da cooperação entre os Parques Nacionais do Iguaçu, Brasil, e Iguazú, Argentina," *Revista latino-americana de estudos avançados* 1, no. 2 (2017): 5–25.

[5] Delegación Técnica Regional NEA, "Primera reunión técnica de trabajo, manejo y conservación de áreas naturales protegidas de la selva paranaense, Argentina-Brazil-Paraguay," Puerto Iguazú, November 1996, NEA; "Reunión Técnica no oficial PN do Iguaçu – PN Iguazú," April 1997, Carpeta "PN do Iguaçu," NEA.

[6] Peter G. Crawshaw Jr., "Comparative Ecology of Ocelot (*Felis Pardalis*) and Jaguar (*Panthera Onca*) in a Protected Subtropical Forest in Brazil and Argentina" (PhD diss., University of Florida, Gainesville, 1995); Karia Schiaffino (zoologist at the Centro de Investigaciones Ecológicas Subtropicales, Argentina), in discussion with the author, August 2014.

[7] Justo Herrera (ranger at Iguazú National Park), in discussion with the author, August 2014; Maurício Savi (former biologist at Iguaçu National Park), in discussion with the author, September 2013.

One of the things preventing greater integration across the border is the recent professionalization of civil servants working at the two parks. Today, park officials are commonly federal career employees originally from other regions to whom Iguazú or Iguaçu is just another stopping point in a career of deployments to different national parks. Such is the case, for example, of Argentine park rangers, who might not have the time or interest to develop transboundary connections before being rotated to another protected area in another corner of Argentina. In the past, park rangers at Iguazú National Park were recruited from among the local population, whereas today, they are part of a national corps of college-trained federal servants who are deployed by the Argentine National Park Agency to different parts of the country. Brazil lacks a federal corps of rangers in the way of the Argentine *guardaparques*, but the technical federal officials working in national parks are also rotated among different parks. Furthermore, as one Argentine park ranger noted, outside park officials commonly lack the interest or knowledge to surmount the linguistic barrier between Spanish and Portuguese – a barrier that, for natives of the borderland, is almost nonexistent – and establish connections across the border.[8]

Another barrier preventing transboundary cooperation has been the development, throughout the years, of entirely distinct Argentine and Brazilian national park systems. The Argentine parks were born as part of a coherent conservation framework, which was supported by robust legislation and proper allocation of funds and counted on a state capable of allocating land for national park use. Argentine national parks in the 1930s had a clear mission: to promote the nationalization of the country's borders. The first Brazilian parks, on the other hand, were created in the 1930s without a system in place. Each park was the result of different circumstances – in the case of Iguaçu, a response in kind to the creation of the Argentine park across the border. In the late 1970s, however, the Brazilian government, with the help of the FAO, invested in creating a legal and institutional framework to unify its parks and orient the creation of new protected areas under a coherent set of conservationist principles. National parks in Brazil would be gazetted after extensive scientific surveys and would follow detailed management plans that were revised every couple of years. Soon Argentina followed suit, adopting management plans as guiding documents in the management of their parks. Iguaçu had its first management plan drafted in 1981 and Iguazú in

---

[8] Herrera, 2014.

1988. Still, despite increasing convergence since the late 1980s, the two
protected areas belong to different national park systems based on distinct
legal frameworks. As parks, they have more in common with the other
national parks within the national system of which they are part than with
their sister park across the border. All of this poses institutional, legal, and
political hurdles to transboundary collaboration, despite the greater integration between the two countries beginning in the 1990s. Many park
officials are, in the end, unwilling to challenge the institutional inertia
keeping the two parks isolated from each other.[9]

Iguazú and Iguaçu were never "peace parks," a term coined in 1932 in
the United States and Canada to describe adjacent border national parks
with some level of transboundary comanagement.[10] Latin America houses
a few examples of peace parks such as the La Amistad International Parks,
comanaged by Costa Rica and Panamá since their inception in 1982.
UNESCO sponsored the establishment of the Costa Rica–Panama protected area, adding the La Amistad parks to its World Heritage Site and
World Biosphere Reserve lists.[11] In the case of the areas planned by
Ecuador and Peru at their shared border in 1998, the goal of promoting
peace was at the forefront of the parks's mission. The two countries went
to war for three weeks in 1995 over a territorial conflict but signed a peace
agreement in 1998 that planned for a series of protected areas in their
disputed borderlands, to be known collectively as the El Condor-Kutukú
Conservation Corridor. The move followed the example of other transboundary protected areas comanaged by two or more countries, mainly in

[9] Instituto Brasileiro de Desenvolvimento Florestal and Jean Paul Poupard, *Plano de manejo Parque Nacional do Iguaçu* (Brasília: Ministério da Agricultura, 1981); Administración de Parques Nacionales and Luis A. Giúdice, *Plan de manejo Parque Nacional Iguazú: Proyecto, planificación y gestión de los parques nacionales (APN-FAO)* (Buenos Aires: Administración de Parques Nacionales, 1988). See also Foresta, *Amazon Conservation in the Age of Development*; and Drummond, "From Randomness to Planning."

[10] The first case of transboundary park was the listing of the Glacier (US) and Waterton Lakes (Canada) national parks, located along the US–Canada border, into "peace parks." The designation in 1932 aimed to foster peaceful cooperation between two friendly nations. The two parks retained their separate administrations, but they integrated their dealings with the public in the 1930s and wildlife management in the 1960s. Neel G. Baumgardner, "Bordering North America: Constructing Wilderness along the Periphery of Canada, Mexico, and the United States" (PhD Dissertation (History), Austin, University of Texas at Austin, 2013); Lieff, Bernard C., and Gil Lusk. "Transfrontier Cooperation between Canada and the USA: Waterton-Glacier International Peace Park." In *Parks on the Borderline: Experience in Transfrontier Conservation*, edited by Jim Thorsell, 39–49. Gland and Cambridge: IUCN Publications, 1990.

[11] Evans, *Green Republic*, 120–25.

Africa. But instead of establishing cross-border parks between friendly nations, the El Condor-Kutukú Conservation Corridor became the first example of using parks as part of a peace agreement between actual warring nations.[12] Iguaçu and Iguazú, despite earlier comanagement proposals and the pressure exerted by UNESCO since the 1980s, were never "peace parks," for they were designed and implemented in competition with each other.

Institutional, geopolitical, territorial, and ideological boundaries kept Iguazú and Iguaçu apart. But the border also acted as an equalizer, channeling flows of information between the political and social forces shaping the two parks on either side of the border. The existence of a border, and a foreign national park just beyond it, led policymakers, parks administrators, and park rangers to adopt discourses, measures, and practices they saw being introduced in the neighboring country. Since their beginnings in the 1930s, the two Iguazu parks have mirrored each other. They followed parallel routes, developing similar features – luxurious hotels, restrictive spatial policies, eviction programs, UNESCO titles – roughly at the same time. All this without ever being managed as a single protected area and in spite of their quite distinct political, social, and economic contexts. Perhaps their most relevant congruence is the similar roles they played in protecting the last contiguous stretches of Atlantic forest in the upper Paraná basin. As bounded spaces of nature that result from an almost century-old experiment in territorial intervention by a diverse array of social and political actors, Iguazú and Iguaçu are both a part of nature and a product of human artifice. The forests, rivers, and animals found inside them have an existence independent from human society. But they are also the fruit of the spatial practices of humans who have made them into places for nature conservation. As such, Iguazú and Iguaçu will bequeath to future generations a forest that is a testament to how twentieth-century Latin American states used conservation to produce territory and nature.

---

[12] Salem H. Ali, "Introduction: A Natural Connection between Ecology and Peace?," in *Peace Parks: Conservation and Conflict Resolution* (Cambridge, MA: MIT Press, 2007); Bankoff, "Making Parks out of Making Wars."

Bibliography and Sources

NEWSPAPERS AND MAGAZINES

Argentina

Ahora
Ayre y Sol
Caras y Caretas
Camping
El Diário
La Acción
La Nación
La Prensa
Leoplán
Week End

Brazil

A Imprensa
A Notícia
Correio Braziliense
Correio da Manhã
Diário da Tarde
Diário de Notícias
Diário do Paraná
Estado de São Paulo
Folha de São Paulo
Jornal de Foz
Jornal do Brasil
Jornal do Commercio

Nosso Tempo
O Dia
O Jornal
O Paiz
Revista Rodovia
Veja

Aerial and Satellite Imagery

Compañia Argentina de Relevamientos Topograficos y Aerofotogramétricos, Set of Orthorectified Aerial Photographs of Northern Misiones, 1:10,000 and 1:20,000, (Province of Misiones), 1962–63. CIES.
Departamento de Geografia, Terras e Colonização, Set of Orthorectified Aerial Photographs of the State of Paraná, 1:25,000 (State of Paraná, Brazil), 1953. ITCG.
Fundação Instituto de Terras e Cartografia, Set of Orthorectified Aerial Photographs of the State of Paraná, 1:25,000 (State of Paraná, Brazil), 1980. ITCG.
Declassified images DS1044–2124DF027, DS1044–2124DF028, and DS1044–2124DF029, November 10, 1967, Sioux Falls, South Dakota: US Geological Survey (USGS) Earth Resources Observation and Science (EROS) Center.
Digital Globe (miscellaneous satellite imagery, 1 m resolution, 2009–13); GeoEye (Ikonos satellite, 1 m resolution, panchromatic, 2000–11); and CNES/Airbus DS (SPOT 5 satellite, 2.5 m resolution, panchromatic, 2004–12); all accessed through ESRI's ArcGIS.

GIS Data

Exército Brasileiro, "SG21XD0000" and "SG22VC0000," GIS shapefiles, accessed in January 2014, www.geoportal.eb.mil.br
INCRA-PR, "Parque Nacional do Iguaçu," GIS shapefiles, INCRA office in Curitiba, 2010.
Open Street Map, "Misiones" and "Paraná," GIS shapefiles, accessed in January 2014, openstreetmap.org
SIB and APN, "Límite del Parque Nacional Iguazú," GIS shapefiles, accessed in December 2013, www.sib.gov.ar

Archives, Libraries, and Other Repositories

AGN – Archivo General de la Nación (Buenos Aires, Argentina)
AHC – Archivo Histórico de Cancillería, Ministerio de Relaciones Exteriores y Culto (Buenos Aires, Argentina)
AIPOPEC – Arquivo da Associação de Integração Comunitária Pró-Estrada do Colono (Realeza, Brazil)
AN-DF – Arquivo Nacional-Brasília (Brasília, Brazil)

AN-RJ – Arquivo Nacional-Rio de Janeiro (Rio de Janeiro, Brazil)
APN – Archivo Administración de Parques Nacionales (Buenos Aires, Argentina)
APN-B – Biblioteca Francisco P. Moreno, Administración de Parques Nacionales (Buenos Aires, Argentina)
APN-P – Archivo Programa Pobladores y Comunidades, Administración de Parques Nacionales (Buenos Aires, Argentina)
APP – Arquivo Público do Paraná (Curitiba, Brazil)
BCN – Biblioteca Congreso de la Nación (Buenos Aires, Argentina)
BGUBA – Biblioteca de Geografia de la Universidad de Buenos Aires (Buenos Aires, Argentina)
BN – Biblioteca Nacional (Rio de Janeiro, Brazil)
BNRA – Biblioteca Nacional de la República Argentina (Buenos Aires, Argentina)
BPEENR – Biblioteca Pública Elfrida Engel Nunes Rios (Foz do Iguaçu, Brazil)
BPI – Biblioteca de Puerto Iguazú (Puerto Iguazú, Argentina)
BPP – Biblioteca Pública do Paraná (Curitiba, Brazil)
CIES – Archivo Centro de Investigaciones Ecológicas Subtropicales (Puerto Iguazú, Argentina)
CPDOC – Centro de Pesquisa e Documentação de História Contemporânea do Brasil, Fundação Getúlio Vargas (Rio de Janeiro, Brazil)
DER-PR – Biblioteca do Departamento de Estradas e Rodagem do Paraná (Curitiba, Brazil)
DGPIH – Archivo Dirección General Patrimonio e Instituto Histórico – Archivo Histórico de la Ciudad de Buenos Aires (Buenos Aires, Argentina)
DR – Documentos Revelados, Arquivo Aluízio Palmar (Foz do Iguaçu, Brazil)
DRNEA – Biblioteca de la Delegación Regional NEA – Administración de Parques Nacionales (Puerto Iguazú, Argentina)
IBAMA – Biblioteca do Instituto Brasileiro do Meio Ambiente e dos Recursos Naturais Renováveis (Brasília, Brazil)
ICMBio – Arquivo do Instituto Chico Mendes de Conservação da Biodiversidade (Brasília, Brazil)
INCRA-Cascavel – Arquivo do Instituto Nacional de Reforma Agrária (Cascavel, Brazil)
INCRA-Curitiba – Arquivo do Instituto Nacional de Reforma Agrária (Curitiba, Brazil)
IPARDES – Instituto Paranaense de Desenvolvimento Econômico e Social (Curitiba, Brazil)
ITCG – Arquivo do Instituto de Terras, Cartografia e Geologia do Paraná (Curitiba, Brazil)
JFP-C – Justiça Federal do Paraná (Curitiba, Brazil)
JFP-F – Justiça Federal do Paraná (Foz do Iguaçu, Brazil)
MA – Biblioteca do Ministério da Agricultura (Brasília, Brazil)
MI – Museu do Índio (Rio de Janeiro, Brazil)
MN-A – Arquivo do Museu Nacional (Rio de Janeiro, Brazil)
MN-B – Biblioteca do Museu Nacional (Rio de Janeiro, Brazil)
PNIA – Archivo Parque Nacional Iguazú (Puerto Iguazú, Argentina)
PNIB-A – Arquivo do Parque Nacional do Iguaçu (Foz do Iguaçu, Brazil)
PNIB-B – Biblioteca do Parque Nacional do Iguaçu (Foz do Iguaçu, Brazil)

SA – Sigrid Andersen's Personal Archive (Curitiba, Brazil)
SU – Stanford University (Stanford, USA)
UFRRJ – Centro de Documentação Ivan de Otero Ribeiro, Universidade
Federal Rural do Rio de Janeiro (Rio de Janeiro, Brazil)

PUBLISHED SOURCES

Acker, Antoine. *Volkswagen in the Amazon: The Tragedy of Global Development in Modern Brazil*, Global and International History. Cambridge, UK: Cambridge University Press, 2017.
Adams, Jonathan S. and Thomas O. McShane. *The Myth of Wild Africa: Conservation without Illusion*. Berkeley: University of California Press, 1997.
Administración de Parques Nacionales and Luis A. Giúdice. *Plan de manejo Parque Nacional Iguazú: Proyecto, planificación y gestión de los parques nacionales (APN-FAO)*. Buenos Aires: Administración de Parques Nacionales, 1988.
Alamandoz, Arturo. "The Garden City in Early Twentieth-Century Latin America." *Urban History* 31, no. 3 (2004): 437–51.
Alcântara, Gustavo Kenner, et al. *Avá-Guarani: A construção de Itaipu e os direitos territoriais*. Brasília: Escola Superior do Ministério Público da União, 2019.
Ali, Salem H., ed. "Introduction: A Natural Connection between Ecology and Peace?" In *Peace Parks: Conservation and Conflict Resolution*. Cambridge, MA: MIT Press, 2007.
Allegretti, Mary, Mauro W. Barbosa de Almeida, and Augusto Postigo. "O legado de Chico Mendes: Êxitos e entraves das reservas extrativistas." *Desenvolvimento e meio ambiente* 48 (November 2018): 25–49.
Alves, Maria Helena Moreira. *State and Opposition in Military Brazil*, Latin American Monographs 63. Austin: University of Texas Press, 1990.
Amend, Stephan and Thora Amend, eds. *National Parks without People? The South American Experience*. Quito: IUCN/Parques Nacionales y Conservación Ambiental, 1995.
Andrade, Theophilo de. *O rio Paraná no roteiro da Marcha para o Oeste*. Rio de Janeiro: Irmãos Pongetti, 1941.
Asturian, Rodrigo and Cássia Morgana Faxina. *INCRA Paraná: Quatro décadas de história*. Curitiba: INCRA, 2011.
Atwood, Wallace W. and Instituto Panamericano de Geografía y Historia. *Publicación Núm. 50: The Protection of Nature in the Americas*. México, DF: Antigua Imprenta de E. Murguia, 1940.
Barker, Mary L. "National Parks, Conservation, and Agrarian Reform in Peru." *Geographical Review* 70, no. 1 (1980): 1–18.
Ballão, Jayme. *A Foz do Iguassu e as cataratas do Iguassu e Paraná: Descripção de viagem 1920*. Curitiba: Typographia da República, 1921.

Bankoff, Greg. "Making Parks out of Making Wars: Transnational Nature Conservation and Environmental Diplomacy in the Twenty-First Century." In *Nation-States and the Global Environment: New Approaches to International Environmental History*, edited by Erika Marie Bsumek, David Kinkela, and Mark Atwood Lawrence, 76–96. New York: Oxford University Press, 2013.

Barreto Filho, Henyo Trindade. "Notas para uma história social das áreas de proteção integral no Brasil." In *Terras indígenas & unidades de conservação da natureza: O desafio das sobreposições*, edited by Fany Ricardo. São Paulo: Instituto Socioambiental, 2004.

Barros, Wanderbilt Duarte de. *Parques nacionais do Brasil*, Série documentária 1. Rio de Janeiro: Serviço de Informação Agrícola do Ministério da Agricultura, 1952.

Basaldúa, Florencio de. *Pasado, presente, porvenir del Territorio Nacional de Misiones*. La Plata: n.p., 1901.

Baumgardner, Neel G. "Bordering North America: Constructing Wilderness Along the Periphery of Canada, Mexico, and the United States." PhD Dissertation (History), University of Texas at Austin, 2013.

Berjman, Sonia and Ramón Gutiérrez. *Patrimonio cultural y patrimonio natural: La arquitectura en los Parques Nacionales Nahuel Huapi e Iquazú (hasta 1950)*. Resistencia, Argentina: Editorial del Instituto Argentino de Investigaciones de Historia de la Arquitectura y del Urbanismo, 1988.

Berjman, Sonia, ed. *Carlos Thays: Sus escritos sobre jardines y paisajes*. Buenos Aires: Ciudad Argentina, 2002.

Bernárdez, Manuel. *De Buenos Aires Al Iguazú: Crónicas de un viaje periodístico á Corrientes y Misiones*, edited by Luis de Boccard, P. Benjamín Serrano, and Francisco Feuilliand, 2nd ed. Buenos Aires: Impr. de "La Nación," 1901.

Bethell, Leslie. "Politics in Brazil under Vargas, 1930–1945." In *The Cambridge History of Latin America*, edited by Leslie Bethell, vol. IX. Cambridge, UK: Cambridge University Press, 2008.

Biggs, David. "Frame DS1050–1006DF129: March 20, 1969." *Environmental History* 19, no. 2 (2014): 271–80.

Biggs, David. "New Spaces for Stories: Technical and Conceptual Challenges to Using Spatial Imagery in Environmental History." *Environmental History Field Notes* (blog), 2014, http://environmentalhistory.net/field-notes/2014-biggs/.

Blanc, Jacob and Frederico Freitas, eds. *Big Water: The Making of the Borderland Between Brazil, Argentina, and Paraguay*. Tucson: University of Arizona Press, 2018.

Blanc, Jacob. *Before the Flood: The Itaipu Dam and the Visibility of Rural Brazil*. Durham: Duke University Press, 2019.

Borba, Nestor and André Pinto Rebouças. *Excursão ao salto do Guayra: O Parque Nacional*. Rio de Janeiro: Casa Mont'Alverne, 1897.

Boyer, Christopher R. *Political Landscapes: Forests, Conservation, and Community in Mexico*. Durham: Duke University Press, 2015.

Brañas, Balbino. *Ayer: Mi tierra en el recuerdo*. n.p.: n.p., 1975.

Bratman, Eve Z. *Governing the Rainforest: Sustainable Development Politics in the Brazilian Amazon*. New York: Oxford University Press, 2019.

Brazil. *I Plano nacional de desenvolvimento (PND) 1972/74*. Brasília: Imprensa Nacional, 1971.

Brito, José Maria de. "Descoberta de Foz do Iguaçu e fundação da Colônia Militar." *Boletim do Instituto Histórico, Geográfico e Etnográfico Paranaense* 32 (January 1977): 45–72.

Brockington, Dan. *Fortress Conservation: The Preservation of the Mkomazi Game Preserve*. Bloomington: Indiana University Press, 2002.

Bryant, William Cullen. *Picturesque America; or, The Land We Live In. A Delineation by Pen and Pencil of the Mountains, Rivers, Lakes, Forests, Water-Falls, Shores, Canyons, Valleys, Cities, and Other Picturesque Features of Our Country*, edited by Oliver Bell Bunce. New York: D. Appleton, [c. 1872–74].

Bublitz, Juliana. *Forasteiros na floresta subtropical: Uma história ambiental da colonização européia no Rio Grande do Sul*. PhD diss., Federal University of Rio de Janeiro, 2010.

Buchinger, Maria and Rodolfo Falcone. "Nota preliminar sobre las especies argentinas del género *Cedrela* L." *Darwiniana* 10, no. 3 (1953): 461–64.

Buchinger, Maria. "Conservation in Latin America." *BioScience* 15, no. 1 (1965): 32–37.

Buchinger, Maria. "El Comité Latinoamericano de Parques Nacionales." *Ciencia Interamericana* 5, no. 3 (1964): 12–16.

Buckley, Eve E. *Technocrats and the Politics of Drought and Development in Twentieth-Century Brazil*. Chapel Hill: University of North Carolina Press, 2017.

Burden, William A. M. *The Struggle for Airways in Latin America*. New York: Council on Foreign Relations, 1943.

Burmeister, Carlos. *Memoria sobre el territorio de Misiones, por el naturalista viajero*. Buenos Aires: Impr. de J. Peuser, 1899.

Burns, Bradford. *The Unwritten Alliance, Rio Branco and Brazilian-American Relations*. New York: Columbia University Press, 1966.

Bustillo, Exequiel. *El despertar de Bariloche: Una estrategia patagónica*. Buenos Aires: Editorial y Librería Goncourt, 1968.

Cabanas, João. *A Columna da Morte sob o commando do tenente Cabanas*. Rio de Janeiro: Almeida & Torres, 1928.

Cabral, Diogo de Carvalho. *Na presença da floresta: Mata Atlântica e história colonial*. Rio de Janeiro: Garamond, 2014.

Câmara, Ibsen de Gusmão. "Breve história da conservação da Mata Atlântica." In *Mata Atlântica: Biodiversidade, ameaças e perspectivas*, edited by Carlos Galindo-Leal and Ibsen de Gusmão Câmara. Belo Horizonte: Fundação SOS Mata Atlântica and Conservação Internacional, 2005.

Cameron, Christina and Mechtild Rössler. *Many Voices, One Vision: The Early Years of the World Heritage Convention*. Farnham, Surrey; Burlington, VT: Ashgate, 2013.

Capanema, Carolina Marotta. "A natureza no projeto de construção de um Brasil moderno e a obra de Alberto José Sampaio." MA thesis, Federal University of Minas Gerais, 2006.

Carey, Mark. "The Trouble with Climate Change and National Parks." In *National Parks Beyond the Nation: Global Perspectives on "America's Best Idea,"* edited by Adrian Howkins, Jared Orsi, and Mark Fiege. Norman: University of Oklahoma Press, 2016.

Carey, Mark. *In the Shadow of Melting Glaciers: Climate Change and Andean Society.* New York: Oxford University Press, 2010.

Carrão, Manuel. *Impressões de viagem à Fóz do Iguassú e Rio Paraná.* Curitiba: Lith. Progresso, R. S. Francisco, 1928.

Carreras Doallo, Ximena A. "Parques nacionales y peronismo: La patria mediante la naturaleza." In *Historia, política y gestión ambiental: Perspectivas y debates,* edited by Alejandra Salomón and Adrian Zarrilli. Buenos Aires: Imago Mundi, 2012.

Carter, Paul. *The Road to Botany Bay: An Exploration of Landscape and History.* Minneapolis: University of Minnesota Press, 2010.

Carvalho, Ely Bergo de. "O estado jardineiro e a gestão das florestas: Uma história do Departamento de Geografia, Terras e Colonização na gestão do sertão paranaense (1934–1964)." In *História ambiental no sul do Brasil: apropriações do mundo natural,* edited by Jó Klanovicz, Gilmar Arruda, and Ely Bergo de Carvalho. São Paulo: Alameda Editorial, 2012.

Carvalho, Maria Alice Rezende de. *O quinto século: André Rebouças e a construção do Brasil.* Rio de Janeiro: Editora Revan, 1998.

Carvalho, Maria Lucia Brant. "Das terras dos índios a índios sem terras, o Estado e os guarani do Oco'y: Violência, silêncio e luta." PhD diss., University of São Paulo, 2013.

Casazza, Ingrid Fonseca. "Ciência e proteção à natureza: A trajetória do botânico Paulo Campos Porto (1914–1939)." In *Anais.* Presented at the 13° Seminário Nacional de História da Ciência e da Tecnologia, University of São Paulo, Sociedade Brasileira de História da Ciência, 2012.

Cavalcanti, Clóvis. "Economic Growth and Environmental Protection in Brazil: An Unfavorable Trade-Off." In *Environmental Governance and Decentralisation,* edited by Albert Breton, Giorgio Brosio, Silvana Dalmazzone, and Giovanna Garrone. Northampton, MA: Edward Elgar Publishing, 2008.

Centro de Pesquisas Florestais da Universidade do Paraná and Instituto Brasileiro do Desenvolvimento Florestal. *Inventário de reconhecimento do Parque Nacional do Iguaçu.* Curitiba, Brazil: IBDF/CPF-UFP, 1968.

Chesterton, Bridget María. "From *Porteño* to *Pontero*: The Shifting of Paraguayan Geography and Identity in Asunción in the Early Years of the Stroessner Regime." In *Big Water: The Making of the Borderlands between Brazil, Argentina, and Paraguay,* edited by Jacob Blanc and Frederico Freitas. Tucson: University of Arizona Press, 2018.

Cloud, John. "Hidden in Plain Sight: The CORONA Reconnaissance Satellite Programme and Clandestine Cold War Science." *Annals of Science* 58, no. 2 (2001): 203–9.

Cloud, John. "Imaging the World in a Barrel: CORONA and the Clandestine Convergence of the Earth Sciences." *Social Studies of Science* 31, no. 2 (2001): 231–51.

Coelho Júnior, Carlos Alberto Teixeira. *Pelas selvas e rios do Paraná.* Curitiba: Guaíra, 1946.

Colnaghi, Maria Cristina. "O processo político de colonização do Sudoeste." In *Cenários de economia e política-Paraná,* edited by Francisco Moraes Paz. Curitiba: Editora Prephacio, 1991.

Colodel, José Augusto. *Matelândia: História e contexto*. Cascavel, Brazil: Assoeste, 1992.

Colodel, José Augusto. *Obrages e companhias colonizadoras: Santa Helena na história do Oeste Paranaense até 1960*. Santa Helena, Brazil: Prefeitura Municipal, 1988.

Comissão Nacional da Verdade. *Relatório*, vol. I. Brasília: Comissão Nacional da Verdade, 2014.

Corral, Mariana. "Espero, Mariana, que tu generación sepa levantar nuestras banderas..." In *Misiones: Historias con nombres propios*, edited by Amelia Báez. Posadas: Ministerio de Derechos Humanos de Misiones, 2011.

Corrêa, Marcos Sá. *Meu vizinho, o Parque Nacional do Iguaçu*. Cascavel, Brazil: Tuicial, 2009.

Correa, Sílvio Marcus de Souza, and Juliana Bublitz. *Terra de promissão: Uma introdução à eco-história da colonização do Rio Grande do Sul*. Santa Cruz do Sul: EDUNISC/UPF, 2006.

Corson, Catherine. "Territorialization, Enclosure and Neoliberalism: Non-State Influence in Struggles over Madagascar's Forests." *Journal of Peasant Studies* 38, no. 4 (2011): 703–26.

Cozzo, Domingo. *La Argentina forestal*. Buenos Aires: Editorial Universitaria de Buenos Aires, 1967.

Crawshaw Jr., Peter G. "Comparative Ecology of Ocelot (*Felis Pardalis*) and Jaguar (*Panthera Onca*) in a Protected Subtropical Forest in Brazil and Argentina." PhD diss., University of Florida, Gainesville, 1995.

Crónica de los gobernantes de Misiones. Posadas, Argentina: Centro de Investigación y Promoción Científico-Cultural, Instituto Superior del Profesorado "Antonio Ruiz de Montoya," 1979.

Cronon, William. "The Trouble with Wilderness; Or, Getting Back to the Wrong Nature." In *Uncommon Ground: Rethinking the Human Place in Nature*, edited by William Cronon. New York: W. W. Norton & Co., 1996.

Cushman, Gregory T. *Guano and the Opening of the Pacific World: A Global Ecological History*. Cambridge: Cambridge University Press, 2013.

Daciuk, Juan. "Consideraciones acerca de los fundamentos de la protección y conservación de la fauna nativa." *Anales de Parques Nacionales* 11 (1966–67): 43–96.

Daughton, J. P. "When Argentina Was 'French': Rethinking Cultural Politics and European Imperialism in Belle-Époque Buenos Aires." *Journal of Modern History* 80, no. 4 (2008): 831–64.

Dawsey, Cyrus B. "Push Factors and Pre-1970 Migration to Southwest Paraná, Brazil." *Revista geográfica* 98 (1983): 54–7.

de Laferrère, Germán. *Selva adentro*. Buenos Aires: Editorial Argentina "Arístides Quillet," 1945.

Dean, Warren. *With Broadax and Firebrand: The Destruction of the Brazilian Atlantic Forest*. Berkeley: University of California Press, 1997.

Dennler de la Tour, Georges, ed. "Introducción." In *La protección de la naturaleza en el mundo: In memoriam doctoris Hugo Salomon*. Buenos Aires: Georges Dennler de la Tour, 1957.

Dennler de la Tour, Georges. "Protección y conservación de faunas de ambientes naturales: Parques nacionales y reservas del norte argentino." *Revista argentina de zoogeografía* 3, no. 1–2 (1943): 33–57.

Deutsch, Sandra McGee. *Las Derechas: The Extreme Right in Argentina, Brazil, and Chile, 1890–1939.* Stanford: Stanford University Press, 1999.

Devoto, Franco E. and Máximo Rothkugel. "Informe sobre los bosques del Parque Nacional del Iguazú." *Boletín del Ministerio de Agricultura de la Nación* 37, no. 1–4 (1935): 129–204.

Diegues, Antônio Carlos Sant'Ana. *O mito moderno da natureza intocada,* 6th ed. São Paulo: Hucitec, 2008.

Dimitri, Milan Jorge, et al. "La flora arbórea del Parque Nacional Iguazu." *Anales de Parques Nacionales* 12 (1974): 1–175.

Dimitri, Milan Jorge. "La protección de la naturaleza en la República Argentina." *Natura: Órgano de la Administración General de Parques Nacionales* 1, no. 1 (1954): 21–41.

Drummond, José Augusto. "A visão conservacionista (1920 a 1970)." In *Ambientalismo no Brasil: Passado, presente e futuro,* edited by Enrique Svirsky and João Paulo R. Capobianco. São Paulo: Instituto Socioambiental/Secretaria do Meio Ambiente do Estado de São Paulo, 1997.

Drummond, José Augusto. "From Randomness to Planning: The 1979 Plan for Brazilian National Parks." In *National Parks beyond the Nation: Global Perspectives on "America's Best Idea,"* edited by Adrian Howkins, Jared Orsi, and Mark Fiege. Norman: University of Oklahoma Press, 2016.

Duarte, Regina Horta. "Pássaros e cientistas no Brasil: Em busca de proteção, 1894–1938." *Latin American Research Review* 41, no. 1 (2006): 3–26.

Duarte, Regina Horta. *Activist Biology: The National Museum, Politics, and Nation Building in Brazil.* Tucson: University of Arizona Press, 2016.

Eidt, Robert C. *Pioneer Settlement in Northeast Argentina.* Madison: University of Wisconsin Press, 1971.

Elena, Eduardo. *Dignifying Argentina: Peronism, Citizenship, and Mass Consumption.* Pittsburgh: University of Pittsburgh Press, 2011.

Escude, Carlos. "Argentine Territorial Nationalism," *Journal of Latin American Studies* 20, no. 1 (1988): 139–65.

Evans, Sterling. *The Green Republic: A Conservation History of Costa Rica.* Austin: University of Texas Press, 1999.

Falcão, João Augusto. *O Serviço Florestal no biênio 1943–1944.* Rio de Janeiro: Ministério da Agricultura, 1945.

Fairhead, James, Melissa Leach, and Ian Scoones. "Green Grabbing: A New Appropriation of Nature?" *The Journal of Peasant Studies* 39, no. 2 (October 2011): 237–261.

Farnham, Timothy. *Saving Nature's Legacy: Origins of the Idea of Biological Diversity.* New Haven: Yale University Press, 2007.

Fearnside, Philip M. "Projetos de colonização na Amazônia brasileira: Objetivos conflitantes e capacidade de suporte humano." *Cadernos de geociências* 2 (1989): 7–25.

Ferreira, Gustavo Henrique Cepolini. "A regularização fundiária no Parque Nacional da Serra da Canastra e a expropriação camponesa: da baioneta à ponta da caneta." M.A. Thesis (Geography), University of São Paulo, 2013.

Figueiredo, José de Lima. *Oéste paranaense, edição ilustrada.* São Paulo: Companhia Editora Nacional, 1937.

Floria, Pedro Navarro. "El *desierto* y la cuestión del territorio en el discurso politico argentino sobre la frontera Sur." *Revista complutense de historia de América* 28 (2002): 139–68.

Foresta, Ronald A. *Amazon Conservation in the Age of Development: The Limits of Providence.* Gainesville: University of Florida Press, 1991.

Foweraker, Joe. "Political Conflict on the Frontier: A Case Study of the Land Problem in the West of Paraná, Brazil." PhD diss., University of Oxford, 1974.

Foweraker, Joe. *The Struggle for Land: A Political Economy of the Pioneer Frontier in Brazil from 1930 to the Present Day.* Cambridge, UK: Cambridge University Press, 1981.

Franco, José Luiz de Andrade and José Augusto Drummond. "História das preocupações com o mundo natural no Brasil: Da proteção à natureza à conservação da biodiversidade." In *História ambiental: Fronteira, recursos naturais e conservação da natureza,* edited by José Luiz de Andrade Franco, et al. Rio de Janeiro: Garamond, 2012.

Franco, José Luiz de Andrade and José Augusto Drummond. "Nature Protection: The FBCN and Conservation Initiatives in Brazil, 1958–1992." *Historia ambiental latinoamericana y caribeña* 2, no. 2 (2013): 338–67.

Franco, José Luiz de Andrade and José Augusto Drummond. "Wilderness and the Brazilian Mind (II): The First Brazilian Conference on Nature Protection (Rio de Janeiro, 1934)." *Environmental History* 14, no. 1 (2009): 82–102.

Franco, José Luiz de Andrade and José Augusto Drummond. "Wilderness and the Brazilian Mind (I): Nation and Nature in Brazil from the 1920s to the 1940s." *Environmental History* 13, no. 4 (2008): 724–50.

Franco, José Luiz de Andrade. "A primeira Conferência Brasileira de Proteção à Natureza e a questão da identidade nacional." *Varia Historia* 26 (January 2002): 77–96.

Franco, José Luiz de Andrade. "The Concept of Biodiversity and the History of Conservation Biology: From Wilderness Preservation to Biodiversity Conservation." *História (São Paulo)* 32, no. 2 (2013): 21–47.

Freitag, Liliane da Costa. *Fronteiras perigosas: Migração e brasilidade no extremo-oeste paranaense (1937–1954).* Cascavel, Brazil: Edunioeste, 2001.

Freitas, Frederico. "A Park for the Borderlands: The Creation of the Iguaçu National Park in Southern Brazil, 1880–1940." *HIB: Revista de Historia Iberoamericana* 7, no. 2 (2014).

Freitas, Frederico. "As viagens de Francisco Moreno: Visões da natureza e construção da nação no extremo sul argentino—1873–1903." *Angelus Novus* 1 (August 2010): 115–43.

Freitas, Frederico. "Terras públicas e política de conservação da natureza: O caos fundiário na formação do Parque Nacional do Iguaçu." In *História ambiental 3: Natureza, sociedade, fronteiras,* edited by José Luiz de Andrade Franco, et al. Rio de Janeiro: Garamond, 2020.

Freitas, Frederico. "Conservation Frontier: The Creation of Protected Areas in the Brazilian Amazonia." In *Frontiers of Development in the Amazon: Riches, Risks, and Resistances*, edited by Antonio Ioris, et al. Lanham, MD: Lexington Books, 2020.

Freitas, Frederico. "The Guarani and the Iguaçu National Park: An Environmental History." *ReVista: Harvard Review of Latin America* 14, no. 3 (2015): 18–22.

Galetti, Mauro, et al. "Palm Heart Harvesting in the Brazilian Atlantic Forest: Changes in Industry Structure and the Illegal Trade." *Journal of Applied Ecology* 35, no. 2 (1998): 294–301.

Gamberale, Humberto and Francisco A. Mermoz. *Caídas del Iguazú, Salto Grande del río Uruguay y Rápidos de Apipé en el Alto Paraná: Estudio sobre su aprovechamiento hidroeléctrico*, edited by Argentina, Dirección General de Navegación y Puertos. Buenos Aires: Briozzo Hnos., 1928.

Garfield, Seth. *Indigenous Struggle at the Heart of Brazil: State Policy, Frontier Expansion, and Xavante Indians, 1937–1988*. Durham: Duke University Press, 2001.

Garfield, Seth. *In Search of the Amazon: Brazil, the United States, and the Nature of a Region*. Durham: Duke University Press, 2013.

Gaspari, Elio. *A ditadura encurralada*. São Paulo: Companhia das Letras, 2004.

Gaspari, Elio. *A ditadura envergonhada*. São Paulo: Companhia das Letras, 2002.

Geisel, Ernesto. *Discursos, Volume I, 1974*. Brasília: Assessoria de Imprensa e Relações Públicas da Presidência da República, 1975.

Giddens, Anthony. *A Contemporary Critique of Historical Materialism*, vol. II, *The Nation-State and Violence*. Berkeley: University of California Press, 1987.

Giordani, Rubia Carla Formighieri. "Os guarani no Oeste Paranaense e a (re) constituição de territórios originários." *Guaju—Revista brasileira de desenvolvimento territorial sustentável* 1, no. 1 (2015): 142–66.

Giraudo, Alejandro R., et al. "Status da biodiversidade da Mata Atlântica de interior da Argentina." In *Mata Atlântica: Biodiversidade, ameaças e perspectivas*, edited by Carlos Galindo-Leal and Ibsen de Gusmão Câmara. Belo Horizonte: Fundação SOS Mata Atlântica and Conservação Internacional, 2005.

Gißibl, Bernhard, Sabine Höhler, and Patrick Kupper, eds. "Introduction: Towards a Global History of National Parks." In *Civilizing Nature: National Parks in Global Historical Perspective*. Oxford: Berghahn Books, 2012.

Gregory, Valdir. *Os eurobrasileiros e o espaço colonial: Migrações no oeste do Paraná, 1940–1970*. Cascavel, Brazil: Edunioeste, 2002.

Grignaschi, Víctor José. *Astas y colmillos: Relatos de caza*. Buenos Aires: Britania, 1983.

Groussac, Paul. *El viaje intelectual: Impresiones de naturaleza y arte, segunda serie*. Buenos Aires: Simurg, 2005.

Grynszpan, Mario. "O período Jango e a questão agrária: Luta política e afirmação de novos atores." In *João Goulart: Entre história e memória*, edited by Marieta de Moraes Ferreira. Rio de Janeiro: Fundação Getúlio Vargas, 2006

Haber, Stephen. "The Political Economy of Industrialization." In *The Cambridge Economic History of Latin America*, edited by V. Bulmer-Thomas, John

H. Coatsworth, and Roberto Cortés Conde, vol. II. Cambridge: Cambridge University Press, 2006.

Halperín Donghi, Tulio. *La República Imposible, 1930–1945*, Biblioteca del Pensamento Argentino 5. Buenos Aires: Emecé, 2007.

Harvey, David. *Justice, Nature, and the Geography of Difference*. Cambridge, MA: Blackwell Publishers, 1996.

Hochstetler, Kathryn and Margaret E. Keck. *Greening Brazil: Environmental Activism in State and Society*. Durham: Duke University Press, 2007.

Hoehne, Frederico Carlos. *Araucarilândia*. São Paulo: Secretaria da Agricultura, Indústria e Commercio do Estado de São Paulo, 1930.

Hoekstra, Jonathan M. and Jennifer L. Molnar. *The Atlas of Global Conservation: Changes, Challenges and Opportunities to Make a Difference*. Berkeley: University of California Press, 2010.

Holanda, Sérgio Buarque de. *Caminhos e Fronteiras*, 4th ed. São Paulo: Companhia das Letras, 2017.

Holdgate, Martin. *The Green Web: A Union for World Conservation*. London: IUCN, Earthscan, 1999.

Hopkins, Jack W. *Policymaking for Conservation in Latin America: National Parks, Reserves, and the Environment*. Westport, CT: Praeger, 1995.

Hoppe, Guillermina. "Ahora en que puedo sacar afuera tanto dolor, empiezo a sentir un poco de paz." In *Misiones: Historias con nombres propios*, edited by Amelia Báez. Posadas: Ministerio de Derechos Humanos de Misiones, 2011.

Howard, Ebenezer. *Garden Cities of to-Morrow (Being the Second Edition of "To-Morrow: A Peaceful Path to Real Reform")*. London: S. Sonnenschein & co., ltd., 1902.

Iglesias, Francisco de Assis. "Os parques nacionais existentes: Descrição e relevância." In *Anais, IX Congresso Brasileiro de Geografia*, edited by Bernardino José de Souza, Cristovão Leite de Castro, and Alexandre Emílio Sommler, vol. III. Rio de Janeiro: Conselho Nacional de Geografia, 1944.

Instituto Brasileiro de Desenvolvimento Florestal and Jean Paul Poupard. *Plano de manejo Parque Nacional do Iguaçu*. Brasília: Ministério da Agricultura, 1981.

Instituto Brasileiro de Desenvolvimento Florestal. "*Plano de ação*." Brasília: Ministério da Agricultura, 1975.

Instituto Nacional de Colonização e Reforma Agrária, INCRA. *Livro Branco da Grilagem de Terras*. Brasília: INCRA, 2012.

Instituto Panamericano de Geografía e Historia. *Publicación Num. 61: Tercera Asamblea General*. Mexico, D.F.: Editorial Stylo, 1941.

Instituto Paranaense de Desenvolvimento Econômico e Social. *O Paraná: Economia e sociedade*. Curitiba: IPARDES, 1981.

International Union for Conservation of Nature and Natural Resources. "Qué es la Unión Internacional para la Conservación de la Naturaleza y de los Recursos Naturales." Translated by Milan Jorge Dimitri. *Anales de Parques Nacionales* 10 (1964): 99–105.

International Union for Conservation of Nature and Natural Resources. *Proceedings of the Latin American Conference on the Conservation of Renewable Natural Resources: San Carlos de Bariloche, Argentina*, IUCN Publications New Series 13.

Morges, Switzerland: International Union for Conservation of Nature and Natural Resources; published with the assistance of UNESCO, 1968.

International Union for Conservation of Nature and Natural Resources. *Tenth General Assembly: Vigyan Bhavan, New Delhi, 24 November–1 December, 1969,* IUCN Publications New Series 27. Morges, Switzerland: International Union for Conservation of Nature and Natural Resources; published with the assistance of UNESCO, 1970.

Jacoby, Karl. *Crimes against Nature: Squatters, Poachers, Thieves, and the Hidden History of American Conservation.* Berkeley: University of California Press, 2001.

Jones, Karen. "Unpacking Yellowstone: The American National Park in Global Perspective." In *Civilizing Nature: National Parks in Global Historical Perspective,* edited by Bernhard Gißibl, Sabine Höhler, and Patrick Kupper. New York: Berghahn Books, 2012.

Karpinski, Cezar. "Navegação, cataratas e hidrelétricas discursos e representações sobre o Rio Iguaçu, 1853–1969." PhD diss., Federal University of Santa Catarina, 2011.

Kelly, Alice B. "Conservation Practice as Primitive Accumulation." *New Frontiers of Land Control,* edited by Nancy Lee Peluso and Christian Lund. London: Routledge, 2013.

Kelly, Matthew, et al. "Introduction." In *The Nature State: Rethinking the History of Conservation,* Routledge Environmental Humanities, edited by Matthew Kelly, et al. Oxford: Routledge, 2017.

Klanovicz, Jó, Gilmar Arruda, and Ely Bergo de Carvalho, eds. *História ambiental no sul do Brasil: Apropriações do mundo natural.* São Paulo: Alameda Editorial, 2012.

Klubock, Thomas M. *La Frontera: Forests and Ecological Conflict in Chile's Frontier Territory.* Durham: Duke University Press, 2014.

Kohlhepp, Gerd. "Tipos de colonização agrária dirigida nas florestas brasileiras: Exemplos históricos." *Fronteiras: Journal of Social, Technological and Environmental Science* 4, no. 3 (2015): 102–21.

Kropf, Marcela Strucker and Alci Albiero Júnior. "Araúcarias do Parque Nacional do Iguaçu: Implicações para sua conservação." In *Fronteiras fluidas: Floresta com araucárias na América meridional,* edited by Eunice Sueli Nodari, Miguel Mundstock Xavier de Carvalho, and Paulo Zarth. São Leopoldo, Brazil: Editora Oikos, 2018.

Kropf, Marcela Strucker and Ana Alice Eleutério. "Histórico e perspectivas da cooperação entre os Parques Nacionais do Iguaçu, Brasil, e Iguazú, Argentina." *Revista latino-americana de estudos avançados* 1, no. 2 (2017): 5–25.

Kupper, Patrick. *Creating Wilderness: A Transnational History of the Swiss National Park,* The Environment in History: International Perspectives 4. New York: Berghahn Books, 2015.

Langfur, Hal. *The Forbidden Lands: Colonial Identity, Frontier Violence, and the Persistence of Brazil's Eastern Indians, 1750–1830.* Stanford: Stanford University Press, 2006.

Lavalle, Aida Mansani. *A madeira na economia paranaense.* Curitiba, Brazil: Grafipar, 1981.

Lazier, Hermógenes. *Análise histórica da posse de terra no sudoeste paranaense*. Curitiba: Biblioteca Pública do Paraná, Secretaria de Estado da Cultura e do Esporte, 1986.

Leal, Claudia. "Behind the Scenes and out in the Open: Making Colombian National Parks in the 1960s and 1970s." In *The Nature State: Rethinking the History of Conservation*, edited by Matthew Kelly, et al. Routledge Environmental Humanities. Oxford: Routledge, 2017.

Leal, Claudia. "National Parks in Colombia." *Oxford Research Encyclopedia of Latin American History*, March 2019.

Lefebvre, Henri. *The Production of Space*. Oxford, UK: Blackwell, 1991.

Leitão, Cândido de Mello. *A vida na selva*. São Paulo: Companhia Editora Nacional, 1940.

Liebermann, José. "Breve ensayo sobre la historia de la protección a la naturaleza en la República Argentina." *Boletín del Ministerio de Agricultura de la Nación* 37, no. 1–4 (1935): 227–44.

Lieff, Bernard C. and Gil Lusk. "Transfrontier Cooperation between Canada and the USA: Waterton-Glacier International Peace Park." In *Parks on the Borderline: Experience in Transfrontier Conservation*, edited by Jim Thorsell, 39–49. Gland and Cambridge: IUCN Publications, 1990.

Linhares, Temístocles. *Paraná vivo: Sua vida, sua gente, sua cultura*. Rio de Janeiro: José Olympio, 1985.

Lira Neto. *Getúlio: Do governo provisório à ditadura do Estado Novo (1930–1945)*. São Paulo: Companhia das Letras, 2013.

Lira Neto. *Getúlio: Dos anos de formação à conquista do poder (1882–1930)*. São Paulo: Companhia das Letras, 2012.

Lopes, Sérgio. *O território do Iguaçu no contexto da Marcha para Oeste*. Cascavel: Edunioeste, 2002.

Lucas, Taís Campelo. "Cortando as asas do nazismo: A DOPS-RS contra os 'súditos do eixo.'" In *Presos políticos e perseguidos estrangeiros na Era Vargas*, edited by Marly de Almeida Gomes Vianna, Érica Sarmiento da Silva, and Leandro Pereira Gonçalves. Rio de Janeiro: Mauad X/FAPERJ, 2014.

Maack, Reinhard and Alexander Marchant. *German, English, French, Italian and Portuguese Literature on German Immigration and Colonization in Southern Brazil*. Cambridge: Harvard University Press, 1939.

Maack, Reinhard. "As consequências da devastação das matas no Estado do Paraná." *Arquivos de biologia e tecnologia, Curitiba* 8 (1953): 437–57.

Maack, Reinhard. *Geografia física do Estado do Paraná*. Curitiba: Universidade Federal do Paraná, 1968.

Macfarlane, Daniel. "'A Completely Man-Made and Artificial Cataract': The Transnational Manipulation of Niagara Falls." *Environmental History* 18, no. 4 (2013): 759–84.

Macfarlane, Daniel. "Saving Niagara From Itself: The Campaign to Preserve and Enhance the American Falls, 1965–1975." *Environment and History* 25 (2019): 489–520.

Maeder, J. A. *Misiones: Historia de la tierra prometida*. Buenos Aires: Eudeba, 2004.

Martins, José de Souza. *A imigração e a crise do Brasil agrário*. São Paulo: Pioneira, 1973.

Martins, José de Souza. *Fronteira: A degradação do outro nos confins do humano*, 2nd ed. São Paulo: Editora Contexto, 2009.

Martire, Agustina. "Waterfront Retrieved: Buenos Aires' Contrasting Leisure Experience." In *Enhancing the City: New Perspectives for Tourism and Leisure*, edited by Giovanni Maciocco and Silvia Serreli. Heidelberg: Springer, 2009.

Matos, Dalva M. Silva, et al. "Understanding the Threats to Biological Diversity in Southeastern Brazil." *Biodiversity and Conservation* 11, no. 10 (2002): 1747–58.

McNeill, John Robert. "Deforestation in the Araucaria Zone of Southern Brazil, 1900–1983." in *World Deforestation in the Twentieth Century*, edited by John F. Richards and Richard P. Tucker. Durham: Duke University Press, 1988.

Melito, Melina Oliveira, et al. "Demographic Structure of a Threatened Palm (*Euterpe edulis Mart.*) in a Fragmented Landscape of Atlantic Forest in Northeastern Brazil." *Acta Botanica Brasilica* 28, no. 2 (June 2014): 249–58.

Mello, Octávio Silveira. "Protecção à natureza." *Rodriguesia* 4, no. 13 (Summer 1940): 151–53.

Méndez, Laura. *Estado, frontera y turismo: Historia de San Carlos de Bariloche*. Buenos Aires: Prometeo, 2010.

Mendonça, Luciana A. "Parques Nacionais do Iguaçu e Iguazú: Uma fronteira ambientalista entre Brasil e Argentina." In *Argentinos e Brasileiros: Encontros, imagens e estereótipos*, edited by Alejandro Frigerio and Gustavo Lins Ribeiro. Petrópolis: Vozes, 2002.

Mertz, Urbano Theobaldo. "Um estudo das transformações sociais e econômicas de uma sociedade de colonos na região Oeste do Estado do Paraná." MS thesis, Federal Rural University of Rio de Janeiro, 2000.

Miller, Shawn William. *Fruitless Trees: Portuguese Conservation and Brazil's Colonial Timber*. Stanford: Stanford University Press, 2000.

Morales, Emilio B. *Hacia el Iguazú, cataratas y ruinas*. Buenos Aires: J. Peuser, 1914.

Morales, Emilio B. *Iguazú, cataratas y ruinas*. Buenos Aires: Talleres Gráficos Argentinos L. J. Rosso, 1929.

Muello, Alberto Carlos. *Misiones, las cataratas del Iguazú, el Alto Paraná y el cultivo de la yerba mate*. Buenos Aires: Talleres s.a. Casa Jacobo Peuser, 1930.

Muller, Arnaldo Carlos. "Proposição de manejo para o Parque Nacional do Iguaçu." MS thesis, Federal University of Paraná, 1978.

Muller, Keith Derald. *Pioneer Settlement in South Brazil: The Case of Toledo, Paraná*. The Hague: Martinus Nijhoff, 1974.

Murgel, Ângelo. *Parques nacionais: Conferência pronunciada na Exposição de Edifícios Públicos do Departamento Administrativo do Serviço Público em 1944, pelo Engenheiro Ângelo Murgel*. Rio de Janeiro: Imprensa Nacional, 1945.

Muricy, José Cândido da Silva. *À Foz do Iguassu: Ligeira descripção de uma viagem feita de Guarapuava à Colônia da Foz do Iguassu em novembro de 1892*. Curitiba: Impressora Paranaense Jesuino Lopes & Ca., 1896.

Myskiw, Antonio Marcos. "A fronteira como destino de viagem: A colônia militar de Foz do Iguaçu, 1888–1907." PhD diss., Fluminense Federal University, 2011.

Myskiw, Antonio Marcos. "Colonos, posseiros e grileiros: Conflitos de terra no oeste paranaense (1961/66)." MA thesis, Fluminense Federal University, 2002.

Myskiw, Antonio Marcos. "Ser colono na fronteira: A colônia militar de Foz do Iguaçu, 1888–1907." In *Campos em disputa: História agrária e companhia,* edited by Elione Silva Guimarães and Márcia Motta. São Paulo: Annablume, 2007.

Nail, Thomas. *Theory of the Border.* New York: Oxford University Press, 2016.

Napolitano, Marcos. *1964: História do regime militar brasileiro.* São Paulo: Contexto, 2017.

Nascimento, José Francisco Thomaz do. "Viagem feita por José Francisco Thomaz do Nascimento pelos desconhecidos sertões de Guarapuava, Província do Paraná, e relações que teve com os índios coroados, mais bravios daqueles lugares." *Revista Trimensal do IHGB* 49 (1886): 267–81.

Nash, Roderick. *Wilderness and the American Mind.* New Haven: Yale University Press, 2001.

Neumann, Roderick P. "Nature-State-Territory: Toward a Critical Theorization of Conservation Enclosures." In *Liberation Ecologies: Environment, Development, Social Movements,* edited by Richard Peet and Michael Watts. London: Routledge, 2004.

Neumann, Roderick P. *Imposing Wilderness: Struggles over Livelihood and Nature Preservation in Africa.* Berkeley: University of California Press, 1988.

Nodari, Eunice Sueli and João Klug, eds. *História ambiental e migrações.* São Leopoldo: Oikos, 2012.

Nodari, Eunice Sueli, Miguel Mundstock Xavier de Carvalho, and Paulo Afonso Zarth, eds., *Fronteiras fluidas: Floresta com araucárias na América Meridional.* São Leopoldo: Oikos, 2018.

Nodari, Eunice Sueli. "Crossing Borders: Immigration and Transformation of Landscapes in Misiones Province, Argentina, and Southern Brazil." In *Big Water: The Making of the Borderlands between Brazil, Argentina, and Paraguay,* edited Jacob Blanc and Frederico Freitas. Tucson, AZ: University of Arizona Press, 2018.

Nodari, Eunice Sueli. *Etnicidades renegociadas: Práticas socioculturais no oeste de Santa Catarina.* Florianópolis: Editora da UFSC, 2009.

Oberg, Kalervo and Thomas Jabine. *Toledo, a Municipio on the Western Frontier of the State of Paraná.* Rio de Janeiro: United States Operations Mission to Brazil, 1957.

Oliveira, Ricardo Costa de. "Notas sobre a política paranaense no período de 1930 a 1945." In *A construção do Paraná moderno: Políticos e política no governo do Paraná de 1930 a 1980,* edited by Ricardo Costa de Oliveira. Curitiba: Secretaria da Ciência, Tecnologia e Ensino Superior; Imprensa Oficial do Paraná, 2004.

Oliveira, Rogério Ribeiro de and Verena Winiwarter. "Toiling in Paradise: Knowledge Acquisition in the Context of Colonial Agriculture in Brazil's Atlantic Forest." *Environment and History* 16 (2010): 483–508.

Olson, David M., et al. "Terrestrial Ecoregions of the World: A New Map of Life on Earth: A New Global Map of Terrestrial Ecoregions Provides an Innovative Tool for Conserving Biodiversity." *BioScience* 51, no. 11 (2001): 933–38.

Olson, David M. and Eric Dinerstein. "The Global 200: Priority Ecoregions for Global Conservation,." *Annals of the Missouri Botanical Garden* 89, no. 2 (2002): 199–224.

Organization of American States. "Convention on Nature Protection and Wildlife Preservation in the Western Hemisphere." Accessed February 10, 2015, www .oas.org/juridico/english/treaties/c-8.html.

Ostos, Natascha Stefania Carvalho. "Terra adorada, mãe gentil: Representações do feminino e da natureza no Brasil da era Vargas (1930–1945)." MA thesis, Federal University of Minas Gerais, 2009.

Packer, Ian and Centro de Trabalho Indigenista. "*Violações dos direitos humanos e territoriais dos guarani no Oeste do Paraná (1946–1988): Subsídios para a Comissão Nacional da Verdade.*" Brasília: Centro de Trabalho Indigenista, Comissão Nacional da Verdade, 2014.

Padis, Pedro Calil. *Formação de uma economia periférica: O caso do Paraná.* São Paulo: HUCITEC, 1981.

Pádua, José Augusto. "Natureza e projeto nacional: As origens da ecologia política no Brasil." In *Ecologia e Política no Brasil*, edited by José Augusto Pádua. Rio de Janeiro: Editora Espaço e Tempo, 1987.

Pádua, José Augusto. *Um sopro de destruição: Pensamento político e crítica ambiental no Brasil escravista, 1786–1888.* Rio de Janeiro: Jorge Zahar Editor, 2002.

Paes, Maria Luiza Nogueira. "A paisagem emoldurada, do Éden imaginado à razão do mercado: Um estudo sobre os parques nacionales do Vulcão Poás, na Costa Rica, e do Iguaçu, no Brasil." PhD diss., University of Brasília, 2003.

Palmar, Aluízio. *Onde foi que enterraram nossos mortos?* Curitiba: Travessa dos Editores, 2012.

Pastoriza, Elisa. "El turismo social en la Argentina durante el primer peronismo: Mar del Plata, la conquista de las vacaciones y los nuevos rituales obreros, 1943–1955." *Nuevo mundo mundos nuevos* (2008), http://nuevomundo .revues.org/36472?lang=pt.

Peluso, Nancy Lee and Christian Lund, eds. "Introduction." In *New Frontiers of Land Control.* London: Routledge, 2013.

Pereira, Osny Duarte. *Direito florestal brasileiro; Ensaio.* Rio de Janeiro: Borsoi, 1950.

Piglia, Melina. "En torno a los parques nacionales: Primeras experiencias de una política turística nacional centralizada en la Argentina (1934–1950)." *Pasos: Revista de Turismo y Patrimonio Cultural* 10, no. 1 (2012): 61–73

Pizarro, Rodrigo. "The Global Diffusion of Conservation Policy: An Institutional Analysis." PhD diss., Stanford University, 2012.

Pusso, Santiago. *Viajes por mi tierra; al Iguazú, a Nahuel Huapí, por las costas del sur.* Barcelona: Casa Editorial Maucci, 1912.

Rau, Maria Fabiana. "Land Use Change and Natural Araucaria Forest Degradation: Northeastern Misiones—Argentina." PhD diss., University of Freiburg, 2005.

Rebouças, André and Francisco Antônio Monteiro Tourinho. *Provincia do Paraná: Caminhos de ferro para Mato Grosso e Bolivia. Salto do Guayra.*, edited by Adolpho Lamenha Lins. Rio de Janeiro: Typographia Nacional, 1876.

Rebouças, André. *Diário e notas autobiográficas; Texto escolhido e anotações,* edited by Anna Flora Verissimo and Inácio José Verissimo. Rio de Janeiro: José Olympio, 1938.

Rebouças, André. *Garantia de juros: Estudos para sua aplicação às emprezas de utilidade pública no Brazil.* Rio de Janeiro: Typographia Nacional, 1874.

Rêgo, Rubem Murilo Leão. "Terra de violência: Estudo sobre a luta pela terra no sudoeste do Paraná." MA thesis, University of São Paulo, 1979.

Ribeiro, Sarah Iurkiv Gomes Tibes. "A construção de um discurso historiográfico relativo aos guarani: Ensaio de teoria e metodologia." *Tempos históricos* 5–6 (2003–2004): 161–83.

Ribeiro, Sarah Iurkiv Gomes Tibes. "Fronteira e espacialidade: O caso dos guarani no oeste do Paraná." *Varia Scientia* 6, no. 12 (2006): 175–77.

Ribeiro, Vanderlei Vazelesk. *Cuestiones agrarias en el varguismo y el peronismo: Una mirada histórica.* Bernal, Argentina: Universidad Nacional de Quilmes Editorial, 2008.

Ricardo, Cassiano. *Marcha para Oeste: A influência da "bandeira" na formação social e política do Brasil.* Rio de Janeiro: José Olympio, 1940.

Rivera, Sebastián Hacher. *Cómo enterrar a un padre desaparecido.* Buenos Aires: Editorial Marea, 2012.

Robin, Libby. "The Rise of the Idea of Biodiversity: Crises, Responses and Expertise." *Quaderni* 76 (Fall 2011): 25–37.

Robinson, Mark, et al. "Uncoupling Human and Climate Drivers of Late Holocene Vegetation Change in Southern Brazil." *Scientific Reports* 8, no. 1 (2018): 7800.

Rocha, Sérgio Brant. "Monte Pascoal National Park: Indigenous Inhabitants versus Conservation Units." In *National Parks without People? The South American Experience,* edited by Thora Amend and Stephan Amend. Quito: IUCN/Parques Nacionales y Conservación Ambiental, 1995.

Rock, David. "Argentina, 1930–46." In *The Cambridge History of Latin America,* edited by Leslie Bethell, vol. VIII. Cambridge: Cambridge University Press, 1991.

Rock, David. *Authoritarian Argentina: The Nationalist Movement, Its History and Its Impact.* Berkeley: University of California Press, 1993.

Rodríguez, José E. *A través del Iguazú y del Guayrá.* Buenos Aires: Talleres Gráficos del Estado Mayor del Ejército, 1917.

Rohde, Hildegarde Maria, Elza Lorenzzoni Biersdorf, and Associação dos Professores Aposentados de Medianeira. *Resgate da memória de Medianeira.* Medianeira, Paraná: CEFET-PR, 1996.

Roncaglio, Cynthia. *Das estradas às rodovias: Meio século de rodoviarismo no Paraná.* Curitiba: DER-PR, 1996.

Sack, Robert David. *Human Territoriality: Its Theory and History.* Cambridge, UK: Cambridge University Press, 1986.

Salles, Apolônio. *As atividades do Ministério da Agricultura em 1942.* Rio de Janeiro: Ministério da Agricultura, 1943.

Salles, Jefferson de Oliveira. "A relação entre o poder estatal e as estratégias de formação de um grupo empresarial paranaense na década de 1940–1950: O caso do Grupo Lupion." In *A construção do Paraná moderno: Políticos e política no governo do Paraná de 1930 a 1980*, edited by Ricardo Costa de Oliveira. Curitiba, Paraná: Secretaria da Ciência, Tecnologia e Ensino Superior; Imprensa Oficial do Paraná, 2004.

Salomon, Hugo. "Nociones generales sobre la protección a la fauna y sugerencas para su preservación." In *La protección de la naturaleza en el mundo: In memoriam doctoris Hugo Salomon*, edited by Georges Dennler de la Tour. Buenos Aires: Georges Dennler de la Tour, 1957.

Sasaki, Daniel Leb. *Pouso forçado: A história por trás da destruição da Panair do Brasil pelo regime militar*. Rio de Janeiro: Editora Record, 2005.

Scarzanella, Eugenia. "Las bellezas naturales y la nación: Los parques nacionales en Argentina en la primera mitad del Siglo XX." *Revista europea de estudios latinoamericanos y del Caribe* 76 (2002): 5–21.

Schaden, Egon. *Aspectos fundamentais da cultura guarani*, 2nd ed. São Paulo: Difusão Européia do Livro, 1962.

Schelhas, John. "The U.S. National Parks in International Perspective: The Yellowstone Model or Conservation Syncretism?." In *National Parks: Vegetation, Wildlife and Threats*, edited by Grazia Polisciano and Olmo Farina. New York: Nova Science Publishers, 2010.

Schlüter, Regina G. *Turismo y áreas protegidas en Argentina*. Buenos Aires: Centro de Investigaciones y Estudios Turísticos, 1990.

Schwarcz, Lilia Moritz and Heloisa Murgel Starling. *Brasil: Uma biografia*. São Paulo: Companhia das Letras, 2015.

Secreto, María Verónica. *Soldados da borracha: Trabalhadores entre o sertão e a Amazônia no governo Vargas*. São Paulo: Editora Fundação Perseu Abramo, 2006.

Sellars, Richard West. *Preserving Nature in the National Parks: A History*. New Haven and London: Yale University Press, 1997.

Seixas, Lara Luciana Leal. "Memória dos desapropriados do Parque Nacional do Iguaçu: As fronteiras do cotidiano em terras (i)legais?" MA thesis, State University of Western Paraná, 2012.

Serviço Florestal. *Regimento do Serviço Florestal*. Rio de Janeiro: Ministério da Agricultura, 1944.

Seymoure, Penny. "The Fight for Mbya Lands: Indigenous Rights and Collective Rights." In *Tourism in Northeastern Argentina: The Intersection of Human and Indigenous Rights with the Environment*, edited by Penny Seymoure and Jeffrey L. Roberg. Lanham, MD: Lexington Books, 2012.

Silva, Alberto Franco da. "Trajetórias geográficas do pioneiro André Antônio Maggi na abertura da fronteira do oeste paranaense." *Geographia* 2, no. 4 (2000): 89–102.

Silva, Evaldo Mendes da. "Folhas ao vento: A micromobilidade de grupos Mbya e Nhandéva (Guarani) na Tríplice Fronteira." PhD diss., Federal University of Rio de Janeiro, 2007.

Silveira Netto, Manuel Azevedo da. *Do Guairá aos saltos do Iguassú*. São Paulo: Companhia Editora Nacional, 1939.

Silvestri, Graciela. "Space, National, and Frontier in the Rioplatense Discourse." In *Big Water: The Making of the Borderland Between Brazil, Argentina, and*

Paraguay, edited by Jacob Blanc and Frederico Freitas. Tucson: University of Arizona Press, 2018.

Silvestri, Graciela. *El lugar común: Una historia de las figuras de paisaje en el Río de la Plata*. Buenos Aires: Edhasa, 2011.

Simonian, Lane. *Defending the Land of the Jaguar: A History of Conservation in Mexico*. Austin: University of Texas Press, 1995.

Skidmore, Thomas E. *The Politics of Military Rule in Brazil, 1964–1985*. New York: Oxford University Press, 1988.

Soluri, John, Claudia Leal, and José Augusto Pádua. "Introduction: Finding the 'Latin American' in Latin American Environmental History." In *A Living Past: Environmental Histories of Modern Latin America*, edited by John Soluri, Claudia Leal, and José Augusto Pádua. Oxford, New York: Berghahn Books, 2018.

Spence, Mark. *Dispossessing the Wilderness: Indian Removal and the Making of the National Parks*. New York: Oxford University Press, 1997.

Sprandel, Marcia Anita. "'Aqui não é como a casa da gente...': Comparando agricultores brasileiros na Argentina e no Paraguai." In *Argentinos e brasileiros: Encontros, imagens e estereótipos*, edited by Alejandro Frigerio and Gustavo Lins Ribeiro. Petrópolis: Vozes, 2002.

Steinberg, Paul F. *Environmental Leadership in Developing Countries: Transnational Relations and Biodiversity Policy in Costa Rica and Bolivia*. Cambridge, MA: MIT Press, 2001.

Stevens, Stan. "The Legacy of Yellowstone." In *Conservation through Cultural Survival: Indigenous Peoples and Protected Areas*, edited by Stan Stevens. Washington, DC: Island Press, 1997.

Strang, Harold Edgard and Henrique Pimenta Veloso. "Alguns aspectos fisionômicos da vegetação no Brasil." *Memórias do Instituto Oswaldo Cruz* 68, no. 1 (1970): 9–76.

Thays, Carlos. "Les forêts naturelles de la République Argentine: Project de parcs nationaux." *Congrès Forestier International de Paris*. Paris: Touring-Club de France, 1913.

Tortorelli, Lucas A. "La lucha por la vida en los bosques argentinos." *Natura: Órgano de la Administración General de Parques Nacionales* 1, no. 1 (1954): 5–20.

Tortorelli, Lucas A. "Lo biológico y lo económico en Parques Nacionales." *Natura: Órgano de la Administración General de Parques Nacionales* 1, no. 2 (1955): 235–55.

Tortorelli, Lucas A. *Maderas y bosques argentinos*. Buenos Aires: Editorial Acme, 1956.

Tourinho, Luiz Carlos Pereira. *Toiro passante: Tempo de República Getuliana*, vol. IV, 5 vols. Curitiba: Instituto Histórico, Geográfico e Etnográfico Paranaense, 1991.

United States National Park Service. *First World Conference on National Parks*. Washington, DC: United States Department of the Interior, 1962.

Urban, Teresa. *Saudade do Matão: Relembrando a história da conservação da natureza no Brasil*. Curitiba, Brazil: Editora da UFPR, 1998.

Vargas, Getúlio. *A nova política do Brasil*, vol. V and VIII. Rio de Janeiro: J. Olympio, 1938.

Velho, Otávio Guilherme. *Capitalismo autoritário e campesinato: Um estudo comparativo a partir da fronteira em movimento.* São Paulo: DIFEL, 1979.

Velho, Otávio Guilherme. *Frentes de expansão e estrutura agrária: Estudo do processo de penetração numa área da Transamazônica.* Rio de Janeiro: Zahar, 1972.

Vencatto, Rudy Nick. "Parque Nacional do Iguaçu: O processo de migração, ocupação e as marcas na paisagem natural." *Revista latino-americana de estudos avançados* 1, no. 2 (2017): 103–17.

Wachowicz, Ruy Christovam. *Obrageros, mensus e colonos: História do oeste paranaese.* Curitiba, Brazil: Gráfica Vicentina, 1987.

Wachowicz, Ruy Christovam. *Paraná, sudoeste: Ocupação e colonização.* Curitiba: Instituto Histórico, Geográfico e Etnográfico Paranaense, 1985.

Waibel, Leo. *Capítulos de geografia tropical e do Brasil.* Rio de Janeiro: Instituto Brasileiro de Geografia e Estatística, 1958.

Wakild, Emily. "Border Chasm: International Boundary Parks and Mexican Conservation 1935–1945." *Environmental History* 14, no. 3 (July 2009): 453–475.

Wakild, Emily. "Environmental Justice, Environmentalism, and Environmental History in Twentieth-Century Latin America." *History Compass* 11, no. 2 (2013): 163–76.

Wakild, Emily. "Naturalizing Modernity: Urban Parks, Public Gardens and Drainage Projects in Porfirian Mexico City." *Mexican Studies/Estudios Mexicanos* 23, no. 1 (2007): 101–23.

Wakild, Emily. *Revolutionary Parks: Conservation, Social Justice, and Mexico's National Parks, 1910–1940.* Tucson: University of Arizona Press, 2011.

Welch, Cliff. *The Seed Was Planted: The São Paulo Roots of Brazil's Rural Labor Movement, 1924–1964.* University Park: Pennsylvania State University Press, 1999.

Westphalen, Cecília Maria, Brasil Pinheiro Machado, and Altiva Pilatti Balhana. "Nota prévia ao estudo da ocupação de terra no Paraná moderno." *Boletim da Universidade Federal do Paraná—Departamento de História* 7 (1968):1–52.

Westphalen, Cecília Maria. *História documental do Paraná: Primórdios da colonização moderna da região de Itaipu.* Curitiba: SBPH-PR, 1987.

Wetterberg, Gary B. and Maria Tereza Jorge Pádua. "*Preservação da natureza na Amazônia Brasileira, situação em 1978,*" Technical Series. Brasília: UNDP/FAO/IBDF, 1978.

White, Richard. "The Nationalization of Nature." *The Journal of American History* 86, no. 3 (1999): 976–986.

White, Richard. "What Is Spatial History?" *The Spatial History Project,* February 1, 2010. Accessed on June 15, 2015, https://web.stanford.edu/group/spatialhistory/cgi-bin/site/pub.php?id=29.

Whitehead, Lawrence. "Latin America as a 'Mausoleum of Modernities,'" In *Latin America: A New Interpretation,* Studies of the Americas. New York: Palgrave Macmillan, 2006.

Whitehead, Lawrence. "State Organization in Latin America Since 1930." In *Latin America: Economy and Society Since 1930,* edited by Leslie Bethell. Cambridge: Cambridge University Press, 1998.

Wilcox, Robert. "Paraguayans and the Making of the Brazilian Far West, 1870–1935." *The Americas* 49, no. 4 (April 1993): 479–512.

Winks, Robin W. "The National Park Service Act of 1916: 'A Contradictory Mandate'?" *Denver University Law Review* 74, no. 3 (1997): 575–624.

Wolfe, Joel. "The Faustian Bargain Not Made: Getúlio Vargas and Brazil's Industrial Workers, 1930–1945." *Luso-Brazilian Review* 31, no. 2 (1994): 77–95.

Wolfe, Joel. *Autos and Progress: The Brazilian Search for Modernity*. Oxford: Oxford University Press, 2010.

Wolfe, Mikael. *Watering the Revolution: An Environmental and Technological History of Agrarian Reform in Mexico*. Durham: Duke University Press, 2017.

Wood, Charles H. and Marianne Schmink. "The Military and the Environment in the Brazilian Amazon." *Journal of Political and Military Sociology* 21 (1993): 81–105.

Index

Other Books in the Series (continued from page ii)